Malthus Past and Present

POPULATION AND SOCIAL STRUCTURE

Advances in Historical Demography

Under the Editorship of

E. A. HAMMEL

Department of Anthropology
University of California, Berkeley

Kenneth W. Wachter with *Eugene A. Hammel* and *Peter Laslett*, Statistical Studies of Historical Social Structure

Nancy Howell, Demography of the Dobe !Kung

Bennett Dyke and *Warren T. Morril* (Editors), Genealogical Demography

J. Dupâquier, E. Hélin, P. Laslett, M. Livi-Bacci and *S. Sogner* (Editors), Marriage and Remarriage in Populations of the Past

Ronald F. E. Weissman, Ritual Brotherhood in Renaissance Florence

J. C. Caldwell, Theory of Fertility Decline

Carl Mosk, Patriarchy and Fertility: The Evolution of Natality in Japan and Sweden, 1880–1960

J. Dupâquier, A. Fauve-Chamoux and *E. Grebenik,* Malthus Past and Present

Selected papers from the International Conference on Historical Demography: "Malthus Past and Present", Paris, Unesco House, 26th–30th May 1980. Organized by the Centre national de la recherche scientifique (France), UNESCO, the International Union for the Scientific Study of Population, the Ecole des hautes études en sciences sociales (France), the Maison des sciences de l'homme (France) and the Institut national d'études démographiques (France).

ORGANIZING COMMITTEE OF THE INTERNATIONAL CONFERENCE
"MALTHUS PAST AND PRESENT"
Jean-Pierre Bardet, Jean-Noël Biraben, Jacques Dupâquier, Antoinette, Fauve-Chamoux, Jacqueline Hecht, Jean-Claude Perrot, Hélène Rénal, Sylvie Sterboul, Jacques Wolff

IUSSP COMMITTEE ON HISTORICAL DEMOGRAPHY
Chairman: Jacques Dupâquier. *Members:* Hubert Charbonneau, Robert Horvath, Soliman Huzayyin, Arthur Imhof, Peter Laslett, Maria Luiza Marcilio. *Co-ordinator:* Marc Lebrun

Malthus Past and Present

edited by

J. DUPÂQUIER, A. FAUVE-CHAMOUX
Ecole des Hautes Etudes en Sciences Sociales, Paris

and

E. GREBENIK
Editor of Population Studies

1983

ACADEMIC PRESS

A Subsidiary of Harcourt Brace Jovanovich, Publishers

London New York
Paris San Diego San Francisco São Paulo
Sydney Tokyo Toronto

Academic Press Inc. (London) Ltd
24–28 Oval Road
London NW1

US edition published by
Academic Press Inc.
111 Fifth Avenue,
New York, New York 10003

British Library Cataloguing in Publication Data

Malthus past and present.—(Population and social structure)
1. Malthus, Thomas Robert — Congresses.
I. Dupâquier, J. II. Series
304.62 HQ/66.7

ISBN 0-12-224670-5

LCCN 82-074008

Typesetting by Kelmscott Press Ltd., 30 New Bridge Street, London EC4.
Printed and bound by T. J. Press (Padstow) Ltd., Padstow, Cornwall.

Contributors

BÉJIN, André,[1] *Centre d'Etudes Transdisciplinaires, 44 rue de la Tour, 75016 Paris, France*

BRETON, Yves,[2] *Centre National de la Recherche Scientifique (CNRS), 162 rue Saint-Charles, 75015 Paris, France*

CHARBIT, Yves, *Institut National d'Etudes Démographiques (INED), 27 rue du Commandeur, 75675 Paris Cédex 14, France*

DEVANCE, Louis, *Université de Dijon, UER Sciences Humaines, 2 Boulevard Gabriel, 21000 Dijon, France*

DIGBY, Anne, *Institute of Social and Economic Research, University of York, Heslington, York YO1 5DD, United Kingdom*

FLINN, Michael W., *Ashdown, Brownshill, Stroud, Gloucester GL6 8AS, United Kingdom*

FRISCH, Rose E., *Center for Population Studies, Harvard University, 9 Bow Street, Cambridge, Massachusetts 02138, USA*

GODELIER, Maurice, *Maison des Sciences de l'Homme, Boulevard Raspail 54, 75270 Paris Cédex 06, France*

GORDON, Linda, *University of Massachusetts, Boston, Massachusetts 02125, USA*

GUILLAUME, Pierre, *IEP Bordeaux, BP 101, 33405 Talence, France*

HEINSOHN, Gunnar, *Universität Bremen, FB 5 Abt. Ökonomie, Bibliothekstrasse, Postfach 330440, 2800 Bremen 33, Federal Republic of Germany*

HOLLINGSWORTH, Thomas, H., *Department of Social and Economic Research, University of Glasgow, Adam Smith Building, Glasgow G12 8RT, United Kingdom*

JEWELL, Peter A., *Physiological Laboratory, University of Cambridge, Downing Street, Cambridge CB2 3EG, United Kingdom*

KEYFITZ, Nathan, *Center for Population Studies, Harvard University, 9 Bow Street, Cambridge, Massachusetts 02138, USA*

[1] Present address: 3 rue Faidherbe, 60800 Crépy-en-Valois, France.

[2] Present address: Université de Paris I, Panthéon Sorbonne, Sciences Economiques, Sciences Humaines, Sciences Juridiques et Politiques, 90 rue de Tolbiac, 75634 Paris Cédex 13, France.

KEYNES, Richard, *Physiological Laboratory, University of Cambridge, Downing Street, Cambridge CB2 3EG, United Kingdom*

LE BRAS, Hervé, *Institut National d'Etudes Démographiques (INED), 27 rue du Commandeur, 75675 Paris Cédex 14, France*

PERROT, Michelle, *UER de Géographie, Histoire et Sciences de la Société, Université Paris VII, 2 Place Jussieu, 75005 Paris, France*

RAUSKY, Franklin, *UER de Lettres, Département de Psychologie, Université de Paris-Nord, Avenue Jean-Baptiste Clément, 93430 Villetaneuse, France*

REBÉRIOUX, Madeleine, *Université de Paris VIII (Vincennes à Saint-Denis), 2 rue de la Liberté, 93 Saint Denis, France*

REMOND, René, *Fondation Nationale des Sciences Politiques, 27 rue Saint-Guillaume, 75341 Paris Cédex 07, France*

RONSIN, Francis, *Université de Paris VII, 30 rue Traversière, 75012 Paris, France*

SEARLE, Geoffrey R., *University of East Anglia, Norwich, Norfolk, United Kingdom*

STAPLETON, Barry, *Portsmouth Polytechnic, Museum Road, Portsmouth PO1 2QQ, United Kingdom*

STEIGER, Otto, *Universität Bremen, FB/Abt. Ökonomie, Bibliothekstrasse, Postfach 330440, 2800 Bremen 33, Federal Republic of Germany*

VALLIN, Pierre, *Centre Sèvres, 35 rue de Sèvres, 75006 Paris, France*

VAN DE WALLE, Etienne, *Population Studies Center, University of Pennsylvania, 3718 Locust Walk CR, Philadelphia, Pennsylvania 19104, USA*

WATERMAN, Anthony,[3] *School of Social Sciences, University of Sussex, Brighton BN1 9QN, United Kingdom*

WOLFF, Jacques, *Université de Paris I, 12 Place du Panthéon, 75005 Paris, France*

WRIGLEY, Edward A., *Cambridge Group for the Study of Population and Social Structure, 27 Trumpington Street, Cambridge CB2 1QA, United Kingdom*

WYNNE-EDWARDS, Vero, *University of Aberdeen, Department of Zoology, Tillydrone Avenue, Aberdeen AB9 2TN, Scotland, United Kingdom*

[3] Present address: St John's College, The University of Manitoba, Winnipeg, Canada R3T 2M5.

Preface

At a time when, as we are told, Marx is well and truly dead, Thomas Robert Malthus, his sworn enemy, seems more than ever alive. The controversy which his ideas continue to arouse — though somewhat obscured by misconceptions — bears witness to his extraordinary actuality.

The International Conference on Historical Demography, which was organized at the headquarters of UNESCO from the 27th to the 29th May 1980 by the Société de démographie historique, had the following objects: to rediscover Malthus's ideas by stripping them of all the misinterpretations and abuse which have rendered them practically unrecognizable; to study their origin and application; and to determine whether they remain applicable now. More than 500 participants from 61 countries attended to hear and discuss the ten reports, based on 164 papers, which dealt with the following themes:

1. The Evolution of Malthus's Thought: Malthus as a Demographer (Nathan Keyfitz)
2. The Fate of Malthus's Work: History and Ideology (Yves Charbit)
3. The Economic Thought of T. R. Malthus (Jacques Wolff)
4. Malthus and His Time (Michael Flinn)
5. Malthus and Ethnography (Maurice Godelier)
6. Malthusianism and Religion (René Rémond)
7. Malthus Today (Etienne van de Walle)
8. Malthusianism and Socialism (Michelle Perrot)
9. Malthus and Biological Equilibria (Richard Keynes)

At the same time, an exhibition was held at the Bibliothèque nationale on the subject "From Malthus to Malthusianism", linking together three topics — Malthus the man, his family and his career; his work; French aspects of neo-Malthusianism.[1]

[1] The catalogue of this exhibition is still available from the Société de démographie historique, 54, Boulevard Raspail, 75006 Paris.

Furthermore, three basic works on Malthus had been published within the space of a year:

Malthus Reconsidered by W. Petersen,[2] which was almost immediately translated into French under the apparently paradoxical title *Malthus, le premier antimalthusien.*
The first French translation of the *First Essay* of 1798[3].
Population Malthus by Patricia James.[4]

The interest aroused by this Conference and these publications prompted several articles and reviews in the press and mass media. Old polemics were revived. At the very doors of the Conference Hall, a few members of an obscure "European Workers' Party" distributed tracts denouncing "this commemoration of the precursor of racial theories, socio-biology and all the ideologies pertaining to genocide which have succeeded him"!

The Conference did, however, help to clarify certain issues by making short shrift of those prejudices which prevented a scientific approach to Malthus's theories:

1. It has by now been clearly established that Malthus was not in the least anti-natalist. As early as 1805, he had himself stated:

> It is an utter misconception of my argument to infer that I am an enemy to population. I am only an enemy to vice and misery, and consequently to that unfavourable proportion between population and food which produces these evils.
>
> In the desirableness of a great and efficient population. I do not differ from the warmest advocates of an increase. I am perfectly ready to acknowledge with the writers of old that it is not extent of territory but extent of population that measures the power of states. It is only as to the mode of obtaining a vigorous and efficient population that I differ from them, and in thus differing I conceive myself entirely borne out by experience, that great test of all human speculations.[5]

2. Malthus has little in common either with "neo-Malthusianism" or with what is commonly called "Malthusianism". He is unfortunate in having been monopolized by his embarrassing admirers — Drysdale

[2] W. Petersen (1979), *Malthus Reconsidered.* Harvard University Press, Cambridge, Massachusetts. Title of French translation: *Malthus, le premier antimalthusien.* Dunod, Paris, 1980.
[3] T. R. Malthus. *Essai sur le principe de population.* French translation by E. Vilquin, Paris INED, 1980, 166pp.
[4] Patricia James (1979). *Population Malthus.* Routledge and Kegan Paul, London, Boston, Henley.
[5] T. R. Malthus. *Essay*, 3rd edition, Appendix, pp. 507–508, 509.

and his disciples.[6] The expression "Malthusianism" has gradually taken on the meaning of "birth control", particularly in the French language. Even when a distinction is attempted between Malthusianism and neo-Malthusianism, the difference is generally reduced merely to the choice of means to be used: moral restraint in the first case, contraception and abortion in the second. Worse still, the French have gone so far as to coin the expression "economic Malthusianism" to describe restrictive practices in production, whereas Malthus was one of the first economists to advocate economic expansion, and was considered by J. M. Keynes as anticipating some of his ideas.

Moreover, if Malthus always rejected contraceptive practices, it was not only because they were "immoral", but above all for demographic reasons: "If, in each household, the number of children were limited voluntarily, an incentive to work would be removed" and "it might happen that neither the various countries nor the entire Earth could reach the degree of population that they should".[7]

3. Malthus was not in the least an enemy of the poor.

No sooner had the *Essay* achieved success than Malthus was violently attacked, or rather insulted, by the Utopians. Socialist writers followed suit, having grasped that the arguments against Godwin had a more general philosophical significance. Instead of counter-attacking on these grounds, for tactical reasons they brought their offensive to bear on one particular aspect of the question — Malthus's attitude towards the Poor Laws.

As we know, Malthus had at first supported the liberal projects of William Pitt and, in a pamphlet which failed to interest any publisher,[8] even advocated aid to households in need. He did, however, change his hand as far back as 1798: ". . . it is to be feared that though they (the Poor Laws) may have alleviated a little the intensity of individual misfortune, they have spread the general evil over a much larger surface." Malthus believed that men were poor because they were heedlessly prolific. To remedy this poverty, England had adopted a system of poor relief whose end result was rather to encourage the poor to be prolific. The consequences were all the more disastrous in that many workpeople, knowing that help would be forthcoming, ceased to make the necessary effort. Thus, Malthus held the opinion

[6] Dr Drysdale founded in 1877 an association advocating the use of contraception to reduce population growth and called it the Malthusian League.

[7] T. R. Malthus. *Essay*, 3rd edition, Book V.

[8] *The Crisis. A View of the Recent Interesting State of Great Britain*, by a Friend of the Constitution.

that "hard as it may appear in individual instances, dependent poverty ought to be held disgraceful"[9].

In the *Essay* of 1803, Malthus went even further. In order to illustrate the idea that paupers had no right to aid, he conceived the famous analogy of the banquet, in which the theme was carried to a ridiculous extreme. This offending passage was cut out of following editions, but was unearthed in 1821 by Godwin who had undertaken, rather late in the day, to refute the Malthusian doctrine. In this he was followed by most of the later writers, either in good faith or otherwise; they thought, moreover, that the text in question had appeared in the *Essay* of 1798.[10]

W. Petersen, in his book, shows why Malthus is termed reactionary by ideologists, and points out the injustice of this accusation:

> Malthus was an active member of the Whig party, and the social reforms he advocated — in addition to the crucial one of universal schooling — included an extension of the suffrage, free medical care for the poor, state assistance to emigrants, and even direct relief to casual labourers or families with more than six children; similarly he opposed child labour in factories and free trade when it benefited the traders but not the public. Apart from such details he was an honest and beneficent reformer, committed throughout his life to the goal that he shared with every liberal of his day — the betterment of society and of all the people in it.[11]

4. The demographic model of Malthus is in no way mechanical.

Whenever Malthus's theory is summarized, there is a tendency to reduce it to the well-known statement about the two ratios — population increases in a geometrical ratio while subsistence increases only in an arithmetical ratio. This contradiction gave rise to the notion which was completely original at that time, that Nature had been niggardly in her distribution of the space and nourishment necessary for life. This idea was quite opposed both to Christian doctrine[12] and to the optimism of the age of enlightenment.

[9] T. R. Malthus. *Essay*, 1st Edition, Chapter V, p.85.

[10] Only a very small number of copies of the *First Essay* of 1798 were published, and it was not reissued until 1923. Consequently, it was almost impossible to find until that date; moreover, it seems to have been rarely consulted in libraries.

[11] W. Petersen, op. cit. in footnote 2, Chapter 10, p.239. *See also* Anne Digby. Malthus and reform of the Poor Law. This volume, pp.97–109.

[12] A century earlier, Fénelon wrote, in *Les Aventures de Télémaque*: "The more men there are in a country, providing they are hard-working, the more can they enjoy abundance. They need never be jealous of one another: the Earth, our good mother, multiplies her gifts according to the number of her children who, by their labour, deserve her fruits." And Godwin wrote, as quoted

Without dwelling on the philosophical aspect of the question, it is interesting to note that this idea of the two ratios has been taken up and used rather naively by many economic historians, who have developed it into a whole theory of crises, cycles and even of pauperization. Now, it is impossible to find anywhere in Malthus's work the idea that there may be a limit to the means of subsistence which would periodically prove an obstacle to the unchecked increase of the population. According to his theory, the two ratios simply describe two unequal forces which need to be kept in balance either by corrective checks (poverty and vice), or by preventive checks (moral restraint, as defined in the *Essay* of 1803).

Far from preventing demographic growth, the Principle of Population acts as a stimulus:

> . . . to further the gracious designs of Providence by the full cultivation of the earth, it has been ordained, that population should increase much faster than food. . . . Consider man, as he really is, inert, sluggish and averse from labour, unless compelled by necessity. . . . We may pronounce with certainty, that the world would not have been peopled, but for the superiority of the power of population to the means of subsistence. . . . The principle according to which population increases, prevents the vices of mankind, or the accidents of nature, the partial evils arising from general laws from obstructing the high purposes of the creation. It keeps the inhabitants of the earth always fully up to the means of subsistence; and is constantly acting upon man as a powerful stimulus, urging him to the further cultivation of the earth, and to enable it, consequently, to support a more extended population.[13]

Thus, not only has this Conference made a contribution towards restoring the true meaning of Malthus's work, but it has also assisted a better definition of his rightful place in the history of demography, economic theory and the social sciences generally.

From the demographic point of view, N. Keyfitz's contribution shows that Malthus cannot be classed with the political arithmeticians; his methods of quantitative analysis are too simple, though he did play a part in changing the emphasis of studies of mortality, as Le Bras shows. His merit lies elsewhere: he concentrated on the most

by Malthus in the *Essay* of 1798, "Three fourths of the habitable globe is now uncultivated. The parts already cultivated are capable of immeasurable improvement. Myriads of centuries of still increasing population may pass away, and the earth be still found sufficient for the subsistence of its inhabitants." (p.180.)

[13]T. R. Malthus (1798). *Essay*, Chapter XIX, pp.361–365.

important problem — how a demographic system works — and devised a model and a general explanation, and this led him to lay the foundations of the sociology of population. At the same time, he called attention to the essential aspect of this system — the extraordinary stability of populations in the past. Nearly two centuries ahead of his time he was able to show that in Europe the institution of marriage furnished the central pivot of the regulating mechanism. As regards the rest of the world, Malthus attempted to interpret the ethnographic data available to him, in order to find out how the principle of population could be applied to them. Unfortunately, as Godelier points out, scientific ethnography did not exist at that time; it was merely a collection of disjointed observations separated from their true meaning within a particular culture, and therefore useless for providing any precise quantitative data. Consequently, in spite of his critical turn of mind, Malthus was unable to free himself completely from the prejudices of his period: his ethnology is still only philosophical anthropology. Nevertheless, the originality of this first attempt at analysis is evident, and it marks an epoch in the history of the social sciences.

In the field of economics, Malthus's approach is much sounder. This is uncontestable, since Keynes acknowledged Malthus as his precursor, but there remain several doubtful points as Wolff points out. We can give a positive answer to the question of whether Malthus properly understood the reality of his time. Flinn shows that, despite the poor quality of the available data and techniques, Malthus's interpretation — unlike that of Ricardo — can be shown to be correct in the light of studies in which modern methods are used for studying the situation in England at the end of the eighteenth and the beginning of the nineteenth centuries.

Many other aspects of Malthus's ideas and influence were examined during the Conference. Most of the papers presented will be published in French by the Editions du centre national de la recherche scientifique. Academic Press has decided to publish an immediate selection for English readers, consisting of the nine most important reports, which are based upon a number of papers, together with such papers as were judged most original by the *rapporteurs* and organizers of the Conference.

For reasons of convenience, these papers have been arranged in six parts: Malthus; Malthus and his Time; Malthus and Religion; Malthusianism; Malthusianism and Socialism; Malthusianism and Darwinism. They could have been arranged in two parts only: one dealing with Malthus himself, and the other with what is more or less correctly called Malthusianism.

There remain, however, a number of outstanding questions. Some are worthy of a special conference, for example, Malthus's ideas on the theory of value and on social problems; what is needed above all is an analysis of his theological system, which was so profoundly influenced by deism and the Scottish moralists.

But perhaps the most urgent task is to publish a synopsis of the successive editions of the *Essay* on the Principle of Population, to enable demographers to follow the evolution of Malthusian thought and to clear up certain difficulties which appear to us like contradictions. Such was the concluding wish expressed by the Conference. Let us hope the near future will see its fulfilment.

JACQUES DUPÂQUIER
February 1983 *Chairman, Société de demographie historique*

Editor's note

References to T. R. Malthus's *Essay on the Principle of Population as it Affects the Further Improvement of Society* (1798) (hereinafter referred to as *First Essay*) are to the Royal Economic's Society's facsimile edition. Unless otherwise stated, references to the later edition of the *Essay* are to the edition in two volumes in the Everyman Library, which was based on the Seventh Edition. Papers submitted to this Conference are referred to as MHA (Malthus hier et aujourd'hui). A summary of these was published in mimeo just after the Conference; it is hoped that the papers will be published in full in the near future.

Acknowledgements

The Editors and authors have been most privileged to have had the expert collaboration of Mr Eugene Grebenik who not only translated most of those papers which were written in French, but also carried out the copy editing of all the texts brought together in the present volume. They would consequently like to express to him their very cordial thanks for many suggestions and for the improvements which he often made to their papers. He was aided in this task by Madame Marylène Chartz-Gustin who retyped the manuscripts most efficiently.

However, the authors wish to mention that they alone are responsible for any possible errors or omissions which may still exist.

Contents

PART 3 MALTHUS AND RELIGION

PART 4 MALTHUSIANISM

PART 5 MALTHUSIANISM AND SOCIALISM

PART 1

Malthus

1 The Evolution of Malthus's Thought: Malthus as a Demographer

N. KEYFITZ

If we overlook the ingenious use of numerical data, the sense of the dilemmas among which policy choices must be made, the profound contribution to reconciling the animal nature of man with his powers of thought and foresight, then the whole of Malthus can be reduced to four words: "population is food-controlled". Such a formula has the advantage of being easily grasped, and a thousand particular cases where it does not fit can be used to attack its author, two reasons for its popularity as against fuller interpretations of Malthus's thought.

No such formulation can possibly be original; this essentially biological one was clearly anticipated both by Adam Smith and by Cantillon before him. "When food increases", wrote the latter, "men will multiply like rats in a barn". Malthus listed classical Greek writers, Montesquieu and Benjamin Franklin among his predecessors.[1] But the biology of population became steadily less important as Malthus extended his observations through his own travels, the reports of the travels of others and national statistical systems that were evolving from primitive beginnings during the same 30 years in which his thought was developing.

In fact, cases in which population is directly food-controlled do not dominate the experience of mankind. For each instance in which nature has applied the ultimate sanction of famine, say in China or India or the Sahel in some recent years, several instances may be cited of populations which have lived comfortably for centuries at densities well below the maximum that their territory could sustain. These are to be found in the writings of De Vore, Lee and Howell on the !Kung of tropical Africa and elsewhere.[2] Godelier in this volume[3] reminds us

MALTHUS PAST AND PRESENT
ISBN 0-12-224670-5

that Malthus selected and sometimes misinterpreted data on primitive communities.

The more subtle and important part of Malthus, the part that is truly original, is not to be found in any second-hand condensation. Many people have been interested in Malthus over the 185 years since the publication of the *First Essay,* but not to the point of picking up his book and reading it. The merit of this Conference is that it includes scholars who are willing to go to the words of Malthus and so discover his originality.

Malthus was practical, and he saw men as neither godlike nor irredeemably wicked. Godwin's scheme of a society based on benevolence seems to him unworkable. Even if it were an ultimate ideal, it is so distant that it cannot give any guidance in practical affairs. If we direct our efforts towards it, we will suffer repeated failures and "impede that degree of improvement in society that is really attainable".[4] And in a footnote, a page later, he explains: "He is a much greater benefactor of mankind, who points out how an inferior good may be attained, than he who merely expatiates on the deformity of the present state of society, and the beauty of a different state, without pointing out a practical method, that might be immediately applied, of accelerating our advances from the one to the other."[5] He was throughout a Whig incrementalist: he promoted universal schooling, extension of suffrage, free medical care for the poor, state assistance to emigrants, more equal distribution of land and of income.

More appropriate to animals than to humans?

The *Essay on Population* is not one book but at least two, the later editions being entirely different from the first. Malthus explains in the 1803 Edition that he would have called it a different book, but he wanted to avoid reference to the first edition.[6] This sounds as though he were repudiating the 1798 work, except for a few parts that he incorporated in subsequent editions.

Thoroughly uncompromising, the first starts from the two postulates that "food is necessary to the existence of man", and that "the passion between the sexes is necessary and will remain nearly in its present state",[7] and proceeds to the conclusion that "the power of population is indefinitely greater than the power of the earth to produce subsistence for man".[8] Human nature and human capacities have little to do with the matter: "the race of man cannot by any efforts of reason, escape from (this great restrictive law)".[9]

Yet, a few pages later, even in the *First Essay,* a qualification is put on this apparent assimilation of people to plants and animals. The preventive check (of late marriage and abstinence) "appears to operate in some degree through all the ranks of society in England".[10] Class distinctions come naturally to Malthus: better-off people are above the animals in their ability to restrain childbearing, while "the positive check to population, by which I mean the check that represses an increase which is already begun, is confined chiefly, though not perhaps solely, to the lowest orders of society".[11] Malthus was neither the first nor the last to see the lower classes as closer to the animal than the upper; but he had every hope, as he clearly states in the later editions, that education would eliminate such differences.

Malthus asks us to look at man as he is: "inert, sluggish, and averse from labour, unless compelled by necessity".[12] "Evil seems to be necessary to create exertion, and exertion seems evidently necessary to create mind".[13] "Leisure is, without doubt, highly valuable to man, but taking man as he is, the probability seems to be that in the greater number of instances it will produce evil rather than good." Humans are not static, but can develop their talents, and hardship is genuinely creative. "The exertions that men find necessary to support themselves or their families frequently awaken faculties that might otherwise have lain forever dormant."

His dour view of the world has never been well received in continental Europe, and to-day it is everywhere out of fashion. It is accepted least of all in the matter of sexual relations, where Malthus expressed himself vigorously against the device of contraception. "If it were possible for each married couple to limit by wish the number of their children, there is certainly reason to fear that the indolence of the human race would be much increased."[14] For him it was the pressure of population that gave individual and social life its tension and significance. To relieve that pressure (as the contraceptive device recommended by Condorcet would do) would destroy the essence of human life and destiny. It is a strange injury that posterity has inflicted on Malthus when it calls contraception "Malthusian" or "neo-Malthusian".

His ideas coincided with the needs of the industrial revolution. In common with Max Weber and his Protestant Ethic a century later, Malthus calls on the individual for endless labour and painful abstinence; there was much capital construction to be undertaken and very little in the way of consumer goods to pass around as rewards. With a different justification that again corresponds to early industrialization, a puritanical view of life has also been taken in the Soviet Union.

The strength of an amateur

Much of the novelty in Malthus's approach, as in that of Einstein, derives from his being a beginner, an amateur, in the field of his specialization. When he wrote the *First Essay* in 1798, he had not even read Süssmilch, let alone more recondite writers of the eighteenth century.[15] In his earliest work Malthus does not consider age-specific fertility, nor does he use a life table, though the life table had been in existence since Graunt. He tries to obtain gross and net reproduction ratios by using only time series of marriages, births and deaths, together with mean ages at marriage and death. To find the number of births, he simply took the deaths e_0 years later, where e_0 is the expectation of life at birth, as though everyone lived out his or her expectation exactly. Yet, Le Bras finds[16] that where a population is nearly stationary, which would have been the case in most epochs, Malthus's crude methods yield good enough results.

Le Bras provides examples of the ingenuity of Malthus's fresh (because he tended to ignore the work of his predecessors) attack on technical problems. He became a demographer in spite of himself by being forced to examine with empirical data one aspect or another of his theory as these came under criticism. Ansley Coale[17] has shown with what ingenuity Malthus analysed the population of the United States in support of his assertion that population was increasing at a rate that would double it within 25 years.

Malthus and data

Both before and since Malthus, China has been a familiar testing ground and source of examples for population theories. Malthus thought that China's population was stationary at a density that corresponded to a low level of subsistence. Cartier examines the statistics, including those that Malthus might, but does not seem to have, consulted, and finds that China's population grew rapidly during the eighteenth and early nineteenth centuries, a situation which had already been perceived by contemporaries and which is in accordance with modern scholarly findings, in particular those of Ho Ping-ti. Malthus falls under the suspicion of having selected his sources to confirm a condition in China that accorded with his general theory of population. He argued that the conventional level of existence was an independent parameter and that the condition which permitted the population to increase and stay at a fixed high density, compared with that of Europe, was that the level of existence should be low.

Cartier takes up a major issue: Does a low standard of living result from population density or does the density result from the standard of living? On the whole, the Malthus of the *First Essay* makes the standard of living the independent variable, while the Malthus of the second and later editions attempts to account for the supposed stability of the population through a combination of demographic and economic factors. In animal populations, of course, the "standard of living" is purely physiological and exogenous, and Demetrius[18], like Darwin, shows the rich consequences that flow from this feature of the *First Essay*.

One question that was much debated during the late eighteenth century concerned the size and rate of population increase. Some, like Montesquieu, argued that actual numbers had decreased since ancient times due to poor government, but they adduced no data, and one suspects that their principal evidence was their conviction that the government of the time was bad. Malthus scorned such circularity of argument and persistently sought numerical evidence during an age when precious little effort went into the collection of data. His use of data seems to have stimulated more systematic methods of collection, and certainly his writings encouraged the beginning of English census-taking in 1801 and of civil registration and the collection of vital statistics in 1837. As better data became available, Malthus made use of them and successive editions of the *Essay* were more solidly empirical.

Demographic conditions of the late eighteenth century

Between 1066, when the population of England and Wales was estimated at 1.1 million, and the Census of 1841, it rose to 15.9 million. Malthus was aware of the pitfalls in the earlier estimates and made some contributions of his own to improving the estimates for 1780 and later. He analysed the downward trend in England's death rate and again was exemplary in his critical approach to data. He was aware of the high death rates in the cities, but unlike Price and other contemporary scholars did not regard urbanization as equivalent to depopulation. All this has been brought out clearly by Petersen. Malthus was one of the first to realize how difficult it is to answer such an easily asked question as: 'Why did the death rate fall during the late eighteenth century?' A less conscientious proponent of the Principle of Population would simply have given the answer "food supplies".

Malthus as a forecaster

It is common to read that Malthus's forecast was a failure, since population has increased since his time, and in the industrialized part of the world this increase has certainly not brought misery. This vulgar treatment of the Principle of Population as a concrete prediction disregards what Malthus never failed to keep in mind — that population — sustaining capacity depends on techniques. Indeed, he wrote at length on the way in which populations grew and became more prosperous in North America as European technology replaced that of the Indians.

Malthus explicitly predicted the future of differential fertility, as we now call it, and of the demographic transition, which would lead to a situation in which birth rates for the whole community would be low. He anticipated that people would come to control their childbearing as they rose in the social scale, and urged that those at the bottom of society be encouraged to rise. Rationality in planning marriage and children, like any other type of planning, depended on faith in the future; as the lower classes achieved a higher standard of living they would also adopt the small-family pattern.

Such forecasts were based on examples found during his travels, where he found that people did accommodate their fertility to resources. The summary of his views provided in the *Encyclopaedia Britannica*[19] quotes Süssmilch's figures which showed that the number of marriages decreased as mortality fell in various parts of Germany and Poland. Malthus quotes figures which show how a supposed depopulation of parts of Switzerland — births which seemed insufficient to maintain the population and, if true, were an instance where his principles did not apply — was really a response to falling death rates, so that fewer births were needed to keep up the population[10]. This is exactly what we, too, regard as progress and describe as the demographic transition.

While most of us have been concerned to show how Malthus contributed to demography, Barry Stapleton turns the tables and provides an account of the influence on Malthus of the demographic conditions of his time[2]. Instead of dealing with Malthus's effect on demography, his contribution deals with the effect that local demography exercised on Malthus. He uses baptismal and other records to show that there was a sharp increase of the population in the area in which Malthus lived, an increase that may have been less general in Europe than Malthus supposed.

Would a rise in wages be turned into children? Vulgar Malthusians have thought that it would, but that was not the view of Malthus himself. "In the vast majority of instances, before a rise in wages can be counteracted by the increased number of labourers it may be supposed to be the means of bringing into the market, time is afforded for the formation of . . . new and improved tastes and habits . . . After the labourers have once acquired these tastes, population will advance in a slower ratio as compared with capital than formerly".[22] In modern terms, Malthus here comes close to suggesting a positive feedback, a kind of virtuous circle, by which the rise in wages results in fewer children, and hence more capital per worker in the next generation, which in its turn will obtain yet higher wages.

Is progress possible?

If Malthus is interpreted as positing an ineluctable force of reproduction that will press against whatever means of subsistence man's ingenuity provides, then he seems to deny the possibility of progress in the welfare of individuals. There are certainly statements to this effect in the first edition, and for anyone who believes in progress, this alone proves Malthus wrong. In the course of his work, Malthus devotes great attention to improvements in the condition of the masses, especially through education. The result would be prudence, especially the preventive check of late marriage, that would avoid the pressure on resources stressed in the *First Essay*

Le Bras emphasizes a more serious difficulty: to the extent to which improvements in the human condition lead to increased longevity, there would be more people and, therefore, more misery. Godwin and Condorcet saw life as becoming indefinitely long, and their answer was birth control. Malthus "wraps himself in the cloak of offended virtue", as Le Bras elegantly puts it,[23] in rejecting this solution.

Schmid asks what brought the change from the severity of the *First Essay* to the more humane perspective of the later editions.[24] He finds the reason in Malthus's observation of the English upper classes and their small families. This convinced him that progress was possible and led him from a biological framework to a sociological one, in which man in society could, indeed, restrain his childbearing.

Moral restraint

That Malthus recommended moral restraint, by which he meant deferment of marriage, should hardly come as a surprise. He saw that in Europe population had, indeed, been held under sufficient restraint during the preceding centuries so that famines had been few in comparison, say, with China. The Chinese peasant may well have been no less skilled and industrious than his European counterpart. The reason for fewer famines in Europe was its smaller population, and the fact that population was held below the carrying capacity of the soil through late marriage. This matter is discussed in Cartier's contribution.[25]

But, with the spread of industry, migration to cities and the weakening of traditional rural associations, this restraint was in danger of breaking down in Malthus's time. In accord with his realistic and anti-utopian outlook he advocated a reversion to tradition. "He was recommending the intensification of a demographic characteristic peculiar, in his day, to Western Europe", writes Coale.[26] "In Western Europe at a given moment, fewer than 50 per cent of women of childbearing age were married: in Eastern Europe the fraction was 65 to 80 per cent, and in African and Asian populations as high as 85 to 90 per cent". Malthus recommended a means of control that he knew was feasible, because it had worked in the past.

Education

Education of the masses is important, because it will make people capable of the restraint in childbearing which was so important to Malthus — the preventive check will operate. And if there is one demographic observation that has stood from his time to ours it is that the better educated have fewer children. But Malthus thought of education also in a broader sense, as contributing directly to welfare, along with liberty; not the welfare of princes and rulers, but that of individual men and women. He was a true child of the Enlightenment, in the sharpest contrast to those of his contemporaries who remained in the tradition of mercantilism.

Few of us would apply the adjective "Malthusian" to connote the education of the masses, yet that is how Elie Halevy[27] uses it: "As concerns the education of the poor in particular, the radical theory of popular instruction is Malthusian in origin." It was not only that educated people would be more capable of exercising the moral restraint that in later editions of the *Essay* was put forward as the solution to the population problem, nor that education would make them better workers (Malthus was not even sure that the workman needed geometry and other academic subjects in his occupation) but that "an instructed and well-informed people would be less likely to be led away by inflammatory writings". Whether or not such confidence was justified, Malthus opposed the majority of his contemporaries who feared that education would only serve to make people rebellious.

Malthus's liberal orientation shows up clearly in his taking the side of the Irish. "The underlying reason (for the poverty in Ireland) was (its) degradation. The peasant, seeing no escape from his lowly condition, spent his life proliferating".[28] It is remarkable that a minister of the Established Church could say: "Let the Irish Catholics have all that they have demanded; for they have asked nothing but what strict justice and good policy should concede to them."

Population pressure and the economy

It is impossible to separate Malthus's demography from his economics. They were related to one another in a classic paper by John Maynard Keynes[28] that was concerned with the two Malthusian devils. Malthus never viewed the world as an easy place. His work comes down to two principles that, for short, might be called population and demand. When population grows, there will be no lack of effective demand. But, as Keynes writes: "When devil P of population is chained up, we are free of one menace; but we are more exposed to the other devil U of unemployed resources than we were before."

The seeming contradiction between the inexorable pressure of population on the standard of living of individuals and the possibility of prudential restraint, the preventive check, has challenged many generations of readers. The answer to the difficulties raised in successive editions of the *Essay*, writes Lux,[30] seems to be given fully in the *Principles of Political Economy,* in which Malthus clearly comes down on the side of progress. In the *Principles* population is no longer the dominant engine of the machine of history, but comes to be attached to the economy, partly as a dependent, partly as an independent variable. The labour market operates in such a way that economic advance increases both the supply of goods and the number of people, but the number of people goes up less quickly than the amount of goods, there being a rise in the conventional minimum standard of living. Population is also an independent variable, but it controls the standard of living to a limited extent only. It is a threat that makes people take thought, a hard school of rationality that progressively teaches restraint.

The Malthus of the *Principles,* who fits population into a complex network of economic factors, appears also in Michel Cartier's contribution.[31] The model that Malthus sketches in his treatment of China recognizes the interplay of such factors as the tax rate, the price level, the proportion of the labour force engaged in non-agricultural activities, and international trade. Above all, Malthus sees the demographic–economic process evolving so that at any given time different countries are in different stages of development. "In stressing the special character of the Chinese case, Malthus was feeling his way towards a theory of underdevelopment".[32]

The poor laws and the poor

Malthus's opposition to the Poor Laws has enabled Utopians and demagogues to portray him as a heartless reactionary. But we must consider what Malthus was objecting to. "Payments of the Spenhamland type, in which wage subsidies and family allowances were confused, meant that the relief received by the pauper-worker was based in part on the number of his children. Employers could, therefore, pay lower wages to those with larger families, and thus . . . preferred to hire fathers . . . Men who receive but a small pittance know that they have only to marry, and that pittance will be augmented in proportion to the numbers of their children."[33] The well-intentioned law looks as though payments were being made to poor workers, but the real beneficiaries were the employers who gained cheap labour immediately and more and even cheaper labour later on.

The humane question, then as now, is how to aid children already born without providing the incentive to bear more children who will also be poor. "If . . . Malthus thus stressed one side of a painful dilemma, he at least saw that it was a dilemma, and not to be resolved with sentimentality."[34]

Equality

By the eighteenth century, bourgeois property was taking its place alongside the hereditary landed property of the nobility. Malthus wavered a little, but on the whole he favoured the break-up of large estates as the French Revolution was doing on the other side of the Channel. He wanted "a greater part of society . . . in the happy state of possessing property"[35] and spoke of the "permanent advantage that would always result from a nearer equalization of property".[36] This, he felt, would further responsibility and liberty as well as needed conservation.

In short, Malthus's thought took account of some dilemmas of policy that face us today, much as they did then. How to discourage excessive childbearing without making life more difficult for children already born is only the first of a series of difficult questions. How can we solve immediate problems of unemployment by emigration without hurting others (for instance, the American Indians) and without encouraging parents to have more children to replace those who depart? How can we provide poor relief in a way that does not merely add to the profits of employers?

In the course of his writings Malthus evolved a framework for the question that has been so much discussed: in what way does man transcend the biological, the animal part of his nature? The early emphasis on the animal side gave way to notions of responsibility, expressed in demography as the preventive check, mentioned in the first edition and more prominently discussed in later ones.

The introduction of much new information into the later editions could not but make the argument more subtle and more complicated. As Walter Bagehot writes: "In its first form the *Essay on Population* was conclusive as an argument, only it was based on untrue facts; in its second form it was based on true facts, but it was inconclusive as an argument."[37]

One way of summarizing the evolution of Malthus's thought is to compare the beginning of the first edition with the ending of the last. The first starts by referring to the progress of science, along with the change of institutions typified by the French Revolution and how these are thought to be decisive for the fate of mankind.[38] In the next few pages he shows that the fate and happiness of mankind depend on quite other considerations embodied in the Principle of Population: our numbers will increase so that neither science nor laws can do much for our individual comfort. In the last sentence of the last edition he writes: "We may confidently indulge the hope that, to no unimportant extent, [the virtue and happiness of mankind] will be influenced by [physical discovery's] progress and will partake of its success."[39]

The contemporary world is faced with a population problem and that inevitably makes us look back to Malthus. But there is a deeper reason why Malthus has an appeal during the late twentieth century; he sees contradictions in every policy proposal. Not only population, but every aspect of existence presented dilemmas to him. That is why he lives again to-day, after the complacent Victorians had seemingly buried him forever.

Notes

1. Preface to the 1803 Edition of the *Essay* reprinted in T. R. Malthus, *On Population* (Edited and introduced by Gertrude Himmelfarb), p.148. Modern Library. New York.
2. Nancy Howell (1979). *Demography of the Dobe !Kung*. Academic Press, New York and London.

3. M. Godelier. Malthus and Ethnography. This volume, pp.125–150.
4. T. R. Malthus. *First Essay*, p.286
5. T. R. Malthus, ibid. p.290.
6. J. Dupâquier (1980). Avez-vous lu Malthus? *Population* **35** 280–290.
7. T. R. Malthus, op. cit. in note 4, p.11.
8. ibid. p.13.
9. ibid. p.15.
10. ibid. p.63.
11. ibid. p.71.
12. ibid. p.363.
13. ibid. p.360.
14. T. R. Malthus. Appendix to 5th Edition of the *Essay*, p.370.
15. H. Le Bras. Malthus and the two mortalities. This volume, pp.31–44. cf. also M. Cartier. Malthus et la Chine. MHA, p.13.
16. H. Le Bras, loc. cit. in note 15.
17. A. J. Coale (1979). The use of modern analytical demography by T. R. Malthus. *Population Studies* **33** (2), 329–332.
18. L. Demetrius. The Malthusian parameter and other measures of growth rate. Their significance in population biology. MHA, p.14.
19. *Encyclopaedia Britannica*, 1824 Edition, p.44.
20. ibid. p.45.
21. B. Stapleton. Malthus: the local evidence and the principle of population. This volume, pp.45–59.
22. Quoted from the *Principles of Political Economy* by W. Petersen in *Malthus*, p.235. Harvard University Press, Cambridge, Massachusetts.
23. H. Le Bras, loc. cit. in note 15.
24. J. Schmid. L'évolution de la pensée malthusienne en tant que source d'une éducation en matière de population. MHA, p.17.
25. M. Cartier, loc. cit. in note 15.
26. A. J. Coale (1978). *T. R. Malthus and the Population Trends in his Day and Ours*, p.8. The Ninth Encyclopaedia Britannica Lecture. University of Edinburgh.
27. Cited by W. Petersen, op. cit. in note 22, p.234.
28. ibid. p.109.
29. J. M. Keynes (1937). Some consequences of a declining population. *Eugenics Review* **29**, 13–17. (The Galton Lecture, delivered on February 16, 1937.)
30. A. Lux. Les principes d'économie politique de Malthus, arbitre du conflit des deux versions du principe de population de l'*Essai*. MHA, p.16.
31. M. Cartier, loc. cit. in note 15.
32. ibid.
33. W. Petersen, op. cit. in note 22.
34. ibid. p.126.
35. T. R. Malthus, op. cit. in note 4, p.345.
36. ibid. p.344.
37. Quoted by Gertrude Himmelfarb, op. cit. in note 1, p.xxxii.

38. T. R. Malthus, op. cit. in note 4, p.2.
39. T. R. Malthus (1826). *An Essay on the Principle of Population*, 6th Edition, p.442. John Murray, London.

2 The Fate of Malthus's Work: History and Ideology

Y. CHARBIT

Malthus is regarded by posterity as a symbol of anti-populationism, if not the declared enemy of the human species. When Proudhon wrote: "To kill or to prevent men from being born, this is where Malthus's theory will lead to, willy-nilly"[1] and when Sauvy, a century later, coined the phrase "Malthusian Spirit",[2] both writers attributed to Malthus responsibility for originating a school of thought which was opposed to population growth.

However, in the 1817 Edition of the *Essay* Malthus affirmed: "There is nothing more desirable than the most rapid increase in population, unaccompanied by vice and misery."[3] Or, even more clearly: "I can easily conceive that this country [England] . . . might in the course of some centuries contain two or three times its present population and yet every man in the kingdom be much better fed and clothed than he is at present."[4]

In an important article published in 1945, Spengler has shown the conditions that Malthus envisaged for success in "uniting the two grand *desiderata,* a great actual population and a state of society in which abject poverty and dependence are comparatively but little known; two objects which are far from being incompatible".[5] The author of the *Principles of Political Economy* thought that it was essential for there to be a strong and sustained effective demand both for labour and for goods, and he systematically described the conditions that would favour growth: a more equal distribution of landed property, the existence of a "non-productive" class, political justice and civil liberty, and, above all, industrialization. In fact, Malthus favoured a society which was composed of the middle classes and had middle-class

MALTHUS PAST AND PRESENT
ISBN 0-12-224670-5

values, a point of view which is far removed from his image as a tool of the landed aristocracy. Although we shall not be concerned with Malthus's theory of economic growth in this chapter, we shall draw upon it in order to explain why he has so often been misinterpreted.

Even though Malthus may have been responsible for these misunderstandings himself, because of the obscurities and contradictions in his argument which even the most sympathetic reader will notice, the *First Essay* constituted only the first stage of his thought. To understand him properly, it is necessary to consider the totality of his views as expressed in successive editions of the *Essay, The Principles of Political Economy* and the *Summary View.* The *First Essay* published anonymously in 1798 was a political and philosophical polemic based on theoretical arguments; it changed in successive editions into a treatise on population, in which empirical observation occupied an important place. And this change resulted in the abandonment of the theory that in Europe the size of the population was determined by the level of subsistence. Through a study of demographic and social conditions Malthus was impressed by the practical importance of the preventive check; it is the individual's attempt to maintain or improve his standard of living that leads to delayed marriage. This interpretation does not agree with that of Eversley who thinks that Malthus stresses the importance of the standard of living in determining fertility, and regards it a spur for the individual to limit his family.[6] Malthus cannot, therefore, be regarded as having anticipated economic theories of fertility.

This very rapid survey of different aspects of Malthus's theory shows its extreme complexity; it is representative of the century in which it was written. As do Adam Smith's *Wealth of Nations* but unlike David Ricardo's *Principles of Political Economy*, Malthus's writings contain metaphysical reflections on evil and on the creation as well as contributions to demographic and economic theories and a discussion of social and political policies which is by no means limited to a consideration of the Poor Laws. It is not surprising, therefore, that he should have been misunderstood. Some of his detractors have concentrated their criticisms on the equilibrium between population and means of subsistence which he describes in the *First Essay* and have not taken account of the important and extensive development of his theory in later editions. Others have neglected his contributions to demographic and economic theory and have limited their interests to the implications of these theories for population policy. Because of the complexity of his argument, a number of conclusions have erroneously been attributed to him. The reason why these errors have flourished during the nineteenth century, and to some extent have persisted even to this day, lies in a number of historical and ideological factors which we shall attempt to trace in this paper.

The diffusion of Malthus's ideas

It is often said of Malthus's work that, like other classics, it has been more frequently cited than read. Because it took some time for it to be translated into other languages, it was not easily accessible to scholars whose mother tongue was not English, and its initial circulation was probably limited. The German and French translations had to serve as a reference for a long time, particularly in Hungary, the Netherlands and Russia. Malthus was not translated into Russian until 1868, the translation being that of the Guillaumin edition of 1845.[7]

We must recognize the high quality of the German translations by Hegewisch Stöpel and Barth, and that of the French translation by Pierre and Guillaume Prévost. However, the first translation into French of the *Principles of Political Economy* was by Francisco Constancio, a Portuguese by origin, who was no doubt influenced by the near-feudal conditions in his own country and reproached Malthus vehemently for his defence of large landowners.[8] Translators and editors often felt the need to add prefaces or introductions, and sometimes notes and commentaries on the original text to their translations, and these must inevitably have influenced the readers, who were frequently given a cut version of the original.[9] But it may be argued that these attempts to clarify and explain were an inevitable consequence of the complexity of Malthus's thought. Moreover, it would be wrong to confine blame for this to the nineteenth century alone. Some recent French translations of Malthus, or articles dealing with his work in encyclopaedias, are strongly polemical and dramatize the discussion of his theories.[10]

Lastly, a considerable responsibility for the misinterpretation of Malthus is due to the neo-Malthusians. In the Netherlands and in Sweden, where Knut Wicksell played a decisive part, Malthus's name became known to the general public as a result of neo-Malthusian propaganda. In England, from about 1820 onwards, Francis Place was one of the principal protagonists in this movement and the Bradlaugh–Besant trial of 1877 helped to give a decisive impetus to neo-Malthusianism.[11] Thus, many years after his death, Malthus's name became linked with a violently controversial subject and the view was wrongly attributed to him that the prevention of births through contraception was desirable or even necessary. In fact, he strongly opposed this attitude, partly for moral reasons, but mainly because he believed that individual effort could only be stimulated by moral restraint. The prudential check, he thought, would only lead to indolence and idleness. Neo-Malthusians have obfuscated one of the essential elements of Malthus's theory by substituting the prudential check for moral restraint. Malthus favoured population growth, provided such growth could be achieved without leading to misery or vice. These considerations lead us to a discussion of a number of fundamental misrepresentations of which Malthus was a victim.

Misunderstandings and inaccuracies

We shall give three examples to show different distortions to which Malthus's theories were subjected.

The most important of these concerns the notion of a "trend" and the very Principle of Population. First, we must correct a gross error. Some writers, such as Chernishevsky, compare the arithmetic and the geometric progressions and suggest that the imbalance was not as dramatic as the numbers suggest, because a doubling of the population could not continue indefinitely.[12] In fact, Malthus spoke of a "tendency to double". In the *First Essay* he wrote in the course of his refutation of Godwin: "I am sufficiently aware that the redundant 28 millions . . . that I have mentioned could never have existed."[13]

Another misunderstanding of the nature of the term "trend" is clearly brought out in the celebrated correspondence between Malthus and Nassau Senior and is more interesting. Senior observed that there was a tendency for subsistence to grow faster than population. Malthus replied that this interpretation of the word "tendency" would reduce his theory to the simple statement that population was determined by subsistence, whereas his reasoning was actually based on the reproductive potential of the human species. Edwin Cannan comitted the same error when he regarded the Principle of Population as "the principle by which population is kept in check by subsistence".[14].

How are we to interpret the important role attributed by Malthus to the human capacity to reproduce despite his recognition that, in practice, this capacity was held in check by the preventive or the positive check? We must look to Malthus's general theory of population for an answer to this question. Effective demand is the driving force of population growth, for as Malthus writes in his *Principles of Political Economy:* " . . . to suppose a great and continued increase of population is to beg the question."[15] Given these assumptions, consistency with the *First Essay* could be attained simply by postulating that population would always respond to an increased demand for labour.

The Principle of Population could then be redefined as a "Principle of Economic Growth"[16] and a social and economic analysis of the nature of effective demand will supply an answer to the fundamental question: How can this vital force be used to the best advantage? We must note the difference between this view and the *First Essay* where population growth was regarded as immediate and necessary, because it was part of the design of the Creator. Though His wishes are clearly stated, mankind's behaviour as revealed by observation runs the risk of negating God's intentions.

> We cannot but conceive that it is an object of the Creator, that the earth should be replenished; and it appears to me clear, that this could not be effected without a tendency in population to increase faster than food; and, as with the present law of increase, the peopling of the earth does not proceed very rapidly, we have undoubtedly some reason to believe, that this law is not too powerful for its apparent object.[17]

Malthus was perfectly clear and consistent in his view of moral restraint. This consists of premarital continence with a postponement of marriage to the time when an individual was in a position where he had a reasonable prospect of being able to care for all the children that would be born of his union. In other words, moral restraint does not involve any control of fertility within marriage. The practice of contraception derives from the prudential check and is characteristic of neo-Malthusianism. French economists, including those who proclaimed themselves the guardians of Malthusian orthodoxy, openly recommended the adoption of the prudential check; far from being immoral, its adoption to them appeared to be a sign of responsible conduct.[18]. This surprising deviation from Malthus's own position can be explained only by a desire on their part for an efficient means of preventing births. Can a worker have any idea of the mean number of children produced in a marriage? Or can he know whether his and his wife's fertility exceeds the average?[19] How is it possible to calculate the costs of a child up to the time that he or she becomes a producer? Is the average price of corn, as used by Malthus, a good index, given the large fluctuations in this figure caused by harvest failures? Again, is it realistic to expect the practice of sexual continence from demoralized individuals? Malthus only advises a preventive check against misery; once an individual has married, he can no longer practise moral restraint. All these objections, some of which were put forward by Malthus's contemporary opponents, show the unrealistic nature of his rules of conduct. The essential features of his theory were perfectly logical. In order to conform with the intentions of the Creator and achieve replenishment of the earth without causing misery, the prudential check must be rejected as an invitation to idleness and the necessity of moral restraint be insisted upon. French economists, however, were more realistic or less inhibited by religious orthodoxy and, therefore, preferred the prudential check.

However, we need to consider the implications of this point of view. Even orthodox Malthusians felt compelled to sacrifice theoretical rigour when it came to the formulation of policy which shows how difficult it is to distinguish between Malthus's original theory and the ideas which were popularized by his followers. It will, therefore, be useful to assess the importance of historical and of ideological factors.

The third example we cite reinforces the need for such an investigation. The notion of "means of subsistence" has suffered less at the hands of Malthus's opponents because there is general agreement on the meaning of this term. Moreover, Malthus himself, following the example of Adam Smith, occasionally refers to "necessaries", i.e. to goods which are essential for the satisfaction of vital needs, such as clothing and housing.[20]

Two important modifications may, however, be mentioned. The first occurred in Germany, where in 1902 Franz Oppenheimer introduced the concept of *Nahrungsspielraum* or "margin of subsistence". The population of every country has come up against and will inevitably come up against the margin of food production. The term *Nahrungsspielraum* for which it is difficult to find an equivalent term in another language, suggests the idea "that a determinate part of the inhabited territory of a nation will be needed to produce its subsistence. From this there follows in the political field, the concept of a pressure of population against national frontiers."[21] We are not far from the concept of *Lebensraum.*

The second modification is the substitution of the concept of "means of existence" for "means of subsistence". Malthus was perfectly aware of the fact that only a section of the population lived at the minimum level of subsistence. A characteristic misunderstanding of Malthus's theory has been to use the concept of "means of existence" as an argument against him; the level of subsistence could not determine the size of a population, because long before a situation was reached where the population was living at the margin of subsistence, the level of growth would come up against the means of existence or conventionally accepted standard of living.[22]. Little need be said about such of superficial interpretation of Malthus's argument. However, the appearance of the concept of 'means of existence' in a number of countries leads us to question the reason for its introduction. The success of this explanatory concept may be regarded as a direct consequence of the change from a primarily agricultural to a primarily industrial society and to consequent increases in the standard of living.

The weight of history

To the extent that the arguments in the *Essay* were based on an impressive array of demographic and social data, it was to be expected that commentators would attempt to verify or falsify Malthus's thesis on an empirical basis. This was the case in Poland, Hungary and Sweden.[23] The central problem investigated was the rate of population growth and the truth of the assertion that population doubled every 25 years. By showing that the population of a particular country was growing more slowly than this it was deduced that the arguments in the *Essay* did not apply to that country. This was the case, for instance, in Germany, Russia and Czechoslovakia.[24] Malthus himself recognized that under certain conditions the population of England could have been much larger than the actual figure. An argument based solely on statistics would not, therefore, be sufficient to refute the Principle of Population. However, it was inevitable that Malthus's ideas would come to be regarded as obsolete, and the existence of a strong anti-Malthusian movement, such as existed in England, Sweden and the Netherlands, resulted in a situation, where the whole of Malthusian theory was rejected. In these circumstances, Malthus's theories and particularly his formulation of the principle of effective demand had little chance of not being regarded as obsolete.

Some Dutch writers were perfectly aware that the age at marriage in Holland was already fairly high, so that the doctrine of moral restraint, if applied, would only have a limited effect on population growth. Moreover, its adoption would result in other evils, such as, for instance, prostitution. However, after 1918 there was a revival of apprehension about absolute over-population and consequently a revival of interest in Malthus.[25] In Sweden, the position was different. During the nineteenth century, emigration from Sweden was so important that fears were expressed about the future continuation of the population. Emigration was relatively neglected in the Malthusian system, and fear of overpopulation was absent in a country whose population was three million in 1850 and which lost one million emigrants during the following 60 years.[26] In England, Malthusian ideas became less important after the reform of the Poor Laws precisely because Malthus himself had been involved directly in the debate.[27]

The decline in fertility that was observed in France during the second half of the nineteenth century and which extended later to other European countries profoundly influenced the development of ideas. It was not so much the demographic facts themselves which were important in this context, as the reaction to them and the significance given to them by contemporary commentators. In this connection, it is of interest to consider the reactions of French economists. Until the revolution of 1848 they, almost to a man, adopted Malthusian views. But when the rate of population growth diminished during the Second Empire and particularly after 1860, they became more populationist: the need to supply manpower for expanding industries, the colonial rivalry with England, the increasing danger of a war with Prussia after the latter's victory over the Austrians at Sadowa, all these facts stressed the relative weakness of France, compared with her more fertile neighbours and brought the subject into the forefront of the discussion.[28] Towards the end of the century populationist pressure groups became very active in their denunciation of Malthusian behaviour on the part of the population. Finally, a very strict law against abortion was enacted in 1920.

The industrial revolution was very important in this context. Improvements in the techniques of agricultural production and the expansion of industry resulted in optimistic and anti-Malthusian views about population growth in a number of countries.[29] Three aspects of Malthus's theory were considered to be obsolete. The concept of "means of existence" replaced the "level of subsistence" as standards of living rose. At a later stage, when it became evident that overpopulation did not constitute a problem in European countries, it was suggested that some social groups — manual workers in particular — had larger families than they could afford. Neither of these two views added anything new to Malthusian ideas. However, the fact that they were used to discredit Malthus once again shows the gap between what Malthus actually wrote and the views that were ascribed to him by posterity.

A more interesting matter is the rejection of the concept of "moral restraint". It was abandoned for two reasons: in the first place it was ineffective for the poor, who most needed it, were unable to practise it, and secondly, it had become unnecessary, for it was believed that economic progress would automatically lead to greater caution and foresight on the part of individuals, anxious not to lose their acquired standard of living.

Theories relating standards of living to population growth became a real alternative to Malthusianism, when it became necessary to explain the decline in fertility and the diminution of the rate of growth. Because the theory was consistent with observations, it was adopted as an explanation.

The role of ideology

No analysis of the consequences of industrialization can be regarded as value-free because social peace depended upon the living conditions of the workers. But, even though changes in ideology are in a large measure the product of historical forces, they, nevertheless, merit our attention. The violence of the polemics associated with the name of Malthus owes much to the central position which he occupied in the ideological controversies of the nineteenth century.

Conservative thinkers in Western Europe frequently used Malthusian arguments in defence of the existing social order. In its crudest form, his doctrine was stated to assert that the principal cause of workers' poverty lay in the excessive size of their families.[30] Malthus was, therefore, invoked as an advocate of self-help; the individual's success was dependent on his own efforts. The stress on the biological aspects of Malthus's theory was a characteristic of social conservatism. The advocacy of the prudential check was introduced into bourgeois ideology in a more subtle fashion: in France and the Netherlands, for example, the poor and the working class were advised to model their behaviour on that of the bourgeoisie, who made sure that their fertility and their resources remained in equilibrium.[31] The decline in French fertility was interpreted as a demonstration that social harmony could be achieved, provided that the working class were prepared to accept a bourgeois model of behaviour in one of the basic aspects of life — reproduction. But liberal thinkers in France, Sweden and the Netherlands were more optimistic, and their belief in the benefits to be derived from economic progress led them to take up intellectual positions which were moderately anti-Malthusian.[32]

Socialists were unanimously opposed to Malthus and stressed causes of poverty which were due to the organization of society. The allegory of the banquet (which it should be noted only figures in the edition of 1803) was always used to reproach Malthus. This was not merely an instinctive reaction against the inhumanity of the doctrine. The allegory was taken as a symbol for the justification of inequalities in the distribution of wealth. This is shown by a reformulation of Malthus's doctrine in 1895 by a Marxist professor of Political Economy in

Holland. Consider the original text:

> No one who is born into this world and whose family are unable to support him, or for whose labour there is no demand, has the least right to subsistence.

Van der Goes changed this sentence to:

> In capitalist society an individual whose labour cannot be used profitably is a surplus individual: this is the true meaning of overpopulation.[33]

Marx's and Engels's criticisms of Malthus were much more fundamental and the difference between them may be described as an "epistemological fissure".[34] Marx thought that it was impossible to construct a theory of population which was independent of economic analysis; there was no natural and universal law of population, but only historical laws which were appropriate to different modes of production. By analysing the law which applied to capitalism, Marx developed the concept of the industrial reserve army. An historical explanation for the difference between Marx and Malthus has been suggested. They lived at different stages of the demographic transition. Malthus wrote his *Essay* in the pre-industrial era, when mortality was the primary determinant of population growth and the age at marriage was also important. Marx, on the other hand, formulated his views in an industrial society, in which the demand for labour determined the size of population growth and this is the reason why he did not consider whether population growth was limited by subsistence.[35] In Marxist terms: "It is not natural reproduction which creates the reserve army of labour, nor does it provide the means of accumulation".[36]

A division between Malthusians and anti-Malthusians can also be found in Eastern Europe during the nineteenth century. In Russia, for instance, the inheritance of ideas from the Enlightenment and the belief in the fundamental goodness of human nature made it difficult to accept the concept of population as a destructive force and led to the support of romantic anti-Malthusian views. The Russian populists developed arguments very similar to those of the Socialists in Western Europe.[37] However, there is one fundamental difference: in France, the Netherlands and England the bourgeoisie had come to be dominant, the regimes in Eastern Europe were still largely feudal. Those liberals who were struggling against autocracy in Hungary suggested that the country was not suffering from overpopulation: the abolition of serfdom, the development of agricultural techniques and of industry and commerce would allow the population to grow under a regime of free capitalism.[38]

When a book has achieved historical importance, it is inevitable that when employed for ideological purposes, the views expressed in it will be distorted in different countries, for they may be used to interpret the world in different ways. In so far as we can analyse Malthus's thought objectively at the present day, it is clear that he has been badly misinterpreted. Whereas he addressed himself to the problem of how population and economic growth could be combined, posterity has come to regard him as a determined opponent of all population growth.

In this paper we have discussed the historical circumstances in which Malthusian ideas were diffused and the ambiguities and obscurities that can be found in his text. But it is important to stress the difference between the renown that he achieved as a demographer, and the relatively limited influence of his economic doctrines, for the contributions that he made to the theory of economic growth remained unrecognized for a long time.

Today, the two central concepts with which Malthus was constantly concerned and which are characteristic of his theory, moral (not prudential) restraint and the Principle of Population, appear most useful in connection with the theory of effective demand. According to Malthus, a strong and sustained demand for labour was necessary to ensure economic progress and happiness, since this was the only means of stimulating population without adversely affecting the living conditions of the people. This was achievable, provided individuals practised moral restraint, the only method of regulating fertility which, in Malthus's view, did not lead to either idleness or misery. Until John Maynard Keynes rediscovered this theoretical contribution by Malthus, the logical connection which existed between moral restraint and the Principle of Population remained unrecognized. This is the reason for the different fortunes of the two concepts; moral restraint was forgotten because it had no value for the formulation of policy, but the Principle of Population and the two progressions were constantly discussed and remained to be cited as an obstacle and counter-argument to the more generous Utopian ideas of the nineteenth century.

These misunderstandings could, in fact, have been foreseen. Malthus's views on effective demand found no immediate support, because they contradicted Say's law, which was used to justify a belief in an harmonious economic order during a century which was marked by economic crises and social conflict and in which conditions were fundamentally unstable, because of the progress of industrialization. Bourgeois ideology found Say's ideas more to its liking than the insecure and pessimistic perspectives opened up by Malthusian theory.

Notes

1. P. J. Proudhon (1923). *Système de contradictions économiques ou Philosophie de la misère*, vol. 2, p.320. Marcel Rivière, Paris.
2. A. Sauvy (1969). *General Theory of Population*, Chapter 10. Weidenfeld & Nicolson, London.
3. Cited by J. J. Spengler (1945). Malthus's total population theory: a restatement and reappraisal. *Canadian Journal of Economics and Political Science*. Quotation from the *Essay*, 1817 Edition, p.550.
4. T. R. Malthus. *Essay*, Everyman Edition, vol. 2, p.174.
5. ibid. p.172.
6. D. E. C. Eversley (1959). *Social Theories of Fertility and the Malthusian Debate*, p.252. Clarendon Press, Oxford. Eversley relies for his interpretation on a passage from Book III, Chapter 13 (Everyman Edition, vol. 2, p.134). However, the interpretation of this passage is not straightforward. Malthus merely states that an increase in the standard of living is associated with a rising age at marriage (see e.g. Everyman Edition vol 2, p.257). Here Malthus analyses the consequences of a rise in the price of corn relatively to other consumption goods; in this case a fall in real wages will probably be compensated for by an increase in purchasing power. "[The labourer] will not indeed have the same power of maintaining a large family; but with a small family he may be better lodged and clothed and better able to command the decencies and comforts of life." Two different cases must be distinguished. For a single individual, an increase in the age at marriage reduces the period of exposure to the risk of having children and this situation is often envisaged by Malthus. But as this change in prices occurs at a given moment it will also affect the level of living of those persons who are already married and they can improve their standard of living by voluntarily restricting their families. Thus, as Eversley suggests, Malthus did consider the possibility of contraception within marriage. One can object to the ambiguity of his formulation and read the passage as applying only to bachelors. In another passage in which he analyses the effect of a change in the price of corn in a specific historical period (England between 1735 and 1755 and between 1790 and 1811), he envisages only a change in the age at marriage (ibid. vol. 2, pp.137–140). A second objection is that the passage cited is the only one in which the relationship between the level of living and fertility control is spelt out. Thirdly, the idea of contraception within marriage is totally alien to Malthus's moral and religious views. Francis Place noted that Malthus avoided the problem by reason of his social conformism. "Mr. Malthus seems to shrink from the propriety of avoiding

conception, not so much it may be supposed from the abhorrence which he or any reasonable man can have to the practice, as from the possible fear of encountering the prejudices of others (cited by K. Smith (1951). *The Malthusian Controversy*, p.321. Routledge, London). Fourthly, Malthus was favourably inclined towards moral restraint for reasons of policy, which we shall discuss later, and, therefore, even in his analytical work favoured changes in the age at marriage as the mechanism to be used for the regulation of population growth.

7. W. Berelowitch. Les lectures de Malthus dans la Russie d'avant la révolution. MHA, p.27. See also the following. Irene Hogen Esch. Malthus in the Netherlands: The reception of his *Essay* during the nineteenth century. MHA, p.33: R. A. Horvath, Les idées malthusiennes, le développement de la population hongroise et son impact sur la démographie historique. MHA, p.35; P. van Praag. Les vicissitudes de Malthus aux Pays-Bas. MHA, p.41.
8. W. Braeuer. Les traductions de l'*Essai* en Allemand. MHA, p.29; Jacqueline Hecht. "Traduttore Traditore?" Les traductions de l'*Essai*" de Malthus en langue française. MHA, p.32; J. G. da Silva. Une lecture méridionale de Malthus. MHA, p.30.
9. W. Berelowitch, loc. cit. in note 7; W. Braeuer, loc. cit. in note 8; J. Hecht, loc. cit. in note 8; I. Hogen Esch, loc. cit. in note 7.
10. W. Berelowitch, loc. cit. in note 7; J. Hecht, loc. cit. in note 8; J. and S. Sterboul. A la lettre M, entre Malte-Brun et Maltitz. MHA, p.39.
11. I. Hogen Esch, loc. cit. in note 7; T. H. Hollingsworth. The influence of Malthus on British thought. This volume pp.213–221; A. S. Kälvemark. Malthus and neo-Malthusianism in Sweden. MHA, p.35.
12. W. Berelowitch, loc. cit. in note 7.
13. T. R. Malthus. *First Essay on Population* (Royal Economic Society Reprint), p.193.
14. R. Minami. An interpretation of the Malthusian Principle of Population. MHA, p.37.
15. T. R. Malthus. *Principles of Political Economy,* 2nd Edition, Book II, Chapter I, Section II, p.313.
16. loc. cit. in note 14.
17. T. R. Malthus, op. cit. in note 4, vol. 2, p.157.
18. Y. Charbit (1981). *Du malthusianisme au populationisme. Les économistes français et la population, 1840–1870.* INED. Travaux et documents. Cahier No. 90, pp.62–65. Presses Universitaires de France, Paris.
19. Malthus refuted this argument. ". . . when a man marries, he cannot tell what number of children he shall have, and many have more than six. This is certainly true; and in this case I do not think that any evil would result from making a certain allowance to every child above this number; not with a view to rewarding a man for his large family, but merely of relieving him from a species of distress which it would be unreasonable in us to expect that he should calculate upon." (*Essay*,Everyman Edition, vol.

2, p.255). In these circumstances, Malthus advocates the granting of an allowance which would put a man with more than six children in the same position as if he had had six.

20. cf. for instance, *Essay,* Everyman Edition, vol. 2, p.153. It would be possible to regard Malthus as a precursor of modern theories of consumption; he clearly describes changes in consumption which are linked to periods of prosperity and particularly in access to convenience and luxury goods. On the other hand, he does not consider the effect of prosperity on fertility and thus ignores a fruitful field of enquiry – the economic theory of fertility, and particularly the argument based on the level of living. For distinction between different categories of consumption goods see *Essay*, Everyman Edition, vol. 2, pp.88, 134, 140.
21. Ingeborg Essenwein-Rothe. Les mésaventures de la pensée de Malthus en Allemagne. MHA, p.31.
22. Y. Charbit. Les économistes français et Malthus; divergences doctrinales et idéologie (1820–1870). MHA, p.30.
23. R. A. Horvath, loc. cit. in note 7; A. S. Kälvemark, loc. cit. in note 11; E. Rosset. Malthus dans la littérature polonaise. MHA, p.39.
24. W. Berelowitch, loc. cit. in note 7; I. Essenwein-Rothe, loc. cit. in note 21; Alena Subrtova. La pensée de Malthus sur le territoire de Tchécoslovaquie. MHA, p.40.
25. P. van Praag, loc. cit. in note 7.
26. A. S. Kälvemark, loc. cit. in note 11.
27. T. H. Hollingsworth, loc. cit. in note 11. "Malthus had won his battle over the Poor Laws and could now be conveniently forgotten."
28. Y. Charbit, loc. cit. in note 18, pp.147–183.
29. W. Berelowitch, loc. cit. in note 7; Y. Charbit, loc. cit. in note 22; T. H. Hollingsworth, loc. cit. in note 11; P. van Praag, loc. cit. in note 7; A. Subrtova, loc. cit. in note 24.
30. W. Berelowitch, loc. cit. in note 7; E. Hofsten. Malthus and discussions on poverty in Sweden during the 1830s. MHA, p.33.
31. Y. Charbit, loc. cit. in note 22; P. van Praag, loc. cit. in note 7.
32. Y. Charbit, loc. cit. in note 18, pp.121–123; E. Hofsten, loc. cit. in note 30; P. van Praag, loc. cit. in note 7; A. Subrtova, loc. cit. in note 24.
33. Cited by I. Hogen Esch, loc. cit. in note 7.
34. L. Behar. Malthus, Marx et la problématique démographique. MHA, p.27.
35. A. C. M. Bots. Population pressure and industrial reserve army: Malthus and Marx on the population issue. MHA, p.28.
36. B. Maris. La loi classique malthusienne de la population et sa critique chez Marx. MHA, p.36.
37. W. Berelowitch, loc. cit. in note 7.
38. R. A. Horvath, loc. cit. in note 7; E. Rosset, loc. cit. in note 23; A. Subrtova, loc. cit. in note 24.

3 Malthus and the Two Mortalities

H. LE BRAS

The use of the term "natural death" implies that there is another type —premature or irregular—which is, in some sense, abnormal. This was recognized in the past when longevity, rather than mortality was studied, i.e. the factors that determined the length of human life. More interest was taken in the reasons why men lived to an old age, i.e. lived out their natural span, rather than in the accidents which cut some down early in their lives. The treatises of Paracelsus, Aristotle, Ficin, Bacon and others all contain advice on how to live for a long time. But, as Vovelle and Ariès[1] have demonstrated, during the course of the eighteenth century the concept of mortality changed. At that time the slow decline of religion led to a de-spiritualization of the concept of life and fate. Mathematics, which had hitherto been applied only to the calculation of the movements of the heavenly bodies, came to be used to discover the laws underlying premature death. The study of longevity was now confined mainly to unscrupulous physicians, and, instead, mortality was studied as a background to death. Malthus was one of the architects of this change. In his writings, he gave a central place to premature death, though he found it very difficult to abandon the old and universally held ideas relating to longevity. His hesitations and the advances that he achieved deserve to be studied in detail.

Progress and stagnation in the study of mortality during the eighteenth century

Until the seventeenth century mortality was not studied by statistics; there were in any case no statisticians. Death was described in all its

MALTHUS PAST AND PRESENT
ISBN 0-12-224670-5

varieties and was attributed to the influence of the stars, the variation of the seasons, magic spells and, above all, to God. A certain regularity in the process of ageing, was accepted, as was the concept of a "natural death" which was achieved when all dangers to life had been avoided and the individual had reached the number of years that David had allotted to man.[2] The works of Graunt, Petty, Halley and Kersseboom showed which of the commonly held views on mortality could be verified by observation (e.g. excess mortality in large towns, higher mortality of men than of women, suspiciously low mortality from certain shameful diseases, such as syphilis, and from crime) and which were untenable. By 1746 Deparcieux had not progressed much beyond the stage that Graunt had reached nearly a century earlier; he had only demonstrated the falsity of some ideas that were current in his time:

> . . . everyone has wrong beliefs about the usual length of life of children, they think it much lower than it actually is[3] [à propos the expectation of life at the age of 10].
> . . .the ages between 40 and 50 are a critical period in women's lives.[4]
> It is a mistaken view that monks and nuns live longer than people outside the religious orders[5]. . .this error comes through judging from appearances.
> . . .there are many other even more ridiculous views, which can be shown to be false, if we were to examine their origins and the illusions which seem to favour them.[6]

This selection of fallacies still leaves the way open for considerable variations in mortality. Mortality will vary in space and time, it will differ in different localities, some years will be healthy and others unhealthy, diseases appear and disappear, the potential life of an individual will vary according to his of her origin.[7] Given all these differences, it was not possible for Graunt to establish a law of mortality.

The empiricism of the first students of mortality was followed by the use of mathematical models. Techniques for constructing life tables were elaborated and took their final form with Deparcieux's work in 1746.

The time was, therefore, ripe for improving observations and changing ideas about mortality. However, this did not happen. On the contrary, some very old views continued to be held for some time even after the new techniques for measuring mortality had been discovered.

As the concept of mortality does not appear in the works of Aristotle, Plato or St Thomas Aquinas, different writers used it in order to avoid inconsistencies in their argument and to bolster up their own *a priori* views. They did not pay much attention to observed mortality nor to methods of measurement, for they regarded the structure of their argument to be more important than mere statistics.

Three different approaches may be distinguished: that of the theologians, the naturalists and the philosophers.

The theologians regarded mortality as part of the manifestation of the divine order in nature. Its regularity bore witness to the perfection of the divine architect's work. Therefore, from very early times, they stressed the unchangeable and unchanging nature of mortality. They write of "natural laws for which the All Highest has a predilection"[8] and they investigate "the multiple aspects of order, which the divine majesty has given proof of, everything is regulated according to certain numbers and proportions".[9] These modern Pythagoreans, therefore, believed in the constancy of mortality. What is most remarkable is not only that man has the capacity of surviving everywere on the globe, but that everywhere he reaches a similar life span. Even 3000 years ago, men lived for as long as they do to-day.[10] Observed differences are but local imperfections which must not lead us to lose sight of the order of the whole. It is possible that the discovery of the law of large numbers may have influenced these views, but it is more likely that empirical studies of mortality were an embarrassment to the theologians. Where mortality exists it must be regular:

> . . .each age, each sex, each profession and each disease must make their pre-ordained contribution to the measure of mortality so that each year there will be exactly one death for every 36 living. If it were otherwise, chaos would reign.[11]

Kepler, Galileo and Newton raised analogous problems. Divine providence is made manifest not through the unexpected actions of the deity, but through the regularity and grandeur of His design. God is the architect, the celestial clockmaker.

The attitude of the naturalists towards mortality can best be illustrated by the works of Buffon and is not unlike that of the theologians. In *The Natural History of Man,* he writes, mortality is constant and

> nothing can change those laws of mechanics which regulate the number of our years, and which cannot be altered either by surfeits or by famine . . . neither differences of race, climate, nutrition nor supplies can make any difference to the length of human life.[12]

The same view was put forward in the *Grande Encyclopédie.* The ordinary length of life has remained unchanged since the world began to be populated; sacred and profane history alike prove this.[13] This surprising statement appears, even though the tables of Deparcieux, Simpson and Halley which are published on another page demonstrate the contrary to be true. This contradiction is apparent in Buffon's remark: "A man who does not die of accidental illness will live for 90 to 100 years."[14]

As a naturalist, Buffon is interested in the fundamental stability of natural phenomena. Any deviation from such stability is random, and it is these random deviations which have been studied by the political arithmeticians. This indicates Buffon's view of the nature of reality. He repeatedly states that the reality of the spirit is superior to that of the body. It also makes it possible to understand some of his passages; both those which are obscure and those which are over simple. For instance: "This law of nature which makes duration of life proportional to growth."[15] Buffon cites examples from the animal and vegetable kingdoms to illustrate his rules, but nowhere does he give a quantitative estimate of mortality. "Man takes 30 years to grow to be an adult and lives to be 90 or 100."[16]

This is the normal length of life, any deviation from this figure is of no interest to him, because it is neither natural nor biological.

> As is well known, men can die at any age, and although in general the length of human life exceeds that of almost all animals, it cannot be denied that it is at the same time more uncertain and more variable.[17]

The factors which cause premature death are social ones. Buffon is interested in a "natural history" which rejects any socio-economic explanation of mortality other than old age.

It therefore becomes necessary to distinguish between the appearance of mortality and its essential nature. The latter cannot be determined by empirical means; it can only be proved by a theoretical study of ageing, and any study of statistics will only provide information about appearances.

The third group whose views we discuss are the philosophers. They took a different attitude both to the concept of mortality and to the methods that need to be used for its study. Condorcet and Godwin, two of Malthus's favourite butts, regarded the world as being in a state of constant change and developed a theory of "organic perfectibility". Man will be transformed and the mean length of human life will increase without limit. However, this view is not based on any published life tables, either.

In the final chapter of the *Esquisse d'un tableau historique des progrès de l'esprit humain,* this point is made quite explicitly. Condorcet proposes an ingenious system of pensions and annuities which is not very different from modern systems of social insurance and recommends that mathematical methods be used to calculate the probabilities of survival and to find the right investment for money. The value of observations and of the application of technical methods for the analysis of mortality is, however, strictly limited. But when outlining the principle of organic perfectibility, Condorcet refers to the general progress of mankind since the savage state, and from these very general principles he derives a theory of the development of mortality.

> One believes that progress in life-saving medicine has exceeded that of reason and social order, and that this will lead to the disappearance of infectious and contagious disease and of those illnesses which are caused by climate, nutrition or the nature of work.[18]

His idea of an indefinite (but finite) decline of mortality is not based on any data, but is arrived at strictly by deductive reasoning.

We could continue to give examples, but the situation is clear. There is a clear difference in approach between the empiricists, calculators and data collectors on one hand, and the scientists and philosophers whose views on mortality are derived from *a priori* theoretical positions on the other. The neglect of numerical data and of life tables is evident in their writings. Condorcet merely proposes to "assemble and order the facts and to demonstrate those useful truths which are embodied in their sequence" because "philosophy is not concerned with guesswork nor does it have to advance hypothetical combinations".[19]

Malthus, too, neglected observational data in the *First Essay,* though he wrote that "experience [is] the true source and foundation of all knowledge".[20].

It might have been expected that once observations on mortality became available they would have been used immediately and the correct conclusions drawn. However, as it happened, they were not used to falsify theories of mortality that were current. The means that were used to construct such theories and those used to support them were very different. By looking at successive editions of Malthus's *Essay,* it is possible to trace how ideas on this subject were changing.

The *First Essay:* change and continuity

In spite of the distance which separates Buffon and Price from Godwin and Condorcet, none take much interest in the problem of premature death. For the first two, the city is the graveyard of mankind. Price, cited by Malthus affirms:

> . . . were there a country where the inhabitants led lives entirely natural and virtuous, few of them would die without measuring out the whole period of present existence allotted to them . . . and death would come upon them like a sleep, in consequence of no other cause than gradual and unavoidable decay.[21]

The two philosophers attribute premature death to social factors and believe that this type of mortality will gradually disappear with social progress. They differ from the naturalists in their views about the ultimate state of mortality; according to Buffon and Price mortality will ultimately reach a constant level, whereas Godwin and Condorcet believe that the decline can continue indefinitely. Whatever their view, neither takes much interest in the study of premature mortality, and this is the main reason why so little attention was paid to the work of the political arithmeticians.

Malthus's genius consists in the fact that he turned the problem upside down and focused interest on premature death rather than on the ultimate biological level of mortality. This made it possible to establish a link between the theory of mortality and observed numbers of deaths and to study mortality by means of the life table. We need to look at this change of attitude in some detail, for the underlying motives for this change of view and its consequences are far from simple.

Malthus's predecessors did not think that premature mortality could be attributed to any specific factor. Epidemics occurred at random, as did wars and famines. Wallace saw "no need to suppose that the number of men on earth should continually increase, and that the number during the present century should be greater than that during any preceding period".[22]

In pointing out the maximum rate of human population growth (doubling every 25 years), Malthus thought that at almost all times, and certainly for a long time in the past, the number of men had been determined by the level of subsistence. This limit operated through the operation of the preventive check (a reduction of general fertility) and the positive check (increased mortality, particularly that of the children of the poor). Premature death is, therefore, the rule rather than the exception, and its mechanics can only be discovered through study.

For this reason, Malthus pleads for a quantitative history of mankind:

> . . . histories of mankind that we possess are histories only of the

> higher classes . . . Some of the objects of enquiry would be in what proportion to the number of adults was the number of marriages, to what extent vicious customs prevailed in consequence of the restraint upon matrimony, what was the comparative mortality among the children of the most distressed part of the community and those who lived rather more at their ease . . .[23]

Although some of this information was available at the time when Malthus wrote, he does not appear to have paid much attention to it, and, like all his predecessors, hardly made use of any of the data that had been collected by the political arithmeticians. He apologizes for this omission at the beginning of his book in much the same way as Fermat did (when he found that there was no space at the margin to scribble down the proof of his celebrated theorem):

> . . . but a long and almost total interruption from very particular business, joined to a desire (perhaps imprudent) of not delaying the publication much beyond the time that he originally proposed, prevented the author from giving to the subject an undivided attention.[24]

Moreover, Malthus falls into the very trap set by this theory and his *a priori* views. For centuries past population had been held down by the level of subsistence, therefore, mortality could not have changed. He holds to this theory while at the same time criticizing Condorcet.

> The average duration of human life will to a certain degree vary, from healthy or unhealthy climates, from wholesome or unwholesome food, from virtuous or vicious manners, and other causes; but it may be fairly doubted whether there is really the smallest advance in the natural duration of human life, since first we have had any authentic history of man.[25]

Note the distinction between the *average duration* of human, life (which is very variable) and its *natural duration* (which is constant). Buffon had expressed similar views. However, because Malthus was obliged to deal with premature mortality, i.e. the average duration of life, he takes a more extreme point of view. Mortality from war, famine, and unhealthy conditions in large towns has replaced that from epidemics.[26] Süssmilch had made a similar point half a century earlier. "The unnoticed losses that the towns cause to the state are equal to the losses from plague."[27] Far from disagreeing with this point of view, Malthus retains it and stresses it in successive editions as, for instance, in his celebrated analogy of

> the channels through which the great stream of mortality is constantly

flowing will always convey off a given quantity. Now, if we stop up any of these channels, it is perfectly clear that the stream of mortality must run with greater force through some of the other channels.[28]

There seems to be some confusion here between premature and natural mortality, both of which now seem to be regarded as constant. However, this idea remains at the centre of Malthus's thought, particularly in the two chapters in which he attacks the ideas of both Condorcet and Godwin. As regards the former, Malthus does not appear to have fully understood the mathematical subtlety of Condorcet's reasoning and believes that he looks forward to a situation when men would become immortal. In fact, Condorcet prudently qualified his conclusions and "it is here that we must distinguish between the two senses of the word indefinite".[29] Progress will ultimately lead to men enjoying a finite span of life, or life may increase without limit. Wishing to deliver a knock-out blow, Malthus, without hesitation, attacks the first interpretation.

With regard to the duration of human life, there does not appear to have existed from the earliest of the world to the present moment, the smallest permanent symptom or indication of increasing prolongation. The observable effects of climate, habit, diet and other causes on length of life have furnished the pretext for asserting its definitive extension.[30]

The term "natural" is not used in this passage, because of premature deaths; the version used by the naturalists, however, reappears when he comes to deal with his opponents. He uses the same argument against Godwin when the latter suggests the possibility of the perfectibility of the human body as a result of spiritual development. To crush these two opponents, Malthus stresses the size of the population that would result from a lengthening of human life and the prompt reaction of nature which could not support such increased numbers. But Condorcet and Godwin had both forestalled criticism on this point by suggesting, in veiled terms, that social and moral progress would result in change when both sexes would behave more rationally. Godwin thought that social progress would lead to a reduction of the passion between the sexes, Condorcet paints a picture where:

. . . the ridiculous prejudices of superstition would cease to impose on morality an austerity which is both corrupting and degrading, instead of purifying and elevating; men will recognize their obligations to as yet unborn generations and these will consist not only of giving them life, but also providing them with happiness.[31]

For Malthus such an eventuality would appear as nothing other than vice, and he wraps himself in his cloak of offended virtue to reject this solution.

The importance given to this quarrel about the indefinite prolongation of human life seems out of all proportion to its importance and reminds one of the interminable debates about the fall of bodies from the moon to the earth between Galileo, Bouillaud, Fermat, Mersenne, degli Angeli, and Riccioli until Newton finally settled the matter by enunciating his famous law. The discussion does not deal with the extension of the actual mean duration of human life or even with the stability of this measure. Malthus wants to deny the possibility of the perfectibility of man. Further on in his work he has some home truths for the philosophers of the previous generation whom he holds responsible for the wicked French Revolution and for all optimists who were drawn to this "fermentation of disgusting passions of fear, cruelty, malice, revenge, ambition, madness and folly as would have disgraced the most savage nation in the most barbarous age".[32] The philosophers are atheists, he is religious; they believe in the possibility of rapid progress in all fields of human endeavour, he thinks progress is possible only in agriculture and then it will be slow; they favour equality, he defends differences between the rich and the poor; they wish to abolish private property, he regards its existence as a factor making for social stability.

His Principle is applied to the growth of population. At the end of the *First Essay* Malthus does no more and no less than develop a system of theoretical social mechanics; it is only through effort that man can become creative. "Necessity has been in great truth called the mother of inventions".[33]

Without a stimulus men will remain ignorant and idle. The Principle of Population rouses man to work. ". . . had populations and food increased in the same ratio, it is probable that man might never have emerged from the savage state".[34]

But in spite of himself and of his refutation of the philosophers, Malthus is in a sense also one of them. His God is no longer the omnipotent architect of Süssmilch, and Malthus is less preoccupied with Holy Scripture. His God is a liberal God, who lays down the laws of nature and then retires from the fray. These laws are unchangeable, for as Malthus argues, if they could be changed, man would never strive to discover them. We have used the term "liberal" deliberately, for the influence of Adam Smith is evident in the very Principle of Population; the demand for and supply of subsistence is included in it. The works of the philosophers have made it possible to discuss some subjects in human terms, and even to compare man with the animal kingdom, subjects which, it used to be thought, had to be left to the divine will or to its substitutes, nature and providence.

It therefore becomes both possible and desirable to collect empirical data about mortality and even to discuss its nature. This is what Malthus did, though, as we have shown, he did not realize the significance of his contribution. His progress came at two levels, viz. by studying premature rather than "natural" mortality, and by considering the two types of mortality together and thus making a unified treatment of the subject possible. He was, as it were, presenting new wine in old bottles.

A poor arithmetician

In the Preface to the second edition of the *Essay,* Malthus confessed that the success of the first had forced him to read about and to develop topics which he had only lightly touched upon in the *First Essay*.

Malthus's success had led him into a trap: he now needed to prove statements which hitherto he had only asserted. Becoming a demographer almost in spite of himself, he tackled this task with great determination; however, he did not acquire a sufficient mastery of the techniques of political arithmetic to apply them properly, and only succeeded in increasing the confusion about mortality.

Let us briefly consider his failures. In the *First Essay,* the checks to population growth were "misery and vice". There has been much discussion about the meaning of these two terms; the first was applied to various kinds of premature death, the second to prostitution and sexual relations outside marriage. It is clear that contraception was not included under either of these headings.

In the second edition Malthus introduced a new "preventive" check, the celebrated concept of "moral restraint", i.e. postponement of marriage. But once moral restraint is admitted into the system, the system becomes indeterminate, for the size of the population is no longer determined by a simple balance between the rate of population growth and the level of subsistence. Instead, it is determined by the positive check — mortality — and the preventive check — reduction of fertility through celibacy. Nowhere did Malthus indicate the relative importance that he attached to each of the two. Sometimes he referred to tyranny, i.e. the political system, at others to the economy or to the state of social progress.

These new conditions of equilibrium modified the part played by mortality completely; although the constancy of mortality suggested that population at all times was at the limit of subsistence, now mortality seemed to be variable.

> . . . the preventive and the positive check must vary inversely as each other; that is, in countries either naturally unhealthy or subject to a great mortality, for whatever cause it may arise, the preventive check will prevail very little. In countries on the contrary naturally healthy and where the preventive check is found to prevail with considerable force, the positive check will prevail very little and mortality be small".[35]

Clearly those regimes in which mortality is low are the most desirable. "I have stated expressly that a decrease of mortality at all ages is what we ought chiefly to aim at."[36]

In this connection Malthus reports the opinion of d'Ivernois that the mortality rates of children in a given country "show the relative merit of the government and the comparative happiness of their subjects".[37] Unfortunately, if the level of mortality is to be regarded as an index of civilization, the view that it is unchangeable will need to be abandoned, a view which was put forward with great vigour in the *First Essay*. Instead, one must draw nearer to the views of the detestable philosophers. Malthus avoided having to have recourse to this extreme by drawing a distinction between differences in time and in space. He admits that there exists a very considerable geographical diversity in mortality.

> Relying, however, too much upon this occasional coincidence, political calculators have been led into the error of supposing that there is generally speaking, an invariable order of mortality in all countries; but it appears on the contrary that this order is extremely variable; that it is very different in different places in the same country, and within certain limits depends upon circumstances which it is in the power of man to alter.[38]

But Malthus plays down the importance of these circumstances and exaggerates the obstacles which stand in the way of reducing mortality in a given place. In this way he can avoid accepting the opinions of those philosophers whom he had so vigorously criticized in the past.

Passages may be found in the later editions which indicate that Malthus had not given up hope of rediscovering an unchanging law of mortality. Thus, having shown that the mean length of life in England had grown by 17 per cent during the past years, he suspects

> that the whole of this proportional diminution of burials does not arise from increased healthiness, but is occasioned in part by the greater number of deaths which must necessarily have taken place abroad.[39]

Moreover, if the positive check were to become more important quickly, mortality would not necessarily fall, for prostitution and vice would result in new diseases which would replace those that had disappeared as a consequence of a more abundant subsistence. When discussing vaccination against smallpox he calls Haygarth's calculations "curious", though they are similar to those of Bernoulli, Duvillard and Laplace, and he suggests that the reduction in the prevalence of smallpox would result in the appearance of new diseases.

> The smallpox is certainly one of the channels and a very broad one, which nature has opened for the last thousand years to keep down the population to the level of means of subsistence. But had this been closed, others would have to become wider, or new ones would have been formed.[40]

Malthus believed that a reduction in mortality would be followed by a further rise and expresses this view by using the analogy of "channels". When one cause of death is suppressed it will be replaced by another. The only way to avoid this would be for the number of marriages to decline. This is a possibility that he does not altogether exclude from consideration. Alternatively, there may be a sudden improvement in the techniques of agriculture, but he considers this to be an unlikely contingency.

In the statistical tables which Malthus quotes from Euler's works, he regards a ratio of one death to every 36 living persons as constant. This is the same ratio of which Süssmilch wrote: "If it were otherwise, chaos would reign."[41]

These few examples show that Malthus did not put forward any theory of mortality. The distinction between natural and premature death has been abandoned, but nothing has been put in its place. Malthus no longer even appears to believe the empirical observation which delimits the role of the positive check and of mortality. In a note in the Appendix to the last edition of the *Essay* he writes:

> It would be a most curious, and to every philosophical mind a most interesting piece of information to know the exact share of the full power of increase which each existing check prevents, but at present I see no mode of obtaining such information.[42]

Notes

1. cf. P. Ariès (1977). *L'homme devant la mort.* Serol, Paris. M. Vovelle (1974). *Mourir autrefois. Attitudes collectives devant la mort au XVIIème et XVIIIème siècles.* Gallimard, Paris.
2. John Graunt uses, as did many of his contemporaries, the verse from the 90th psalm: "The days of our years are three score and ten, or even by reason of strength, four score years."
3. M. Deparcieux (1746). *Essai sur les probabilités de la durée de la vie humaine,* p.74, Guerin, Paris.
4. ibid. p.83.
5. ibid. p.85.
6. ibid. p.85.
7. An extensive list of these factors may be found, for example, in John Graunt's work, or in R. Price (1773). *Observations on Reversionary Payments,* particularly in the third edition, published in London.
8. J. Süssmilch (1775). *Die göttliche Ordnung im menschlichen Geschlecht,* 4th Edition, p.13. Berlin.
9. ibid.
10. ibid. p.101.
11. ibid. p.28.
12. G. Buffon (1792). *Histoire naturelle de l'homme*, p.188. Plassau, Paris.
13. Article on "Espérance de vie" in the *Grande Encyclopédie* of Diderot and d'Alembert.
14. G. Buffon, op. cit. in note 12, p.189.
15. ibid. p185.
16. ibid. p.185.
17. ibid. p.210.
18. Marquis C. de Condorcet (1933). *Esquisse d'un tableau historique des progrès de l'esprit humain,* p.236. Editions Boivin, Paris.
19. ibid. p.9.
20. T. R. Malthus. *First Essay*, p.17.
21. R. Price, op. cit. in note 7, vol. 2, p.243, cited by Malthus in the *First Essay.*
22. R. Wallace (1754). *A Dissertation on the Numbers of Mankind.* London.
23. T. R. Malthus, op. cit. in note 20, p.32.
24. ibid. Introduction, p.ii.
25. ibid. Chapter 9, pp.157–158.
26. ibid. p.113.
27. J. Süssmilch, op. cit. in note 8, p.114.
28. T. R. Malthus. *Essay*, 6th Edition, p.467.
29. Marquis C. de Condorcet, op. cit. in note 18, p.237.
30. T. R. Malthus, op. cit. in note 20, pp.161–162.
31. Marquis C. de Condorcet, op. cit. in note 18, p.237.
32. T. R. Malthus, op. cit. in note 20, pp.144–145.
33. ibid. p.338.
34. ibid. p.364.

35. T. R. Malthus. *Essay*, Everyman Edition, vol. 1, p.15.
36. T. R. Malthus, op. cit. in note 28, Appendix, p.549.
37. From d'Ivernois (1801). *Tableau des Pertes*, vol. II, p.16. Paris.
38. T. R. Malthus, op. cit. in note 28, vol. 2, p.342.
39. ibid. p.299.
40. ibid. p.469.
41. J. Süssmilch, op. cit. in note 8, p.101.
42. T. R. Malthus, op. cit. in note 28, Appendix, p.552.

4 Malthus: The Local Evidence and the Principle of Population

B. STAPLETON

Thomas Robert, son of Daniel Malthus Esquire, and Henrietta Catherine, was privately baptized on February 14th 1766 having been born on the 13th.[1] This entry in the parish register of Wotton indicates that the Malthus family then resided at the Rookery which just lay in the neighbouring parish of Dorking. Daniel Malthus was clearly no ordinary local resident. The title "Esquire" and the private as opposed to church baptism were both indicative of some social standing in the community. As the eldest child and only son of Sydenham Malthus he had inherited the family estate on his father's death in 1757. Sydenham had been a successful lawyer at Lincoln's Inn, a Director of the South Sea Company, and had acquired land in Hertfordshire and Cambridgeshire. His son Daniel went to Oxford, leaving without a degree, then followed his father into Lincoln's Inn, but abondoned the law. Two years after coming into his inheritance Daniel, then a married man with two children, bought Chert Gate Farm west of Dorking in Surrey and converted it into the Rookery. There, Robert Malthus was born, the second son and sixth child of the seven which Daniel and Henrietta were to produce.

From 1768, when Daniel sold the Rookery, to 1786, the Malthus family appear to have been highly mobile and thus difficult to trace. In 1773, they were tenants of part of Claverton House, near Bath in Somerset, where Robert also attended school. At the age of 16 in 1782, Daniel sent Robert to be educated by Gilbert Wakefield at a Dissenting Academy, located mid-way between Liverpool and Manchester at

MALTHUS PAST AND PRESENT
ISBN 0-12-224670-5

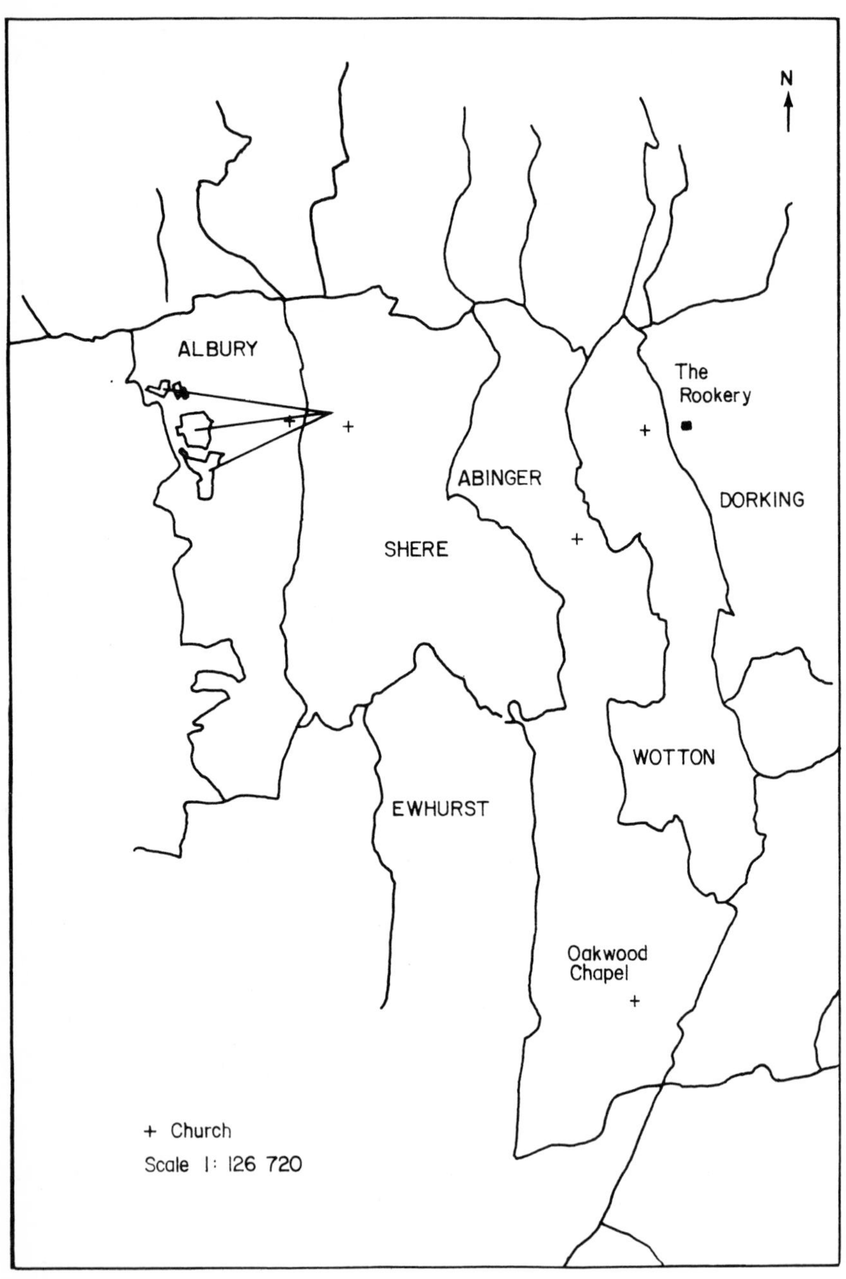

Surrey: The Malthus Parishes

Warrington in Lancashire, and the following year when the school closed he moved with Wakefield to continue his education at the latter's home in Bramcote near Nottingham. In 1784, when Daniel was living at Cookham, Berkshire, Robert became a student of Jesus College, Cambridge, and graduated early in 1788 as ninth Wrangler, the equivalent of a first class honours degree in mathematics. Later that year he was ordained at the age of 22.[2]

The year before Robert's graduation, his father returned to live in that part of Surrey where Robert was born and had spent the first two years or so of his life. In 1787 Daniel bought a house in an outlying part of Shere parish which was situated to the west in the parish of Albury, and there he remained until his death in 1800.[3] Little is known of Robert's movements between 1788 and 1798 but it would seem that it was at this house that he was to spend much of his time for the decade which passed between his graduation and the publication of the first *Essay on the Principle of Population.* Such a view can perhaps be supported firstly by the fact that in 1798 he was appointed curate of Oakwood, a chapel in the southern wooded part of the parish of Abinger which lay between Shere to the west and Wotton to the east; secondly by his references in the *First Essay* to "the labourers of the south of England", and to "those who live much in the country"[4]; and thirdly by a comment in the preface to the 1803 second edition of the *Essay* where, writing of the *First Essay,* Malthus stated: "It was written on the impulse of the occasion, and from the few materials which were then within my reach *in a country situation.*"[5]

Thus the environment from which the *First Essay* emerged was that of a comfortable middle-class family in the heart of rural Surrey where its author could indulge his pastimes of walking, riding, hunting and shooting.[6] It was this background and this locality which, along with "the few materials", would seem to have influenced Malthus's thinking when he was producing his famous *Principle of Population.* Accordingly, though he had clearly been busying himself with very little in the years between leaving Cambridge and becoming a curate[7], he was able to write of the stratum of society into which he was born that "the middle regions of society seem to be the best suited to intellectual improvement"[8] and, furthermore, that "extreme poverty, or too great riches may be alike unfavourable"[9] to the growth of mind. Having asserted the mental superiority of those with whom he associated, country gentry, clergy and professional men, he turned his attention to the social group which was at the centre of his thoughts:

> . . . the principal argument of this essay tends to place in a strong

point of view the improbability that the lower classes of people in any country should ever be sufficiently free from want and labour to obtain any high degree of intellectual improvement.[10]

Thus, the result of raising the wages of labourers from 18 pence (7.5p) to five shillings (25p) a day "would make every man fancy himself comparatively rich and able to indulge himself in many hours or days of leisure",[11] in much the same way presumably as the wealthier middle class behaved. To support his view he quotes some local evidence: "The labourers of the south of England are so accustomed to eat fine wheaten bread that they will suffer themselves to be half starved before they will submit to live like the Scotch peasants."[12] This comment is curiously at variance with his observation about those who live in the country noticing that:

. . . the sons of labourers are very apt to be stunted in their growth and are a long while arriving at maturity. Boys that you would guess to be fourteen or fifteen are, upon enquiry, frequently found to be eighteen or nineteen. And the lads who drive plough, which certainly must be a healthy exercise, are very rarely seen with any appearance of calves to their legs: a circumstance which can only be attributed to a want either or proper or sufficient nourishment.[13]

It is also at variance with his recognition of the advantages accruing from higher wages paid to workers in America:

". . . where the reward of labour is at present so liberal, the lower classes might retrench very considerably in a year of scarcity without materially distressing themselves."[14]

However, the major reason for his interest in the lower classes is their crucial role in the operation of the central principle of the *First Essay:*

"Population, when unchecked, increases in a geometrical ratio." Subsistence increases only in an arithmetical ratio."[15]

Having indicated the operation of the preventive check of later marriage in all ranks of society in England,[16] Malthus asserts that the positive check, infant and child deaths through malnutrition and disease, "is confined chiefly . . . to the lowest orders of society",[17] because it is these people who continue to have more children than they can support, and, citing Adam Smith in corroboration, Malthus states:

. . . if potatoes were to become the favourite vegetable food of the

> common people, and if the same quantity of land was employed in their culture as is now employed in the culture of corn, the country would be able to support a much greater population, and would consequently, in a very short time have it.[18]

Population thus invariably increased when the means of subsistence increased, and that increase, if unchecked, would be in a geometrical progression with population doubling in 25 years, a figure arrived at because it was the "ratio of increase which is well known to have taken place throughout all the Northern States of America."[19] American colonial population is said to have grown from some 400 000 in 1715 to about 2 500 000 in 1776,[20] mostly as a result of immigration, a factor which also contributed to the growth of 50 per cent between the first census in 1790 in which 4 000 000 people were recorded and that of 1820, in which the number was 10 million, although the major cause in this 30-year period was natural increase. Since the population grew from a relatively small size in a vast and underutilized geographical area, America was statistically and spatially a somewhat exceptional example for Malthus to use, but clearly one which would aptly demonstrate his theory.

Thus, as a result of actual experience, this ratio of increase of American population Malthus says "we will take as our rule and say that population when unchecked goes on doubling itself every twenty-five years or increases in a geometrical ratio."[21] The ratio of increase is then applied to Britain, "the population of the Island is computed to be about seven millions"[22] and at the end of a century would have reached 112 million whereas the means of subsistence would support only 35 million.

Problems, however, would have arisen before the population had reached 28 million since there would have been sufficient increase in food supply to feed only 21 million people.[23] The consequent rise in food prices "would immediately turn some additional capital into the channel of agriculture"[24] but agricultural output would only be able to respond very slowly to the rising prices of provisions, and increasing poverty would be inevitable. Such problems were inescapable since Providence had "ordained that population should increase much faster than food". The Principle of Population is thus elevated to a part of natural law ordained from above, and exists, because man is naturally "inert, sluggish, and averse from labour, unless compelled by necessity"[25] to be otherwise.

Consequently any development which interfered with the operation of the Principle by tending to raise the level of population without increasing food supply would by definition be harmful. And in England Malthus was certain that such was the result of the operation of the Poor Laws that the condition of the poor was actually worsened in two ways. First, by their tendency "to increase population without increasing the food for its support", and secondly because "the quantity of provisions consumed in workhouses upon a part of the society that cannot in general be considered the most valuable part diminishes the shares that would otherwise belong to more industrious and more worthy members".[26] Furthermore, the Poor Laws resulted in a weakening of the spirit of independence among the peasantry inducing men "to marry from a prospect of parish provision with little or no chance of maintaining their families in independence". They "diminish both the power and the will to save among the common people" who seem "always to live from hand to mouth" and "seldom think of the future".[27] Without the Poor Laws men would be more prudent since thoughts of death or sickness would deter them from going to the alehouse and dissipating their earnings for fear their families would starve. Thus the Poor Laws removed one of the strongest checks to idleness and dissipation and allowed men "to marry with little or no prospect of being able to maintain a family in independence."[28]

What was required was the encouragement of agriculture to provide more employment whilst raising the levels of food supply.[29] However, England's recent historical experience was quite different. Instead, Malthus notes "the commerce of this country, internal as well as external, has certainly been rapidly advancing during the last century". But because increasing wealth has been mainly the produce of labour and not land, the funds for maintaining labour have only risen slowly and the increasing national wealth "has had little or no tendency to better the condition of the labouring poor" and a much greater proportion of them "is employed in manufactures and crowded together in close and unwholesome rooms".[30] And the greater the proportion of population in manufacturing, and the fewer consequently in agriculture, meant the poor were worse off. Furthermore, Malthus argues that enclosure and related expansion of pastoral farming plus the growth of large farms had reduced the numbers employed in agriculture in the last century. Consequently, any increase in population must be employed in manufacturing, in which economic fluctuations and changing fashions had resulted in increasing numbers of paupers who had exchanged "the healthy labours of agriculture for the unhealthy occupation of manufacturing industry".[31] This prejudice against manufacturing industry was perhaps the result of his stay in

Warrington at the impressionable age of sixteen, since that town, manufacturing sailcloth, glass, ironwares and linens,[32] must have presented a stark contrast to rural Somerset. However, trade fared no better in Malthus's economic thinking since he stated that foreign commerce "will be found ... to have contributed but little to the increase of the internal funds for the maintenance of labour".[33] With such negative views on the economic contribution of manufacturing industry and overseas trade it is hardly surprising that Malthus was concerned about population growth. It is clear he was aware that economic growth was taking place, but was unable to recognize the advantages of the production of surplus manufactures for export in exchange for imported foodstuffs. He tended to view the economy as a closed one, despite the knowledge that Holland was dependent on food imports.[34] Growth, unfortunately for Malthus, was occurring in industry and trade, not agriculture, and the result was poverty. Hence, the "great increase of the poor rates is, indeed of itself a strong evidence that the poor have not a greater command of the necessaries and conveniences of life".[35] Malthus's solution was the total "abolition of all the present parish laws" because they interfered with the Principle of Population, plus premiums for expanding and encouraging agriculture and the weakening of institutions which caused agricultural labourers to be paid less than the labourers in trade and manufacture. Additionally he advocated the establishment of county workhouses.[36] Thus, the Principle of Population meant that the tradition established in Elizabethan times of the relief of poverty by public assistance was unacceptable, except in the most extreme cases.

The references to the labourers of the South of England make it clear that in the formulation of his views Malthus was influenced by the people he saw around him and the events he encountered. Some of those events, in his capacity as curate at Oakwood, would have brought him into contact with the labourers and their families, since the baptism of their children would have been one of Malthus's duties. Those baptisms are recorded in the registers of Oakwood chapel and in the decade from 1788 to 1798 show an average of 16 each year, a figure over three times greater than the average annual number of burials for the same period, which numbered only five. It seems impossible to believe that Malthus could have been unconscious of, or be uninfluenced by, such evidence. Yet there is no indication that, despite his first-class honours degree in mathematics, he ever used the local parish register information in a numerate manner, notwithstanding the fact that he demonstrated his awareness that at least two of his predecessors had made demographic calculations based on parish register baptism and burial entries. Malthus referred to Richard Price's use of such data in his *Observations on Reversionary Payments* and to Thomas Short's attempts to compare the proportion of baptisms to burials in the century before 1650 with the proportion from the late seventeenth century to 1750.[37] He criticized Price for using extracts from the registers for periods of insufficient extent by which to judge the real growth of population because it was not possible to infer the "increase for the twenty years before or . . . for the twenty years after". This was sound demographic comment and when applied to the registers of those parishes with which Malthus would have been most familiar, Wotton, Shere and Abinger with Oakwood chapelry, it produces interesting results.

At Wotton, for the whole of the seventeenth and eighteenth centuries little noticeable population growth occurred when baptism entries are compared with burials, especially between 1670 and 1740. Between 1780 and 1800 there was actually a surplus of burials, After 1730, Shere registers indicate steady but unspectacular growth of the parish's population, and at Abinger, after baptism surpluses in the early seventeenth century to the mid 1630s, the next 80 years indicate an almost stationary population, before it appears to rise steadily (with the exception of the 1740s when the levels of baptisms and burials are much the same). Only in Malthus's own curacy at Oakwod does an unequivocal rise in population occur, which is sufficiently large to ensure that when the baptisms and burials of Wotton, Abinger and Oakwood are aggregated, there appears a quite clear and marked rise in the population of the combined parishes after 1740[38] (see Figs 1, 2 and 3).

This trend of rising population was undoubtedly one of concern not

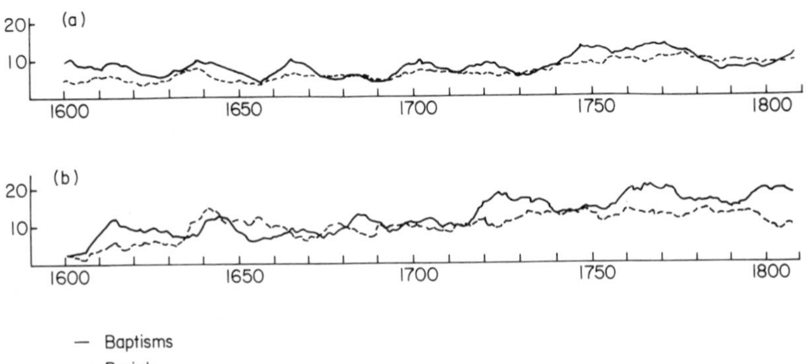

FIG. 1. Nine-year moving averages for (a) Wotton and (b) Abinger.

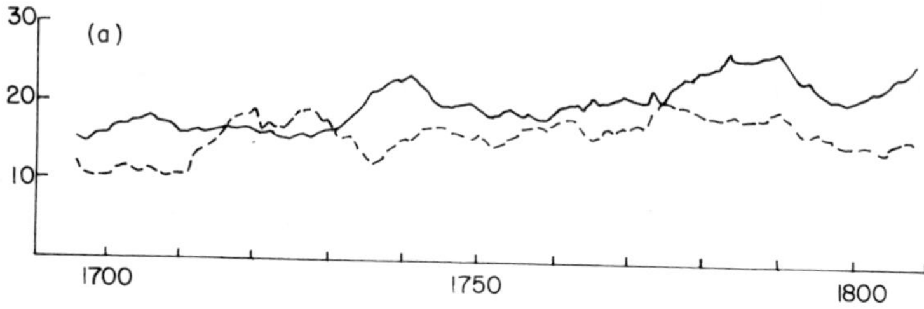

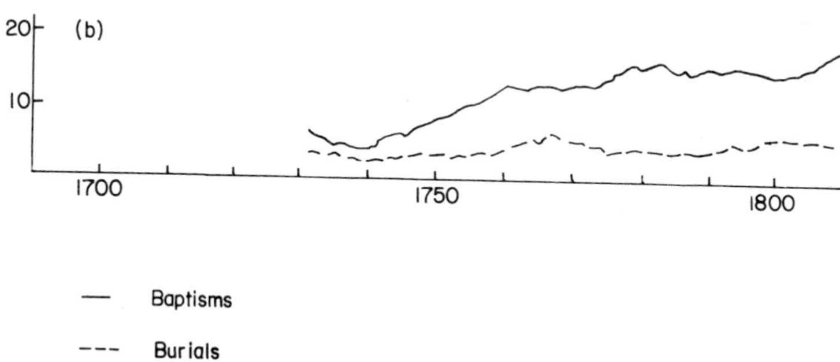

FIG. 2. Nine-year moving averages for (a) Shere and (b) Oakwood Chapel.

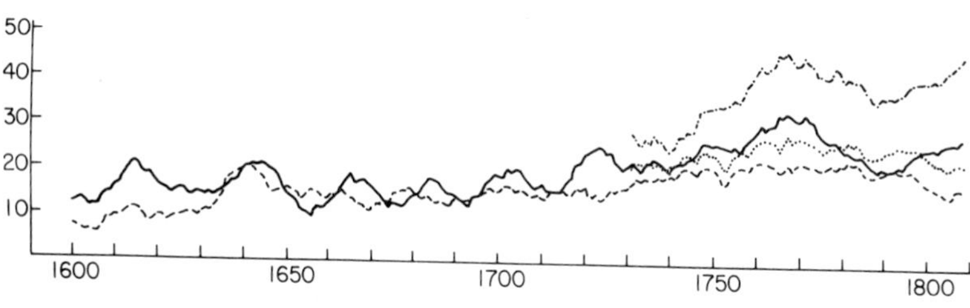

— Baptisms (Wotton and Abinger)
--- Burials (Wotton and Abinger)
-·-· Baptisms (Wotton, Abinger and Oakwood Chapel)
···· Burials (Wotton, Abinger and Oakwood Chapel)

FIG. 3. Cumulative totals of nine-year moving averages for Wotton, Abinger and Oakwood Chapel.

only to Malthus but to others in the locality with whom he would have associated. A letter written in November, 1794, to the Bray family at Shere from Mr Duncomb at Newdigate, a parish some 13 kilometres south-east of Shere, gave figures of births and burials from the parish register for every tenth year from 1693 to 1793 inclusive, indicating that the number of births for the eleven specified years totalled 138 and burials 71. Duncomb wrote that the population of Newdigate was greatly increased, but building had not kept pace, only one house having been built in 40 years.[39]

Malthus knew the Brays well (his younger sister had married into the family) and Duncomb was confirming what the families already knew to be a problem in their own locality, since it was being highlighted by the considerable increases in poor rate assessments which they were required to pay. There could be no clearer demonstration of the Principle of Population in operation.

The accounts of the expenditure on poor relief for Wotton, Abinger and Shere parishes all survive for various parts of the eighteenth century. Wotton's, beginning in 1708, show an increase of almost three hundred per cent (296 per cent) from the first five years' (1708-1712) total expenditure of £540.5*s*.2*d* (£540.31) to the last five years' of the eighteenth century (1796-1800) total of £2139.0*s*.6$\frac{3}{4}$*d*, (£2139.03) but the decade with the largest increase was that of 1790-1799 in which expenditure soared by some seventy-five per cent. Abinger's Overseers' the Poor disbursements commence in 1732 and produce an increase of 186 per cent between the annual average expenditure of £175. 12*s*.8*d* (£175.63) and that of 1796-1800 which averaged annually £502.12, although the increase was more evenly spread out over the years with a more modest rise of almost one-third in the 1790s.[40] Information about payments to the poor at Shere have survived for a much shorter period, only beginning in 1776. In the first five years (1776-1781) £1681.61 was expended. During the last five years of the century that sum rose to £2804 with the increase in the 1790s amounting to 37 per cent. Fortunately, at Shere the survival of the Overseers of the Poor Receipt Book affords us a minor insight into the Malthus family since among the payers is listed for the first time on the ninth of January, 1787, "Mr Malltiss" (the name became Malthus in 1792) who was rated at £34, plus £4 for "Oughtreds Meadow", and in the parish as a whole he was the seventeenth-highest payer. Daniel Malthus's first half dozen six-monthly payments totalled £28.6*s*.0*d* (£28.30), and the last six, prior to the publishing of the *First Essay*, £37. 3*s*.0*d*, an increase of just over 30 per cent.[41] Although the percentage increase in annual relief payments in the 1790s was lower in Shere than in Wotton, this smaller increase would seem to reflect the fact that levels of poor relief in Shere were then much higher than in the neighbouring parishes. For instance, the proportion of the population of Shere receiving relief was higher and the proportion being assessed for payment was lower than in either Wotton and Abinger. Consequently, the average contribution of each assessed individual in Shere was higher than elsewhere (see Table 1). In addition Daniel Malthus's payments amounted to almost twice the average for the parish as a whole (e.g. in February 1800 Daniel's widow Henrietta paid £6.13*s*.0*d* (£6.65) on a rate of 3*s*.6*d* in the pound when the average payment for all those assessed was £3.8*s*.10*d* (£3.44). With such considerable increases in the payments for poor relief during the eighteenth century it is perhaps not surprising that Malthus would find it necessary to comment on them in the *First Essay*,[42] since the sums paid were mainly obtained from families like his own. And it was clearly not too difficult to forge a link between the rising poor rates and the growing population, without attempting any analysis of the structure or causes of poverty.

The evidence suggests that Malthus was perhaps too strongly influenced by some contemporary events. Even so, had he taken account of his own criticism of Richard Price's use of parish register material and looked at the entries over a much longer time span, the indications in the *First Essay* suggest he would not have found any evidence which could have led him to form a conclusion other than the one he enunciated. For, when he examined Price's statement that the proportion of births to deaths was higher at 124 to 100 from Queen

TABLE 1

Contributors to and Recipients of Poor Relief in 1801

	Population 1801 Census	*Contributors*	*Proportion of population (contributors X 4.75)*	*Recipients*	*Proportion of population (Recipients X 4.75)*	*Total sums paid 1801*	*Average contribution*
Abinger	632	70	53%	35	26%	£308.6.4	£4.8.1 3/6 rate
Wotton	441	48.	52%	35	38%	£148.15.9	£3.2.0 2/6 rate
Shere	871	78.	43%	75	41%	£403.7.6	£5.3.5 5/– rate

It has been assumed that both contributors and recipients represent households; hence a multiplier of 4.75 for mean household size has been applied to produce the percentages. (See P. Laslett and R. Wall, 1972. *Household and Family in Past Time,* pp. 125–158. Cambridge University Press, Cambridge.)

Elizabeth's time to the middle of the seventeenth century, by comparison with the 111 to 100 from the late seventeenth century to the middle of the eighteenth, he finds this wholly to be expected as more good land would have been available for cultivation during the earlier stages than later when the population of England "had accommodated itself very nearly to the average produce of [the] country".[43]

Malthus, although he knew of Gregory King's work, [44] was not in any position to quantify the size of the nation's population. Nevertheless, he shows that he was aware of the reduction in the rate of population growth which occurred in England between approximately the mid-seventeenth and mid-eighteenth century, a century in which it is now thought that the national population grew from some five and a half million people to only six million.[45] His explanation for this trend was that discouragements to marriage, war, depopulation of large towns, the close habitations and insufficient food of many of the poor had prevented population from increasing beyond the means of subsistence.[46] He had discounted the possibility that any agrarian developments "could remove the pressure of it [population] for a single century."[47] Yet the evidence of the expansion of agricultural output at a pace faster than population growth during the century is inescapable. The price of wheat fell steadily. In the 1640s the average price for the year at Eton College, some 32 kilometres from Abinger, was 51*s*. 7*d* (£2.58) per quarter, whereas by the 1740s it had fallen to 26*s* (£1.30).[48] Wimpey wrote: "All history cannot furnish twenty such years of fertility and abundance as from 1730 to 1750 when the average prices were the lowest ever known."[49] Not surprisingly, the average price of the loaf in London fell over the same period from 6.6*d* to 4.6*d* producing real savings for the poorer members of the community. Since from the 1670s to the late 1760s England became a substantial exporter of surplus grain (there were only four years, 1728, 1729, 1757 and 1758, when any significant imports of wheat or flour occurred before 1765),[50] at a time when there were more, not fewer, people to be fed, the evidence clearly points to considerable improvement in agricultural output.

Furthermore, it is apparent that for long periods, of up to a century, the major principle of the *First Essay,* that population should increase much faster than the means of subsistence, did not apply, since despite increasing real incomes for the majority of the population there was no tendency to earlier marriage and the consequent production of surplus population over subsistence which Malthus stated would be the result of improved circumstances.[51] The poor of England had not always behaved as the Principle of Population stated they would, and had

Malthus used his mathematical skills to explore the local parish registers with a more open mind he might have arrived at a conclusion rather different from the monocausal explanation into which he made all historical change fit. But then, like all of us, he was a man of his time and knowing what he could see happening around him to the population and the associated rising payments of poor relief he neglected to use some of the most valuable of those few materials which were then within his reach in a country situation.

Notes

1. Wotton Parish Register; *see also* The Parish Registers of Abinger, Wotton & Oakwood Chapel, Co. Surrey. *Surrey Record Society*, London, **25**, 159.
2. The bibliographical details are taken from Patricia James (1979). *Population Malthus*, pp.13–34. Routledge & Kegan Paul, London. I am grateful to Patricia James for making some of her material available to me in advance of publication.
3. The burials of Daniel and his wife Henrietta are both recorded in the Wotton Parish Register as follows:
   January 14th 1800, Daniel Malthus, Esquire, of Albury in this county, aged 70; April 12th 1800, Henrietta Catherine, widow of Daniel Malthus, Esquire, late of Albury in this county, aged 67.
   See also Surrey Record Society **25**, 218.
4. T. R. Malthus (1798). *First Essay*, pp.73, 132.
5. T. R. Malthus (1973). *Essay,* 7th Edition, p.1. Everyman, Dent, London.
6. T. R. Malthus, op. cit. in note 4, chapter XII, p.225.
7. P. James. *Population Malthus*, pp.40–41.
8. T. R. Malthus, op. cit. in note 4, p.367.
9. ibid. p.367.
10. ibid. pp.217–218.
11. ibid. p.78.
12. ibid. p.132.
13. ibid. p.73.
14. ibid. p.131.
15. ibid. p.14.
16. ibid. pp.63–66.
17. ibid. p.71.
18. ibid. pp.136–137; and Adam Smith (1950). *The Wealth of Nations* (Ed. Cannan), 6th Edition, p.179. Methuen, London.
19. T. R. Malthus. *First Essay*, pp.185–186. This statement was later supported by census figures of the white population of America from 1790 to 1800 and 1810 in Malthus's *Summary View*, published in 1830 – *see* D. V. Glass (ed.) (1953). *Introduction to Malthus*, p.128. Watts, London.
20. E. B. Green and V. D. Harrington (1932). *American Population before the Federal Census of 1790*, pp.4–7.

21. T. R. Malthus, op. cit. in note 4, p.21.
22. ibid. p.23. Malthus's computation when compared with the 1801 Census underestimates the population of Britain by over 50 per cent.
23. ibid. p.189.
24. ibid. p.310.
25. ibid. p.363.
26. ibid. p.84.
27. ibid. p.86.
28. ibid. p.89.
29. ibid. pp.96–97.
30. ibid. p.313.
31. ibid. p.321.
32. John Aikin (1795). *A Description of the Country from Thirty to Forty Miles Round Manchester*, pp.300–304. London.
33. T. R. Malthus, op. cit. in note 4, p.336.
34. ibid. p.310.
35. ibid. p.313.
36. ibid. p.97.
37. ibid. pp.122–123.
38. In view of the fact that the Oakwood baptism register states that many of the parents lived in Wotton or Abinger, aggregating the baptism totals would seem sensible. Clearly the Chapel was catering for families in the southern parts of both parishes since it was nearer than the two parish churches. Note also that baptism/marriage ratios fell in the early eighteenth century by comparison to earlier and later peaks in the combined parishes.
Guildford Muniment Room, PSH/SHER/1/1–2, Shere Parish Registers.
Guildford Muniment Room, PSH/OK/1/1, Oakwood Chapel Registers.
39. Guildford Muniment Room, 85/2/8 (642), Bray Collection,
40. Surrey Record Office, LA4/17/5,6,7,8, Wotton Overseers' Disbursements, 1708–1800; P1/7/1,2,3,4 Abinger Overseers' Disbursements, 1732–1800.
41. Surrey Record Office, P10/1/1–2, Shere Poor Books 1776–1800.
42. T. R. Malthus, op. cit. in note 4, p.320.
43. ibid. p.125. In the light of this observation, Malthus's solution of the problem of rising poverty by expanding agricultural employment and productivity (*First Essay*, p.96) appears somewhat paradoxical, since presumably less good land would have been available at the end of the eighteenth century than in 1750.
44. ibid. p.125.
45. E. A. Wrigley and R. S. Schofield (1981). *The Population History of England, 1541–1871. A Reconstruction.* Edward Arnold, London.
46. T. R. Malthus, op. cit. in note 4, p.126.
47. ibid. p.16.
48. B. R. Mitchell and Phyllis Deane (1962). *Abstracts of British Historical Statistics*, pp.486–487. Cambridge University Press, Cambridge.

49. J. Wimpey (1775). *Rural Improvements*, pp.492–493, quoted in G. E. Mingay (1956). The agricultural depression, 1730–50. *Economic History Review* **8** (3), 336.
50. B. R. Mitchell and Phyllis Deane, op. cit. in note 48, p.94.
51. T. R. Malthus, op. cit. in note 4, pp.30–31; *and see* E. A. Wrigley (1966). Family limitation in pre-industrial England. *Economic History Review* **19**, (1), 82–109; and R. B. Outhwaite (1972). Age at marriage in England from the late seventeenth to the nineteenth century. *Transactions of the Royal Historical Society* 55–70.

5 The Economic Thought of T.R. Malthus

J. WOLFF

The economic theories of any author may be described under a variety of headings. In the case of Malthus, our discussion will be divided into four parts. First, we shall consider an aspect which has been relatively neglected in the discussions on the history of economic thought. This is the diffusion of Malthus's economic views, the reason why some have survived and others have been rejected in different periods and different places. Why are some economic doctrines accepted immediately they are put forward? Why are other theories forgotten only to reappear after varying periods of delay? Why does a particular author tower over his contemporaries? Many similar questions could be asked, and raise problems in the theory of knowledge. They are all aspects of the same problem: how best to study the history of economic thought.

In the second section of this paper we shall consider the extent of the originality of Malthus's views, that is to say the features which distinguish his theories not only from those of his contemporaries, but also from those of economists who preceded and those who followed him. What is Malthus's place in the history of the general development of economic doctrines? Is he part of a wider school of thought, or does he stand apart from the dominant ideas? If the latter, are the differences between him and other economists limited to specific points, or is his entire conception of the economy different? These are some of the questions that will be discussed in this section.

Thirdly, we shall be concerned with the consistency of the ideas put forward by Malthus at different periods of his life. An author's views can change during the course of his life. Is there a unity in them or does his work consist merely of a fragmented number of different

MALTHUS PAST AND PRESENT
ISBN 0-12-224670-5

pieces which have little or no connection with one another? If there is a common element throughout his work, does this take different forms, so that a careful study of different texts becomes necessary in order to recognize it? Which aspects of Malthus's works are worth retaining? Should we look at the earlier editions, or the later ones? Can they be reconciled with each other? There cannot be a task which is more complex, constructive, instructive (and, it may be said attractive) than to trace the evolution of an author's ideas.

Fourthly, we shall examine the philosophical bases of Malthus's ideas. Behind any economic theory, there is a *Weltanschauung,* an ideology. How does Malthus see the real world? What is the interaction between the different variables that he has selected for his analysis? Is the model that he puts forward self-regulating? Does it include recurrent processes, oscillations or transformations? In the latter case, what is the final state towards which his system is moving? A knowledge of these fundamental aspects of an author's thought is indispensable for an understanding of his contributions.

We shall try to consider all these aspects in this paper and suggest answers to the questions we have put forward, insofar as these relate to Malthus.

I

Even in his own country, England, the diffusion of Malthus's views has had a curious history.[1] We may distinguish between three different periods. Until 1870, Malthus occupied an ambiguous place in economic theory. He was not regarded as an economist of the first rank, and this could not be otherwise as Ricardo dominated the classical school, and Malthus had opposed Ricardo on a number of issues. However, Ricardo accepted Malthus's theory of rent, as well as the "hard" version of his Principle of Population; on the other hand, it would seem that Malthus recognized the superiority of the concept of the "labour embodied" theory of value over the "labour commanded" theory. Perhaps the main reason for the relatively subordinate place that Malthus occupied in English economic theory is related to the fact that as one of the principal members of the anti-Ricardian school of thought (which also included Lauderdale and Chalmers), Malthus favoured balanced economic growth, maintaining agriculture as an important sector, at a time when political and economic power was passing into the hands of entrepreneurs and businessmen. This interpretation is supported by the fact that towards the end of the period John Stuart Mill rejected Malthus's views on value and on gluts, but placed the "hard" Principle of Population at the centre of his theory of distribution, in much the same way as Jevons used the "soft" version.[2]

Between 1870 and 1930 British economists paid little attention to Malthus's views on economic matters. Even his ideas on population came to be regarded as less important, as production increased faster than population and real income per head rose. However, his eclipse was only a partial one, for Jevons thought that the main line of development of economic doctrine from Adam Smith to Nassau Senior passed through Malthus, whilst in 1885 James Bonar was the first writer to provide a complete presentation of Malthus's economic ideas.[3]

Malthus had to wait for nearly a century after his death before being permitted to leave purgatory and be admitted to paradise. His theories began to be re-evaluated after the 1930s, largely as the result of the interest shown in them by John Maynard Keynes. The latter's *General Theory*[4] was the most important contribution to the economic literature of the period, and Malthus's ideas came to be studied in the light of Keynes's re-formulation of economic theory. The relevance of his ideas continued to be recognized: the ratio between population and subsistence was once again considered as an important variable, as was the view that economic analysis should be concerned with long-term trends. Today, Malthus and Ricardo are regarded as the founders of the two distinct branches of English political economy which are distinguished by their methodology.

Reactions to Malthus in other countries were similar to those in England. In Italy, the *Principles of Political Economy* was only rarely referred to during the first half of the nineteenth century, and no summary of Malthus's work was published.[5] The first translation, as well as that of *Definitions in Political Economy* was published in 1854 with an introduction by Ferrara, who underestimated its importance. It is clear that Fuoco was the only Italian economist to be influenced by Malthus's views and recommendations on the method to be followed in economic analysis, on the distinction between the science of political economy and the art of economic policy, and on the need to verify both one's hypotheses and one's conclusions. On the subject of profit, the views of J.B. Say, who distinguished between profit and interest, were much more influential than those of Malthus, and those Italian economists who accepted the views of their English colleagues followed Adam Smith rather than Malthus. The discussions by Say and Sismondi on economic crises were also more influential than those by Malthus. The ratio between production and consumption did not occupy an independent place in economic theory, and the view that there might be a deficiency in aggregate demand was not generally accepted.

However, towards the end of the century[6] an important debate began about the relations between Malthusianism, social Darwinism and socialism whilst Loria put forward a theory of capitalist development which was based on the Principle of Population.

The situation was different in the United States.[7] During the *ante bellum* period, the first synthesis of English economic theories published in 1820 by D. Raymond[8] was strongly anti-Ricardo and pro-Malthus. Raymond put forward a theory of balanced growth, insufficiency of demand and social responsibility, but his work met with a mixed reception. The generality of American economists were opposed to Malthus; Raymond's work sold badly even though it went into four small editions. However, he was highly esteemed both by President John Adams and President John Quincy Adams, and it should be recalled that Raymond was particularly impressed by Malthus's ideas on the abolition of tariffs, and that his arguments influenced M. Carey, H. Carey and F. List. On the other hand, H. Clay who was responsible for the interregional compromise which dominated American politics from about 1820 to 1850 was inspired by Malthus through reading Raymond's work; his plan which came to be called the "American System" envisaged a balance in the growth of the agricultural and the industrial sectors, each acting as an outlet for the other, and the introduction of an effective tariff which would not, however, be so high as to be prohibitive.

In Yugoslavia little interest was taken in Malthus's ideas until the end of the nineteenth century,[9] partly because the country was under-populated and partly because of the predominance of cameralist ideas. Though Malthus's views, particularly those relating to population, were known and discussed during the second half of the nineteenth century, free traders and protectionists, socialists and Marxists alike were critically sceptical, though for different reasons. It was only during the period between the two world wars, and particularly during the 1930s that Malthus's contributions were recognized as being among the most important of those of the nineteenth century. Since the end of the second world war they have been continuously and actively studied.

II

How can Malthus be placed in context and the originality of his ideas appreciated? To do this, we must mention the principal features of his work and compare it with that of other economists.

One of his predecessors was Galiani. It is easy to establish the points on which Malthus and Galiani agreed, as well as those where they differed.[10] Both were interested in population, but whereas Malthus's interest extended both to the theory of population and its development in the real world, Galiani did not consider theory. The two were clearly on opposite sides of the fence, for whereas Malthus preferred a slower rate of population growth accompanied by an increase in national income per head, Galiani advocated rapid growth, believing that population and national product would react upon one another. In addition, he stressed the value of a large population for a country's defence. The two writers also differed in their treatment of the theory of value. Galiani stressed value in use, demonstrated the roles played by utility and scarcity and believed that value was created by land and labour. He understood the nature of the inverse relationship between the quantity of demand for a good and its price, and accepted the proposition that "man can be regarded as a measure of value". Malthus, on the other hand, stressed value in exchange and adopted first a labour theory of value and, later, a theory in which value was related to cost of production. He measured (though with some qualifications) value in terms of precious metals.

But there was also a similarity in the views of the two authors, for Galiani did not ignore value in exchange and put forward a theory of long-term price equilibrium, and both he and Malthus agreed that the choices of consumers and producers were determined by their personal interests.

On the subject of distribution there was again some difference of opinion. Galiani puts forward a theory of equilibrium profit and of the real rate of interest in terms of time preference, whereas Malthus advances a complete theory of income distribution (and together with West and Ricardo) originated the theory of rent which was based on differences in the fertility of the soil.

Lastly, it was Malthus alone who took an interest in economic crises and recessions. He does not appear to have believed in the theories of political arithmetic, whereas Galiani accepted them.

The position could be summarized in modern economic terminology by stating that whereas Galiani was mainly interested in microeconomic questions, Malthus was essentially concerned with problems of macro-economics.

We can find similar differences between Malthus and his contemporaries. Although the friendship between Ricardo and Malthus produced a large and important correspondence, it is well known that neither succeeded in convincing the other of the error of his ways.

We can best compare Malthus and Ricardo by indirectly using Adam Smith as a reference point.[11] Ricardo's principal disagreements with Smith concerned value — both the determinants and the correct measure of value — and the theory of profit. Malthus saw Ricardo's work as threatening to undermine Smith's wonderful construction. If this point is borne in mind, then much falls into place. Malthus insisted, in opposition to Ricardo, on taking account of a plurality of causes rather than a single cause, and on the need to submit theoretical speculation to empirical verification. Malthus concentrated on short-run analysis against Ricardo's preoccupation with the long run. Malthus looked to the interaction of supply and demand for an explanation of value, whilst Ricardo looked to labour. Even though both included labour in their discussion of a measure of value, Ricardo proposed to use the amount of labour embodied in a commodity against Malthus's amount of labour commanded by the commodity. For Ricardo, the rate of profit was determined by the conditions of production of wage goods, but for Malthus by the relative value of output and advances. Ricardo saw the possibility of an end to economic growth in the changing conditions of supply of commodities consumed by workers, whilst Malthus looked to insufficient effective demand for consumption goods. Ricardo put the problem of crises on one side, whereas Malthus recognized the possibility of their existence. On all these counts, Malthus held that Ricardo had strayed too far from the teachings of Adam Smith.

The parallelism between Malthus and Ricardo can also be seen directly by considering their "style".[12] One important similarity is immediately apparent: both were sceptical about the value of economic changes and took a commonsense view of affairs. They both agreed that it was the function of a economist to apply rational arguments to conditions in the real world, but there was also an important difference between them. Whereas Ricardo was mainly interested in the conclusions drawn from the argument, Malthus preferred the argument itself, where he could demonstrate his dialectical skills, his ingenuity and his mental agility. But this is not all. Malthus was an original thinker who made use of paradox; Ricardo was always lucid, direct and incisive. Their difference can best be illustrated in their correspondence on the subject of profit. Though Malthus could never be considered to be a radical, this is not true of Ricardo; Malthus did not much like a society which was composed mainly of businessmen and which relied on market forces, Ricardo did not share this dislike.

Malthus was sensitive to criticism by his friends (as may be seen from the changes which he made in successive editions of his works), whereas Ricardo was almost completely indifferent to criticism — indeed, it may be thought that he had too high an opinion of himself.

We turn to the affinities between Malthus and another great economist of his period, Sismondi.[13] They shared a common attitude towards effective demand, and both preferred the consideration of practical problems to abstract theorizing. Their analysis of the causes of economic crises was closely linked to the study of economic growth; an increase in production did not lead to an automatic increase in the demand for the additional goods produced. But there were also important differences between them. Malthus never forgot the likelihood of greater indolence as production increased; profit, which is the motive force of accumulation will not be sufficient if demand for the extra product comes only from those workers who produce it; there has to be an extraneous source. Overinvestment occurs when there is no matching increase in demand: it is accompanied by losses and part of the investment is wasted. For Sismondi, who was committed to the refutation of Say's law, wants are limited and once scarcity has disappeared, there is nothing to guarantee the operation of Say's law. Changes in demand, whether from inside or from outside the economy, will lead to disequilibrium and, therefore, to change, and the importance of the agricultural sector in the economy is bound to diminish. Their differences are equally deep when it comes to a discussion of the role played by money in the causation of disequilibrium. Malthus in the *Principles of Political Economy* is more allusive; he merely shows that an exogenously caused rise in demand (caused, for instance, by an increase in government spending) is the principal factor in economic recovery and will affect the distribution of incomes.

Malthus's affinities with his contemporaries do not stop with Sismondi or Ricardo.[14] Say and Everett are equally important. Say's position is close to that of Malthus, for although he had not read Malthus's work, the first edition of his treatise contains a Principle of Population. According to Say, the relation between population and subsistence is fixed, and the limiting factor will be subsistence. Therefore, the proper object of economic policy should not be the encouragement of a higher birth rate, but an increase of production. Say takes account of human suffering, as well as of the effects of wars and epidemics on the average duration of human life.

Everett also deserves to be mentioned, because of the originality of his views. He believes that far from being regarded as a cause of scarcity, an increase in population should be considered a sign of abundance, and that this is consistent with the views of both Malthus and Say. According to him, population is an outlet for production and overproduction is impossible, and, therefore, there can never be too many producers, or too large a population. He maintains that Say's position on the population problem is not capable of being regarded as Malthusian without implying an internal contradiction. Malthus's and Say's views on the subject of outlets for production cannot be made compatible.

Our difficulties are greater when we attempt to compare Malthus's views with those of his successors. Many economists considered Malthus's works in relation to their own, or in relation to the subjects that preoccupied their attention, and they may, therefore, consciously or unconsciously, have been carried away by their own passions and prejudices. This applies both to Marx and to Keynes.

Marx's aversion to Malthus is well known[15] and is made manifest in the panoply of rich and uncomplimentary epithets which he applies to Malthus. Equally famous is Keynes's celebrated article in which he places Malthus on a pedestal and praises him as the greatest economist of all time. It is better to consider Malthus's position with greater detachment than did either of these two celebrated men. It cannot be denied that Malthus provided a link between the level of population and welfare (or misery) and that in doing so he made a most important contribution to demographic science. Nor must we forget his influence on Ricardo, for the latter accepted Malthus's theory of population and was inspired by his views on rent and on diminishing returns. Moreover, Malthus broke new ground in his *Principles of Political Economy* by pointing out the risk of overproduction and insufficiency of effective demand, and in this he distanced himself from other members of the classical school. In short, neither Marx nor Keynes succeeded in giving a correct appreciation of Malthus's importance. Marx's attack on Malthus's ideological and political position fails to give credit to his contribution to the development of the science of political economy and to Marx's own thesis in particular; Keynes overstresses the similarities between Malthus's theory and his own. The true Malthus was a more complex figure than either of them is prepared to admit.

However, a number of remarks on specific points will be in order. Keynes is by no means uniform in praising Malthus;[16] he does not hesitate to criticize him for neglecting the important part played by the rate of interest, nor for his failure to realize that the situation which he envisages could only arise if the rate of interest were zero. Similarly, Marx reproaches Malthus for his theory of population. The

Malthusian position may be stated simply: fertility within marriage is not controlled; it can be checked only by delaying marriage and by the operation of the positive check; population will adjust to the rate of real wages, i.e. the size of the working population is determined by the size of the wages fund. Marx rejected the concept of a wages fund; overpopulation *was* possible and an industrial reserve army *could* appear. There was no natural law of population, only social laws corresponding to a particular mode of production and, therefore, in particular, one which was specific to capitalism.

III

Having discussed the significance of Malthus's place in the history of economic ideas, we can proceed to a general consideration of his work. This analysis will raise a number of different questions. This could not be otherwise, when we take account of the volume of his writings, the modifications which he made in successive editions of his works and the fact that his theories developed over a period lasting for one-third of a century. We shall attempt to proceed systematically.

There is general agreement on a number of points. Malthus's economic thought is characterized by three aspects.[17] The first is methodological: Malthus viewed society as a collection of individuals who are motivated by self-interest. But he preferred an inductive and empirical approach to economic problems to the deductive method. Secondly, Malthus introduced a new concept — effective demand. He did not believe that an individual's abstinence from consumption would necessarily lead to a new act of investment.[18] Thirdly, he thought that the rate of new investment would depend on the rate of profit, which, like Keynes, he tended to view in a financial framework.

Thirdly, Malthus puts forward an original theory of economic growth, that is concentrated on adjustment processes rather than on long-run prospects; on inter-sector relations rather than on aggregate properties of the economy.[19] He takes some structural data as given, e.g. the right to property, the fact that suppliers offer either products or their labour on the market, a circular flow between different sectors of the economy, the division of society into groups, the dependence of production on demand, the organization and customs of society. From these data he proceeds to construct a dynamic short-period model of the economy, which may result in disequilibrium. He shows that it is possible for the economy to be in equilibrium even though there is unemployment, that a rise in the size of the working population will result in a fall in real wages, so that the same amount of capital will be employed for the payment of wages, but increased production will lead to a fall in prices so that profits will remain constant (which would not have been the case, if the previous price level had been maintained). Similarly, a growth in investment, or the conversion of income into capital[20] might result in a reduction of the total demand of capitalists (or in overinvestment) which would again reduce prices and profits, because the growth of incomes and of production would be delayed.[21] Accumulation of capital and growth in employment are, therefore, bounded by the socio-economic structure within which they occur.

Malthus's ideas on the subject of value and markets seem more ambiguous. What is his theory of value and what is its purpose?[22] It results from the adaptation of Adam Smith's labour theory of value to the conditions of the industrial revolution and of capitalism in England, and takes account of the interests of the landed aristocracy. When it became clear that the implications of Ricardo's theories were subversive for the existing social order, these had to be opposed. When at a later stage, Malthus came to agree with Ricardo and showed that only part of the value of a product was returned to its producers he, nevertheless, differed from him in his assessment of the fraction which went to the exploiting classes by suggesting that a substantial element of rent would stimulate demand for and the sale of the goods that had been produced. Later he came to use Adam Smith's idea that the value of a good is indicated by the amount of labour it can command (the labour content of the goods for which it is exchanged) and explains the unequal position of labour and capital on the basis of equivalence. He concludes that there will only be a market for goods, if there exists a social class whose members receive income without having to work, who are consumers without being producers; consumption by non-producers was a necessary condition for the realization of profit and this could only be achieved by maintaining a parasitic class. He preferred this solution to one which involved increasing costs of production, diminishing profits and restricting saving. His arguments can, therefore, be read as a justification for the continuation of the social order of his period.

What are the links between the theory of value and effective demand?[23] This subject can be treated both at micro and at macro level. As the labour that can be purchased by the exchange of a good is a measure of its effective demand, this evaluation is independent of the condition of production of other goods. Thus, the special significance of labour is that it measures effective demand prior to production and independently of exchange. To maintain that effective demand can be measured by the amount of labour a good can command implies that labour itself cannot be regarded as a good. However, it is possible to hold that nothing has changed when other goods are added to labour for purposes of production; if the proportion represented by direct labour in the value of any one good depends on the value of other goods, then the expression of effective demand for that good in labour terms cannot be the sole measure of its intrinsic value. It is not, therefore, possible to accept the contention that the effective demand for a good can be measured in terms of the labour that it can command in the general case, when labour is not the sole input. However, although the explanation may not hold for any specific good, it is the only possible one when the global situation is considered, for the capitalists as a whole the total quantity of labour (or more accurately of productive labour) that can be commanded is the only measure of demand which can be used before production and, therefore, exchange has actually taken place. Unless we make a distinction between productive and unproductive labour, effective demand would be underestimated, for otherwise there would be nothing to distinguish the power to command productive labour (or the possibility of putting individuals to work to produce their own subsistence and that of those who can command their labour) from that possessed by any other owner of wealth.

How did Malthus treat the problem of markets in his *Principles*?[24] He was one of the first to criticize Say's law of markets by demonstrating the important part played by money and by the need to sell all the goods that were produced, and he stressed that it was possible for expenditure on consumption by landlords and managers to be insufficient to maintain effective demand. Thus, he made the realization of profit the central issue of his investigation of markets. This was the positive aspect of his theory. However, the question might be asked (though Malthus did not ask it) whether it would not be useful to consider expenditure on investment as well as on consumption in this connection. An increase in expenditure on investment implies a rise in the share of the national product going to capitalists, because investment goods are bought by capitalists rather than by workers. Malthus did not realize that investment might make savings possible. Therefore, he believed that equilibrium between savings and expenditure, between supply and demand, could only be established by a reduction of production and diminution of employment. It was, therefore, necessary for a group of unproductive consumers to exist if the realization of profit was to become possible. Like Keynes, he criticized the view that a reduction in wages would lead to a restoration of full employment; the results of such savings would depend on the conditions of demand, i.e. whether or not demand was sufficient. Conversely, he ignored the time-lag between the production of capital goods and production of consumption goods (or that demand increases and profits are realized before investment actually occurs). Moreover, it is not possible to agree with him that a reduction in taxation will lead to an increase in savings and accumulation and to a reduction in total demand, for according to him, savings are not used for any other purpose than investment.[25]

Consider, next, some more general aspects of Malthus's work. Are the different parts of his thought internally consistent? In other words, are there two Malthuses or is there one? From the very moment of publication, it was recognized that Malthus's economic theories were complex and even contradictory. Torren's phrase is well known: "As presented by Mr Ricardo, political economy shows a regularity and simplicity which is more pronounced than that found in nature; as presented by Mr Malthus it is a chaotic assembly of specific and independent facts." Economists would still differ today about whether this is a true statement of the situation.

Some think that there is only one Malthus. But even those who believe that his views are consistent do so for different reasons and they differ in their account of how different aspects of his theories can be reconciled. Some start with the concept of overinvestment.[26] At first sight, it would seem as if Malthus provides different explanations for different periods of time: in the long run it is pressure of population on subsistence which constitutes the main threat to human happiness; in the short run it is economic crises, or the maladjustment between supply and demand, caused largely by insufficiency of demand. If total demand and total supply are considered to be inelastic with respect to price, they can be seen to vary around a long-term equilibrium level. Supply is more sensitive (e.g. to fluctuations in harvests) and can be adjusted more quickly and easily than demand. An ingenious diagram (which is not reproduced here) makes it possible to demonstrate the importance of both productive and unproductive labour that is used, of the equilibrium point between supply and demand, of the possibility of underemployment and the consequences of using savings. If savings were to rise because the employment of unproductive labour is reduced, there will be an increase in the investment of productive capital and, thus, an increase in the demand for investment goods and in total demand. The economy will expand and unemployed workers will be absorbed in the productive sector. As fixed capital has been installed, total demand will be reduced and unemployment increased. If investment were to remain constant, the same effect in the long run would be produced by the pressure of population.

Other economists discuss the theory that value is determined by the amount of labour that a good can command.[27] Just like Adam Smith and Ricardo, Malthus considered the relationship which existed between capital accumulation, technological development and population movements, i.e. a dynamic equilibrium between growth and distribution. If it proved possible to determine the quantity of labour that the national income could command, or conversely, the share of the national income that could be commanded by labour at different levels of employment, this relationship would provide a link with the accumulation of capital. In other words, an appreciable change in the amount of labour commanded would involve a change in the distribution of income, because changes in the demand for and supply of labour will follow. This is a different situation from that which exists in the market for other goods, because in the labour market buyers and sellers belong to distinct social groups. The Principle of Population may be used to explain whence and how landlords derive their incomes. It is concerned specifically with the distribution of incomes and wealth in a society, and affects productivity as well as demand. Malthus's work, therefore, consists of a series of models which, in today's terminology, would be considered as being subject to supply constraints, i.e. the conditions that are necessary for goods to be brought on the market.

A third group considers the unity of purpose found in Malthus's thought.[28] To explain this phrase, we must note that Malthus was not a Malthusian in the sense that this term has acquired.[29] In his *Essay* he does not oppose population growth, but tends to discuss the rate of growth rather than the total size of the population and favours a moderate but sustained increase in numbers. This is part of his ideology; it justifies the superiority of the fundamental values of Protestantism — work and foresight — over the common neglect of the population problem by other Christian Churches, and it can be used to blame the poor themselves for their misery and irrational behaviour. It also has important implications for economics; population growth plays a fundamental part in providing outlets for production and maintaining a ratio between the supply and demand for labour which favours the entrepreneur. However, although population growth is a necessary condition to ensure economic expansion, it is not fundamental, for numbers must not be confused with income and it is the source of incomes (whether from productive or from unproductive labour) which is important. Population growth is a necessary but not a sufficient condition for ensuring the growth of the national product. In Malthus's theory, however, this conclusion could be upset, provided numbers increased in households with means that exceeded their needs for subsistence. Such an increase would be equivalent to an increase in the numbers of unproductive workers. Its effect would be more beneficial, because it would favour productive workers. Increases in population which are brought about through increases in income can, therefore, play an important part, and population growth may occur in part of a population only. Malthus may not have foreseen this eventuality, because only by ignoring it was he able to justify the superiority of applying a commercial rationality to human reproduction and thus legitimize the merits of those who accepted this degree of conformity.[30] This unity of purpose may be a reason for the apparent contradictions in his work.

A fourth group appeals to his description of the real world.[31] The unifying factor in his thought may be his readiness to consider concrete phenomena. His inconsistencies could be explained by the complexity of the real world which he is trying to describe and which cannot be explained by reference to one single principle. Wealth does not increase uniformly; there are fluctuations in prices and in economic activity. We must remember that Malthus lived at a time when prices began to decline (about 1815-1817) and when there was overinvestment and insufficient demand to absorb industrial production.[32] Capitalists, motivated by their desire to invest, did not appreciate the limitations inherent in the situation and overinvested, thereby upsetting the correct proportions between capital and labour. It thus seemed right to distinguish between the analysis of the short run and the long run, and between economic and other motives. Malthus may be regarded as a theoretician who favoured balanced growth, and in which certain rhythms and structures which are difficult to analyse quantitatively are preserved. To study disequilibrium, as he did, means that he considered the reverse aspects of economic growth as it were. One should not fall into the trap of believing that Malthus spread his efforts too wide, and he must be read a second time.

However, it is also possible to find arguments to the contrary, for there are at least two demographic—economic models to be found in his writings.[33] The first is well known. In a poor country with a high birth rate, an increase in income per head will in the short run be vitiated by population growth which would be kept in check by the level of resources. Real incomes would vary around subsistence level. A rise in real incomes would not last for long enough to bring about modifications in demographic behaviour and a reduction in the birth rate. There cannot, therefore, be any period of transition. The correct policy is for government to economize, to restrict consumption, to advocate a delay in marriage and to conserve natural resources.

The second model is completely different. It incorporates a safety valve: a sufficient level of unused resources to make it possible for the preventive check (moral restraint) to operate to reduce the birth rate and thus the growth in population. This safety valve operates because the demand for labour would result in permanent unemployment, a reduction in the incomes of the workers which will prevent them from marrying and raising a family. Different policies are, therefore, desirable to encourage moral restraint: a just and enlightened system of government, civil and political liberty and improvements in education, particularly given "the prodigious powers of production". At the same time, a programme of public works, growth of consumption by non-producers and redistribution of wealth, should make it possible to stimulate demand and to increase employment. Thus, the limits set by nature would not be attained for several centuries. Malthus was aware of the contradictions in his argument and tried to find two methods of resolving them, but neither was very satisfactory. One stressed the limits of physical resources, which would check the growth of population, the second was based on insufficiency of demand.

However, it may be more satisfactory to admit that Malthus could be simultaneously consistent and inconsistent. When considering this method of analysis we shall find some indications of a split personality.[34] Some differences in analysis are easily demonstrated. The Principle of Population links the *Essay* and the *Principles of Political Economy*. However, there are some significant differences between the two works: the concept of rent is introduced and the law of diminishing returns replaces the arithmetical progression of subsistence. However, when he considers distribution, both the doctrine of population and of diminishing returns are rejected, so that Malthus may be able to maintain that there exists a harmony of interest between landed proprietors and the forces of progress. As regards effective demand, Malthus suggests in the *Essay* that increased saving would be a remedy for economic depression, but in the *Principles* he recommends that expenditure should be increased. Even though he suggests later that the principle of effective demand is important in the short run and that of population in the long run, it remains true that the two views are difficult to reconcile.

However, in regard to doctrine there is only one Malthus. Though he takes an interest in the conditions of the workers, he is always addressing one question: which group in society can and will benefit from labour. He consistently defends the landowning classes and absolves them from responsibility for the misery of the people by showing that the latters' distress is entirely due to their own lack of prudence; he rejects any policies designed to redistribute or reduce the inequality in incomes; he stresses the importance of the landlord class for the maintenance of effective demand, because by receiving rents they are enabled to consume more than they produce and are, therefore, able to maintain non-productive workers.

Malthus's argument may be regarded as an analysis of economic underdevelopment of his time.[35] This becomes clear when we look at the part of his *Principles* in which he discusses the fertility of the soil. Do the ideas put forward in that book and in the *Essay* form a coherent doctrine? In fact, Malthus provides two different analyses of the phenomenon of underdevelopment. That in the *Essay* depends on the Principle of Population and is institutional in character. It is beneficial that a man should need to provide for his family, because this forces him to undertake productive work and to curb his sexual impulse. Population pressure is one factor which makes for progress, but it can only operate in a favourable environment, i.e. in the presence of two important social institutions — private property and marriage. If these did not exist, population pressure would act as a brake on development, because it would lead to incomplete and imperfect utilization of resources. Differences in wealth may be related to differences in social institutions.

In the *Principles,* the analysis is based on effective demand and the importance of individual preferences is stressed. Because human wants are limited, the natural resources of production are not fully exploited. This is the result of the "natural tendency to indolence" and of its consequences on the fertility of the soil and the methods of production. The disutility of effort is particularly important, and the influence of human capital exceeds that of physical capital.

A priori, there would not seem to be any incompatibility between these two analyses; they can both be used to establish a typology of underdeveloped economies. Such economies suffer from considerable chronic underemployment of productive resources. Malthus's view of underdevelopment is, therefore, consistent; it is based on a postulate about human nature, the tendency to indolence, which can only be overcome by appropriate social institutions which force men to overcome the obstacles that nature sets them.

Thus, Malthus's work cannot be considered as monolithic and the controversy about his views is unlikely to be settled, but may be expected to continue to produce lively discussion.

IV

Finally, it is impossible to understand Malthus without having a clear view of the purposes of his analysis. He is searching for regularities in demographic and economic behaviour, that is to say for adjustment mechanisms which are at one and the same time inherent in the structure of society, conform to natural laws and can explain human conduct in a number of different fields and which may be used to formulate policy.[36]

According to Malthus, societies are governed by definite laws. Specifically, two complementary principles can be seen at work. On the one hand, there is a restrictive principle, that societies face scarcity. Here the main issue is the survival of the species which is naturally linked to the problem of subsistence. Economics should be regarded as the struggle against scarcity: population and wealth must not get out of step. On the other hand, there is the principle that tends to bring about this adjustment, viz. the principle of competition. This is simply an extension of the principle of the survival of the species and expresses itself in the laws of supply and demand. However, the adjustment mechanism may fail to bring about equilibrium. Things can go wrong in two ways: on the one hand a lack of synchronization between the economic and population cycles, and on the other a species of "overshooting". Pressures, such as the difficulties of production stimulate human activity, invention and capital accumulation, but they may also lead to an overreaction which will result in an economic crisis.

Malthus attempts to reconcile the requirement that the society be adaptable in the manner just indicated with the preservation of social cohesion and the existing relations between social classes. This means that the most advantageous form of social and economic organization would be one in which there are a large number of relatively small and self-sufficient units of production. However, social systems are never still and cannot be frozen by the requirement of stability.

Can we speak of a cybernetic model in relation to Malthus's work?[37] We must recall Malthus's position in the development of economic thought, the great explosion in economic thought which had already occurred. Economic activity was seen as governed by two empirical laws: supply and demand and profit. The lines of analysis were established: the need to exploit the environment to ensure the development of the economic system and the complementarity between process and outcome, were well-established principles. There existed a two-sided dynamic (the circular flow and the tendency towards equilibrium) and two different models: one administrative and centralized and the other decentralized. Theories of the self-regulating private economy had been developed from Boisguilbert to Adam Smith.[37]

Malthus provides a cybernetic Principle of Population. There is negative feedback between changes in wages and changes in population, which will maintain wages at subsistence level. However, by regarding the supply of labour as being to some extent independent of the adjustment process, the tendency of the economy towards equilibrium can be modified and a rise in wages becomes possible.

It is unlikely that this negative relationship will be modified in the economic domain alone. At the micro-level the relation between supply and demand implies that a small reaction will occur because prices will rise. The natural price will then no longer be determined by a cybernetic process but will settle at some average equilibrium level between supply and demand. At the macro-level, the relation between total supply and total demand will result in economic cycles in the medium term.

Thus, Malthus both criticizes the cybernetic model and reinterprets it. The regulatory mechanism which he describes is only a special case of a general dynamic which articulates positive and negative movements and leads to tension.

Form and content cannot be separated. Some special features of Malthus's theories can only be understood by showing that he followed a programme of research in economic semantics.[38]

Malthus suggests rules relating to the definition of economic terms and their use. Three different categories are defined: mathematical, natural and moral. Each of these uses a different terminology because each of them is designed for statements of a different nature. Every definition is complex and contains elements of deduction, classification and denomination. Different procedures are used depending on the type of statement that it is desired to make.

The search for rules of definition in economics makes it necessary to investigate the special characteristics of economic terminology. Malthus regards economics as being a moral and political science and notes that there are uncertainties in economic terminology.[39] The reason is that economic vocabulary is used not to identify or describe but to explain and consists of a small number of terms. (Definitions require the use of an elaborate set of conventions) to ensure their consistency.) The statements that may be deduced from these definitions are pragmatic in character, and this explains the relationship between economic terminology and everyday language. But they are also positive and normative and depend on moral values. The Newtonian idea of causality cannot be applied to economics.[40]

In other words: it is impossible to construct a complete vocabulary of technical terms which would be adequate for the expression of every possible economic proposition. The complex and unstable dynamic link between different economic phenomena, resulting from random elements, needs to be stressed. Alternatively, we must identify the domains in which different systems of causal relationships are valid and produce evidence to show why a particular set of conditions is more probable than another

V

One obvious conclusion follows at the end of this discussion. Because of its breadth and complexity, Malthus's work makes him one of the greatest of the great economists. The treasures to be found in his writings are inexhaustible.

Notes

1. A. W. Coats. Malthus and British economics. Classical, neo-classical and Keynesian interpretation. MHA, p.114.
2. By the "hard" version, we mean a theory which uses the concept of a "natural" or wage "subsistence" and which assumes that labour is homogeneous. In the "soft" version there are two additional points: population growth is regarded as an index of economic and social development and is controlled by the pressure of population on subsistence, or by failure of the distribution system to maintain full employment.
3. J. Bonar (1885). *Malthus and his Work.* London. (Reprinted 1924.)
4. J. M. Keynes (1935). *The General Theory of Employment Interest and Money.* Macmillan, London.
5. P. Bini. Malthus, économiste en Italie dans la première moitié du XIXème siècle. MHA, p.110.
6. R. Fucci. Malthusianism in Italian economics, 1880–1890 MHA, p.115.
7. M. Perlman. Malthus's economics and its early American reception. MHA, p.125.
8. D. Raymond (1820). *Elements of Political Economy.*
9. L. Pejic. Malthus and economic thought in Yugoslavia. MHA, p.123.
10. P. R. Toscano. The economics of Ferdinando Galiani and Thomas Malthus. Similarities and differences. MHA, p.128.
11. P. Barruci and P. Roggi. Malthus, économiste smithien, anti-ricardien. MHA, p.109.
12. W. D. Grampp. Malthus versus Ricardo. MHA, p.118.
13. M. Herland. Rubans, dentelles et batistes. Cuique suum. MHA, p.118; J. Weiller. Malthus et Sismondi. MHA, p.129.
14. E. Schoorl. Say, Everett and Malthusianism. MHA, p.127.

15. T. Szmrecsanyi. The real Malthus: Somewhere between Marx and Keynes. MHA, p.128.
16. S. Fernandez. Malthus, Proudhon and Boisguilbert in the struggle for a world free from economic disequilibria. MHA, p.116.
17. A. J. Field. Malthus, method and macro-economics. MHA, p.117.
18. Some of the problems which occupied the attention of Malthus and his contemporaries have been clarified by Keynes's analysis. Thus, if not all income derived from production is spent on consumption, deflation does not necessarily result, provided the government follows a policy of deficit budgeting.
19. J. P. Gern. Structure sociale et équilibre économique chez Malthus. MHA, p.117.
20. This means that workers would have to move from unproductive into productive employment, or the creation of a wages fund, or the substitution of demand for production goods for that for consumption goods.
21. Two points may be added: a reduction in the production of luxuries may lead to an increase in the production of essentials, and the distribution of income between capital and labour may change.
22. I. Nicolae Valeanu. T. R. Malthus et sa théorie sur la valeur; sa signification d'hier et d'aujourd-hui. MHA, p.122.
23. J. Cartelier. La demande effective comme quantité du travail productif commandé. MHA, p.114.
24. A. Matyas. Malthus and social theorising. MHA, p.120.
25. In this connection, the contributions by Cartelier and Gern to this symposium should be compared. They look at this problem from different points of view.
26. M. Bronfenbrenner. On Malthusian macro-economics. MHA, p.111.
27. G. W. Zinke. A reconciliation of Malthus's rigid population principles with the flexibility of his Keynes-type short-period analysis. MHA, p.130.
28. G. Meublat. Peuplement et croissance économique. Malthus était-il malthusien? MHA, p.121.
29. [Translator's note] The term *"Malthusien"* in French has acquired a wider connotation than in English and is used to imply a restrictionist view.
30. It can be argued that Malthus is not attempting to seek an optimum population, but a particular distribution or social structure. His ideal society would be one dominated by middle-class values. cf. L. Calabi. Le principe de population comme principe d'une théorie de l'economie politique. MHA, p.113.
31. M. Lutfalla. T. R. Malthus: Corneille de l'économie politique. MHA, p.119.
32. Fluctuations in prices do not depend on changes in the quantity of money, but on changes in economic activity, although there may be side effects to changes in the money supply.
33. M. Paglin. The Malthusian safety valve and its economic policy correlation. MHA, p.123.
34. G. Caire. Un ou deux Malthus? MHA, p.112.

35. J. P. Platteau. De l'existence de deux principes contradictoires d'explication du sous développement dans la pensée économique de Malthus. MHA, p.126.
36. C. Menard. Régulation et direction: le projet économique de Malthus. MHA, p.120.
37. An integrated demonstration of the law of supply and demand and of the law of profit shows a self-regulating economic process in each sector, based on the equalization of supply and demand on one hand and an equilibrium between price and cost of production on the other.
38. C. Schmidt. Malthus et la sémantique économique. MHA, p.126.
39. This could be interpreted as a symptom of an unconscious introduction of definitions which have been wrongly presented as objective and value-free.
40. The principle of causality, as put forward by Newton, makes it possible to deduce the state of a system at time t' by calculation, when the state of the system at time t, which is often taken as the origin, is known.

PART 2

Malthus and his Time

6 Malthus and his Time

M. W. FLINN

In this section we were asked to look at those aspects of economic growth and social development in Britain, and, where relevant, in Europe, which particularly stirred the interest of Malthus, and at the cultural and intellectual background to his mental activity, again in respect of his economic and social ideas, though not of his demographic thought. Shortly after invitations to rapporteurs and authors were issued in the late autumn of 1978 and early spring of 1979 two major books about Malthus were published — Patricia James's admirable biography,[1] and William Petersen's erudite study of Malthusian themes and interpretations.[2] These two books complement each other splendidly and go a long way towards meeting the requirements of the second of this section's two remits — the examination of Malthus's cultural and intellectual background. On the other hand, they left largely untouched the first remit — the economic and social background — and there seemed much to be said, therefore, for keeping the emphasis in this section more specifically on the social and economic aspects rather than the cultural and intellectual.

Since his first unpublished essay was written in 1796 and he died in 1834, the period of his intellectual activity, let us say roughly from 1790 to 1834, spans a distinctive and important period of Britain's social and economic development. It was a period of rapid, if fluctuating, economic growth — of war with its inflation, and peace bringing deflation. The simultaneity of the processes of population growth and industrialization produced problems of adjustment between the agricultural and industrial sectors that were exacerbated by the erratic price movements. In short, rapid and often bewildering change was the order of the day, and it was a stimulating, if not exciting time for the professional economist, which, for all practical purposes, Malthus had

MALTHUS PAST AND PRESENT
ISBN 0-12-224670-5

become after his appointment to the East India College in 1805. But if it was exciting, it was also frustrating, for the raw material of the analytical economist — hard, preferably statistical facts about the whole range of economic inputs and outputs — was to a large degree missing in his day. Quite apart from the population problem, Malthus was interested in and wrote about a wide range of economic and social issues — the factors of production and their rewards, economic growth in both the short and the long run, investment, saving, overseas trade, and state policy, particularly in relation to poverty and the grain supply. In very few of these areas was statistical evidence available in his day, so that speculation necessarily took the place of informed reasoning. Malthus may well have insisted to Ricardo, "I certainly am disposed to refer frequently to things as they are, as the only way of making one's writing practically useful to society",[3] but in too many essential areas he lacked the means of knowing exactly "how things were". As Wrigley[4] has shown, he underestimated Britain's population at the time of the *First Essay* by a modest 56 per cent.

Since this period initiated the faster economic growth that carried Britain's steadily growing population through the nineteenth and into the twentieth century with increasing income per head, it is a natural focus of study for British social and economic historians. That much said, it has to be admitted that this crucial period in British economic history attracts less interest nowadays than it used to. A glance through the contents pages of the *Economic History Review* in recent years reveals few articles dealing with principal themes in this period: the classic studies by Ashton[5] and Mantoux[6] are respectively 32 and, unbelievably, 74 years old, while even the modern standard texts by Phyllis Deane[7] and Mathias[8] are respectively 15 and 11 years old, and the great Deane and Cole[9] and Rostow[10] studies that did so much to set us thinking on new lines are respectively 18 and 20 years old.

If some of the grander themes of economic growth do not at present seem to attract the attention of scholars that they would appear to merit — the works of Crouzet[11], Feinstein[12] and Pollard[13] are honourable and important exceptions — nonetheless, some of the particular themes that attracted Malthus are, by good fortune for this Congress, currently being studied — the economic role of the landed proprietors, the operation of the Corn Laws, the role of overseas trade, particularly of manufactures, in British economic growth, and trends in prices and wages.

Though he concerned himself in all areas of economics with concepts of mathematical relationships between economic variables, outside the field of demography Malthus only rarely adopted a quantitative approach to the economic developments of his days for the very obvious reason that few of the necessary statistics were publicly available. Working, however, very often from unpublished governmental and other sources, and using interpretative techniques not available to Malthus, and with the advantages of hindsight and a longer perspective, modern economic historians have been able to provide a firmer picture than was available to contemporaries of the course of development in the various sectors of economy and society.

Wrigley observes that "it was Malthus's fate to frame an analysis of the relationship between population, economy and society during the last generation to which it was applicable" because from the beginning of the nineteenth century the progress of the Industrial Revolution in Britain, by producing a growing surplus of manufactures to trade for imports of food, freed the country from its dependence upon what food could be produced at home, and hence from both the operation of the positive check and the need to operate the preventive check. The problems of interpreting the available statistics of British overseas trade during the eighteenth and early nineteenth centuries to illustrate this development have teased successively Imlah,[14] Elizabeth Schumpeter[15], Ashton[16] and Davis[17], but in a recent paper[18], summarized in his contribution to this Congress, Crouzet has produced a remarkably precise account of the actual course of British exports and their share of the national product. While Malthus was obliged to speak in the vaguest terms about "the general and powerful tendency of foreign commerce to raise the value of the national income", Crouzet is able to illustrate the substantial chronological and sectoral variations in the feedback of exports to industrial development. Crouzet's paper examines, in effect, the foundation of this major change during Malthus's lifetime. Malthus, indeed, attached great importance to the growth of foreign trade, but as a prime stimulant to economic growth, not as a means of making good the widening gap between the geometric progression of population growth and the arithmetic one of food supplies. The growth of foreign trade, he observed in the *Principles of Political Economy* had been "a most powerful agent" in the growth of national income between the 1780s and 1814. Moreover, as Crouzet points out, this was an area in which there was already in Malthus's day a regular publication of trade statistics. It is unlikely, however, that the problems of interpreting these statistics were fully appreciated at the time, while the violent movement of prices during Malthus's lifetime added a further complication for trade statistics which were based (at least until 1796) on fixed values of goods rather than on their changing real values. The careful study of these figures, with the aid of the work of Imlah and Davis, enables Crouzet to produce an analysis of the growth of British exports from the 1780s to the 1820s that modifies and adds precision to the picture available both to Malthus and to students of British economic history until very recently. It seems that the cotton exports, which Malthus thought to be of the greatest importance, did not really assume a "leading" role until the 1790s. Crouzet is also able to illustrate the fairly sharply fluctuating pattern both of total trade and of its geographical distribution during the war period (1793-1815), whereas Malthus had tended to assume a fairly steady growth.

In spite of the many technical problems involved in the interpretation of the trade statistics of Malthus's day, Crouzet is able to conclude: "... most of [Malthus's] remarks about [exports and foreign trade] appear quite sensible to the economic historian of his time." On the problem of capital formation, however, a field of great importance in Malthus's thinking, the position was very different: absolutely no statistics were available, while the criteria and methodology for assessment were almost equally non-existent. Anderson's paper performs two valuable services in this context: first, it surveys succinctly Malthus's theoretical view of the determinants of the level of capital accumulation and its role in the process of growth; secondly, it examines recent historical estimates of rates of investment over the late eighteenth and early nineteenth centuries, culminating in Feinstein's important new estimates.[19] These estimates, in sharp contrast to the earlier and much-used estimates of Deane and Cole, indicate, as Anderson says, "more strongly than ever before the crucial transformation in the composition of industrial and commercial capital in the industrial revolution". The recent work, while confirming Malthus's opinion as to the centrality of investment in the great acceleration of the Industrial Revolution, is at last beginning to bring some precision to the study of both the chronology and the sectoral distribution of capital formation.

Though they differ as to precise magnitudes, all the sectoral studies of capital formation reveal, as might be expected, the relative importance of agriculture in the British economy of Malthus's time. It was a major area of interest to Malthus, who spent most of his life in rural areas, and whose controversial views on the protection of agriculture attracted a great deal of attention. The general issue of food supplies, is, of course, central to Malthus's conception of the population problem, and the regulation of the corn trade was probably the major policy issue of his lifetime. Malthus's birth coincided very closely with the point in time when Britain ceased to be a net exporter of grain and became a net importer, but even at the time of his death, Britain was still able, possibly thanks to some extent to the Corn Laws, to produce substantially the greater part of its grain requirements. In the short run, however, as Turner shows in a valuably detailed paper, the natural fluctuations in the grain supply created recurring urgent and virtually insoluble problems. When Malthus wrote his two pamphlets on the Corn Laws in 1814 and 1815 memories of the acute wartime scarcities with their exceptionally high prices must still have been fresh in people's minds. The early wartime crises of 1795 and 1800 were important in the evolution of Malthus's thought in that they reinforced his adverse views about the effects of the Poor Laws. The tendency of grain prices in these crises, Malthus believed, to rise more than could be accounted for merely by the extent of the harvest deficiency, was the result (in Turner's words) of "a demand situation artificially created by more generous parish allowances in the face of a fixed supply, a situation of too much money chasing too few goods". While Turner accepts that this may have contributed to the crisis inflation of grain prices, and accepts Malthus's paradoxical view that, while the allowances "had forced a greater number to suffer partial scarcity", they also reduced the number who faced actual or potential starvation, he is able to show that the middlemen may well have had more responsibility for pushing up crisis prices than Malthus was willing to concede. Certainly, as Turner shows, contemporaries believed their activities to have been decisive in this context, and hostility to them was an important element in the social disturbances that followed the high prices. But even if speculation played some part in the market instability, there were few serious suggestions that reliance on capitalist organization in this sector should be ended: there was, therefore, a tacit general acceptance of the price to be paid for the continuance of private enterprise in this market in the form of some premium for the operators in times of scarcity.

Malthus believed that encouragement for home production of grain must be given to ensure an adequate supply at all times in an age when war, the trading policies of other countries, and market imperfections were liable to disrupt imports and leave a nation dependent, even only in part, upon imports, temporarily or for longer periods, without adequate food supplies. It is worth bearing in mind that in 1815 nearly 30 of Malthus's 49 years had been years of war. The protective principle he recommended was embodied in the 1815 Corn Law, and this measure is generally believed to have significantly altered the position of British agriculture as well as of grain prices during the last 20 years of Malthus's life. In her important article of 1969,[20] Susan Fairlie showed that for some years, or even decades, after 1815 there was probably a European grain surplus that, even with the addition of freight costs, could have severely undercut British producers, captured a significant share of an unprotected market, and turned British farmers away from grain production. By the time grain protection was abondoned in 1846 this European surplus, thanks probably to population increase in the exporting countries, had very largely evaporated, so that it was not until cheap shipping and prairie railways had made the transatlantic grain trade possible during the last third of the nineteenth century that British grain farmers were seriously threatened by free trade. Neither Malthus nor anyone else could have foreseen these post-1846 developments in 1815, and, indeed, it is worth noting that, whatever it was that affected the fortunes of British grain farmers later in the century, it was not what Malthus had feared — temporary interruption of supply by war or embargoes. There was, of course, no major European war after 1815 until the twentieth century when the danger against which Malthus had warned at last transpired, though his warning had by then been long forgotten. If there was a reason for protecting British grain producers after 1815 it was surely on the grounds of the population principle. Without the transatlantic supplies, quite unforeseeable in 1815, and with the degree of reliance on home grain production still prevailing at the levels of Malthus's lifetime, Malthus's ratios would surely sooner or later have brought real problems of feeding a population that during the late nineteenth century was still growing, despite heavy emigration, at over one per cent per year. One might say that on the issue of the Corn Laws in 1815 Malthus was right for the wrong reasons.

Susan Fairlie has caused us to revise our assessment of the impact of the Corn Laws in 1969, and Vamplew's paper argues for a further diminution of the protective effect of the Laws by scrutinizing their precise method of operation. The failure of both the 1815 and 1828 Laws to determine average prices (which in their turn determined imports) by a *weighted* average system allowed, as Vamplew skilfully demonstrates, the protective intention of the Corn Laws to be mitigated once again by the activities of the same merchants whom Turner has already shown to be shrewd manipulators of the imperfections of the grain market. "Clearly", writes Vamplew, "the predictability of the duty, the time lags . . ., and the bonded warehouses . . . gave dealers in foreign grain the opportunity to minimise the amount of duty which they had to pay within any cycle of duties."

Grain prices and the Corn Laws were important elements, as Mingay's paper shows, in the determination of levels of rents. For

Malthus, as Cannadine says, "the landed classes were at the centre of the stage." Malthus insisted, as is well known, on the need for a body of "unproductive consumers", who by their excessive spending "give a stimulus to production by developing the wants which the manufacturers are to satisfy". Cocks has set the background to this issue very nicely for us by showing, in particular, how post-war conditions after 1815 contributed to the development of this strand in Malthus's thinking, and has illustrated also the breadth of Malthus's concept of unproductive consumers. In a fascinating paper Cannadine illustrates the ways in which, with or without Malthus's encouragement, the landed classes followed these precepts. But he believes that Malthus greatly exaggerated the power of the "unproductive consumers" to stimulate economic growth. Both he and Mingay also show that Malthus was guilty of underestimating the importance of landowners as industrial capitalists.

The foundation of the landowners' influence on the economy, whether through investment or consumption, was, of course, the level of rents, and Mingay has performed a valuable service for us, first, in analysing the determinants of rent levels, and, second, in assessing the chronological course of rents over Malthus's lifetime. If, as he shows, rents probably rose in the inflation of 1790-1813 by about 90 per cent, this was not greatly in excess of the general price rise, and rather less than that for wheat; and if, as he also demonstrates, rents did not fall greatly after 1813, allowing the faster fall of general prices to drive up landowners' real incomes, their fortune in this respect was unlikely to have been sharply different from that of many wage-earning groups.[21]

Another major issue on which Malthus's views were decidedly controversial was the Poor Law. Here recent scholarship enables us to put at least some of Malthus's assumptions to the test. Broadly, he assumed that relief of poverty, whether arising out of unemployment or inadequate wages, particularly relief that took account of a man's wife and children, tended to encourage early, "improvident" marriage and excessive fertility within marriage. Because "a poor man may marry with little or no prospect of being able to support a family without parish assistance", the Poor Law tended, in his view, to breed the very poverty it aimed to cure. Blaug challenged this assumption in 1963,[22] and in an article of 1969[23] Huzel tested it statistically. He succeeded in tracing some 17 rural parishes and five towns in all of which allowances were known to have been discontinued at a stated point in time (mostly a date during the 1820s). In his present paper he is able to show that crude marriage and birth rates in these groups of parishes and towns were marginally higher without allowances than they had been with them. The small differences are probably not very meaningful, given the imperfections of the sources, but there is no clear positive correlation between allowances and high marriage and birth rates required by the Malthusian assumptions, if anything the reverse is true. He is able to confirm his earlier finding that "the allowance system does not encourage rising births and marriage rates", and goes on to assert, as Blaug had tentatively suggested in 1963, that "the Malthusian proposition should be turned on its head since the allowance system was more likely to be society's response to the pressures of faster population growth than the reverse". This leads him to conclude: "Malthus, in spite of his often meticulous emphasis on empirical data, failed to test sufficiently assumptions which guided English social policy not only in his own time but also for generations to follow."

It is well known that Malthus's reasoning from these assumptions led him to suggest that, in the long run, poverty would be much reduced by the total abolition of the Poor Laws. But if this was where his logic drove him, his humanity dictated otherwise. Anne Digby has made a valuable contribution in surveying the whole range of Malthus's views in this area, showing, as might be expected, that the view of Malthus as a simple abolitionist is an over-simplification. She explores, in particular, the conflict between the intellectual and humanitarian considerations that underlay his sometimes confused thinking about poverty. "It was", she says, with reference to his unpublished essay of 1796, "Malthus's concern for the condition of the poor that had set him thinking about population in the first place". And Stapleton's paper shows vividly how the experience of the Surrey parishes most familiar to Malthus during the last years of the eighteenth century must have brought him very immediately face to face with these issues. Malthus's fundamental humanitarianism would not permit him to follow, as policy recommendations, the extremes to which his logic as an economic analyst pushed him, and Anne Digby considers that it would be more accurate to describe him as a reformist than as an abolitionist. Her paper brings out fascinatingly the conflict between "Population Malthus" and "Parson Malthus".

The link between real incomes and marriage and fertility also forms the subject of Wrigley's paper. His aim, in line with most of the other contributors to this section, is to test Malthus's assumptions against the facts as revealed by modern statistical study. He draws his information on real wages from the well-known Phelps Brown and Hopkins index.[24] The danger with all wage statistics is of over-simplification: it is well known that much more work is needed at the local level to establish a pattern of regional and occupational variations and how these differentials varied over time. For this reason the regional work of Eccleston is particularly valuable. He makes a skilful attempt to reconstruct from a wide range of original wage and price data for the English Midlands the course of Malthus's measure of "corn wages". What Eccleston's detailed local study succeeds in showing is that, inevitably, the picture is more complicated than Malthus's or even Wrigley's interpretations imply: there were on the one hand important occupational variations in trends determined by supply and demand as well as by differences in the organization and bargaining power of workers, while on the other hand the chronology of trends was sharply influenced by the inflationary and deflationary phases of wartime and post-war movements. The disparities of experience of different occupational groups and the contrast between the stagnation of real wages until the inflationary peak of 1812-1813 and the gains during the deflationary period make it difficult to sustain any single generalization about the relationship between real wages and demographic trends.

Huzel, Anne Digby and Wrigley all raise explicitly or implicitly the question of the trend, assumed to be downward in Malthus's time, of the age at first marriage. Malthus was, of course, concerned that the Poor Law and its allowance system tended to encourage early marriage, or at least not to discourage it. Petersen has recently suggested,[25] moreover, that a breakdown of the institutional checks on the age at marriage in the late eighteenth century was a powerful stimulant to the production of the *First Essay* in 1798, and that the information made available to Malthus by the first census of 1801 assisted in the process of developing his change of emphasis in favour of the preventive check. Clearly, when Malthus was writing in 1798 he was almost entirely in the dark in respect of levels and trends of "age at first marriage" so far as Britain was concerned, nor did the Census of 1801, in spite of Rickman's "Parish Register Abstracts", shed much light in this area. At first sight there appears to be a conflict between Huzel, who demonstrates on the basis of several samples of parishes operating and parishes not operating allowance schemes that marriage appeared not to be influenced by such schemes, and Wrigley who, drawing on the immense resources of the Cambridge Group's data bank, shows at the same time a rising crude marriage rate and accordingly rising fertility. The resolution of these disparities may perhaps lie in the phenomenon investigated by Levine[26] of occupational variations in age at marriage. He establishes, I think beyond question, that by the late eighteenth century the group of domestic workers he investigated — Leicestershire frame knitters — married appreciably earlier than the farmers and agricultural workers he also studied. This opens the possibility that Wrigley's rising marriage rate (and the lowering of age at marriage to which he also refers) may be explained by a shifting of the balance of occupational groups, as employment in domestic industry rose, in favour of those groups with lower ages at first marriage. Before this explanation may be accepted, however, we would need to know more about parallel changes (if there were any) in the marriage habits of other occupational groups like miners, factory workers, or agricultural labourers (as opposed to "servants in husbandry") that might also have been increasing in relative importance at this time: it would be misleading to generalize from just one such group whose marriage habits happen to have been studied.

The papers presented in this section do not, of course, aim to offer a comprehensive survey of the economic history of Britain in Malthus's lifetime. The intention has been to review the principal areas of the economy that most interested Malthus and to consider, in the light of modern scholarship, how far contemporary prejudices and the unavailability of information handicapped Malthus in his analysis. The gain in recent years, as the majority of these papers show, is the degree of precision brought about by skilful and often ingenious exploitation of statistics, some of which were available to, but in general not used by, Malthus. In some areas the evolution of concepts and analytical techniques has permitted a more rigorous analysis than Malthus's looser framework could ever have done. But if Malthus suffered from a notably inferior access to both information and technique, his understanding of the economy of his day stands up extraordinarily well to scrutiny under the searchlights of modern methods, better, arguably, for example, than Ricardo's, in discussion with whom many of his ideas had been forged.

Notes

1. Patricia James (1979). *Population Malthus. His Life and Times.* London.
2. W. Petersen (1979). *Malthus*, Cambridge, Massachusetts.
3. Letter to Ricardo, 26 January 1817, quoted by Anne Digby.
4. All papers presented at the Congress and referred to in this Report may be found in the microfiche edition of the Congress *Proceedings*. Selected papers are published also in this volume.
5. T. S. Ashton (1948). *The Industrial Revolution.* Oxford.
6. P. Mantoux (1928). *The Industrial Revolution of the Eighteenth Century.* London. First French edition 1908.
7. Phyllis Deane (1965). *The First Industrial Revolution.* Cambridge.
8. P. Mathias (1969). *The First Industrial Nation.* London.
9. Phyllis Deane and W. A. Cole (1962). *British Economic Growth, 1688–1959.* Cambridge.

10. W. W. Rostow (1960). *The Stages of Economic Growth.* Cambridge.
11. F. Crouzet (1972). *Capital Formation in the Industrial Revolution.* London; Angleterre et France au XVIIIe siècle. Essai d'analyse comparée de deux croissances économiques', *Annales ESC*, 1966.
12. C. Feinstein (1978). Capital formation in Great Britain. In *The Cambridge Economic History of Europe* (Eds P. Mathias and M. M. Postan), vol. VII. Cambridge.
13. S. Pollard (1978). Labour in Great Britain. In *The Cambridge Economic History of Europe* (Eds. P. Mathias and M. M. Postan), vol. VII. Cambridge.
14. A. H. Imlah (1958). *Economic Elements in the Pax Britannica.* Cambridge, Massachusetts.
15. Elizabeth B. Schumpeter (1960). *English Overseas Trade Statistics, 1697–1808.* Oxford.
16. T. S. Ashton. "Introduction" to Elizabeth B. Schumpeter, *English Overseas Trade Statistics,* cited in note 15.
17. R. Davis (1978). *The Industrial Revolution and British Overseas Trade.* Leicester.
18. F. Crouzet (1980). Toward an export economy: British exports during the Industrial Revolution. *Explorations in Economic History* **17**.
19. C. Feinstein, loc. cit. in note 12.
20. Susan Fairlie (1974). The Corn Laws and British wheat production, 1829–76. *Economic History Review*, 2nd ser. **27**.
21. M. W. Flinn (1974). Trends in real wages, 1750–1850. *Economic History Review*, 2nd ser. **27**.
22. M. Blaug (1963). The myth of the Old Poor Law and the making of the New. *Journal of Economic History* **23**, 176.
23. J. P. Huzel (1969). Malthus, the Poor Law and population in early nineteenth century England. *Economic History Review*, 2nd ser. **22**.
24. E. H. Phelps Brown and Sheila V. Hopkins (1956). Seven centuries of the prices of consumables compared with builders' wage-rates. *Economica*, n.s. **23**..
25. W. Petersen, op. cit. in footnote 2, p.180.
26. D. Levine (1977). *Family Formation in an Age of Nascent Capitalism*, pp.61–63, 97. New York.

7 Malthus and Reform of the Poor Law*

ANNE DIGBY

> A pamphlet on the poor laws generally contains some little piece of favourite nonsense, by which we are gravely told this enormous evil may be perfectly cured... Every man rushes to the press with his small morsel of imbecility; and is not easy till he sees his impertinence stitched in blue covers.[1]

This apt comment by Sydney Smith applies to many of Malthus's contemporaries but not — we are so often told — to Malthus himself. Malthus's contribution is alleged to be the vigorous application of a scientific principle in place of piecemeal, meliorist reform of the Poor Law.[2] This interpretation is based on Malthus's *Essay on the Principle of Population* of 1798, where the application of the Poor Law had led Malthus to the conclusion that there should be a "total abolition of all the present parish-laws".[3] Yet while this early abolitionist stance is well known his later reformist views have received less attention. This article suggests that it was as a reformer, as much as an abolitionist, that Thomas Robert Malthus (1766-1834) was to influence the shaping of the new Poor Law.

I

For contemporaries the Poor Law appeared to be one of the most interesting of Malthus's applications of the Principle of Population. His views on poor relief at this time had much in common with those of a group who adhered to natural law principles in political economy. They saw the Poor Law as a distortion of the free market, and the poor

*I am very grateful to Dr Avner Offer and Dr Peter Searby for their helpful comments on earlier versions of this paper.

MALTHUS PAST AND PRESENT
ISBN 0-12-224670-5

rates (which financed relief) as an undesirable diversion of money from the wages fund which reduced the amount of employment and wages available for the poor.[4] In the *First Essay* of 1798 Malthus advocated the "abolition of all the present parish laws" since, although they were instituted for "the most benevolent purpose", they produced "irremediable" evils.

> Their first obvious tendency is to increase population without increasing the food for its support. A poor man may marry with little or no prospect of being able to support a family in independence. They may be said therefore in some measure to create the poor which they maintain[6]

His objections to the Poor Laws were to be developed in the second *Essay* of 1803, and elaborated still further in the fifth edition of the *Essay* of 1817. In these and other writings he criticized the impact which the Poor Laws had on the labour market and on wages. Since poor relief encouraged the growth of population, it increased the supply of labour beyond demand, and hence lowered wages.[7] Malthus condemned a permanent system of allowances because they destroyed the "necessary connexion between the apparent corn wages of day labour and the real means which the labouring classes possess of maintaining a family".[8] The parish poor rate thus became a subsidy for labourers' wages; an accelerating process of ever-increasing pauperism was set in motion which could end only in "the great body of the community" becoming paupers.[9] His conclusion in 1827 was still that "no essential improvement can take place without the denial of a legal claim" to poor relief to the unemployed able-bodied poor.

It was not only poor-law allowances that Malthus viewed with a critical eye. He had reservations about other public interventions into the labour market, although his opinions often changed on these issues. By 1827 he was opposing public schemes for employing the poor which he had supported ten years earlier. He concluded that the short-term gains were more than counterbalanced by bad long-term results, because labourers were encouraged to marry and have children, whom they were unable to support when the public works ceased.[11] The alarming propensity of the poor to marry and breed made Malthus excessively cautious about colonial emigration: another fashionable contemporary remedy for removing surplus population and reducing pauperism. He would concede that the emigration of redundant labourers would be advantageous, but only if the emigrants' houses were pulled down so that those left behind were not encouraged to marry early and set up home.[12]

A similar concern about the supply of cottages led to ambivalence in his later views on the settlement laws of the Poor Law. In this case, uncharacteristically, the Principle of Population made him prefer the retention of the laws of settlement to their abolition. Yet earlier, in 1798, he had felt that one of the principal gains in abolishing the Poor Laws would be to end the settlement laws. This would free the labour market, and so "give liberty and freedom of action to the peasantry of England", thus finishing "a most disgraceful and disgusting tyranny" of poor people by parochial officers. Also, in their obstruction of the labour market, the settlement laws were criticized because they had "a constant tendency to add to the difficulties of those who are struggling to support themselves without assistance".[13] Later, Malthus deviated from conventional economic thinking on this subject and declared: "I think that anything like an abolition of the present laws of settlement would be accompanied with more evil than good."[14] By this he meant that it was better to countenance an impediment to a free labour market than the increased cottage building and encouragement to marriage that abolition of the settlement laws might bring. For similar reasons he defended existing inequalities in the financial incidence of the burden of the poor rate because they encouraged ratepayers to be vigilant over the administration of poor relief.[15]

"I certainly am disposed to refer frequently to things as they are, as the only way of making one's writings practically useful to society."[16] This personal observation by Malthus is valid in so far as it refers to the way in which he applied his Principle of Population to a central issue of social policy, the system of poor relief, and read contemporary publications in order to understand it. His interest in the day-to-day management of the Poor Law appears to have been rather limited and his failure to link systematically the application of his Principle to poor-law policy with the actual operation of poor relief helps to explain some lack of consistency in his writing on the subject. It also gives an insight into the reasons why Malthus periodically admitted that the theoretical tendency of the Poor Law to increase population and aggravate poverty was not actually happening in practice. For example, in 1807 he conceded that "the operations of the Poor Laws are so complicated that it is almost impossible to take in at one view all their different bearings and relations... [and] that the Poor Laws do not encourage early marriage *so much* as might naturally be expected".[17]

II

Malthus's advocacy of the abolition of the Poor Laws stemmed both from elements in his economic theorizing, and from his first statement of the Principle of Population. However, the subtle evolution of his views led to a fundamental restatement of the Principle of Population and hence to different emphasis when this was applied to the subject of poor relief. In his first version of the Principle of Population Malthus had stated:

> . . . the power of population is indefinitely greater than the power in the earth to produce subsistence for man. Population, when unchecked increases in a geometrical ratio. Subsistence increases only in an arithmetical ratio.[18]

In 1798 Malthus had argued that population increase might be reduced by positive checks (of misery and disease) and preventive checks (of postponement of marriage with consequent vice), but by 1803 he had developed his thinking on preventive checks with the idea of moral restraint.[19] This preventive check was defined as "the restraint from marriage which was not followed by irregular gratification".[20] The introduction of this moral element made his Principle of Population an indeterminate one, which depended for its operation on individual character. Moral restraint, involving a prudential postponement of marriage, was thus dependent on educating the poor and inculcating habits of self-reliance and self-respect. Malthus's views on poor relief reflected this concern for the elevation of the labourer's moral character.

In his view — and those of several other classical economists — the distribution of poor relief involved profound moral issues. Probably their most influential legacy in shaping the new Poor Law was the theory of unstable moral equilibrium in the life of a poor man: he might be subverted into pauperism or encouraged to retain his independence.[21] The starting point for Malthus's thinking on poverty and its relief was : "It is by no means to be wished that any dependent situation should be made so agreeable, as to tempt those who might otherwise support themselves in independence."[22] Social policy should tip the balance in that it should create a situation in which "dependent poverty ought to be held disgraceful".[23] Yet the institutional framework of the Poor Law, or its alternatives, should only hold the ring in stimulating desirable virtues of prudence and thrift in the labourer. "The very admission of the necessity of prudence, to prevent the misery from an overcharged population, removes the blame from public institutions to the conduct of individuals."[24]

It was the superior virtues of voluntary charity over the forced public charity of the Poor Law that made it preferable in Malthus's view.

Since the incidence of voluntary charity was uncertain, no poor man could depend on it, but must rely on his own industry and forethought. Voluntary charity was better than poor relief because it exercised moral discrimination in selecting deserving objects for assistance; these were industrious, prudent individuals who needed help to overcome unmerited misfortunes. These worthy labourers would show gratitude for the assistance, rather than the indifference which characterized the recipients at the parish pay table. The charitable donor would benefit from fulfilling his moral obligation to practise the virtue of charity. Society would be improved as well, since the rich would increase their personal knowledge of the poor and closer bonds would be forged between different social ranks.[25] While the objects of charity retained self-respect, pauperism involved subjection and the extinction of honourable feelings. Malthus argued that the Poor Law should be replaced because it "powerfully contributed to generate. . . carelessness and want of frugality"; by diminishing the will to save it weakened "incentives to sobriety and industry, and consequently to happiness"; and removed "one of the strongest checks to idleness and dissipation".[26] Abundant poor relief effectively tilted the moral scales in society tempting the poor man down into improvident dependence and making more difficult his assimilation of bourgeois virtues.

For Malthus (like the Rev. Joseph Townsend before him) a very important objective of social policy was to "draw a more marked line between the dependent and independent labourer"[27] and in consequence he opposed many of the reforms for assisting the poor put forward by his meliorist contemporaries. Even those which had as their avowed aim the immediate encouragement of self-help might encounter his hostility, because Malthus felt that their long-term effect would be increased dependence. Both Arthur Young's suggestion for a potato ground and a cow for the labourer, and Samuel Whitbread's proposed legislation on the parochial provision of cottages were rejected by Malthus, since in his view they encouraged marriage and procreation, while not increasing resources proportionately.[28] Townsend's plan for universal, compulsory subscriptions to Friendly Societies to replace the Poor Law brought the predictable response that this would have the same undesirable attributes as a compulsory poor rate, while even voluntary subscriptions to these societies were condemned by Malthus in his most pessimistic mood.[29] The same reasoning might possibly have been applied to Savings Banks, but Malthus retained his belief in these institutions in helping prudence and thrift, and indeed served as a "manager" of the Provident Institution for Savings in West London.[30]

Malthus believed fervently in the "moral obligation imposed on every man by the commands of God and nature to support his own children". Pauperism was thus a practical consequence of the failure to exercise moral restraint. Hence, it was upon the moral understanding and moral character of the labourer that he felt the most lasting causes of improvement in the labouring classes were to be found.[31] It is not surprising to find him pinning his hopes on educating the poor rather than relieving them. Even a modified Poor Law "would have a tendency to depress the independent labourer, to weaken in some degree the springs of industry and good conduct, and to put virtue and vice more on a level than they would be in the natural course of things".[32]

III

Malthus's views on the Poor Law were complex. They involved both theoretical and practical analyses of the administration of poor relief, and policy prescriptions which included long-term ideal solutions and short-term realistic ones. In the short term Malthus had to concede the practical necessity for poor relief in times of social distress. "I hardly see what else could have been done" he commented on the allowances given to the poor by the magistrates during the time of very high bread prices from 1799 to 1800.[33] His admission that poor relief was necessary during times of social distress was not just expediency but also reflected his underlying humanitarianism. It appears that it was his concern for the poor that had set him thinking about population in the first place.[34] We can see from the surviving fragments of his unpublished work of 1796, entitled *The Crisis*, that his views were similar to those of a humanitarian group of reformers who sympathized with the poor.[35] At this time Malthus wished to relieve the poor in their own homes since "it is certainly desirable that the assistance in this case should be given in the way that is most agreeable to the persons who are to receive it".[36] Malthus felt that in times of high bread prices, such as 1800 or 1817, allowances could be justified since in sharing hardship they averted starvation.[37] Here "the great moral duty of assisting our fellow creatures in distress" triumphed over abolitionist principle.[38] It was in distressed years such as 1816-17 that Malthus's conscience was most sensitive; the employment of the poor on temporary public works was useful "to avoid the bad moral effects of idleness".[39] To a limited extent Malthus was able to justify his humanitarian policies by economic reasoning. For example, when prices were high, temporary poor relief avoided an increase in wages which would be difficult to take back when prices came down again.[40]

The years of distress after the Napoleonic wars gave a practical demonstration, in Malthus's opinion, of Sir Frederick Morton Eden's previous conclusion that the legal right to relief under the English Poor Law could not be fulfilled.[41] But if it could not fulfil its promises then Malthus argued, as had Townsend earlier, that voluntary charity should replace the forced "charity" of the Poor Law. This was an ideal prescription, but Malthus recognized that immediate abolition was not realistic. He appreciated that "the relief given by the Poor-Laws [is] so widely extended, that no man of humanity could venture to propose their immediate abolition". From this came the view that legitimate children who were born a year after legislation (or two years, if illegitimate), should have no right to relief. Therefore, abolition would come about very gradually.[42] But on the level of short-term policy Malthus, as we have seen, conceded that allowances or employment schemes under the Poor Law were justified in years of social distress, and that the settlement laws did more good than harm. He conceded that abolition must wait upon a changed public opinion, including that of the labouring poor, who should "be made to understand that they had purchased their right to a provision by law, by too great and extensive a sacrifice of their liberty and happiness".[43]

In advocating abolition as a long-term and ideal policy objective which would ensure the happiness of the labourer. Malthus was prepared to accept that the price that would have to be paid, for this involved individual hardship.[44] This led to charges of inhumanity, and an understandable identification of an apparently harsh policy with the character of its author. Malthus himself commented that "I feel that I have no occasion to defend my character from the imputation of hardness of heart".[45] Also, that "I am not conscious of ever having said anything to countenance calumnious reports against the poor, and most certainly I never intended to do so".[46] Contemporary admirers were at pains to distinguish the man from popular misunderstandings of his work. Bishop Otter eulogized Malthus as "the most humane and considerate of men" who aimed to increase the poor's "comforts, and to raise their moral and intellectual condition".[47] Yet Malthus's defenders conveniently forgot the large group of helpless poor on whose fate Malthus maintained a deafening silence in nearly all his testimony. In his earliest work he took a sympathetic line towards the relief of the aged, children, or widows who could not maintain themselves through no fault of their own. Thereafter, he implicitly included them with the able-bodied poor, for whom hardship was a necessary spur to industry. This was a harder line than that of admirers, including Ricardo, who, although in agreement with the main lines of Malthusian abolitionism, still felt that these helpless poor needed relief.[48] However, Malthus typically offered a concession on this issue in 1827, when testifying to the Select Committee on Emigration. He was asked if a Poor Law system restricted only to the aged, infirm, and children would still be prejudicial and replied "Perhaps not".[49]

IV

Alternately reviled and praised, Malthus's views were of central intellectual significance in shaping the debate over poor-law policy for nearly 40 years before the decisive reform of 1834. Pitt's Bill of 1796-1797 which would have given relief as of right to families with more than two children, had been criticized by Malthus and by Bentham; their views convinced Pitt, and he became an opponent of poor-law allowances.[50] During the opening years of the nineteenth century his abolitionist views attracted widespread support, as the following accolade in the *Edinburgh Review* of 1807 suggests: "While other writers busied themselves in criticizing and amending paltry details, Mr Malthus went to the bottom of the evil, and showed that the system was so vicious in its principle, that no amendments could render it beneficial."[51] In the same year, Samuel Whitbread, in introducing his Bill on the Poor Laws in the Commons, paid tribute to Malthus in having argued from sound principles.[52] A decade later, Malthus's influence was at its height, when the Select Committee on the Poor Laws of 1817, under its Malthusian Chairman, Sturges Bourne, accepted much of the abolitionist case. In 1826, Wilmot Horton, who had corresponded with Malthus for several years on emigration, chaired the Select Committee on this subject. Its *Third Report* spoke of the empirical testimony of other witnesses having "been confirmed in the most absolute manner by that of Mr Malthus", and advocated emigration as a means of reducing redundant labour and decreasing pauperism.[53]

The narrow focus of Malthusian argument on the able-bodied poor—on their moral condition, and redundant numbers — was to be repeated by the Royal Commission on the Poor Laws of 1832-1834 and in the legislation which followed it. In the *First Essay* Malthus had contemplated providing deterrent workhouses in each county for the able-bodied where "the fare should be hard, and those that were able obliged to work".[54] Later, he abandoned this idea because he argued that the dependent poor in workhouses consumed provisions, and that this diminished the resources available to sustain the independent poor.[55] His opposition to workhouses was caricatured in 1818 by

Thomas Love Peacock, in his novel *Melincourt*, where Malthus, personified as Mr Fox, denounces the fact that paupers marry even in the workhouse so making of it "a flourishing manufactory of beggars and vagabonds". Yet the workhouses set up under the Poor Law Amendment Act of 1834 were identified in the popular mind as Malthusian instruments, in which the separation of members of the family under the workhouse classification scheme would restrain the poor from breeding.[56] This stemmed from radical opinion, shaped to a considerable extent by William Cobbett, whose attacks on Malthus over the years had culminated in 1831 in his satirical melodrama *Surplus Population*. Here the fanatical Malthusian, Peter Thimble, pens a "Remedy Against Breeding" in which he argues against "that great national scourge, the procreation of the human species".[57]

For contemporaries there seemed no doubt of Malthus's influence on the new Poor Law, whether they were critics of the Poor Law Amendment Act of 1834[58] or admirers like Malthus's old friend Bishop Otter. In 1836 Otter wrote that "the Essay on Population and the Poor Laws Amendment Bill, will stand or fall together".[59] Yet recent writers have been less confident about the nature, or degree, of Malthus's influence on this decisive reform of the Poor Law. Patricia James's comment on Otter's statement was that "nothing could be further from the truth", J.R. Poynter stated that "the case for describing the Amendment Act as Malthusian is weak", while W. Petersen referred to Malthus's "indirect" influence and concluded that "in some respects he left no doubt he was opposed to the 1834 Act".[60]

It has been suggested in this article that Malthus's views on the Poor Law were complicated, and further that over a period of 34 years they changed on several important issues. Thus, if one wishes to ask to what extent the 1834 Act was influenced by Malthus it is possible to make a case out of either the similarities or the divergences between his opinions and the provisions of the 1834 legislation. If the 1834 Act is defined by reference to its provision for emigration subsidies, its creation of a more complex administration of the Poor Law, and its failure to take radical measures to abolish poor relief, the new Poor Law cannot be termed Malthusian. In contrast, the new Poor Law might be thus characterized if the stringent reforms of the Poor Law Amendment Act are taken as a step towards abolition, which, as we have seen, tended to Malthus's later position. This is the case, too, if the bastardy clauses (penalizing unmarried mothers), and the workhouse classification scheme of the Poor Law Commission (which separated husbands and wives), are taken as applications of the Principle of Population. Also, the ending of outdoor allowances to the able-bodied may be viewed in the Malthusian moral context of strengthening the labourers' independence and prudence. Thus, on balance, the Poor Law Amendment Act might be considered a Malthusian measure because it reflected moral and reformist elements that were central to Malthus's later prescriptions for a practicable social policy.

The Poor Law Amendment Act had followed many of the conclusions of the Royal Commission on the Poor Laws of 1832-1834. In spite of the presence of abolitionists such as Sturges Bourne, Bishop Summer, and Bishop Blomfield on the Commission, its *Report* had come out in favour of a reform of poor relief. The reformist ideas of the two authors of the *Report*, Nassau Senior and Edwin Chadwick, decisively shaped the legislation which followed. Nassau Senior was not an orthodox Malthusian: he did not believe that population was out-stripping subsistence because he emphasized to a far greater extent than did Malthus the force of the desire to better oneself, and hence the psychological drives of ambition and the achievement of self-respect as key factors in keeping the growth of population and resources in step. Unlike Malthus, he did not think that increased population *necessarily* produced poverty. Moreover, he thought abolition of poor relief impracticable.[61] His fellow-author, Chadwick, commented that the enquiries of the Poor Law Commissioners had disproved the pessimistic conclusions of the Population Principle as it had been applied to the Poor Law.[62] He thought that it was the old poor-law application of relief, and not the principle of relief, that was wrong. Hence, he advocated reforming the Poor Law in order to remove its pernicious tendency to seduce labourers into pauperism, and create a positive framework of law which encouraged the labourer to choose moral and economic independence.[63]

Total abolition was rejected but the moral arguments of Malthus were to help fashion the mechanism of reform. The *Report* of the Royal Commission concluded that "under strict regulations, adequately enforced, such relief may be afforded safely and even beneficially". The essential precondition of reformed relief was to be that the pauper's situation "on the whole shall not be made really or apparently so eligible as the situation of the independent labourer" and that "every penny bestowed that tends to render the condition of the pauper more eligible than that of the independent labourer, is a bounty on indolence and vice".[64] The workhouse test of the new Poor Law was designed as the practical application of this moral principle; those who from lack of prudence and forethought were forced to seek relief would receive assistance in the deterrent conditions of the union workhouse. This was in accord with Malthus's final views on the subject:

"If it be generally considered as so discredible to receive parochial relief, that great exertions are made to avoid it, . . . there is no doubt that those who were really in distress might be adequately assisted."[65] Those who entered the new union workhouses after 1834 were imprinted with the moral stigma of pauperism; their misfortunes were their own responsibility since the better-off had fulfilled their responsibility to them in underlining the necessity for prudence and thrift. The abrasive class character of the new Poor Law was thus rooted in the moral sentiments of Malthus.

V

Malthus admitted that public opinion was not ready to embrace his ideal policy of abolishing the Poor Laws and that he would settle for their reform: "Practically, therefore I am inclined to look forward to the first improvement as likely to come from an improved administration of our actual laws, together with a more general system of education and moral superintendence."[66] This moral element gives us the key to much of Malthus's thinking on the Poor Law; he advocated the elevation of the labourer so that it would increase his moral restraint and hence reduce pauperism. In doing so Malthus posed the question (which is still with us today), of how far a collectivist system of social benefits would modify an individual's attitude to work. He concluded: "To what extent assistance may be given, even by law, to the poorest classes of society when in distress . . . depends mainly upon the feelings and habits of the labouring classes of society and can only be determined by experience."[67] Malthus's own experience gave him a view of pauperism as a moral disease whose contagious qualities provided a built-in multiplier to an ever-increasing, dependent population. His pessimistic vision of expanding poor relief increasing moral and social degradation lent urgency to the discussion on a necessary reform of the Poor Law in the years before 1834, and influenced the reforms adopted in the new Poor Law. It was neither the originality nor the consistency of his views on social welfare which gave them such relevance. Rather they commanded support because of their apparent inevitability when linked to his Principle of Population.

Notes

1. Sydney Smith (1820). Poor Laws. *Edinburgh Review* 65, pp.91–92.
2. See, for example, S. and Beatrice Webb (1963). *English Poor Law History* (reprint, 2 vols), part 2, vol. I, pp. 21–25; S. E. Finer, (1952). *The Life and Times of Sir Edwin Chadwick,* p.44; R. G. Cowherd (1977). *Political Economists*

and the English Poor Laws, pp.19–20, 32. Athens, USA. See also the views of contemporaries cited in notes 51 and 59.

3. T. R. Malthus *First Essay*, p.95.
4. R. G. Cowherd, op. cit. in note 3, pp.19–20; R. G. Cowherd (1960). The humanitarian reform of the English Poor Laws from 1782–1815. *Proceedings of the American Philosophical Society* **104,** 339–340.
5. T. R. Malthus, op. cit. in note 4, pp.93, 98.
6. Ibid, p.83.
7. T. R. Malthus. *Essay*, 5th Edition (3 vols, 1817), vol. 2, p.371.
8. T. R. Malthus (1836). *Principles of Political Economy*, 2nd Edition, p.232.
9. T. R. Malthus, op. cit. in note 7, p.368.
10. Select Committee on Emigration, Parliamentary Papers, 1826–1827, V, Q. 3369.
11. Ibid. Q.Q. 3343–4.
12. Ibid. Q.Q. 3252–3.
13. T. R. Malthus, op. cit. in note 3, p.92.
14. Malthus to Rev. T. Chalmers, 21 July 1822, quoted in P. James (1979). *Population Malthus*, p.450.
15. T. R. Malthus, op. cit. in note 7, vol. 3, pp.265–267.
16. Letter from Malthus to Ricardo, 26 January 1817, quoted in G. F. McCleary (1953). *The Malthusian Population Theory*, p.167.
17. A Letter to Samuel Whitbread, Esq. M. P. reprinted in D. V. Glass (ed.), (1959). *Introduction to Malthus*, pp. 192–193.
18. T. R. Malthus, op. cit. in note 3, pp.13–14.
19. Ibid. pp.63–73.
20. T. R. Malthus (1803). *Essay*, 2nd Edition, p.14.
21. A. W. Coats (1971). The classical economists and the labourer. In *The Classical Economists and Economic Policy* (Ed. A. W. Coats), pp.156–157.
22. *The Crisis, a View of the Present Interesting State of Great Britain by a Friend to the Constitution.* Extract quoted in Bishop Otter's *Memoir of Robert Malthus* appended to T. R. Malthus (1836), *Principles of Political Economy*, 2nd Edition, p.xxxvi.
23. T. R. Malthus, op. cit. in note 3, p.85.
24. Letter from T. R. Malthus to W. Godwin n.d. quoted in Patricia James (1979). *Population Malthus*, p.69.
25. T. R. Malthus, op. cit. in note 7, vol. 3, pp.216–223.
26. T. R. Malthus, op. cit. in note 3, pp.86–87.
27. D. V. Glass (ed.), op. cit. in note 17, p.191.
28. Ibid. pp.192–193; T. R. Malthus, op. cit. in note 7, vol. 3, pp.238–250.
29. Ibid. pp.229–233, 270–272.
30. Patricia James, op. cit. in note 25, p222; D. V. Glass (ed.), op. cit. in note 17, p.203.
31. Ibid. pp.202–3; T. R. Malthus, op. cit. in note 7, vol. 2, p.277.
32. G. V. Glass (ed.), op. cit. in note 17, p.198.
33. T. R. Malthus (1800). *An Investigation of the Causes of the Present High Price of Provisions*, 3rd Edition, p.13.
34. W. Empson (1837). Life, writings and character of Mr. Malthus. *Edinburgh*

Review, **64**, 479–483.
35. R. G. Cowherd. *Political Economists*, pp.2–23.
36. *The Crisis* in *Principles of Political Economy*, p. xxxvi.
37. *An Investigation*, p.19.
38. T. R. Malthus, op. cit. in note 7, vol. 2, pp.354–355.
39. Ibid. p.357; T. R. Malthus, op. cit. in note 7, vol. 3, pp.272–274.
40. T. R. Malthus, op. cit. in note 7, vol. 2, p.324.
41. Ibid. pp.351–3.
42. T. R. Malthus, op. cit. in note 7, vol. 3, pp.176–179.
43. G. V. Glass (ed.), op. cit. in note 17, p.188.
44. T. R. Malthus, op. cit. in note 7, vol. 3, pp.181–2.
45. G. V. Glass (ed.), op. cit. in note 17, pp.189–190.
46. Malthus to D. Ricardo, 13 September 1821, in P. Sraffa (ed.), (1952). *Works of David Ricardo*, vol. IX, p.64. Cambridge.
47. "Memoir of Robert Malthus" appended to Malthus, *Political Economy*, p.xlv.
48. M. Blaug (1958). *Ricardian Economics*, p.198. New Haven.
49. *S. C. on Emigration*, PP. 1826–1827, V. Q. 3255.
50. J. Bonar (1924). *Malthus and His Work*, 2nd Edition, pp. 29–30, 43.
51. *Edinburgh Review* **11**, (1807), III.
52. S. Whitbread (1807). *Substance of a Speech on the Poor Laws*, pp.10–11.
53. Patricia James, op. cit. in note 15, pp.388–396.
54. T. R. Malthus, op. cit. in note 3, p.97.
55. T. R. Malthus, op. cit. in note 7, vol. 2, pp.332–333.
56. For example, F. H. Maberley (1836). *To the Poor and their Friends;* T. Marsters (1835). *Reform and Workhouses*, 2nd Edition. Lynn.
57. Quoted in H. Ausubel (1952). William Cobbett and Malthusianism. *J. of History of Ideas* **13**, 253–256.
58. For example, A Friend to the Poor (1835). *The Malthusian Boon Unmasked*, p.11. Maidstone.
59. "Memoir of Robert Malthus" appended to Malthus, *Political Economy*, p.xix.
60. Patricia James, op. cit. in note 14, p.451; J. R. Poynter (1969). *Society and Pauperism: English Ideas on Poor Relief, 1795–1834*, p.325; W. Petersen (1979). *Malthus*, p.114.
61. Marian Bowley (1937). *Nassau Senior and Classical Economics*, p.311; G. F. McLeary, op. cit. in note 16, pp.116, 129; S. E. Finer, op. cit. in note 2, p.23.
62. *Edinburgh Review*, 63, 1836, 491–492.
63. S. E. Finer, op. cit. in note 2, pp.22–23, 44–45.
64. S. G. and E. O. Checkland (eds) (1974). *The Poor Law Report of 1834*, Penguin Edition, pp.334–335. Harmondsworth.
65. T. R. Malthus (1830). *A Summary View of the Principle of Population*, 1st Edition (Pelican Classics Edition, Harmondsworth, 1970), p.269.
66. Malthus to Rev. T. Chalmers 21 July 1822, quoted in Patricia James, op. cit. in note 14, p.450.
67. T. R. Malthus, op. cit. in note 65, p.269.

8 Malthus's Model of a Pre-industrial Economy

E. A. WRIGLEY

When Malthus wrote his first *Essay on the Principle of Population* one of his chief aims was to refute the views expressed by Condorcet and Godwin about the perfectibility of man and of human society. Another was to demonstrate the unfortunate effects of the English Poor Law, not least on those who were intended to benefit most from its operation. About half of the book is taken up with these matters. His general purpose in writing the *First Essay* is well captured by its full title, *An Essay on the Principle of Population as it Affects the Future Improvement of Society*. Since his arguments were powerful and their influence was very widely felt, it is scarcely surprising that he should have been so frequently discussed and judged as a social prophet. Even in this context he has often failed to receive well-informed or charitable treatment. It was recently remarked of him, indeed, that "in the whole development of the social sciences, there has probably never been anyone attacked and defended with so little regard for what he had written as Malthus".[1]

The trenchant prose of the *First Essay* and its polemical purpose, however, tended to obscure the analytical strength of the brief sections of the book in which Malthus first set out his understanding of what he termed the Principle of Population. In the later editions of the *Essay* the balance changed. They are heavier reading, containing long passages consisting largely of empirical observations, distinguished neither by wit nor elegance of prose. The emphasis becomes more scholarly, the discussion more historical and the title changes to reflect the new emphasis. The second edition, for example, published in 1803, is entitled, *An Essay on the Principle of Population; or, a View of its Past and*

MALTHUS PAST AND PRESENT
ISBN 0-12-224670-5

Present Effects on Human Happiness; with an Inquiry into our Prospects Respecting the Future Removal or Mitigation of the Evils which it Occasions.

It is to Malthus's discussion of population history that I wish to draw attention. The passage of time has shown that his forebodings about the limits of future economic growth (and hence real income for the mass of the population) were not justified. In this, however, he was in excellent company since the most penetrating of his near contemporaries, such as Adam Smith and Ricardo, shared the same view. All rejected the possibility of general exponential economic growth because the supply of cultivable land was limited and increasing its productivity tended to require large and larger inputs of other production factors to secure a unit increase in output.[2]

The reason for the general failure to appreciate the possibility of what would now be called an industrial revolution (defined to include comparable parallel changes in agriculture) may be simply expressed. There was no warrant in past experience for the belief that such a radical break could occur, and abundant evidence of the extreme difficulty of securing it. As Malthus put it, when arguing against Godwin's facile belief in overcoming all current obstacles to progress by an appropriate improvement in material technology:

> "I expect that great discoveries are yet to take place in all the branches of human science, particularly in physics; but the moment we leave past experience as the foundation of our conjectures concerning the future; and still more, if our conjectures absolutely contradict past experience, we are thrown upon a wide field of uncertainty, and any one supposition is then just as good as another."[3]

As it happened, it was Malthus's fate to frame an analysis of the relationship between population, economy and society during the last generation to which it was applicable. Once the world had changed, the very cogency and clarity of his argument, now that it could be seen to miss the mark, made him an easy prey to those who disliked his conclusions. But the reputation of all social analysts is contingent only. As the world changes, the relevance of their remarks tends to decline *pari passu*.

It is important to judge them, in part at least, on the basis of the evidence available to them when they wrote, for it was on this evidence that they formed their theories and drew their conclusions.[4] Malthus spent much effort in the years following the publication of the *First Essay* in assembling historical evidence, and modified the argument of the *First Essay* substantially as a result. It is, therefore, especially apposite in his case to consider how far his model of population behaviour holds true for early modern Europe, and for England in particular.

The essence of Malthus's analytic framework can be grasped by considering Fig. 1. Malthus held that population would tend to grow exponentially in the absence of the checks imposed by the fixed supply of agricultural land, noting that in North America the population of the British colonies and of the youthful United States had consistently doubled every quarter-century since the early years of settlement there.[5] But at some stage, however favourable the initial circumstances, growth must be arrested as the land becomes fully occupied. Once this stage is reached, any further growth in population necessarily causes the price of food to rise and real incomes to fall.[6] The diagram in Fig. 1, therefore, shows a positive relationship between population size and food prices and a negative one between food prices and real incomes. At this point the negative feedback system may take one of two routes (or, of course, may follow both either alternately or simultaneously). The outer path (the positive check) shows that falling real incomes may cause mortality to rise, thus restoring once more a balance between population and available resources. Or the same result may be achieved by following the inner path (the preventive check). In this case, the effect of falling real incomes is to discourage marriage (either by causing individuals to marry later or to refrain from marriage entirely), which reduces fertility and so again reverses

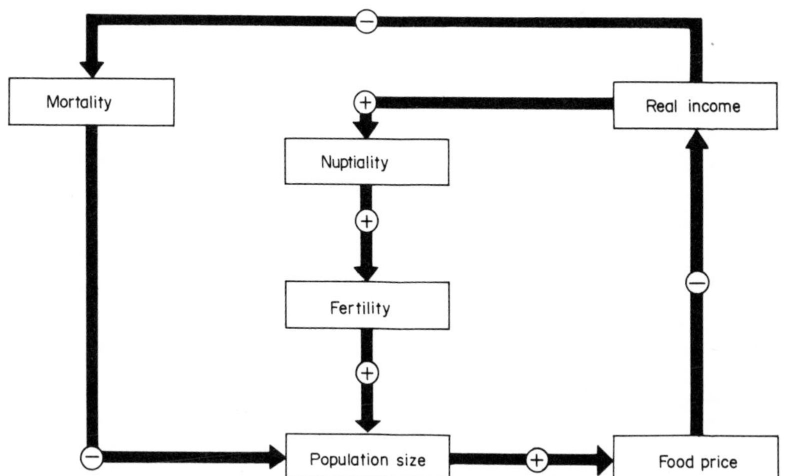

FIG. 1. A diagrammatic representation of Malthus's argument.

the population trend. Equally, of course, an initial fall in population by lowering food prices and thus causing an improvement in real incomes will also be corrected. Population will thus oscillate round some equilibrium level, or, assuming a slow growth in agricultural production (Malthus's arithmetic increase), round a secular trend line.[7]

Malthus set out this model clearly in the *First Essay* and did not thereafter change his view of its logical composition, but he did substantially modify and amplify his discussion of its application to the history of the countries best known to him. In this essay, for brevity's sake, I shall concentrate on his discussion of English history, taking advantage of the fact that it has recently become possible to measure much more fully and accurately trends in fertility and mortality in England from the mid-sixteenth century onwards as a result of work recently completed at the S.S.R.C. Cambridge Group for the History of Population and Social Structure.[8]

The most important change of emphasis made by Malthus between the first and later editions of the *Essay* was a much increased emphasis upon the operation of the preventive as opposed to the positive check in recent English history (or in terms of Fig. 1, on the inner rather than the outer path around the diagram). Between the publication of the first and second editions, the first English census was taken, and, as part of the same operation, Rickman, the organizer of the first four English censuses, secured a vast mass of empirical data about totals of baptisms, burials and marriages during the eighteenth century.[9] When Malthus wrote the first edition he was ignorant even of the most elementary facts about the English population. He supposed, for example, that the population of Britain was about seven million.[10] Three years later the census showed the true total to be 10.9 million, or 56 per cent larger than he had supposed. Once the Census of 1801 had been published he had available to him the bulk of the data which have been used since then, for the parish register returns collected by Rickman have been the empirical foundation of most subsequent work.

Reflection upon the newly available census and parish register data, combined with a much more extensive acquaintance with comparable information from other countries, convinced Malthus that in the English case the preventive check played the predominant role in restraining population growth. In the first edition he laid stress upon the evidence of malnutrition visible among the labouring classes,[11] and displayed great concern about their ability to withstand the temptation of an imprudently early marriage, given the way in which the Poor Laws operated, though he noted that "a spirit of independence still remains among the peasantry",[12] which helped them to resist such temptation. The nature of the problem he expressed in the following passage:

> "Every obstacle in the way of marriage must undoubtedly be considered as a species of unhappiness. But as from the laws of our nature some check to population must exist, it is better that it should be checked from a foresight of the difficulties attending a family, and the fear of dependent poverty, than that it should be encouraged, only to be repressed afterwards by want and sickness."[13]

He was not, however, very optimistic that foresight would prevail.

Later Malthus came to see matters in a different light. The positive check was relegated to a comparatively minor role in his analysis of recent English experience, and more generally that of Europe, compared with other parts of the world. As he put it, " . . . in modern Europe the positive checks to population growth prevail less, and the preventive checks more than in past times, and in the more uncivilized parts of the world",[14] or again, " . . . an infrequency of the marriage union from the fear of a family . . . may be considered . . . as the most powerful of the checks, which in modern Europe, keep down the population to the level of the means of subsistence."[15] In his discussion of mortality Malthus laid increasing stress upon its wayward and unpredictable impact and tended to promote overcrowding above malnutrition as the prime agent in increasing the death rate amongst the poor. A typical passage from the later edition of the *Essay* runs as follows when discussing the effects of famine and death:

> How far these "terrible correctives to the redundance of mankind" have been occasioned by the too rapid increase of population, is a point which it would be very difficult to determine with any degree of precision. The causes of most of our diseases appear to us to be so mysterious, and probably are really so various, that it would be rashness to lay too much stress on any single one; but it will not perhaps be too much to say, that *among* these causes we ought certainly to rank crowded houses, and insufficient or unwholesome food, which are the natural consequences of an increase of population faster than the accommodation of a country with respect to habitations and food will allow.[16]

Reverting to the representation of the logic of Malthus's argument as set out in Fig. 1, therefore, it may be said that the later Malthus, while continuing to stress the closeness of the links between population growth, changes in food prices, and fluctuations in real income, favoured the inner track rather than the outer, or marriage rather than mortality, as the factor primarily responsible for keeping population and economic resources in balance so far as early modern England is concerned. How far does modern scholarship substantiate this interpretation?

Fortunately, it is now possible to plot changes in population size, nuptiality, fertility and mortality in England from 1541 onwards, and the work of Phelps Brown and Hopkins has made available indices of changes in the price of a basket of consumables and in real wages over the same period, though there is a greater margin of uncertainty about the accuracy of these measures, especially in the case of real wage trends. The strength of each link in the feedback loops shown in Fig. 1 can, therefore, be tested for early modern English history.

In Fig. 2 the relationship between rates of population growth and changes in the consumables' price index is shown (the index weights of the food components were as follows: farinaceous food, 20, meat and fish 25, butter and cheese $12\frac{1}{2}$, drink $22\frac{1}{2}$; making a total of 80 for food items out of the total of 100 for the consumables index as a whole).[17] The rates of population growth are those prevailing between each date indicated and a date 25 years later, while the rates of growth in the price index are taken from a 25-year moving average of the individual annual figures over identical periods (a 25-year moving average was used to remove the effect of the very sharp annual fluctuation in food prices). In both cases compound annual rates are shown. Thus, the first point in the figure shows that between 1541 and 1566 the compound annual rate of growth in population was 0.48 per cent while that of the price index was 1.85 per cent.[18] Figure 2 leaves little room for doubt that the growth rates of population and food prices were closely related until the end of the eighteenth century, and it is reasonable to suppose that the former largely determined the latter. The relationship between the two series was surprisingly tight. Periods of rapid growth in the later sixteenth and eighteenth centuries were accompanied by accelerating rises in the price index, while during the later seventeenth century, when for a time population declined, the index fell in sympathy. A line epitomizing the relationship between 1550 and 1800 would pass through the origin of the graph and then rise or fall at an angle reflecting the fact that the price index was more volatile than population growth approximately in the ratio 3:2. When Malthus wrote the *Essay* it was entirely rational for him, on the basis of recent history, to detect a strong link between the population growth rate and food price rises and to fear the effect of rapid population growth. He stood approximately at the point marked 1781 in the figure (covering the period 1781-1806), and his retrospect was, therefore, the long sweep of years in which the relationship between the two variables was uniformly close, and by implication forbidding for any period of rapid population increase.

Figure 2, however, also shows with equal clarity that this fundamental aspect of the functioning of the economic-demographic system was about to change with astonishing rapidity. Secular food price

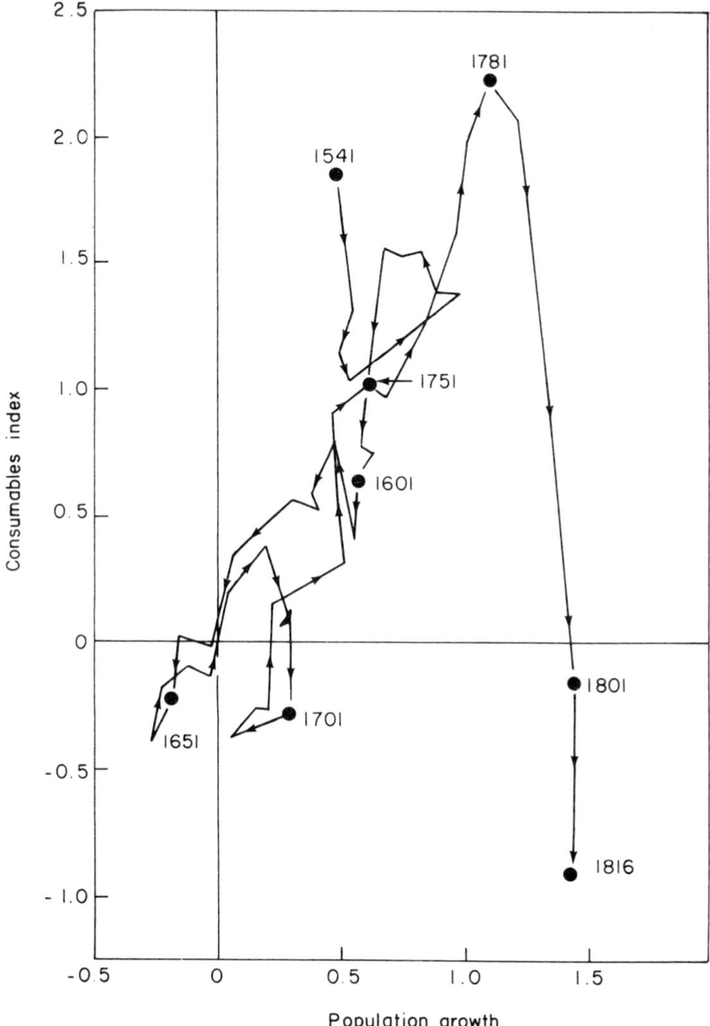

FIG. 2. Compound annual growth rates of population and an index of the price of consumables (per cent per annum). See text for fuller explanation.

trends lost all connection with those of population. Previous experience in this instance was a fallible guide to further behaviour.

The second link in the feedback loop takes us from food prices to real incomes. It need not detain us long, for in any society in which the bulk of all consumer expenditure is devoted to food, any change in its price is almost certain to be mirrored by an opposite change in real incomes. In Fig. 3 the same method as in Fig. 2 is used to set out the

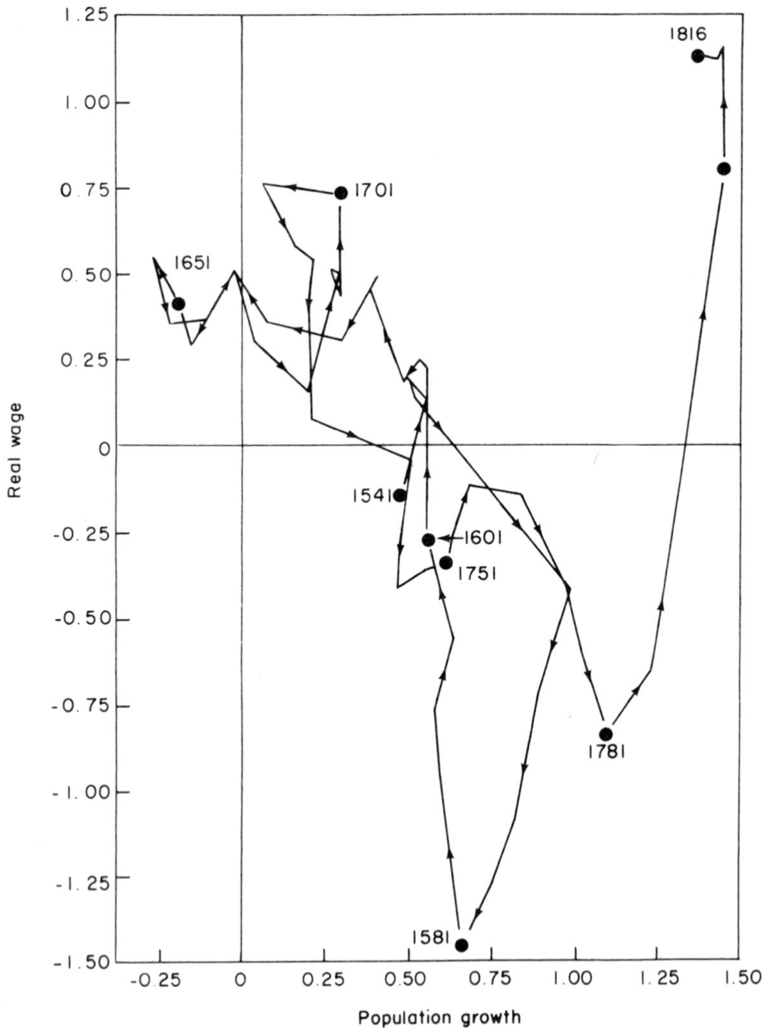

FIG. 3. Compound annual growth rates of population and an index of real wages (per cent per annum). See text for fuller explanation.

relations between population growth and real wage changes. It is so closely similar to Fig. 2 that it calls for little comment in this context. The trend in the cluster of points representing growth trends before 1800 does not, in this case, pass through the origin of the graph. Instead, it implies that there was a secular rise in productivity in early modern England at a rate of between one-quarter and one-half of one per cent annually, since real wages rose at about this rate when population was stationary, or, alternatively, a population growth rate of this order or magnitude could be sustained without provoking a fall in real wages. At higher rates of population growth, on the other hand, real wages fell increasingly sharply. Once again it is clear that very soon after Malthus turned his mind to this question, the pattern which he detected, and which he thought to be permanently imprinted on the socio-econimic system, abruptly disappeared. Exceptionally high population growth rates proved consonant with rising real wages after 1800.

At this point the two negative feedback paths in Fig. 1 diverge. Either the falling real incomes must induce a rise in mortality to check population growth, or marriage behaviour must change in a way which reduces fertility sufficiently to secure the same outcome by a different route, or perhaps some combination of the two may occur. As we have seen, Malthus, while never disclaiming the potential significance of the positive check, tended to discount its importance compared with the preventive check in recent English history. He probably had chiefly in

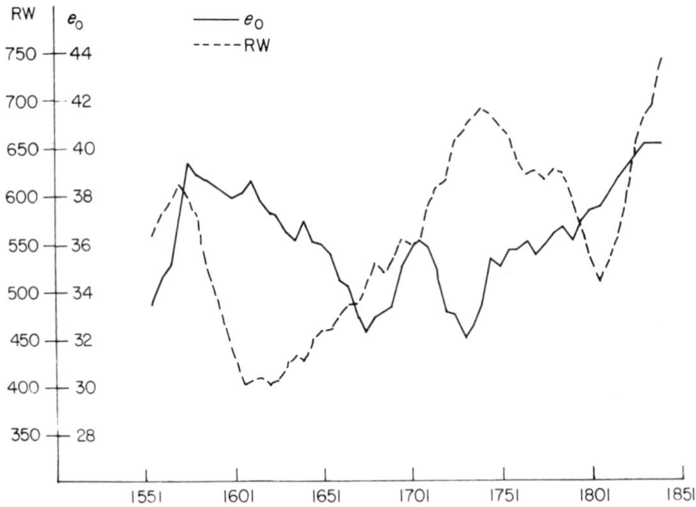

FIG. 4. Secular trends in real wages and expectation of life at birth (25-year moving averages centred on years shown).

mind the eighteenth century, since this was nearest to him in time and was the period covered by the returns made to Rickman in 1801, but, as with prices and wages, it is convenient to survey a longer period in this discussion.

The secular relationship between real wages and mortality in early modern England is shown in Fig. 4.[19] Once again, in order to simplify the consideration of very long-term trends, the data refer to 25-year periods centred on the dates shown. Thus, the impact of even the most severe mortality crises, such as those of 1557-1559 and 1727-1729, is limited. If mortality levels had been strongly affected by the level and trend of real wages, the two lines in the figure would have moved in sympathy. Low real wages and a low expectation of life at birth would have been closely associated with one another, while in periods of improved wages the reduced level of mortality would have caused expectation of life to improve. There is little evidence of this relationship in Fig. 4. During the late sixteenth and early seventeenth centuries there was a similar tendency in the two curves. Expectation of life was falling slightly as real wages plunged to extremely low levels. But apart from this brief period, the lack of evidence for the "expected" relationship is striking. Mortality worsened steadily for half a century

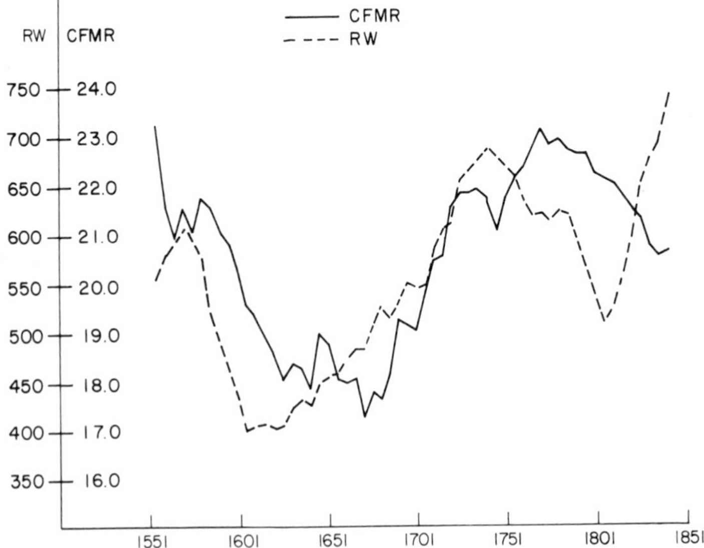

FIG. 5. Secular trends in real wages and the crude first marriage rate (25-year moving average centred on years shown: see text for method of calculating the marriage rate).

after real wages had begun to recover in the seventeenth century, improved sharply but then again worsened between *c.* 1680 and *c.* 1730 while real wages rose without interruption, and in the next three-quarters of a century down to Malthus's day improved steadily, though real wages fell sharply towards the end of the eighteenth century. Clearly mortality in early modern England did not act as an equilibrating mechanism preserving the balance between population and resources.

We may turn finally, therefore, to nuptiality and fertility as the presumptive agents in achieving the balance. Figure 5 repeats once more the real wage graph shown in the last figure, but also shows a measure of nuptiality rather than mortality. The latter takes the form of a 25-year moving average of a modified crude marriage rate, representing the number of first marriages per 1000 persons aged 15-34.[20] Fluctuations in the rate reflect the combined impact of changes in marriage age and proportions who never married. While the "fit" of the two graphs is not perfect, it strongly suggests that nuptiality responded to changes in the trend of real wages with a lag of about 30 years.[21] The extent of the change in nuptiality was very considerable. It can be shown that age at

FIG. 6. Secular trends in the crude first marriage rate and the gross reproduction ratio (25-year moving averages centred on years shown).

first marriage for women probably varied by about $3\frac{1}{2}$ years from *c.* 23 to *c.* $26\frac{1}{2}$ years between its minimum and maximum, and that the proportions who never married (both sexes combined) may have ranged from *c.* 5-8 per cent to *c.* 16-20 per cent.[22] The timing of the changes in these two nuptiality variables were such as to reinforce one another in their effect on fertility.

Back projection allows the calculation of the gross reproduction ratio. In Fig. 6 its fluctuations are compared with those in the marriage rate already shown in Fig. 5. It appears that the secular changes in trend of the gross reproduction ratio accord closely with those in the marriage rate, though changes in fertility tend to lag slightly behind those in nuptiality. In a fuller discussion there would be much to be said about the detailed behaviour of the two graphs and their relation to each other, but constraints of space prohibit an extended treatment in this short paper. Nor is such a discussion necessary in order to establish the strength of this final link in the chain of negative feedback which restrained population growth in early modern England through the preventive check. It may, however, be noted that analysis of fertility and mortality produced by back projection demonstrates that changes in fertility exercised a substantially greater influence than changes in mortality on population growth rates throughout most of the early modern period. It was not simply the case, therefore, that fertility moved in sympathy with economic trends whereas mortality did not: the fertility changes were also decisive in changing population growth rates. The fluctuations in fertility were in turn almost solely a function of changes in the timing and incidence of marriage since age-specific marital fertility rates varied only trivially. Marriage commanded the demographic stage in early modern England.[23]

There is, of course, far more to be said about the operation of the positive and preventive checks in the centuries immediately before the *First Essay* than is contained in the six figures which have been used here as a means of summarizing a mass of data. Nothing has been said, for example, of short-term variations in prices, nuptiality, fertility, and mortality. Nor have changes in relationships over time been discussed; nor regional variation. Only a gross and summary picture has been attempted. But perhaps this is broadly appropriate. Malthus did not attempt a rigorous and comprehensive treatment of his subject. He contented himself in the main with an examination of its chief, strategic features. And in this respect his judgement has been proved remarkably sound, especially as he expressed it in the later editions of the *Essay*. As an historian he emerges largely unscathed from the tests made possible by the subsequent accumulation of greater knowledge of early modern England, though, in common with his contemporaries, he clearly failed to foresee the effects of the changes which were already in train in his day.[24] Unless, therefore, the stature of an historian and social scientist is to be judged by his success in predicting the future, rather than by the accuracy of his analysis of the present and the past, Malthus's standing deserves to be high.

Notes

1. W. Petersen (1969). *Population*, 2nd Edition, p.151. London.
2. The issue was given its classical formulation by Ricardo, but Smith held similar views. The relevance of Smith's views on economic growth generally to this point is discussed in E. A. Wrigley (1972). The process of modernization and the industrial revolution in England. *Journal of Interdisciplinary History* **3**, 225–259.
3. T. R. Malthus (1798). *First Essay*, p.232.
4. In this light H. L. Beales's dismissal of Malthus is not only ungenerous but oddly grounded for an historian. "The historian's estimate of the *Essay on Population*", he wrote, "is usually far this side of idolatry. He sees it in relation to contemporary fact and to *post-Malthusian development* (my italics), and to his pragmatic sight it appears largely irrelevant to both". H. L. Beales (1953). The historical content of the *Essay on population*. In *Introduction to Malthus* (Ed. D. V. Glass), pp. 21–22. London.
5. T. R. Malthus, op. cit. in note 3, pp.105–107.
6. ibid. pp.29–30.
7. This process is very clearly set out by Malthus in op. cit. in note 3, pp.29–31.
8. The demographic data used in Figures 2 to 6 were drawn from this work (population totals, age structure, gross reproduction ratios, expectations of life, etc.). Their derivation is described in E. A. Wrigley and R. S. Schofield (1981). *The Population History of England 1541–1871: A Reconstruction*. London.
9. Rickman secured returns from each parish of the annual totals of baptisms and burials for every tenth year from 1700 to 1770, and for each year 1780 to 1800; and of marriages for each year from 1780 to 1800. Their characteristics are discussed at length in E. A. Wrigley and R. S. Schofield, op. cit. in note 8, Appendix 7.
10. T. R. Malthus, op. cit. in note 3, p.23.
11. See, for example, his remarks about the sons of labourers: T. R. Malthus, op. cit. in note 3, p.73.
12. T. R. Malthus, op. cit. in note 3, p.84.
13. ibid. pp.89–90.
14. T. R. Malthus (1807). *Essay*, 4th Edition, vol. 1, p.579. London.

15. ibid. vol. 1. p.580.
16. ibid. vol. 1. p.565.
17. E. H. Phelps Brown and Sheila V. Hopkins (1962). Seven centuries of the prices of consumables, compared with builders' wage-rates. In *Essays in Economic History* (Ed. Eleanora M. Carus-Wilson), vol. ii, p.180. London. The data taken from Phelps Brown and Hopkins's work used in Figs. 2 and 3 are discussed and the operations carried out on them are described in E. A. Wrigley and R. S. Schofield, op. cit. in note 8, Appendix 9.
18. Malthus died in 1834. The last point in the diagram is for 1816 and, therefore, relates to the quarter-century 1816–1841; it may be regarded as covering the latest period of which Malthus could have had personal knowledge.
19. In Figs 4 and 6 the graphs are taken to 1841 for the reason given in note 18.
20. English parish registers very seldom record the marital status of all brides and grooms consistently and from an early date. The evidence enabling the proportion of first marriages within total marriages to be identified is discussed in E. A. Wrigley and R. S. Schofield, op. cit. in note 8, chapter 7.
21. There is a much fuller discussion of the lag and of the imperfections in the data which make its measurement difficult in E. A. Wrigley and R. S. Schofield, op. cit. in note 8, Chapter 10.
22. See Table 7.26 and Fig. 7.15 in E. A. Wrigley and R. S. Schofield, op. cit. in note 8.
23. The evidence to substantiate the brief epitome of English population history given in this paragraph may be found in E. A. Wrigley and R. S. Schofield, op. cit. in note 8, especially Chapters 7 and 10.
24. Malthus's historical judgement was not, however, infallible. For example, his assumption that population invariably reacts to an opportunity for increase by a rapid rise in numbers does not square well with English population history in the century and a half following the Black Death.

9 Malthus and Ethnography

M. GODELIER

This chapter will seek to present a synthetic view of the eleven papers delivered at this Congress which deal with the relation between Malthus and ethnography. The discussion will keep close to the authors' arguments, but as different authors worked independently of each other and did not know each other's conclusions, an attempt will be made to show where their work is complementary and where they disagree. I shall, of course, also add my own comments on the problems that the authors have considered and the views that they have expressed.

The eleven papers can be divided into two parts with different theoretical perspectives. Three authors[1] (Broc, Stagl and Duchet) have systematically studied Malthus's work as well as the ethnographic sources that he used to support his argument. However, the majority of the authors have attempted to throw light on Malthus's work from the point of view of present-day ethnographic knowledge. They use modern research findings about the different types of society which Malthus classified, as did his contemporaries, according to the ways in which their members made a living; in other words, by the nature of their economy: hunters, herdsmen gatherers of the South Seas, and those engaged in agriculture in Africa or Asia. They compare Malthus's work with the results of the most recent analyses of societies of hunters and gatherers. Following the congress held in Chicago in 1965 under the title *Man the Hunter*[2] our views on the way in which men lived during the longest period of their history, the middle and late palaeolithic, i.e. before the domestication of plants and animals and the emergence of agriculture and stock breeding, have changed. The

MALTHUS PAST AND PRESENT
ISBN 0-12-224670-5

researches of anthropologists and archaeologists have provided a new explanation of the process of change and the reasons for the economic and social changes that have occurred in society. The two papers by Annette Hamilton and Alain Testart[3], which complement one another, contain an interesting attempt to construct such an explanation. Bernard Saladin d'Anglure and Joëlle Lamblin[4] analyse two Eskimo hunting societies, whose members make their living in very difficult and special conditions, the Inuit in the Canadian Far North and the Ammasalimiut in Greenland. Saladin d'Anglure shows (and I shall return to this point later in the paper) that the mythology of the Inuit provides an almost perfect example of a Malthusian system, and that they have tried to achieve a stationary population whilst maintaining a constant ratio between human populations, those of other species and of natural resources. They regard the renewal of populations and the replacement of the past by the present as a type of cyclical relationship. However, they have not been able to avoid continuous population growth. Yengoyan[5] has studied Australian aborigine societies and compares the practice of infanticide among them with that of the Eskimos and completes the analysis.

Another method of applying modern ethnology to Malthus's analysis is to study pastoral nomadic societies, to whom Malthus devoted two chapters in his *Essay* (Chapter 6, which was historical and contained an account of the invasion of Northern Europe by the barbarians, and Chapter 7 which is more ethnological in character and deals with the pastoral societies of his time). Such societies provide particularly good illustrations because their material standards of living depend upon the relations between human populations and those of the animals which they exploit. Pierre Bonte in his paper[6] examines this problem by studying the population dynamics of some East African pastoral societies about which practically nothing was known in Malthus's day, but where a great deal of knowledge has accumulated during the last 20 years or so as a result of ecological, anthropological and historical researches by English and American scholars. These results may be compared with those recorded for the pastoral societies of the Sahara by French researchers. Bonte does not consider the pastoral societies of the near East nor those of Central Asia, which are also mentioned by Malthus.

Two other problems have been chosen for discussion because of their theoretical importance. Malthus wrote:[7]

> There is probably no island yet known the produce of which could not be further increased. This is all that can be said of the whole earth.

> Both are peopled up to their actual produce. And the whole earth in this respect is like an island.

For this reason, and because much rich ethnographic material had been collected by Cook, de Lapérouse and other explorers, and because their description of the Polynesian way of life did much to make popular the idea that the savage was living in a natural paradise, Malthus devoted a chapter of his *Essay* to the populations of the South Sea islands. He thought that the descriptions given were misleading, and regarded it as important to correct false impressions. It is necessary to recall Diderot[8] to understand the importance that Malthus attached to "correct the views of travellers who seemed to think all apprehension of dearth seems at first sight to be banished from a country that is described to be fruitful as the garden of the Hesperides".[9]

Michel Panoff has stressed this point in connection with eighteenth-century Tahiti and has shown that Malthus was himself guilty of distortion and selective quotation from his sources.

The last problem chosen because of its epistemological importance is that of the demographic effects of the African slave trade on the populations that were its victims, as well as the effects on their economy. Whilst recognizing that the wars caused by slavery paralysed the economy of these societies and constituted an obstacle to the achievement of prosperity, Malthus did not doubt "that it would be difficult to find the gap that has been made by a hundred years' exportation of negroes which has blackened half America".[10]

In spite of the slave trade, continuous warfare and the vices and improvidence of the blacks it seemed to Malthus that the Principle of Population was verified, for

> notwithstanding this constant emigration, the loss of numbers from incessant wars and the checks to increase from vice or other causes, it appears that the population is constantly pressing against the limits of means of subsistence.[11]

The validity of this statement which has found some defenders is, however, questioned in the last paper by Manning[12] based on his researches on the effects of slavery in Dahomey. However, Manning does not contest that Malthus was right in his views about those parts of Africa where only the populations living near the coast were affected by the slave trade and where the trade did not extend over long periods of time. John Thornton who has studied the situation in Angola[13] had come to the same conclusion.

I now proceed to discuss these points in more detail.

Malthus and the ethnology of his day

It is well known that the main difference between the *First Essay* and subsequent editions, which made the latter what Malthus called a "new work", consisted of a systematic examination by the author of much of the ethnographic literature which he found in the accounts of contemporary travellers and explorers and of their predecessors during the preceding two centuries. Chapter 3 of the *First Essay* which was devoted to a short review of savage, hunting and pastoralist societies and of the tribes of barbarians which overran the Roman Empire is replaced in subsequent editions by no fewer than 12 chapters. These are based on a systematic review of all corners of the world known to those who had travelled there, before Malthus wrote. The only way of getting to know the world was by travelling, and soon after the publication of the *First Essay* Malthus himself made two journeys in Europe visiting Scandinavia and Russia in 1799 and France and Switzerland in 1802. Between his own travels, he also followed the travels of others. However, in the *First Essay* there is only one explicit reference to ethnographic literature and Malthus takes all his examples from ancient history or the discussions of philosophers and economists. However, Chapter 3 could not have been written unless the author had possessed some knowledge of ethnography. Malthus himself tells us the reason for his own travels and for citing those of others. They are

> to understand the Principle of Population as it affects the past and present state of society; that, by illustrating the subject more generally, and drawing those inferences from it, in application to the actual state of things, which experience seemed to warrant, I might give it a more practical and permanent interest.[14]

This is ambiguous, for Malthus seeks to prove empirically a principle which he had already put forward as being of universal application for theoretical and philosophical reasons. Moreover, it was a principle which he had not discovered himself. The question, therefore, arises whether Malthus used ethnography to "illustrate" a principle which in his view had already been proved to be both necessary and sufficient, to show that experience supported theory in proving its validity, or whether he used it to probe whether experience could wholly or partially falsify his thesis.

That Malthus made use of ethnographical knowledge cannot be doubted. He could not have done otherwise at a time when scientific ethnology did not yet exist and when it could not, therefore, be used to oppose the abstract theorizing of philosophers and others on the subject of social progress. In Malthus's time, ethnography consisted of reports and descriptions which Numa Broc in his paper[15] divides into six categories. This categorization is based on the different sources of observation and judgements, which were frequently violently ethnocentric and on which theorists could only comment because they felt that they were obliged to do so for theoretical reasons.[16]

These six categories are: reports of voyages, reports of official expeditions organized by the European powers, accounts of solitary voyages, reports by diplomats sent on special mission to China, Burma or other distant countries (such as Australia), accounts of missionaries, and, finally, the works of historians and statisticians. The boundaries between these categories are often indistinct; for instance, Broc asks how to classify Father du Halde's work[17] which contains a plethora of information taken from letters, accounts and recollections of Peking, which were put together by du Halde without his ever leaving Paris. The task was later completed by the Abbé Grosier,[18] whose work is in some respects new. What can be said about the Abbé Raynal's history of India?[19] But, conversely, among the accounts by missionaries is included that of François Xavier Charlevoix[20] which is based on his journeys in Canada where he served as a missionary. Among the great accounts of voyages which began with the Renaissance and became more numerous during the eighteenth century, Malthus does not quote the Abbé Prévost's *L'histoire des voyages*,[21] but bases himself on the 34 volumes of the Jesuits' *Lettres édifiantes et curieuses*[22] which contain unique material about America and China. He also uses the Président de Brosses *L'histoire des navigations aux terres australes* (1756)[23] and among English sources the *Compleat Collection of Voyages and Travels*[24] containing works of above 600 of the most authentic writers collected by John Harris, as well as Thomas Astley's *New Collection of Voyages and Travels*[25] which served as a model for Prévost's work. Among the accounts of the great official expeditions there is that by Antonio de Ulloa, who was commissioned by the Spanish government to accompany the French academicians in their journey to Peru in 1735-1736.[26] But it is above all during the second half of the eighteenth century that we have the accounts by Cook,[27] de Lapérouse,[28] de Barthélémy de Lesseps,[29] Entrecasteaux[30] and Vancouver,[31] as well as that of the great Danish expedition of 1761-1767 to Arabia, Egypt, Persia and India of which Carsten Niebuhr was the sole survivor and of which he published an account in the French language in Copenhaguen in 1773.[32]

Among the solitary voyagers whose accounts Malthus read and cited were Bruce on Egypt and Abyssinia, Engelbert Kaempfer on Japan and

China,[33] and the Swedish scholar, Thunberg[33] who became Linnaeus's successor in the Chair of Botany at Uppsala after having explored Japan, Mungo Park who explored Africa from Senegal to Ségou on the Niger[34] and the Frenchmen Volney who travelled in Egypt[35], and Le Vaillant who travelled in Africa.[36] The great diplomatic missions included Lord Macartney's British mission to China in 1793 which consisted of 95 persons in four warships.[37] Lastly, Daniel Collins, a magistrate in Port Jackson, Australia, between 1788 and 1796, furnished Malthus with important information on the Australian aborigines.[38]

The missionaries included the Jesuit father Jean François Lafitau, one of the precursors of scientific ethnology who published his work entitled *Moeurs des sauvages américains comparés aux moeurs du premier temps* in 1724, in which he tried to demonstrate that the Canadian "savages" could be compared with the ancient Greeks and the "barbarians" of ancient Europe. In this work he tried to construct a bridge between history and ethnology and his researches were the forerunner to the comparativism and evolutionism of the nineteenth century.

The last category consists of the works on statistics and political arithmetic. Early works on statistics were not necessarily numerical in character but consisted of descriptions from different sources of the territory, population, customs, administration, armed forces and educational systems of different European countries, with which every statesman (Italian: *statista*) should be familiar.[39] This particular branch of knowledge began in Italy, where statesmen felt the need to obtain information about the conditions of the nation and to classify this information which grew more and more voluminous following the discoveries of the renaissance period and the wider use of printed material. In Germany, the subject was introduced into higher education of the higher civil servants by Conring,[40] and during the eighteenth century the term "statistics" was used for it by Gottfried Achenwall, Professor at the University of Göttingen, where also the study of physical anthropology was pioneered with Blumenbach's work on different human races,[41] and where the term "ethnology" was invented. However, Malthus does not cite Blumenbach.

The term "Political Arithmetic" was first used in the celebrated work by Sir William Petty, whom Marx regarded as the founder of the science of economics. The subject developed beyond the collection of simple descriptive ideas and Petty's successors attempted to apply mathematics, and above all the calculus of probabilities, to the study of social phenomena and to construct a "natural science of society" which would discover constant ratios between different quantities as well as natural laws. Stagl reminds us that these methods were used during the eighteenth century, for example in the University of Jena, as means to discern the design of the Creator and to discover the immanent laws of his Creation which were independent of mankind's will.[42] He demonstrates that this view was also held by Malthus, for in the final chapter of the *First Essay* Malthus attempts to deduce a justification of God and his sacred design from the pitiless mechanism of the Principle of Population. In this sense, his work is a type of theodicy. However, the same science of political arithmetic could also serve as a vehicle for revolutionary ideas such as those of Price and Godwin whose opinions were opposed by Malthus.

The three authors who deal with the use that Malthus made of contemporary ethnographic material agree that his reading was wide and catholic and that he had consulted the principal works that had been published just before he completed the second edition of his *Essay*. Broc and Stagl, however, point out some surprising omissions, for instance, the neglect of Blumenbach and Buffon whom Malthus cites only once on the subject of Africa to the effect that "the negro-women are extremely prolific" and that "the shortness of life [of the natives] is attributed to the premature intercourse of the sexes, and very early and excessive debauchery".[43] One is struck by the number of references to French writers and by the fact that even during the French revolution their work was widely known in England. Malthus also makes use of the Jesuits' *Lettres édifiantes et curieuses* at a time when the Order was much criticized in Europe, resulting in its suppression by Rome in 1773, and whose views on colonial policy in America were very different from that of the Puritan and Protestant exaltation of work and virtue as manifested in the colonization of North America.[44]

However, Broc and Stagl disagree on one important point. The former suggests that Malthus's interest in exotic societies continued after 1803 and seeks a confirmation of this view in the fact that in his *Summary Review of the Principle of Population,* Malthus repeatedly cited Alexander Humboldt's remarkable *Essai politique sur le royaume de la Nouvelle Espagne* (1811). Stagl, on the other hand believes that Malthus was not interested in either savage or primitive societies and he notes that although he was a Professor at the East India Company's college for the training of administrators at Haileybury, Malthus only cited the work of one colonial administrator, Sir William Jones, who died in 1794.[45]

Personally, I do not believe that Malthus used the accounts of voyagers only for the purpose of illustrating the universality of a principle which he had not invented himself but had merely taken over without having systematically examined the ethnographic literature of his time. Rather, he proceeded to a serious examination of ethnographic data, but rapidly reached the conclusion that it was not worth while continuing the effort and he explained his reasons: "In drawing similar inferences from the state of society in a number of different countries, I found it very difficult to avoid some repetitions."[46]

It is probably, because Malthus was convinced that the facts supported his thesis, that he sometimes offered generalizations without empirical proof: "Of the large islands of New Guinea, New Britain, New Caledonia and the New Hebrides, little is known with certainty. The state of society in them is probably very similar to that which prevails among many of the savage nations of America."[47]

This citation shows clearly that it was common for philosophers and theorists even in the era preceding Darwin and evolutionary biology towards the end of the eighteenth century to regard the history of human society in terms of a succession of different stages: savage society, barbarian society and civilized society. A brief examination of the stage which a particular society has reached can be used to put it into one or other of these classes and the experience of other societies in the same class can then be brought to bear upon it. Even before ethnography existed as a science, concrete ethnographic observations were being fitted into theoretical schemes which, to use the expression of Michèle Duchet, were "summary and totalitarian".[48] In ethnology, as in other sciences, philosophical synthesis preceded the scientific analysis of empirical data. But the data must have been of a nature to lend themselves to such an analysis. Stagl shows that there was a change in the nature of the material gathered by travellers during the eighteenth century.[49] Expeditions of different sizes were organized to provide a systematic inventory of the world's resources and to contribute to the establishment of a "natural history of man", such as was advocated by Buffon.

However, the information that was collected on social practices and customs was included in a variety of curious observations which seemed enigmatic, absurd or even grotesque in spite of being fitted into philosophical or theological systems based on the natural history of man. A scientific analysis only emerged when some social institutions were chosen to be analysed by themselves and compared with analogous institutions in different societies. This, for instance, was the method used by one of the founders of modern anthropology, Lewis Morgan, when he compared some 200 different systems of kinship and discovered that they could be grouped under two headings "classificatory" and "descriptive" kinship systems. But his *magnum opus*[50] was only published in 1871, when the beginning of a scientific analysis of kinship systems, i.e. of the social aspects of reproduction, can be dated. Without such an analysis, an essential link in the construction of a science of human population, demography, is missing. Malthus hardly refers to the diversity of marriage systems and when he does so, he merely reaffirms his European and Christian preconceptions: "Whether the law of marriage be instituted, or not, the dictate of nature and virtue seems to be an early attachment to one woman."[51]

Malthus, therefore, approaches the facts with a prejudice in favour of the monogamous patrilineal European family, which he regards as a norm and in accord with the laws of nature and the principles of Christian morality. Matrimonial customs in other societies can only be regarded as a form of vice or even of prostitution. He was not, of course, the only scholar to hold these prejudices and it would be both easy and tedious to cite passages in which he accuses the savage of indolence, improvidence, ignorance, toleration of prostitution and a degrading submission to their chiefs. He goes as far as to write: "We could not expect to find among savages in such climates any degree of moral restraint."[52]

In what sense, therefore, could it be said that Malthus treated his ethnographic sources in a scientific manner? I would suggest that his main contribution did not lie in his recognition that populations tend to grow faster than the means of subsistence, but rather that he found it strange, curious and interesting to analyse the reason why population *did not grow* in many exotic societies as was noted by a number of travellers.

> The question that is asked in Captain Cook's first voyage with respect to the thinly scattered savages of New Holland, 'by what means the inhabitants of this country are reduced to such a number as it can subsist?' may be asked with equal propriety respecting the most populous islands in the South Sea or the best peopled countries in Europe and Asia. The question, applied generally, appears to me to be highly curious, and to lead to the elucidation of some of the most obscure, yet important points, in the history of human society. I cannot so clearly and concisely describe the precise aim of the first part of the present work as by saying that it is an endeavour to answer this question so applied".[53]

Malthus, therefore, became a scientist when he recognized a general problem where others before him only saw particular situations and when he began to study the literature to obtain a list of the reasons which authors had used to "explain" the obstacles which prevented the spontaneous tendencies of population to grow from operating.

He believed that "we shall be able to trace some very powerful checks to population in *the habits of the people*".[54]

The different reasons that he discovered included infant mortality, the limitation of means of subsistence and their consequences, scarcities, famines, malnutrition and epidemic diseases, the climate, female sterility, the sexual coldness of American Indians, the hardships and fatigues of life in the primitive state, the impoverishment that it causes, the constant movements of nomadic peoples, prolonged lactation, sexual abstinence, polygyny, castration, the infibulation of females, the care for honour and the preservation of virginity, late marriages, short life spans, infanticide etc. The major scientific value of Malthus's work is, therefore, that he noted the absence of population growth and searched systematically for reasons to explain this phenomenon. Nor did he stop at this, but attempted to summarize all the reasons under two general headings which he called misery and vice. This terminology demonstrates the ethnocentric and ethical bases of his analysis of social facts, but it seems clear to me that Malthus regarded misery as the strongest check to human population growth. However, for him misery and vice were not independent. Misery had a moral basis too: the effect of ignorance, improvidence and indolence of the savage, whose vices can be compared to those of the lower classes in civilized societies. Here again, Malthus's prejudices become apparent, but this time they relate to the poor and to the labouring classes.

Malthus's theory requires numerical information for verification, and the ethnographers of his day did not, as a rule, provide this. Malthus regrets this fact, but when numerical information comes his way he does not accept it uncritically. Thus, he criticizes Cook's figures relating to the total population of Tahiti as probably being an overestimate and, conversely, those of the missionaries as being an underestimate of the true value. Panoff[55] believes that Malthus was not far from the truth and had reasons for suggesting that the population of Tahiti had declined in the interval between Cook's voyages.

However, as Michèle Duchet suggests[56], Malthus sometimes gives a false impression of understanding by considering together very different institutions all of which are explained as being a check to population growth. Thus, he cites Raynal who himself bases his remarks on a passage in Diderot's *Histoire des Indes,* when he discusses islanders in general:

> It is among these people that we trace the origin of that multitude of singular institutions which retard the progress of population. Ant-

> hropophagy, the castration of males, the infibulation of females, late marriage, the consecration of virginity, the approbation of celibacy, the punishments exercised against girls who become mothers at too early an age.[57]

Moreover, and this is even more important, Malthus often ignored or refused to regard seriously facts which were at variance with his thesis. He does cite Raynal, but entirely ignores the latter's violent criticism of European colonialism and his description of the genocide and ethnocide of the population of American Indians. He is self-contradictory in his willingness to "correct the observation of those who seem to describe the gardens of the Hesperides" when they write about the more favourable aspects of savage life. The "corrected" view that he gives us is one of incessant famines and warfare, devastations, cruelty, degrading customs, prostitution and vice. But he goes too far in places. He emphasizes Cook's observation that the Australian aborigines "spend all their time in looking for food", a statement which we know to be false today but which was already contradicted in Malthus's own time by certain witnesses whose testimony he refused to accept. He accuses the Abbé Raynal of

> reasoning most inconsistently in his comparisons of savage and civilized life, though in one place he speaks of the savage as morally sure of a competent subsistence.[58]

But later when he assesses the description of savage life he concedes that

> . . . the only advantage in it above civilized life that I can discover is the possession of a greater degree of leisure by the mass of the people . . . When we consider the incessant toil to which the lower classes of society in civilized life are condemned, this cannot but appear to us a striking advantage; but it is probably overbalanced by much greater disadvantages . . . In all these countries where provisions are procured with facility, a most tyrannical distinction of ranks prevails.[59]

This is a degrading submission to the despotism of chiefs, or for women, to the despotism of men. "That women are indebted to the refinement of polished manners for a happy change in their state is a point which can admit of no doubt."[60]

This is exactly the opposite of what Morgan affirmed in his *Ancient Society* and Engels in his *Origin of the Family, the State and Property*, which was published in 1884.

Malthus does not deny that there is often a considerable degree of equality in savage societies. But he also believes that classes exist in these societies, an aristocracy which he calls a "feudal system", such as in the Sandwich Islands where the chiefs live in abundance, whilst their subjects live in misery. He admits that overpopulation can only be defined in relation to the distribution of wealth. But he also believes, and here he is strongly criticized by Marx, that the existence of classes and the antagonism between the rich and the poor is inevitable. He regards overpopulation as "the effect of a grand cause intimately united with the very nature of man which, though it has been constantly and powerfully operating since the commencement of society,"[61] does not result from social structure, the pattern of production or the distribution of wealth. This theoretical view leads him to state: "... we shall be compelled to acknowledge that the poverty and misery which prevail among the lower classes of society are absolutely irremediable."[62] It is true that Malthus did not altogether exclude the possibility that some of these evils might be remedied, but he did not think that they could ever be entirely abolished. In the light of experience and of science, he proposed to look for remedies to relieve the sufferings of the lower classes, provided that such remedies were not useless or even worse than the evils that they were designed to relieve.

These are the reasons why Malthus did not examine new ethnographic data. He was not interested in primitive societies as such, nor in producing a science which would explain the state of affairs in such societies. His interest lay in his own society which he believed to be menaced by misery and vice among the lower classes, who though needed to undertake society's labours were also dangerous, and among whom the subversive ideas of the French revolution fell on fertile ground. This is Stagl's conclusion with which I agree. Malthus's fears and his desire to find the most efficient remedies for the dangers which threatened his own society caused him to turn away from an ethnography which did not teach him anything new and could not contradict his thesis, and to take up political economy and social policy instead. Fundamentally, he used ethnography as a source of primary data and as a justification of a philosophy of anthropology which explored the unchanging elements in human nature and laid open the mysteries of man's relations with God. Ethnography became part of a philosophy of man which led simultaneously to a theodicy and a conservative economic policy. Malthus regards misery and vice in a contradictory, ambivalent and ambiguous fashion, being both the destiny of man and the instrument of his salvation and redemption. "A state of sloth and not of restlessness and activity, seems evidently to be the natural state of man; and this latter disposition could not have been generated but by the strong goad of necessity".[63]

However, we must go beyond these generalities. In the course of his researches Malthus obtained results which remain valid in the light of today's knowledge and which are, at least, worth discussion. This is what the eight other authors of papers in this section have done and I shall summarize their contributions briefly.

Malthus in the light of present ethnology

Eight papers delivered at this Congress are concerned with the Malthusian thesis in the light of present day anthropological science, and with a theoretical interpretation of these data. All the authors show little interest in Malthus's general theory, but they all agree that he pointed out some important aspects of the societies which they themselves had studied and that he suggested some explanations which have been found to be valid. Five of the papers deal with societies of hunters and gatherers. These societies posed a fundamental problem for Malthus: he wondered how the population of Australian aborigines could have been reduced to so low a figure. In this connection, Annette Hamilton's paper is of particular theoretical importance.[64] She recollects that recent archaeological researches have demonstrated almost without doubt that the aborigines arrived in Australia a little less than 40 000 years ago, but that the size of their population, though not as low as 300 000 as was suggested in Captain Cook's time, probably did not exceed one million. She uses the researches of Polgar, Hassan and others to show that the example of the Australian hunters helps us to understand the transformation in the world's population which occurred with the emergence of agriculture. According to Deevey[65] this amounted to some three million persons during the late palaeolithic, a figure which 41 000 years later, after agriculture had developed, had risen to 90 million. This increase implies a relatively low rate of population growth of less than 0.003 per cent.[66]

Malthus gave four reasons for the small size and the lack of growth of the Australian population: lack of resources leading to a high mortality from famine, the cruel treatment meted out by men to women, polygyny, and the effects of the nomadic life on women's fertility. However, the papers delivered at the 1965 Congress on *Man the Hunter*[67] show that the aborigines did not live at mere subsistence level. They "worked" little, ate well, and were only rarely affected by scarcities or famines. The same has been shown to hold true for the pygmies of the Congo and the Bushmen of the Kalahari.[68] How can this long-term stability of the population be explained? Annette Hamilton sees it as the result of three factors, two of which are unconscious and non-volitional. She reminds us that in those societies in which there is neither agriculture nor cattle breeding, mother's milk is the sole nourishment of infants during the early part of their lives. This intense lactation acts as an inhibitor of ovulation. It is not lactation alone that has the effect so much as the intensity and repetition of the stimulation of the breast by suckling which increases the secretion of prolactin and of the gonadotrophic hormones which inhibit ovulation.

However, this factor by itself would not be a sufficient explanation for the absence of population growth. Infant and child mortality which can affect as many as 35 per cent of infants and children under the age of five years is an additional factor which becomes more important during periods of drought and scarcity. And a third factor to be considered is also volitional — infanticide. However, infanticide does not seem to have been a collective strategy adopted for the purpose of regulating population growth. It was an individual rather than a social response to a particular situation and was used by women rather than by men. In Australia, men were not permitted to interfere in the responsibilities and activities of women and any matters connected with childbirth were within the exclusive and secret domain of women.

The combined effect of these three factors: intensive and prolonged lactation, infant and early childhood mortality, and infanticide must be at the basis of the stability of Australian populations. In contrast, the introduction of agriculture and stockbreeding led to the use of new types of food and new methods of food preparation, which reduced the frequency of suckling by infants and thus the inhibiting effect of lactation on ovulation and resulted in shorter intervals between successive births and an increase in the importance of mortality as a check. Moreover, in the majority of agricultural societies and in all those based on the possession of cattle, women lost some of the control they used to exercise over their own reproductive functions. Infanticide became less important as it proved economically and politically beneficial for families to be large.

Testart's paper[69] complements Hamilton's but goes further to explain the reasons for the growth of populations which followed the end of the palaeolithic period. Instead of linking this increase entirely to the emergence of agriculture and keeping of cattle, he shows that such an increase had already begun to occur in some hunting and food gathering societies once these ceased to be nomadic and became wholly or partially sedentary. He begins his account with an analysis of the lack of growth and low density of the populations of Australian aborigines, bushmen, pygmies etc. and looks for an explanation of this phenomenon in some of the factors that Hamilton, too, discusses. He emphasizes the importance of mobility in the mode of life of these societies and its part in the regulation of population size and praises Malthus for having recognized the importance of this factor. But he goes on to consider other hunting and food gathering peoples with a high density of population, often higher than that of agricultural societies. He mentions the Indians of California and the North West coast of America, two regions which were among the most densely populated of the continent before the arrival of the Europeans. Kroeber and Driver[70] gave a figure of 43 inhabitants per square kilometer for California and 28 inhabitants per square kilometer for the North West coast. Both regions provided abundant resources: in California the acorns, on the North West coast the salmon which returned to the rivers during each season. Both societies were sedentary and both possessed a complex structure.

Testart reminds us that it is not sufficient to explain the process of settlement to stress the relative abundance of natural resources, for they were only available at certain seasons of the year. To make use of these resources it was necessary that there should be a system of storage, because only this made it possible to ignore Liebig's law which states that the size of population is determined not by the total quantity of resources available to sustain it, but by the minimum amount that is available during months of scarcity. Testart concludes from his analysis that the use of storage and the conservation of grain were fundamental economic innovations which preceded the emergence of agriculture and made agriculture possible. Many groups of hunters were able to give up their nomadic life and settle, and their populations could be stabilized at new and higher levels. His findings support Binford's hypothesis[71] that the settlement of some hunting groups at the beginning of the last post-glacial age led to economic and demographic disequilibria between different regions which encouraged the development of agriculture.

Saladin d'Anglure[72] considers Malthus's thesis in relation to another population of hunters who lived under particularly difficult conditions: the Inuit in the Far North of Canada. In his paper he used both the explanations that we have discussed, and in the first section he considers the social and ideological context of Malthus's work. He maintains that every theory of population is based on a particular ideology and that conversely every ideology more or less explicitly assumes a certain explanation of demographic change. He demonstrates this important general point in the second part of his paper where he analyses the demographic ideas which are implicit in Inuit mythology. These show that the argument that population and subsistence are related did not originate with Malthus, or even with Aristotle, and that it is the duty of anthropologists to point this out to a public which is ignorant of this fact and, therefore, retains its prejudices. Here is the summary given by Saladin d'Anglure:

> At the beginning of time, night reigned permanently on earth. Two male adults emerged; the first two human beings. When they wanted to reproduce one changed into a woman and humanity began with the first couple, whose descendants multiplied rapidly, for at that time there was no death. When women were sterile, as was not infrequently the case, they could look for their babies to emerge from the earth; it was easy to find girls in this way, but boys were scarcer and took a long time to find.
>
> The earth was, therefore, essential for mankind, it provided not only subsistence but also produced descendants, for game was rare and men lived on the proceeds of the soil.
>
> The first Inuit lived on an island; when they reached old age, they squatted on the edge of their living platforms and performed a somersault reaching the ground head first, and this returned them to the state of a young adult. However, under the weight of this very rapid increase of population this island became too heavy and began to sway. At this threat of engulfment due to the increase of population, an old woman prayed for the arrival of death and of warfare and, in spite of a contrary prayer by an old man, her magic prevailed and assured that mankind's survival would now depend exclusively on procreation. Death and warfare prevented the excessive concentration of mankind on earth.
>
> At a later stage men wished to put an end to permanent darkness, so that they might be able to develop their knowledge and improve their techniques and one of them prayed for the arrival of daylight. In spite of a contrary prayer by a woman, the man's magic prevailed and mankind now became exclusively dependent for their food on hunting and gathering.
>
> Mother earth was, therefore, excluded both from the provision of food and from reproduction; humanity had seen the light of day after a long period of gestation.

These are the major aspects of the demographic myths of the Inuit. They relate to the social customs of their lives right up to the beginning of modern times.

In the mythology of the Inuit it was the female conscience which became aware of the need for control of population. The male conscience on the other hand regarded it as necessary to develop reproduction, and this view is nearer to that of the social philosophers. Surely, this is nothing other than the Principle of Population which asserts that the capacity of a population to survive and its well-being depends on production and reproduction. The difference between Malthus and the mythology of the Inuit is that in the latter disequilibrium was brought about by too high a rate of reproduction, rather than by too low a rate of production. After this situation changed, men lived in a state in which sometimes production was too low and sometimes reproduction too high, and these states are mirrored in the social customs of the Inuit.

This example shows us that myths do not only have a connection with social reality, but may be used to legitimize practices which have contributed to the stability of the population over time. Infanticide and the adoption of children are used to assure the proper spacing of births and distribution of families by size, and not necessarily to affect the rate of growth. This is rare among the Eskimos and postulates that these means must be used intelligently. Saladin d'Anglure reminds us that although it was generally believed that the Eskimos practised infanticide, the institution existed only among the Netsilik who were visited by Rasmussen in 1930 and again investigated by Balicki in 1967.[73] Today, we know that the Netsilik form an altogether exceptional group among the Eskimos, among whom quarrels, suicide and homicide also occur more frequently than among other groups. Among the Eskimos, just as among the Australian aborigines, infanticide is a limited individual response to extreme situations and not a generally practised means of population control.

Aram Yengoyan studies the practice of infanticide among hunting societies by considering the Pitjandjatjara people of Australia. He begins his paper with a critical examination of the available information dealing with infanticide among all Australian tribes and compares these with data on the selective infanticide of girl babies among the Eskimos. He shows that with the possible exception of the Yir Yoront studied by Lauriston Sharp[74] systematic infanticide of female children was not practised in Australia, but that infanticide may have accounted for up to 40 per cent of all children born in certain tribes near Adelaide. However, these figures are based on observations made during the nineteenth century which were lacking in precision. He suggests that both non-selective infanticide in the Australian tribes and selective infanticide among the Eskimos could be explained in terms of the differing roles of men in these societies. The contribution of men to the subsistence of their families is essential among the Eskimos whereas in Australia women contributed as much as or more than men did to subsistence. He shows that Divale and Marvin Harris[75] who attempted to explain the role of warfare in primitive Australian society as a means of restoring the balance of the sexes in the population which had been disturbed by the selective infanticide of female children were wrong, and that their explanation was a reconstruction of the state of primitive society based on ideology. He also shows that the practice of female infanticide among the Eskimos resulted in a great variety of methods by which a man could obtain a wife and that the practice, therefore, exercised considerable influence on the kinship structure. Female infanticide is incompatible with a system in which the exchange of women is regulated or with the privileges that old men enjoyed among the Australian aborigines. This provides a logical and structural justification for the belief that selective infanticide could not have been practised in Australia.

Joëlle Lamblin provides additional evidence for the stability of hunting and gathering populations[76] by considering another Eskimo society, that of the Ammasalimiut of West Greenland which was discovered by a Danish officer in 1884. She shows that in that society population density played an important part until the eighteenth century when the whale populations were decimated by Europeans. During the nineteenth century, therefore, the hunters had to turn from whales to seals, and the equilibrium which had existed between population and resources became precarious, so that shortly before their discovery at least 15 per cent of the population had died in a famine. However, and this result is in agreement with Saladin d'Anglure's, there is no evidence of intentional birth control or systematic infanticide. Infant mortality was very high, and births were widely spaced. There were also many suicides.

After this population had been colonized and became settled, it increased to more than six times its original size within a period of 75 years, and was progressively transformed into a society which was dependent on social assistance and a bureaucracy and which lacked any dynamic. This experience confirms in an historical context during a period very near to ours the effects of settlement on a hunting population and the effects of changes in the economic structure and nutrition on the development of population. Since 1968, the Danish government has followed what might be termed a Malthusian policy, to slow down the population explosion. Whilst the measures relating to abortion were rejected by this population, those relating to contraception were found to be acceptable.

Pastoral nomadic societies also provide an interesting example for examining Malthus's idea on population critically. The survival and wealth of these societies depends upon the number of their domestic animals, cattle, sheep or camels, who themselves depend on ecological systems in which man rarely, if ever, intervenes. In his paper, Pierre Bonte[77] examines the reproductive dynamics of human populations and their herds. He chooses his examples from the vast number of pastoral nomadic societies of East Africa, societies which were practically unknown in Malthus's days but which have been studied in great detail by American and English Scholars during the last 20 years. Bonte's paper has considerable theoretical importance. He reminds us that Malthus, who shared the general view of pastoral societies of his time, was wrong. He considered pastoralism as an archaic stage of production, intermediate between savagery and civilization, the state of barbarism. Today, however, we have learned that, more often than not, pastoralism is a highly specialized form of technological and economic organization which followed, rather than preceded, certain forms of mixed agriculture. But, as Bonte points out, Malthus did put his finger on a number of important facts, such as, for instance, the explosive nature of population growth in some pastoral societies and the brutal nature of the adjustments which followed such growth. But here again Malthus did not try to explain the essential reasons for such movements in terms of the social structure of these populations. Bonte shows that some pasturage, water and minerals are a necessary condition for the existence of pastoral societies, but that changes in the availability of these resources do not suffice to explain the population dynamics of these societies, which can only be understood in the context of the social functions of the pastoral method of production and not by the constraints on its environment.

Each member of such societies produces for two reasons: to reproduce himself directly and also to reproduce all those who are associated with the daily exploitation of natural resources. In order to continue the conditions of social life and his relations within his tribe, political, matrimonial and religious, his production helps to reproduce tribal society as a whole. He must, therefore, adjust his production not only to variations in the size of his own family, but also to maintain the production and reproduction of his political, economic or religious relations between his own domestic unit and others in the tribe. And, in addition, the production of the whole tribe is constrained by the possibilities offered by its environment, the potential of the ecosystem in which his society operates. Thus, the degree of specialization and the productivity of workers will depend on the dynamics of social relations between different domestic units in the fields of production, kinship, or political or religious solidarity.

The rates of growth of population in these societies — both those of humans and of animals — can vary very quickly, because animals reach maturity rapidly and animals are accumulated for purposes of competition or for social reasons. These rapid movements occur within an unstable ecosystem because it is a highly specialized one and this results in the explosive character of changes in populations and the brutal nature of the adjustments which follow such changes: epidemics, migrations, wars or a partial conversion of the society to a settled agriculture which leads to an increase in the productivity of work. In this respect, the analysis comes back to Malthus and it is interesting to note that he quotes the population of Ethiopia as one of his examples, a population which bordered on the great cattle-breeding societies of East Africa, those of the Masai, the Jie and the Turkana of whose existence Malthus was unaware.

Panoff[78] who has worked on Polynesian societies considers Malthus's chapter on the Pacific islands. We have already stressed the importance of the discovery of these islands on European thought, because of the high quality of the accounts of early travellers such as Cook and Lapérouse and also because these accounts were used to show the ways in which European civilization was superior or inferior to the natural state of the savages. Recall the argument in Diderot's *Supplément au Voyage de Bougainville.*

Panoff shows that Malthus had read the most important accounts and was aware of the inconsistencies and contradictions between different authors. He tried to explain the stability of these island populations as being caused by four factors: infanticide, continuous warfare, prostitution and lack of resources. Panoff examines the importance of each of these factors in the light of present-day knowledge and concludes that the state of demographic stagnation which Malthus postulated has not been proved to exist. Moreover, even if there had been stagnation, none of the four factors which Malthus mentions could have been sufficient to bring it about. There is no evidence for infanticide in Tahiti. Some infanticide of female babies was practised, but mainly in aristocratic, semi-religious and semi-artistic isolates such as the Arioi, whom Malthus cites, but there is no proof whatever that the practice was prevalent among the common people. Tribal warfare, far from being continuous in these societies, was a wholly exceptional feature. It resulted from the appearance of a new cult in Tahiti at the beginning of the century which led to a political realignment of communities into antagonistic blocks. In 1768, Cook described the island as being divided into two camps, but this situation was probably very different from that found in preceding centuries. The wars of 1788 and 1789 which were observed by missionaries and the crew of the Bounty were probably the result of direct intervention by Europeans who evangelized and manipulated local groups.

To regard the sexual freedom which existed both before and after marriage and the rules of hospitality of the Tahitians as a form of prostitution is highly ethnocentric. Moreover, it is far from proven that a correlation exists between sexual freedom and a low birth rate.

Lastly, it cannot be demonstrated that resources in Tahiti were insufficient to maintain the population. Malthus refused to accept the views of missionaries who had lived there for many years and who had pointed out this fact. He also ignored the enormous productivity of the horticultural producers of tubers. Variations in yield and lack of resources which Malthus noted and commented on was often caused by the practice of placing a provisional taboo on their use in order to accumulate stocks for large feasts or warlike expeditions. Norma MacArthur[79] has shown that this method of production allowed the population to treble during the nineteenth century. Therefore, during the eighteenth century it was not true that the population of Tahiti was kept in check by the pressure of subsistence. And it is difficult to understand how Malthus can have regarded Tahitian society as a closed system when the natives were counted amongst the most skilful long-distance navigators in the world, whose prowess in this field was greatly admired by Cook. Whenever facts contradicted Malthus, he either ignored them or presented them in a light more favourable to his own theory

The last paper is by Patrick Manning[80] and deals with the consequences of the African slave trade, the greatest forced migration of the eighteenth century and the only example in modern times of a migration instituted to develop a system of production based on slavery. The trade can be compared in some respects to that practised in ancient Greece and Rome. Manning distinguishes two aspects of Malthus's thought, the first technical, the second ideological. In his technical account Malthus relied on the work of Mungo Park[81] who described the situation in Senegambia, a region in which the slave traffic was not very important and where it had only recently begun. He thought that the slave trade alone was not sufficient to reduce population, but that the wars, destruction of property and famines which were its accompaniment added to the negative effects of slavery. But he did not think that the slave trade had affected the overall demographic situation of Africa. On the ideological plane, Manning holds that Malthus did not consider that the African situation was worth greater attention and that he saw no hope that Africans would ever be free of their poverty or sufferings. Though he condemned slavery and expressed his abhorrence at the traffic in human beings, he also provided some partisan excuses for the practice. In 1793 Dalzel, a slaver, published his *Histoire du Dahomey,* a work which was very similar to Malthus's in its views. The debate continues to the present day. John Fage believes that the slave trade was sufficient to stabilize the populations of Africa who were subjected to it.[82] Manning shows that in Dahomey there was, in fact, a decline in population and he thinks that this state of affairs would arise whenever the slave trade had continued for at least two centuries and when its effects were not limited to the coastal regions as was the case in Mungo Park's Senegambia, but extended to the interior. He suggests that the effects of the slave trade may have been very different in different places and at different times, but believes that his findings for Dahomey probably apply also in the Congo and Angola. However, Thornton would contest this view as ragards Angola. The problem still awaits a solution.

This, too, must be our conclusion. Malthus's heritage is both ambivalent and inconsistent. His general theory has not been verified by history, but some of his remarks continue to inspire critical researches. I doubt, however, whether any anthropologist would subscribe to his general statement that: "In drawing similar inferences from the state of society in a number of different countries, I found it very difficult to avoid some repetition."[83]

Contrariwise, almost all would subscribe to the idea that by making a serious study of the causes which regulate human populations "we may promise ourselves a clearer insight into the internal structure of human society".[84]

It is paradoxical that Malthus who wished to be remembered as a demographer rather than as a comparative ethnologist and who turned to economics and social theory is likely to be remembered for the remarks he made on societies with which he had little sympathy, rather than for the remedies that he suggested for his own society and which, of all, he regarded as least imperfect.

Notes

1. Numa Broc. Malthus et la géographie. MHA, p.52; J. Stagl. Les sources ethnographiques de "l'*Essai sur le principe de population*" de Malthus. MHA, p.58; Michèle Duchet. Malthus et l'ethnographie. MHA, p.52.
2. R. B. Lee and T. Devore (eds) (1968). *Man the Hunter.* Proceedings of a

Symposium held at the University of Chicago. April 6-9, 1966, pp.415; Aldine Publishing Company, Chicago 1968.

3. A. Testart. Mobilité et démographie chez les chasseurs-cueilleurs. MHA, p.58; Annette Hamilton. Australian aboriginal population. Malthus and the theory of transition. MHA, p.53.
4. B. Saladin d'Anglure. L'idéologie de Malthus, les "sauvages" d'Amérique et la démographie mythique des Inuit d'Igloolik. MHA, p.58; J. R. Lamblin. Les mécanismes de régulation démographique dans un groupe de chasseurs arctiques, les Ammassalimiut du Groenland oriental. MHA, p.55.
5. A. A. Yengoyan. The question of female infanticide in aboriginal Australian societies. MHA, p.59.
6. P. Bonte. Les lois de population dans les sociétés d'éleveurs nomades. MHA, p.51.
7. T. R. Malthus. *Essay*, Everyman Edition, vol. 1, p.44. (Unless otherwise stated all page references are to this edition.)
8. D. Diderot. *Supplément au voyage de Bougainville*. First published in *Oeuvres de Diderot*, Paris, 1800.
9. T. R. Malthus, op. cit. in note 7, vol. 1, p.47.
10. ibid. p.91.
11. ibid.
12. P. Manning. Malthusianism and the demography of the African slave trade. MHA, p.56.
13. John Thornton, Professor at the University of Zambia, quoted by P. Manning, loc. cit. in note 12. Thornton argues, on the basis of evidence from Angola, that the African population responded rapidly and successfully to the losses caused by the slave trade, and thus implies that depopulation did not occur. Manning, basing himself on evidence from the Bight of Benin, comes to the opposite conclusion.
14. T. R. Malthus, op. cit. in note 7, Preface, p.1.
15. Numa Broc, loc. cit. in note 1.
16. Michèle Duchet, loc. cit. in note 1.
17. J. B. du Halde (1735). *Description géographique et historique de l'empire de la Chine* (4 vols) Paris. (English translation by R. Brooker, London, 1736.)
18. J. B. G. A. Grosier (1785). *Description générale de la Chine* (2 vols). Paris. (An English translation was published in London in 1788.)
19. G. T. F. Raynal (1770). *Histoire philosophique et politique des établissements et du commerce des Européens dans les deux Indes* (6 vols). Paris. (An English translation by J. Justamond appeared in 1776.)
20. P. F. X. de Charlevoix (1744). *Histoire et description générale de la Nouvelle France, avec le journal historique d'un voyage fait par ordre du Roi dans l'Amérique septentrionale* (3 vols). Paris.
21. A. F. Prévost d'Exiles (1746–1770). *Histoire générale des voyages* (with additions by Meusnier *et al.*) (20 vols). Paris.
22. *Lettres édifiantes et curieuses*. Edité par C. Le Gobien *et al.* (1707–1773). (30

vols). Paris. A later edition edited by Y. M. M. Querbeuf in 26 volumes was published in Paris between 1780 and 1783.

23. C. de Brosses (1756). *Histoire des navigations aux terres australes* (2 vols). Paris. (English edition by J. Callender. *Terra Australis cognita* (3 vols). London, 1766.)
24. J. Harris (1745). *Navigantium atque itinerantium bibliotheca.* Compleat Collections of Voyages and Travels (2 vols). London. Later editions with large additions to 1764 (Ed. J. Campbell).
25. T. Astley (1747). *A New General Collection of Voyages and Travels* (compiled by J. Green), published by Thomas Astley. London. The work by Prévost referred to in note 21 is a translation of this text into French.
26. A. De Ulloa (1748). *Relacion historica del viaje a la América meridional* (5 vols). Madrid.
27. J. Cook (1773). *An Account of a Voyage round the World in the Years MDCCLXVIII, MDCCLXIX, MDCCCLXX and MDCCLXXI* (2 vols). John Hawkesworth, Dublin; *A Voyage towards the South Pole and round the World, Performed in His Majesty's Ships The Resolution and Adventure in the Years 1772, 1773, 1774 and 1775* (2 vols). London, 1777.
28. de Lapérouse (J. F. Galaun, Compte de) (1797). *Voyage de Lapérouse autour du monde* (rédigé par M. L. A. Milet-Mureau). Imprimerie de la République. Paris.
29. J. B. Barthélémy Baron de Lesseps (1790). *Journal historique du voyage de M de Lesseps depuis l'instant où il a quitté les frégates françaises au Port Saint Pierre et Saint Paul du Kamtschatka j'usqu'à son arrivée en France, le 17 octobre 1788.* Imprimerie royale. Paris.
30. J. A. Entrecasteaux (1808). *Voyage de Dentrecasteaux envoyé à la recherche de Lapérouse* (2 vols). Imprimerie nationale, Paris.
31. G. Vancouver (1798). *Voyage of Discovery to the North Pacific and round the World in the Years 1790–1795* (Edited by J. Vancouver) (2 vols). London.
32. C. Niebuhr (1774). *Reisebeschreibung nach Arabien und anderen umliegenden Ländern* etc. Hamburg. (An English edition translated by R. Heron appeared in Edinburgh in 1792 entitled *Travels through Arabia and Other Countries in the East* (2 vols) and a French version was published in 1773 entitled *Description de l'Arabie d'après des observations et recherches faites dans le pays même.* Copenhaguen.)
33. J. Bruce (1791). *Travels to discover the Sources of the Nile in the Years 1768–1773.* (5 vols). London; E. Kaempfer (1727). *History of Japan with a Description of the Kingdom of Siam* (translated from the Dutch MS by J. Scheucher) (2 vols). London. (A French version was published in the Hague in 1729); C. P. Thunberg (1795). *Travels in Europe Africa and Asia from 1770–1779.* London. Published in Swedish in Uppsala, 1799–1793 and in French in Paris in 1794.
34. M. Park (1799). *Travels in the Interior Districts of Africa in the Years 1795-1796 and 1797.* London.
35. C. F. de Volney (1787). *Voyages en Syrie et en Egypte pendant les années*

1783–85 (2 vols). Paris. (An English edition was published in the same year.)

36. F. Le Vaillant (1790). *Voyages dans l'intérieur de l'Afrique par le Cap de Bonne Espérance dans les années 1780–85*. (Edited by G. Varon) (2 vols). Paris. (An English translation by E. Helme was published in the same year.)
37. G. (Earl) Macartney (1797). *An Historical Account of the Embassy to the Emperor of China* (Edited by G. L. Staunton). London.
38. D. Collins (1798). *An Account of the English Colony in New South Wales* (2 vols). London.
39. J. Stagl, loc. cit. in note 1.
40. cf. H. Westergaard (1932). *Contributions to the History of Statistics*, pp.6–7. P. S. King, London; cf. also J. Stagl (1977). Zur Geschichte der Statistik und Staatsbeschreibung in der Neuzeit. *Zeitschrift für Politik* **24** (1), 81–86.
41. Johann Friedrich Blumenbach (1752–1840), (1777). *De Generis Humanis Varietate Nativa Liber*. Vanderhoeck, Göttingen.
42. J. Stagl, loc. cit. in note 1.
43. T. R. Malthus, op. cit. in note 7, p. 90.
44. Saladin d'Anglure, loc. cit. in note 4.
45. T. R. Malthus. *Essay*, Book I. chapter II, *passim*.
46. T. R. Malthus. *Essay* vol. 1, p.2.
47. ibid. p.45.
48. Michèle Duchet, loc. cit. in note 1.
49. J. Stagl, loc. cit. in note 1.
50. L. Morgan (1871). *Systems of Consanguinity and Affinity of the Human Family*. Washington. (Republished by Oosterhout in 1970). *See also* L. Morgan (1877). *Ancient Society*. London.
51. T. R. Malthus, op. cit. in note 7, vol. 1, p.7.
52. ibid. p.55.
53. ibid. p.45.
54. ibid. p.48. My italics.
55. M. Panoff. Malthus devant les insulaires du Pacifique. MHA, p.57.
56. Michèle Duchet, loc. cit. in note 1.
57. T. R. Malthus, op. cit. in note 7, vol. 1, p.44.
58. ibid. pp.38–39.
59. ibid. p.57.
60. ibid. p.28.
61. ibid. vol. 1, p.5.
62. ibid. p.3. vol. 1.
63. ibid. p.59.
64. Annette Hamilton, loc. cit. in note 3.
65. E. S. Deevey (1958). The equilibrium population. *In The Population Ahead* (Ed. R. G. Francis). University of Minnesota Press, Minneapolis.
66. Polgar.
67. loc. cit. in note 2.
68. Colin Turnbull, a specialist on the pygmies, lived with the Mbuti, a group

of pygmies in the equatorial forests of Zaïre. *See* Colin Turnbull (1961). *The Secret People.* Anchor Books, New York; (1965). *Wayward Servants.* Eyre & Spottiswoode, London; For the Bushmen, *see inter alia* R. B. Lee (1972). Population growth and the beginnings of sedentary life among the !Kung Bushmen. In *Population Growth. Anthropological Implications* (Ed. B. Spooner). MIT Press, Cambridge, Massachusetts; (1979). The *!Kung San.* Cambridge University Press, Cambridge.

69. loc. cit. in note 3.
70. A. L. Kroeber (1939). *Cultural and Natural Areas of Native North America.* University of California Press, Berkeley; H. E. Driver and W. C. Massey (1957). Comparative studies of North American Indians. *Transactions of the American Philosophical Society* **47**, 163–465.
71. L. R. Binford and W. J. Chasko (1976). Nunamiut demographic history: A provocative case. In *Demographic Anthropology* (Ed. E. B. W. Zubrow). University of New Mexico Press, Albuquerque.
72. loc. cit. in note 4.
73. A. Balicki (1967). Female infanticide on the Arctic coast. *Man* **2**, 615–625.
74. R. Lauriston Sharp (1940). An Australian aboriginal population. *Human Biology* **12**, 481–507.
75. W. T. Divale (1970). An explanation for primitive warfare: Population control and the significance of primitive sex ratios. *The New Scholar*, pp.173–192; (1972). Systematic population control in the Middle and Upper Paleolithic: Inferences based on contemporary hunter–gatherers. *World Archaeology* **4**, 222–243; M. Harris (1977). *Cannibals and Kings. The Origins of Culture.* Random House, New York.
76. J. R. Lamblin, loc. cit. in note 4.
77. loc. cit. in note 6.
78. loc. cit. in note 55.
79. Norma MacArthur (1968). *Pacific Island Populations.*
80. loc. cit. in note 12.
81. M. Park, op. cit. in note 34. Malthus quotes Park extensively in book I, chapter VIII.
82. J. D. Fage (1969). Slavery and the slave trade in the context of West African history. *Journal of African History* **10** (3), 393–404; (1975). The effect of the export slave trade on African population. In *The Population Factor in African Studies.* (Eds. R. P. Moss and R. J. A. Bathbone), pp.15–23.
83. Preface to 2nd Edition of the *Essay.*
84. T. R. Malthus, op. cit. in note 7, vol. 1, p.17.

PART 3

Malthus and Religion

10 Malthus and Religion

R. REMOND

Any attempt to synthesize the contributions to a Congress such as this must contain considerable gaps. These become particularly apparent when attempts are made to compare the attitudes of different religions. The original subject proposed for this section was "Malthus and the Christian religion", but the organizers have rightly attempted to extend its scope to include other religions as well. The original title was chosen both because Christianity was the prevailing religion in those parts of the world where Malthus's work originally made an impact and also because Malthus himself was a clergyman of the Established Church. However, although the attempt to broaden the discussion was laudable, it proved difficult to realize. At the time of writing, only one paper dealing with a religion other than Christianity has been received, this is Judaism which shares with Christianity the exhortation contained in Genesis "Be fruitful and multiply and replenish the earth", an exhortation which seems to be at variance with Malthus's views. The absence of any reference to other religions and particularly to Islam must, therefore, not be taken as an indication of indifference to their views; rather it reflects my own personal lack of qualifications to write about these matters. It is my hope that the scope of this report will be extended during the discussion; responsibility for its inadequacies is mine alone.

Even though only a small number of contributions has been received, these have led me to modify some of the views which I set out in a note to the authors and in which I raised certain questions. Some of these questions have been answered, others have been shown to lack interest or importance, and some questions which had not occurred to me on first consideration have been raised. A number of major points may serve as a basis for discussion.

MALTHUS PAST AND PRESENT
ISBN 0-12-224670-5

First, the papers show the ways in which Malthus's views ran counter to religious orthodoxy and the reasons for these differences, particularly with the tenets of the Christian and Jewish religions. These may be discussed on a number of different levels. This problem is of interest to theologians. Two different methods which correspond to different theological points of view are contrasted. Malthus suggests that God can only be known through observation of the nature of His laws. This is the point of view of natural theology. Dogmatic theologians, on the other hand, cite Scripture and reproach Malthus for not taking account of revelation. This controversy in which religious attitudes are related to certain epistemological views has resulted in confronting religious writers, possibly for the first time, with demographic problems that have been put into a statistical framework, and with the results of empirical social research.

Malthus's Principle of Population also provides an occasion for theological considerations. The view that there is a natural tendency for population to grow beyond the means of subsistence must surely contradict the concept of a benevolent God. How can Malthus's observations, assuming they were true, be reconciled with the injunction in Genesis: "Be fruitful and multiply"? Malthus's pessimism conflicts with the notion of Providence. It is this pessimistic view, the denial or confidence in God that would seem to conflict with religious doctrine.

A system of faith normally also implies a system of morals. Malthus's theory raises certain problems for religions concerning men's private conduct. Malthus commends moral restraint; he regards it as a matter of conscience for individuals to practise self control within marriage and to delay marriage. The Churches which have their own point of view on the nature of marriage cannot be indifferent to the consequences for the personal conduct of their members which Malthus deduced from the truths that he believed he had demonstrated.

Lastly, the theory also has certain social consequences. Malthus condemns any effort to help those improvident individuals who have contracted marriage without having the means necessary to support a family and he is opposed to organized charity. Here again, there is a point of disagreement with religion and Malthus's theory leads to conclusions which are opposed to those of religious thinkers in the middle of the nineteenth century, when they took account of the consequences of industrialization, pointed out the sufferings of the labouring classes and progressively developed a moral and social doctrine.

There are, therefore, four distinct aspects of the dialogue or the misunderstandings between Malthus and religion, which are interdependent.

Malthus should have asked these questions himself, for he was in Holy Orders and had studied theology. A number of writers who have studied Malthus and the religious and social thought of his time have taken an interest in the basis of his work and in the relationship between his theory of population and his understanding of the Bible and of Christian doctrine. However, they have not always come to the same conclusion. Crawford from a parallel reading of Malthus's *Essay* and the Bible notes a number of points of concordance and concludes that some of Malthus's views were based on his study of Scripture. Waterman, on the other hand, gives Malthus a bad mark as a theologian and believes that he was influenced by the theism of his time. This is also the view of the majority of other authors. Malthus's work is not only self-contradictory at times, but also heterodox on a number of points. In his view of God he takes no account of revelation and limits His functions to the enforcement of a strict application of the laws that He has laid down for mankind. Perhaps the differences between different authors will be brought out during the discussion.

Turning now to the heart of the matter, the position of different religions, and particularly that of the Roman Catholic Church (the subject with which most of the contributors are concerned), a number of points are raised which are not immediately obvious. It would appear, that, contrary to popular impression, Catholics who read Malthus soon after the publication of his *Essay* did not express any antagonism to his position. The position of the Catholic Church on the population question was not unchanging. Father Vallin points out that the Church has never regarded large numbers and an abundant population as good in itself. It is afraid of overpopulation. Moreover, its views have changed with different circumstances; some of the contributors stress that the attitudes of the magisterium to demographic problems have been different in different periods. During the last two centuries, when population trends have changed, these trends have had repercussions on attitudes to the Principle of Population and to the consequences which Malthus deduced therefrom. A number of different reactions can be distinguished, and I would like to submit to following attempts to distinguish different periods for discussion.

During the first, which lasted until the middle of the nineteenth century. Catholics did not oppose Malthus's views; they agreed that his intention was apologetic. The danger of overpopulation pointed out by Malthus could be used as an argument in favour of the celibacy of the clergy and the religious orders against the attacks of the populationists; the Church in her wisdom had foreseen the dangers of overpopulation. Because of the tendency for population to exceed means of subsistence, the Christian faith could support the practice of abstinence. There was a certain parallelism between the practice of moral restraint and the virtue of chastity which had traditionally been esteemed by the Church.

Disagreement began when the social consequences of the Malthusian doctrine came to be considered. Catholics objected to their lack of humanity: Malthus's views were far removed from the duty to help the poor and were in opposition to Christian thought which had come to stress the social implications of the evangelical message and which had developed a social doctrine. This Christian social doctrine was equally opposed to Malthusianism and liberalism, and for the same reason: both were regarded as an unconditional submission to natural, demographic and economic laws.

The disagreement extended. Malthus's pessimism was contrasted with the optimism of the Christian which was based on a belief in the goodness of Providence. Catholic social thinkers refused to admit that there could be a disequilibrium between population and resources, though they did not examine the problem scientifically, on the pretext that adequate and reliable statistics were not available. Temporary or local disequilibria might exist, but this could not be the case on a global scale. Such disequilibria were merely a consequence of defective organization which could be modified by men. This optimistic view, was based on faith in divine providence and fortified by an historic vision of the progress of humanity and by a certainty that civilization would develop. Malthus was reproached for not having taken account of man's increasing capacities, his inventive genius, the power of his industry and the virtually unlimited possibilities of expanding resources. In summary, it was thought that his views were too limited to his own time. This was the perspective which inspired the encyclical *Mater et Magistra* (1961) of John XXIII and *Populorum progressio* (1967) of Paul VI. Within the period of one century, the teaching of the Roman magisterium was transformed from one which was tinged with pessimism to one of collective hope. It is not, therefore, surprising that the Church's views on the Principle of Population underwent modification.

In this report no mention has been made of the movement which is today, quite wrongly, called neo-Malthusianism. Though public men, moralists and preachers often confuse Malthusianism with neo-Malthusianism and reproach the author of the *Essay* with having advocated forbidden practices, neither the theologians nor the ecclesiastical authorities have ever committed this error. Given that there is an objective difference between the Principle of Population and the teaching of Malthus which on the one hand calls upon men to practise virtue, and the practice of contraception which has been called neo-Malthusianism on the other, I have preferred to exclude this subject from discussion in this paper. It is better studied by students of collective behaviour than by theologians. The relationship between Malthusianism and religious ideas seems to me to be a sufficiently broad subject, even though it is limited to a confrontation between his ideas and religious teachings, and should generate an interesting discussion.

11 French Roman Catholics and Malthusianism before 1870

P. VALLIN

Though this paper is limited to the views of French Roman Catholics, I shall refer also to some writers in other countries whose works circulated in France. It is probable that an examination of the views of Roman Catholics in other countries, particularly Latin countries, would yield similar results, but I have not checked this assertion carefully.

The period considered ends in 1870; this date has been chosen because it marks a significant watershed in a number of other areas.[1] It will be shown that a new attitude towards Malthusian ideas began to evolve around that time.

The paper will be divided into four sections, which deal respectively with the knowledge of Malthusian ideas and the moral aspects of conjugal life; the reception of Malthusian ideas by Roman Catholics; the reservations against the social views put forward in the *Essay,* and the evolution of thought on this subject.

1. Malthus and ethics

The first translation of Malthus's *Essay* into French was published by Pierre Prevost in Geneva in 1809; another by the same translator cooperating with his son Guillaume appeared in 1823 and was reprinted in 1836; in 1845 Joseph Garnier published a revision of the Prevosts' translation containing a notice by Charles Comte and an introduction by Pellegrino Rossi; this volume was reprinted with new notes by Garnier in 1852.[2] Henceforth, I shall cite from that edition.

I have mentioned all these versions not merely to illustrate the large

MALTHUS PAST AND PRESENT
ISBN 0-12-224670-5

circulation that the *Essay* enjoyed in France during that period, but also to support a point which is directly pertinent to my argument. The Prevosts added a note to Chapter 14 of Book 1 in which they explained that the term "moral restraint" should be interpreted "in a general sense to mean a purely prudential check, i.e. it does not involve strict chastity within marriage and is, therefore, tinged with vice, without being in itself vicious."[3] In the edition of 1845, Garnier pointed out that Malthus would not have agreed with this interpretation and added: "It has not yet been proved that this type of abstinence which prevents misery without running counter to the laws of physiology, is immoral."[4]

This comment roused Proudhon's anger. He devotes the last chapter of his *Système des contradictions économiques, ou philosophie de la misère* to Malthus. He refers to Garnier's note to show that Malthus's disciples regarded moral restraint as "a purely physical restraint with little restriction on pleasure" and adds that "the general public who accept this view and have no liking for subtleties interpret Malthus's theory in this sense".[5] Garnier wrote a rejoinder to this in the 1852 edition of the 1845 translation, particularly in a final note.[6]

Catholic authors, too, alluded to this interpretation. Félix Martin-Doisy refers to the "violation of the natural law which the economists have concealed under the name of prudence within marriage".[7]

It is, therefore, evident that there is a direct relationship between the circulation of the *Essay* in France and the discussion of the concept of "onanism within marriage" by Catholic moral theologians.[8] It is possible that Garnier's note of 1845 provided the occasion for a reply from the Holy Office in 1851, which stated that the thesis that conjugal onanism was not contrary to the natural law was false and scandalous.[9] However, at that time the *Essay* was not generally mentioned in treatises on moral theology, nor does the problem seem to have preoccupied the attention of authors.[10] At a more general level, they did not seem to attach great value to the procreation of children as such. In successive editions of the classic manuals by the Jesuit Busenbaum,[11] the classical view is put forward in which the marriage of Joseph and Mary is cited as an example to show that a true marriage is possible even when the spouses have taken a vow of continence; such a vow does not mean that the spouses have violated the commandment to continue the human species.[12] Busenbaum also taught that it was licit for the poor to practise abstinence from procreation and fear the arrival of future children, always provided that they did not commit any positive acts which would make their physical union sterile.[13] This leads us to Section 2.

2. Favourable reactions to Malthusian ideas

I have shown previously that some of the more renowned Catholic authors of the first half of the nineteenth century[14] expressed concern about overpopulation and suggested that Christian continence was one method of avoiding this danger. This traditional view was restated towards the end of the eighteenth century in reply to the populationist attacks on Christian morality and the celibacy of the clergy and of religious orders.[15] It is in their opposition to populationist attacks, too, that Catholic authors have argued that the state does not have the right to interfere in family life. This is the view expressed by Fr Martin in the volume already cited and also that of his Italian colleague Taparelli.[16]

In this context, Malthus's ideas can be accepted, provided moral restraint is interpreted in the sense originally intended by the author and not in the way of his French disciples. Luigi Taparelli d'Azeglio cites Malthus as an apologist for Christian morality.[17] However, he refers to the danger of overpopulation without making any special reference to Malthus.

Those authors who took an interest in the Malthusian system frequently mentioned the support which his views on demographic subjects gave to the Catholic teaching on chastity and the religious life and to the revival of monastic institutions. Villeneuve-Bargemont proposes the setting up of new celibate communities[18] and Rossi, in his introductory note to the *Essay,* suggests that the traditions of communal life should be revived in the form of communities of five, six or ten families living together for mutual support and mutual moral education.[19]

It is easier for these writers to express a favourable reaction to Malthus, as some of his more extreme views had already been criticized by German and English economists. Catholic authors often refer to these criticisms, whilst stressing Malthus's arguments. However, in these discussions they never range themselves on the side of Malthus's opponents.

Sismondi suggested that the application of Christian morality would lead to over-fast population growth; Villeneuve-Bargemont attempts to refute him.[20] He receives some support in his views from Proudhon who is astonished by this attitude of "Christian economists": how can they not recognize that the remedy proposed by Malthus was "an accusation against Providence, an expression of mistrust in nature"?.[21] However, given that they did not do so clearly, this interpretation cannot have been obvious for the Christian conscience. In the *Economie politique chrétienne* it is admitted[22] that the Principle of Population is valid and this means that "population will always press against means of subsistence",[23] "a wise government must try to counteract this tendency."[24] Presumably Pellegrino Rossi was to be included among the Christian economists; he was soon to be shown papal confidence by being entrusted with the government of the papal states.[25]

A well-known Catholic militant author said of Malthus that "some of his defenders can not be regarded in any way as suspect".[26] He follows Villeneuve-Bargemont in affirming that Roman Catholicism "far from imprudently encouraging the Principle of Population, moderates and regulates its application."[27] In his view, "there is no need for any government to take measures to encourage population growth . . . its interest lies in the population being healthy, affluent, intelligent and moral, rather than large".[28]

3. Some reservations against social Malthusianism

The Vicomte de Villeneuve is strongly opposed to Malthus's views on assistance given to the poor, whether by the state or by charitable association.[29] He reproaches Malthus for not drawing attention to the concentration of wealth and capital, to "the egotism and greed of the leaders of British industry", and to the "theories of British political economy", as well as to the absence of any "religious or charitable sentiments";[30] all these have done more to reduce the lower classes to a state of misery than any geometrical progression or improvidence of the working classes.[31] He believes that assistance to the poor, by charitable associations and employers, must continue; he is not, however, opposed to the view that public opinion might encourage the government to adopt measures which would lead to a delay in marriage.[32]

The author, whom I have not been able to identify, of the article on Population in the *Encyclopédie catholique,* published in 1840 and edited by the Abbé Glaire, Dean of the Faculty of Theology at the Sorbonne, does not refer to Malthus, on whom there is a brief note in Volume 14, but he implicitly refutes the Malthusian argument by stating that "Providence will not allow men to be born, unless the possibility of life exists for them".[33] He agrees with Villeneuve-Bargemont's social views that "it is the duty of government to increase the amount of work available for the lower classes. If this is done, large population will never become a burden; on the contrary, the population will contribute to the country's strength".[34]

Charles François Chevé takes a similar view and, relying on Châteaubriand, writes in his article on "Population"[35] that in the middle ages France was relatively more densely populated than at present, but the horrifying material poverty which is caused by moral poverty and lack of faith was then unknown.

Henri Baudrillart in an article on "Malthus" for the second edition of the *Biographie universelle Michaud*[36] writes that "Malthusian ideas not only form an important part of economics, but also of the passionate polemics of socialism". Baudrillart was influenced by the social reformism of Michel Chevalier and reproaches Malthus for one-sided views "which will lead the spirit into a slough of despond",[37] for being uncritical and for risking bringing about an excessive pessimism.[38] His views are not dissimilar from those of Villeneuve-Bargemont on the social conclusions of Malthusian doctrine, but he also deals with some new problems.[39]

4. The evolution of thought

Baudrillart remains a member of the school favourable to Malthus but nevertheless criticizes him on two counts. First, "moral restraint is easier the higher a man stands on the social scale"; the rationalism which leads men to moderate their fertility has grown to a point among the upper classes where it has become deadly.[40] Secondly, Malthus is criticized for thinking only in terms of statistics, instead of considering men as a capital asset which could be improved.[41] Given the nature of human industry, where are the limits to the productive capacity of the earth?[42] The first criticism raises the spectre of a fall in the birth rate: the second is an expression of faith in the progress of civilization. It is these two aspects which are increasingly discussed by other writers and which signal an evolution in the way of thinking about demographic problems.

Martin-Doisy to whom we have already referred, opposes the Abbé Dourif.[43] He says that the latter is "frightened by the growth of population". He is looking for an outlet to this rising flood. He does not realize that greed will lead to a reduction in the size of households through violations of the natural law, which economists have concealed under the name of "marital prudence". This is the beginning of the pro-natalist school which takes account of the fall in the number of births.[44]

Auguste Ott[45] is more careful. He does not believe that the number of births in France is declining dramatically, merely that it is stationary and that the population is only increasing because of a fall in the number of deaths. However, he does not agree with Proudhon that the number of men will ultimately reach a stationary state, nor does he find Malthus's views convincing. As regards the latter, he does not agree that overpopulation is a cause of misery; on the contrary it is misery that leads to people marrying early and having large families.[46] He points out that Malthus's view that subsistence can only increase in arithmetic progression is based on the assumption that the fertility of the soil cannot be increased, whereas "the better soils have normally been those that have been continuously cultivated, and their quality is the result of men's labour. Because of the invention of machinery, men's labour, far from becoming heavier, will prove more and more productive."[47] This conclusion again differs from Proudhon's, because capital can be accumulated to improve the productivity of the soil. "Nothing in the real world justifies Malthus's theories; neither the development of population nor that of subsistence will follow the path that he has mapped out".[48]

Proudhon thought "that work will become progressively more onerous, for men".[49] Ott refutes this thesis. Proudhon also believes that a weakening of the sexual impulse will lead to a reduction in the number of births. Ott doubts this as well. Moral progress implies that people will marry later and have fewer children, but in the world as a whole the number of births may well increase. It must, therefore, be admitted, as Rossi does, that Malthus's fears are justified on a global scale. There is an upper limit to the fertility of the soil which cannot be overcome.[50] But, although economic science can foresee this stage of man's history, it cannot prophesy what will happen then. Ott ends on an apocalyptic note. "Man is only a passenger on this earth, one day his destiny will have to change completely . . . any speculation about this, however, would be both useless and sterile."[51] This argument is followed by less alarming statistics about the population of France!

Up to this last mystic or messianic element, Ott's work illustrates the second new aspect that we have already met in Baudrillart's work; discussions of Malthus's theory now generally include an optimistic view of the possibility of human progress, both in the economic and the demographic field, a view which is not out of keeping with the anti-Malthusianism of some socialists.

Fr Alphonse Gratry[52] gives an almost lyrical expression to this view of a more complete development of humanity to master the resources of the world. Whilst manuals of moral theology continued to put forward the traditional view that man was in this world only temporarily, other Catholic thinkers developed an almost messianic vision which attributed moral value to human development.[53] The social teachings of Catholicism were affected by this view, particularly their opposition to the social implications of Malthusian doctrine. As an example of this school, we may cite the Jesuit Matteo Liberatore, one of those who inspired the encyclical *Rerum novarum*.[54]

Between 1860 and 1870, another group of Catholic writers developed an interest in empirical studies which dealt with education and the family. In this context we may cite the works of Monseigneur Dupanloup and the somewhat sentimental work of edification published by Madame Craven in 1866 under the title *Le récit d'une soeur,* which was extremely successful. After 1870, Henri Baudrillart devoted most of his attention to the social aspects of population studies and family institutions, and Frederic Le Play studied the same topics from a somewhat different point of view.

These studies were almost of a polemic character, the ideal of the Christian family was put forward as a remedy for modern disorder. Catholic authors presented an original model of the family to the French public, in which a large family was regarded both as a spiritual ideal and as a response to the challenges posed by modern society. During the first half of the nineteenth century, members of Catholic elite groups ignored the favourable reception that Catholic theorists had given to Malthusian ideas and had large families. After about 1870, the ideal of a large family was proclaimed explicitly and was increasingly adopted by the new *haute bourgeoisie*. The ideal was also in accord with may aspects of rural family patterns in regions where religion continued to have an important influence.[55]

This image of the family as a manifestation of spirituality marked the evolution of ideas which I have described. Account was taken of the fall in the French birth rate and a new ethic of the development of mankind appeared.

Our analysis shows that a knowledge of Malthusian ideas played an important part in forming Roman Catholic opinion. This was true of the *Essay* itself and of the ideas that it generated. The reception given to the ideas of a Protestant English writer, far from being negative, was appreciative and welcoming and this remained the dominant reaction until about 1860. The only reservations expressed related to the wrong interpretation which certain authors put on the concept of moral restraint and which favoured conjugal onanism, and to the conclusions for social policy which Malthus deduced from his general theory. Catholic authors took a different view of this theory, and this distinguished their reaction from that of other economists with a different philosophical or religious background. But, in about 1860, the reservations became stronger, and an anti-Malthusian reaction developed which corresponded with the observed behaviour of practising Catholics which has been analysed by Philippe Ariès.

Notes

1. cf. my contributions to the article "Jésuites" in *Dictionnaire de Spiritualité*, reprinted in *Les Jésuites, Spiritualité et activités*. Beauchesne, Paris, 1974.
2. In particular cf. p.lvi which contains a note about Rossi who was assassinated in Rome in 1848, having been called there to assume ministerial office by Pope Pius IX.
3. Garnier's translation, 1852, p.149.
4. ibid.
5. See the edition of Proudhon's work published by Rivière in Paris, 1923, vol. 1–2, p.349.
6. Garnier, op. cit. in note 3, pp.662–664.
7. F. Martin-Doisy (1857). *Dictionnaire d'économie charitable*, vol. 4, col. 439. We shall have occasion to refer to this work again later.
8. J. T. Noonan (1965). *Contraception. A History of its Treatment by the Catholic Theologians and Canonists*, pp.397–403. Harvard University Press, Cambridge, Massachusetts. These discussions have been summarized by Jean Louis Flandrin (1970) in *L'église et le contrôle des naissances*, pp.79–83. Paris,
9. Garnier also expressed his views on moral restraint in his *Eléments d'économie politique* (1st Edition, 1846) and in *Du principe de la population* (1855), chapter 5, no. 2. In the latter work he relied on Mill and Dunoyer. See the criticism of his views by the Jesuit writer Matteo Liberatore in his *Principes d'économie politique*, published in 1889. (French translation Paris, 1894, pp.128ff.)
10. One of the problems which occupied the attention of Catholic moralists was the attitude to be taken by confessors to married persons: should they question their married penitents about the practice of onanism? The Jesuit Jean Pierre Gury deals with this question in a course of lectures for young priests of his order, which was lithographed between 1840 and 1850 (a copy of this course may be found in the library of the Centre Sèvres, 35 rue de Sèvres, 75006 Paris). He takes the point up again in his *Compendium theologiae moralis* (the first edition cited by Noonan is dated 1850), and he takes account of the reply by the Holy Office in 1851 in later editions (e.g. the ninth edition, dated 1857). His position, both before and after the publication of the Holy Office's reply, is one of extreme reserve. In the 1857 edition of the *Compendium* he states: "The confessor should generally keep silent about these matters, but he cannot always refrain from asking questions." (*Semper ab omni questione abstinere non potest*, op. cit. vol. 2, p.634.)
11. Busenbaum, *Medulla theologiae moralis*. cf. e.g. the 1863 Edition, Paris and Tournai.
12. This thesis is further developed in a more technical argument by the Jesuit Jean Pierre Martin in his *De matrimonio et potestate ipsum dirimendi ecclesiae soli exclusive propria*. (Lyons and Paris, 1844, vol. 1, pp,. 88–89.)
13. Busenbaum, op. cit. in note 11, pp.605 and 609.
14. I refer to Châteaubriand, *Génie du christianisme*, and the writings of

Bonald, Maistre and Lacordaire. cf. my "La famille en France. Esquisse d'histoire religieuse", in *Etudes* (Aug-Sept. 1973), pp.283–301, and "La croissance de l'espèce humaine selon la tradition chrétienne" in *Recherches de Science Religieuse* (1974), pp.321–346.

15. In his article "Célibat" in the *Encyclopédie méthodique* (1788), vol. 1, the Abbé Nicolas Sylvestre Bergier (1718–1790) writes: ". . . it is said that if celibacy became general, the human race would perish. We reply that if marriage were to become general, the earth would not be able to produce sufficient nourishment for its inhabitants; the population does not exist solely to fill the world, but to produce subsistence." (p.285.) This work was reprinted several times, e.g. in 1863 with the help of the Abbé Migne; in his edition, the passage cited will be found in column 733 of volume 1. A posthumous edition of the articles and papers by the former Jesuit François Xavier de Feller (c.1802) is entitled *Cours de morale chrétienne et de littérature religieuse*. He refers to the population problems several times: ". . . the artificial zeal for population . . . which is nothing else than hatred . . . of religious celibacy" (2nd Edition, Paris, 1824, vol. 4, p.163; also vol. 2, pp.136ff, pp.460ff; vol. 3, pp.284ff, 384ff). However, he does not express any fear of overpopulation.
16. op. cit. in note 7, vol. 2, p.226. L. Taparelli (1857). *Traité de droit naturel basé sur les faits*, vol. 2, pp.328ff, Paris and Tournai; the original Italian edition was published in the 1840s.
17. cf. *Traité*, p.338.
18. cf. *Economie politique chrétienne, ou recherches sur la nature et les causes du paupérisme,* vol. 1, p.236. Paris, 1834.
19. Rossi, op. cit. in note 2, p. liv.
20. Villeneuve-Bargemont, op. cit. pp. 207 and 244.
21. op. cit. in note 5, p.348.
22. Book 1, chapters 5 and 6.
23. p.232.
24. p.234.
25. A long note on Pelegrino Rossi can be found in Henri Baudrillart's book *Publicistes modernes*, published in 1862 (though my citations are to the edition of 1863). In this note he provides a eulogy for Rossi's introductory note to the *Essay*, published in 1845 (pp.429–431), though he mentions the objections by Louis Reybaud in his book on modern economists. Baudrillart states that he himself takes a more favourable view of Malthus than does Reybaud. He praises Rossi for having been the first economist to have given attention to the "relation between the family and the production of wealth" (p.443), a subject which became a major preoccupation for Baudrillart. Note that Baudrillart cites with approval a remark by Rossi to someone who informed him of the danger of assassination: ". . . the Pope's cause is God's cause" (p.452); even though Baudrillart is far from taking an ultramontane (Vaticanist) position; for instance, he reproaches Joseph de Maistre for having introduced party politics into religion. *Publicistes modernes*, p.173.

26. The author was Martin-Doisy (cf. Jean Baptiste Duroselle (1967). *Les débuts du catholicisme social en France: 1822–1870.* Paris), writing for the *Encyclopédie théologique*, published by the Abbé Migne. cf. *Dictionnaire d'économie charitable.* (Four volumes, Paris 1857), vol. 4, col. 312.
27. op. cit. in note 26, col. 315.
28. ibid. col. 316. Villeneuve-Bargemont's attitude to Malthus is also summarized in his *Histoire de l'économie politique*, vol. 2, pp.273ff. Paris 1841. (Published by Guillaumin, who edited the *Essay* in 1845 and 1852.)
29. *L'économie chrétienne et le paupérisme.* Book 3, chapter 24.
30. ibid. p.382.
31. ibid. pp.381–382.
32. For the limits to governmental action on the regulation of marriage see p.235.
33. This is not exactly the "dogma" mentioned by Proudhon.
34. op. cit., vol. 16. Paris, 1848, p.82. There are many other articles in the *Encyclopédie catholique* on related topics, e.g. celibacy, continence, marriage, and there is also a brief article on Malthus. In the "General Introduction" (vol. 1, 1840), Edouard Alletz gives a synoptic view of the sciences. In discussing political economy, he contrasts the two laws of growth and adds: "Malthus saw the cause of misery of mankind as the tendency of population to press on the means of subsistence. The truth in this view shows the excellence of the teachings of Christianity which erects a barrier against excessive population by stressing the sanctity of marriage and by counselling celibacy. However, the exaggerated nature of Malthus's calculations has been well shown by Messrs Ricardo, Mill and Everett." loc. cit. pp.lxxxii–lxxxiii.
35. He was a contributor to the journal *L'Atelier* (cf. Duroselle, op. cit.) and published the *Dictionnaire des bienfaits du christianisme* (which followed that of Martin Doisy in the *Encyclopédie théologique*). See col. 1256.
36. 2nd Edition, vol. 26, p. 280. This volume must have been published in about 1860, because between vol. 12 and the last volume, vol. 45, there was a period of ten years (1855–1865). cf. the note at the beginning of the final volume. In the 1852 Edition of the translation of the *Essay*, Garnier reminds us that during the discussion at the National Assembly in 1848, dealing with the right to work, Proudhon wrote a sharp pamphlet directed against the opponents of this right, called *Les Malthusiens* (loc. cit. Note to pp.xi–xii). The reference is to an article by Proudhon published in the *Représentant du peuple* of August 11, 1848 (and reprinted in vol. 17, pp.105–110, of the Collected Works, edited by Lacroix). An excerpt was cited by Jules L. Puech in his edition of *Du principe de l'art* and *La pornocratie ou les femmes dans le monde moderne*. Cf. vol. 11 of the Collected Works in the Rivière édition, Paris, 1939, p.448. The *Pornocratie* was published posthumously in 1875; it contains a number of strong anti-Malthusian passages, and the celebrated sentence: "One does not marry in order to make love. Love for love, love for pleasure. Any woman who thinks in this way is a prostitute." (p.435.)

37. loc. cit. p.285.
38. ibid. pp.286–287.
39. Baudrillart's note on Malthus is a summary of his writings in the *Manuel d'économie politique* (1857, 1864, 1872, 1878). Silvestre de Sacy in his preface to the French translation of Liberatore's *Principes d'économie politique*, notes that Baudrillart's work enjoyed a huge success, particularly in religious circles. The Baron de Sacy was a close relative by marriage of Baudrillart. Liberatore's *Principes* contains a strongly anti-Malthusian chapter; in the French translation (Paris, 1894, pp. 131–132), de Sacy cites a passage from Baudrillart's *Manuel* to provide a French counterpart. A passage which is common to the *Manuel* and to Baudrillart's note in the *Biographie universelle* and which relates to our subject is worth citing: "The religious precept 'Go forth and multiply' does not mean that man should reproduce without thought and without limit. Religion has made a virtue and not a vice of virginity, chastity and continence. Evil does not consist of not giving life to as many children as is physiologically possible, it is evil to give life to children whom one has not the means to feed or educate." (p.430 of the 1872 edition of the *Manuel*, p.283 of the article in the *Biographie*).
40. Baudrillart, op. cit. p.285.
41. ibid.
42. ibid. p.286.
43. The Abbé Dourif was the author of a work entitled *Philosophie chrétienne, loi de la charité*, Paris, 1855. Martin-Doisy attacked him in the *Dictionnaire*, op. cit., vol. 4, col. 439.
44. Baudrillart had noted Ross's interest in the connection between family systems and production and devoted part of his unflagging energy to this subject. The main results of his labours were the three volumes on *Les populations agricoles de la France*, Paris, 1855–1893. The last volume was edited by his son Alfred Baudrillart, the future cardinal, after his father's death. The first volume contains a study on Normandy which had been presented to the Académie des sciences morales et politiques in 1880. In this study, the author pointed out the gravity of Normandy's demographic situation (pp.123–137 of the 1885 edition) and raised the alarm in the Preface. "France is suffering from depopulation." (p.x.) The matter was first raised, he wrote, in a paper on the Département of the Eure, which was presented to the same Academy in 1862 by Louis Passy. Baudrillart presented his own work as a complement to that of Louis Reybaud on the factories, but did not mention Le Play's *Ouvriers européens*. Baudrillart distances himself from Le Play in *La famille et l'éducation en France dans leurs rapports avec l'état de la société*, 1874, pp.82ff.
45. Ott was the author of the *Dictionnaire des sciences politiques et sociales*, (1855), Paris, 3 vols, which preceded the work of Martin Doisy in the *Encyclopédie théologique*. cf. Duroselle, op. cit. for further details on Ott, who was a pupil of Buchez. See the article "Population" in vol. 3, col. 355, of his work.

46. loc. cit. cols. 348–349.
47. ibid. col. 353.
48. ibid. col. 355.
49. ibid. col. 351.
50. ibid. cols. 357–358.
51. ibid. col. 359.
52. See his work entitled *La morale et la loi d'histoire*, Paris, 1868. On this subject see also my paper "Genèse des idées du socialisme et de développement au XIXème siècle". In *Projet*, May 1971, pp.540–552.
53. For instance, the work of the Jesuit Henri Ramière, *Les espérances de l'église* Lyon, 1861, and Paris, 1867.
54. cf. M. Liberatore, *Principes d'économie politique*. The original Italian edition was published in 1889, a French translation appeared in 1894. It was the work of a close kinsman of Henry Baudrillart, the Baron Sylvestre de Sacy, who compared Liberatore's criticism of Malthus with the more measured views of Baudrillart. See the notes to pp.131–132.
55. See my papers "La famille en France" and "L'enfance et la jeunesse dans la société française, 1800–1950" in *Etudes* (Aug.-Sept. 1979, pp.201–213).

12 The Principle of Population and the Teaching of the Roman Catholic Church during the Twentieth Century

P. GUILLAUME

The "mastery of the self" extolled in *Humanae Vitae* inevitably brings to mind the practice of moral restraint as advocated by Malthus. Both Malthus and the Catholic Church needed to reconcile a new view of procreation with the traditional respect given to the precept "Go forth and multiply". The similarity of the problems that they faced leads us to consider the relationship between the present attitude of the Church and that of Malthus.

A mere glance at the encyclical *Mater et Magistra* makes it clear that the Church does not accept the validity of Malthus's Principle of Population, but looks to the benevolence of God and to technical progress to resolve the problems posed by population growth. Malthus's moral vision of the destiny of mankind does not allow him to believe in the possibility of progress nor to rely on the workings of providence. Though he repeatedly affirms his attachment to the rights of the individual, these do not seem to include the rights of the poor, women or children. The Church's doctrine, on the other hand, has for the last half-century recognized the rights of the couple to full development. Taken as a whole, Malthus is concerned with celibacy, the Church with matrimony; the Church believes that human relations should be settled by discussion and dialogue, whereas Malthus's vision is one of an entirely hierarchic society.

Neither view is timeless or unchanging. Malthus's ideas are not derived from the Protestant tradition, but refer to a specific society of

MALTHUS PAST AND PRESENT
ISBN 0-12-224670-5

the past. The position of the Church today, too, must be viewed in the context of an age of growth and of decolonization.

During the nineteenth century, Malthus's position as an Anglican clergyman could be used to make him into an Aunt Sally for Catholic writers. His views, which related to the world as a whole and which were devoid of any analytical content, could be presented as one of the aberrant manifestations of the ethics of the Reformation. But, in an age of ecumenism, it no longer seems incongruous to look at the similarities between Malthus's approach to population problems and those of the Catholic Church of today. Both are concerned with the effects of a troublesome problem for the Christian conscience, a problem which concerns the present and future condition of mankind. And, on two important aspects, there seems to have been a convergence of views. Thus, in *Humanae Vitae,* Paul VI declares:

> But the right and lawful ordering of the births of children presupposes in husband and wife first and foremost that they fully recognize and value the true blessings of family life, and secondly, that they acquire complete mastery over themselves and their emotions. For, if with the aid of reason and free will they are to control their natural drives, there can be no doubt at all of the need for self-denial.[1]

Malthus defines moral restraint as "the only virtuous mode of avoiding the incidental evil arising from this principle [of population]"[2] and adds: "The Christian cannot consider the difficulty of moral restraint as an argument against its being his duty."[3]

Whilst recognizing that no two individuals ever face completely identical situations, it is, nevertheless, clear that in both cases the solution proposed faces the difficulty that it involves mastering a natural human desire, and that this can only come about through the internalization of Christian values. From this fundamental affirmation, there follows a condemnation, both by Malthus and by the Church, of contraceptive practices. In *Humanae Vitae,* they are referred to as the "unlawful ways of regulating birth".[4] Malthus refers to "promiscuous intercourse, unnatural passions, violations of the marriage bed, and improper arts to conceal the consequences of irregular connections [as] preventive checks that clearly come under the head of vice".[5] He also mentions "irregular artifices" as the only means available for men to avoid procreation, in the absence of moral restraint.

There is another similarity between the views. Malthus, in his own time, and the Roman Catholic Church during the present century, have both found difficulty in reconciling new propositions with the traditional interpretation of Scripture. The importance attached to the precept "Go forth and multiply" cannot be denied. But, whilst their difficulty is the same, their reactions are very different. Malthus puts the situation clearly when he writes: "We cannot but conceive that it is an object of the Creator that the earth should be replenished",[6] otherwise man would neither have peopled the earth nor worked the soil and would not have realized God's potential destiny for him, unless he had been subject to necessity, i.e. the pressure of population. The object of the Creator having been achieved, it is, nonetheless, necessary for man to attempt to relieve a pressure which even in God's eyes seems to have lost its purpose. During the discussion of Schema 13 at Vatican II, the Council Fathers debated what importance was to be given to the precept: "Go forth and multiply." Cardinal Suenens during the debate asked if the Church had maintained a perfect balance between "Go forth and multiply" and "they will be two in one flesh". These two scriptural doctrines must illuminate each other. Suenens urged that the Commission set up by the Pope "tell us whether we have excessively stressed the first end, procreation, at the expense of another equally important end, that is growth in conjugal unity".[7]

In both cases, an evangelical precept, which had hitherto been considered absolute, needs to be related to the requirements of the real world, but the methods of doing so and the approaches to the population problem are quite different and, as we shall show, the two views cannot be reconciled.

We should note that Malthus is no longer regarded as the spokesman of the devil by the Catholic Church. Joseph Folliet, whose work achieved a wide circulation, admits this explicitly when he writes:[8]

> Malthus's ideas are not lacking in depth, and his work has the merit of posing, for good or ill, certain questions which are important, and he suggests solutions which need to be discussed and some of which are lacking neither in loyalty, courage, nor even in moral idealism.

However, the author adds: "As regards the Malthusian mentality, this is a different kettle of fish altogether."

From the necessary to the possible

A deliberate postponement of marriage must be accompanied by moral restraint, but mastery of the self relates to married persons. Moral restraint excludes any sexual activity and, therefore, births.

Mastery of self makes it possible to practise "responsible parenthood" and could lead couples "to have no more children for the time being or even for an indeterminate period".[9]

The Church does not regard the regulation of births as a good in itself, even when this is accomplished by lawful means, because the Church does not accept the validity of the Malthusian analysis; it believes the Principle of Population to be in error. This is apparent from the encyclical letter of July 14, 1961, where John XXIII declares:

> Truth to tell we do not seem to be faced with any immediate or imminent world problems arising from the disproportion between the increase in population and the supply of food. Arguments to this effect are based on such unreliable and controversial data that they can only be of very uncertain validity.[10]

The Pope's position is both moderate and firm. He does not claim to provide a scientific analysis but declares a faith in both God and man, as is shown by the following passage:

> Besides the resources which God in his goodness and wisdom has implanted in Nature are well nigh inexhaustible, and He has at the same time given man the intelligence to discover ways and means of exploiting these resources for his own advantage and his own livelihood. Hence, the real solution of the problem is not to be found in expedients which offend against the divinely established moral order and which attack human life at its very source, but in a renewed scientific and technical effort on man's part to deepen and extend his dominion over Nature. The progress of science and technology that has already been achieved opens up limitless horizons in this field.[11]

This is the opposite view to the suspicion of science which the Church used to hold and which was so brilliantly stated by Pius IX. This text preceded the Green Revolution which may be regarded as a positive illustration of the benefits of science which are mentioned in *Mater et magistra* as well as an answer to the obsession with the scarcity of non-renewable resources which was such a feature of the late 1970s.

None of this belief in providence can be found in Malthus's work, nor does he have much faith in the capacity of science to help find a solution. He states on the last pages of his work:

> . . . from a review of the state of society in former periods compared with the present, I should certainly say that the evils resulting from the Principle of Population have rather diminished than increased, even under the disadvantage of an almost total ignorance of the real cause.[12]

But he does not believe that mankind can escape the effects of scarcities and does not question the inevitability of this phenomenon in his view of the world. "Man cannot live in the midst of plenty. All cannot share alike the bounties of nature."[13] Note that Malthus refers to the "bounty of nature" and not to the "bounty of God". This choice of words is almost certainly deliberate as it makes it possible for him to ignore the question of the limits of divine generosity. But, although Malthus does not have great faith in science, he does not ignore scientific progress either. On the last page of his book, he writes: " . . . the views of physical science are daily enlarging, so as scarcely to be bounded by the most distant horizons."[14] Elsewhere in his book he evokes the notion of technical progress and, in particular, shows that the movement of workers from agriculture to industry "will probably be compensated for by improvements in tools and methods"[15] Nor does he neglect the role of fertilizers in the agriculture of his time. But though he is aware of the scientific and technical progress of his age, he does not foresee the consequences of this on the standard of living. Rather than blame a lack of foresight for the misery of his times, he seems to elevate it to the status of a moral principle. Having spoken of the progress of physical science, he continues:

> " . . . it is a melancholy reflection . . . that the science of moral and political philosophy should be confined within such narrow limits, or at best be so feeble in its influence, as to be unable to counteract the obstacles to human happiness arising from a single cause."[15]

Thus, Malthus encloses himself in a moralist perspective which does not permit him to accept that salvation, even material salvation, might be obtained in another way than as a reward for virtue. On several occasions he repeats that he regards virtue and happiness as being indissolubly linked. To dissociate the search for happiness from the practice of virtue, both of which have been joined together by God's will, is nonsensical and scandalous for the Christian conscience.[16]

At the same time Malthus takes a static view of society. All his references relate to rural society which, in his view as in that of all the physiocrats, is the only good society. Manufactures only provide a dangerous illusion of wealth and the development of a merchant class is seen as a threat to a balanced society.

During the twentieth century, the Catholic Church, on the other hand, has come to regard scientific progress as being of benefit to mankind and to be used not only for problems posed by underdevelopment but also for the "mastery of the self" by the individual. In his celebrated declaration of October/November 1951 which legitimized the use of the so-called "natural" method of birth control (the rhythm method based on temperature), Pius XII declared:

> . . . we have affirmed the lawfulness and at the same time the limits — in truth quite broad — of a regulation of offspring. Science, it may be hoped will develop for this method a sufficiently secure base.[17]

In 1963, J.Folliet summarized the hopes put in scientific progress in one sentence: " . . . following scientific and technical discoveries, [the Christian] can envisage both regulation of births and a world population policy."[18] At that period before the Pope had pronounced in *Humanae Vitae* the distinction between artificial and natural methods of birth regulation was often forgotten.

It is because the mastery of the self incorporates the knowledge obtained by science that scientific progress affects the life of the couple. Moral restraint implies total abstinence, but, once marriage had taken place, Malthus in effect said, let nature take its course. Malthus was, therefore, forced to a position in which he viewed human life as being divided into two radically separate parts by marriage. In the Pauline tradition, he regarded marriage as the least objectionable remedy for concupiscence. However, it is clear that the "mastery of the self" would restore integrity to the moral life of the individual.

The individual and his rights: from the necessary to the possible

Malthus does not appear to have been worried by the break in man's life which, paradoxically enough, is brought about by marriage. This may be due to the fundamental ambiguity of his analysis. It is couched in global terms, but although the Principle of Population is said to apply to humanity as a whole, its operation also affects individual behaviour. Having stated at the beginning of his work that his analysis was designed to "investigate the causes that have hitherto impeded the progress of mankind towards happiness",[19] Malthus then declares that "the happiness of the whole is to be the result of the happiness of individuals; and to begin first with them".[20] Repeatedly, Malthus rejects contrary views which, according to him, have been put forward in the interests of the state or the nation. "He has always been told that to raise up subjects for his king and country is a very meritorious act. He has done this and yet is suffering for it."[21] Malthus found this populationism unacceptable, even criminal, because "wealth and the power of nations are of no avail, unless they contribute to the happiness of men".[22]

The Catholic Church, on the other hand, has often regarded group interests as equally important with the happiness of the individual. We may cite the declaration of the French bishops of May 7, 1919, where they stated:

> . . . the principal end of marriage is the procreation of children . . . the war has forcefully impressed upon us the danger to which they [theories and practices that encourage the restriction of births] expose our country. Let that lesson not be lost. It is necessary to fill the spaces made by death if we want France to belong to Frenchmen and to be strong enough to defend herself and prosper.[23]

At first sight the difference between the two positions seems clear. Protestant individualism is opposed by Catholic concern for the interest of the group, However, the situation seems more confused, since after the publication of *Casti Connubii* the Church has re-defined morals relating to the family as stemming from the position of the couple. On the other hand, a reading of Malthus's works soon leads to a perception of the limit of his concept of individual rights. These are subject to numerous exceptions. Though the interest of the nation is not to prevail over that of the individual, the interest of what we may call "social class" will affect those of its members. Thus when writing about the noxious effects of charity, Malthus states: " . . . it is in the highest degree important to the general happiness of the poor that no man should look to charity as a fund on which he may confidently depend."[24] Malthus is quite clear on this point; any action which is designed merely to alleviate an individual's misery, is meaningless: it comforts the donor without helping the recipient. In his hierarchic view of society it is difficult to escape the conclusion that Malthus thinks that the right to happiness of the poor is limited.

When it comes to the rights of women and children, Malthus's views are more ambiguous. In places he has written some almost lyrical passages about family life.

> The evening meal, the warm house, and the comfortable fireside, would lose half their interest, if we were to exclude the idea of some object of affection with whom they were to be shared. We have also great reason to believe that the passion between the sexes has the most powerful tendency to soften and meliorate the human character, and keep it more alive to all the kindlier emotions of benevolence and pity. Observations . . . have generally tended to prove that nations, in which this passion appeared less vivid, were distinguished by a ferocious and malignant spirit . . . If this bond of conjugal affection were considerably weakened it seems probable, either that the man would make use of his superior physical strength and turn his wife into a slave, as among the

> generality of savages . . . and this could hardly take place without a diminution of parental fondness and care which would have the most fatal effect on the happiness of society.[25]

But who were the women and children that Malthus was thinking of? Certainly not those who had been abandoned, for in regard to them Malthus is extremely hard-hearted. Nothing must be done to help abandoned women or foundlings, because it is wrong for society to take over responsibilities which belong to the individual. He adds:

> . . . it may appear hard that a mother and her children who have been guilty of no particular crime themselves should suffer for the ill conduct of the father, but this is one of the invariable laws of nature.[26]

Society must not infringe this law, because "the infant is, comparatively speaking, of little value to the society, as others will immediately supply its place. Its principal value is on account of its being the object of one of the most delightful passions in human nature — parental affection. But if this value be disregarded by those who are alone in a capacity to feel it, the society cannot be called upon to put itself in their place.[27] As regards the injustices suffered by women who have been abandoned, this is only the limiting case of the female condition.

> . . . that a woman should at present be almost driven from society for an offence which men commit nearly with impunity seems undoubtedly to be a breach of natural justice. But the origin of the custom, as the most obvious and effectual method of preventing the frequent recurrence of a serious inconvenience to the community, appears to be natural, though not perhaps perfectly justifiable.[28]

Thus, although the individual's happiness must not be sacrified in favour of the interest or pseudo-happiness of the group, that of women can be abandoned in order that social equilibrium may be maintained. We find in Malthus's work a certain indifference to the fate of wives and children, which Philippe Ariès considers to have been general during the eighteenth and at the beginnings of the nineteenth century. No doubt this explains his complete neglect of the problems faced by the couple. Once a marriage has taken place, it can be left to the random buffetings caused by human and natural desires.

The position of the Catholic Church, on the other hand, results from long reflection on the problems and nature of the family, for whose well-being the happiness of the couple is essential. The traditional view of the family unequivocally subordinated the individual's happiness to the primary end of marriage — procreation. This view was reaffirmed in the encyclical letter *Casti Connubii* of December 31, 1930, where we read:

> The act of wedlock is of its very nature designed for the procreation of offspring; and, therefore, those who in performing it deliberately deprive it of its natural power and efficacy, act against nature and do something which is shameful and intrinsically immoral.
>
> Any use of marriage whatever, which during its exercise is deprived by human artifice of its natural effect to create life is offensive to the law of God and to the natural law, and those who have committed similar acts are guilty to a grave fault.[29]

In this view the sexual act has no significance in itself. However, in the development of thought from this very traditional position, the work of Herbert Doms has played an important part. He distinguishes between the meaning and the purpose of the conjugal act and writes:

> . . . the personal end is the accomplishment of spouses as individuals of the different aspects of their being. The final biological end is procreation and this is distinct from the personal end.[30]

Reflection on this point results in the demand formulated by Cardinal Leger in the discussion on Schema 13 at Vatican II to

> clearly present human conjugal love — I stress human love which involves both the soul and the body — as a true end of marriage, as something good in itself, with its own laws and characteristics. The schema should proclaim that two ends of marriage are equally good and holy.[31]

Thus, from a conception of the duty of the spouses to their group, their family and to society as a whole, there emerges the right to self-fulfilment through the conjugal act, which as recently as 1949 was described by Monseigneur A. Martin in his classic work[32] as a "remedy for concupiscence" and relegated to a secondary objective of marriage.

This synthesis can be seen clearly when parenthood is presented as a duty to educate children within a harmonious family. The Catholic Church, therefore, supports the rights of individuals — both men and women. In so doing, it advocates a very different kind of individualism from that expressed by Malthus.

Such different perceptions of the individual also lead to a different view of personal relations. In the language used in *Mater et magistra,* which was composed at a time when attempts were made to define co-operation, "a worldwide co-operation among men with a view to a fruitful and well-regulated interchange of useful knowledge, capital and manpower"[33] was desirable. This would presuppose a recognition of the equal dignity of both partners. For Malthus, personal relations in a hierarchic society provide an occasion for the exercise of moral authority. He writes: "It is necessary that receipt of charity should be accompanied by a sense of shame".[34] And again:

> . . . the poor should be taught that his own exertions, his own industry and foresight, are his only just grounds of dependence . . . that in the distribution of our charity we are under a strong moral obligation to inculcate this lesson on the poor by a proper discrimination is a truth of which I cannot feel a doubt.[35]

The notion of fraternity is conspicuously absent in Malthus's work. Even in the exercise of benevolence the rights of the rich against the poor are stressed.

Our comparison between moral restraint and mastery of the self is, therefore, brief. One is struck by the historicity of the texts which, separated in time by 150 years, provide two different expressions of Christian thought on the problem of population. In Malthus's work, there is little attempt to conceal a view of society which is inegalitarian, in which women and children play a subordinate role, and which expresses an individualism which is both hesitant and self-contradictory. In *Mater et magistra*, on the other hand, we find the expression of hope in technical progress and the emancipation of mankind. It is a text which is appropriate to an age of growth and of decolonization. In *Humanae Vitae*, this optimism is slightly muted. Perhaps, after some 12 years, the optimism has waned.

Our comparison has shown a number of cross currents which lead us to question classifications which have hitherto been accepted. It is not in the writings of the Protestant clergyman Malthus that we find confidence in the individual or in the possibility that the benevolence of the Creator will become manifest in His works. 150 years later, Catholic teaching consists of faith in man and in his actions in this world. A comparison of these two texts does not confirm the Weberian contrast between the Protestant and the Catholic ethic. One can only return to the historical context in which these two attitudes arose. Both attempt to interpret a common Christian inspiration relating to the human condition, social relations and the rights and hopes of individuals, but the nature of their vision is determined by the period during which they were put forward.

Notes

1. *The Regulation of Birth.* Encyclical Letter of Pope Paul VI. *Humanae Vitae*, 1968, Part III, para. 21.
2. T. R. Malthus, *Essay*, Everyman Edition, vol. 2, p.159.
3. ibid. p.164.
4. cf. ibid. p.15.
5. T. R. Malthus, op. cit. in note 2, vol. 1, p.14.
6. ibid. vol. 2, p.157.
7. cf. J. T. Noonan (1965). *Contraception. A History of its Treatment by the Catholic Theologians and Canonists*, p.503. Cambridge, Massachusetts.
8. J. Folliet (1961). *La régulation des naissances*, p.212. Lethilleux, Paris.
9. *Humanae Vitae*, p.10.
10. Encyclical Letter *Mater et magistra.* Article 188.
11. *Mater et magistra.* Article 189.
12. T. R. Malthus, op. cit. in note 2, vol. 2, p.261.
13. ibid. p.13.
14. ibid. p.262.
15. ibid. p.262.
16. This is no doubt one of the reasons why Malthus rejects the apparently easy solution to the population problem provided by colonization.
17. J. T. Noonan, op. cit. in note 7, p.446.
18. J. Folliet, op. cit. in note 8.
19. T. R. Malthus, op. cit. in note 2, vol. 1, p.5.
20. ibid. vol. 2, p. 169.
21. ibid. p.170.
22. Livre IV, chapter 10, 2nd Edition.
23. J. T. Noonan, op. cit. in note 7, p.422, citing *Documentation catholique* (1919), pp.578–579.
24. T. R. Malthus, op. cit. in note 2, vol. 2, p.220.
25. T. R. Malthus, op. cit. in note 2, vol. 2, p.155.
26. ibid. p.203.
27. ibid. p.203.
28. ibid. p.20.
29. *Casti Connubii.* Article 54.
30. Herbert Doms (1937). *Du sens et de la fin du mariage*. Paris.
31. J. T. Noonan, op. cit. p.502.
32. Mgr A. Martin (1949). *Le mariage,* 472 pp. Rennes.
333. *Mater et magistra*, para. 192.
34. T. R. Malthus, op. cit. in note 2.
35. ibid. pp.220-221.

13 Malthusianism and the Secularization of Jewish Thought: Towards an Historical Psychology of the Religious Mentality

F. RAUSKY

A study of the relationship between Malthusianism and Jewish thought is not new. One of the first to discuss it was, the Utopian Christian socialist, Pierre Leroux, in a book published in 1849[1] that is critical of English political economy (which the author equates with Malthusianism), the Protestant ethic, the new attitudes of the French clergy to economic matters and of Judaism, which Leroux identifies with capitalism, bankers and usury.

However, as regards Jews, Leroux confines himself to the economic activities of the Jewsish *haute bourgeoisie* at the time of the July monarchy. He completely ignores the traditional world view taken by traditional Judaism, as well as the economic role which the Jews played in history. However, he stresses one of the latest tendencies which became apparent in Jewish circles during his time, an acceptance of Malthusianism on the part of a community whose traditional ideology was opposed to such views.

The classical Jewish doctrine on world population

The traditional Jewish attitude to population problems is neither well known nor correctly understood. The verse in the bible in which the Creator blessed Adam and Eve with the words "Be fruitful and multiply and replenish the earth"[2] was considered by Christian exegesis as a divine command, which was binding on the whole of humanity from

MALTHUS PAST AND PRESENT
ISBN 0-12-224670-5

the time of the Creation to that of the Second Coming, when this commandment as well as many others in the Old Testament would become outmoded. However, the interpretation of this verse by the rabbis and talmudic scholars, as well as by the Pharisees is completely different. According to this interpretation the "peoples of the world", that is all non-Jews, were obliged to keep seven commandments, the "commandments of the children of Noah", which included the establishment of courts of justice, the prohibition of blasphemy, idolatry, incest, murder and theft, and the consumption of "any part cut from a living animal". (Prohibitions designed to avoid excessive and unnatural cruelty against other living beings.)[3]

Contrariwise, the reproduction of the species, considered as a religious duty, does not appear in the rabbinical tradition of ethics and universal laws. Moses Maimonides (1135-1234) does not include the duty to reproduce in his tables of universal and eternal divine commandments, included in his codex of Jewish law *Mishne Torah.* Maimonides's text was designed to put an end to all further discussion of talmudic problems which had remained open during the middle ages, and the omission of the duty to reproduce is significant. In this attempt to produce a definitive statement of rabbinical laws, it was established that there was no duty for man to assure the survival of the human species. The verse which appeared in the first chapter of *Genesis* was interpreted as a divine blessing given to man, not as an obligation laid on man by God. It is true that the injunction to be fruitful and multiply is repeated in another part of *Genesis,*[4] but in the context of a blessing given to Noah and his sons after the flood. It can be argued that this injunction may have been more than a benediction, and imposed an obligation on the human species to grow and replenish the earth. But one of the great rabbinical authorities of the eighteenth century, the Turkish Rabbi Judah Rozanes, stated that reproduction must not be taken as a definitive and eternal duty, but was strictly limited to Noah's sons *sensu stricto,* i.e. Sem, Ham and Japhet, who, in the exceptional circumstances of an empty earth after the flood, were commanded to replenish the earth. The force of this commandment lost its strength later.[5]

However, the people of Israel are obliged to reproduce as a religious duty, this being one of the 613 commandments of the Mosaic law.

However, the theological and philosophical problem of man's place in the universe and of his responsibility for the transmission of human life extends beyond formal religious legalism. What part does the benediction on Adam and Eve play in the plan of the Creator and what is its meaning? An explanation by a modern orthodox Jewish theologian, Rabbi Manahem Kasher, explains it thus:

> the instinct and the desire to reproduce the human species is part of the general plan of the Creator and is present in all human beings without distinction of sex, religion, or origin and exists in all periods and civilisations. But for the Jew, the Mosaic law has elevated this instinct and desire to the status of a sacred duty.[6]

These discussions lead us to the fundamental conclusion that the Jewish interpretation of the injunction in *Genesis* differs fundamentally from that of the Christian of whatever persuasion. European writers, who regarded the Old Testament as a pre-Christian book, could only interpret *Genesis* in a pro-natalist sense. This was the interpretation commonly taught in English theological seminaries to the young Thomas Robert Malthus.

Malthus and the Jewish character

There are three significant omissions in Malthus's *Essay*. The first of these refers to the history of religion. Malthus analyses the relationships that exist between religious views, ethics and population growth and reviews the teachings of the great religions and their influence on the development of population. He deals with Islam and its views on the religious value of human multiplication, with the views of St Paul and the Christian churches on marriage, with Zoroastranism and Persian dualism, Menou and Hinduism, Tibetan Buddhism and the doctrine of celibacy. However, in spite of this encyclopaedic knowledge of different religions, Malthus does not once mention Judaism. Alone among the great religions of the world, Judaism is ignored by this divine, who must surely during his Anglican theological education have come across Judaism as the faith of the Old Testament.

We turn to the second omission. Malthus dealt with the correspondence between certain aspects of ancient civilization and population growth, which he regarded as being determined by the social rather than by the natural history of man. After examining the ancient civilizations of the East and the Mediterranean, Malthus deals with Greece (making a special reference to Sparta), Rome, China and Japan. But nowhere does he mention the Jews or the Kingdom of Israel, whose history was well known in England in Malthus's time. In discussing past civilizations, he excludes the study of a people in whose past there was a particularly rich body of teaching on what Malthus called "obstacles to population growth", e.g. the massacre of the first-born in Egypt, the banishment of the ten lost tribes to Assyria, as well as massacres and expulsions.

The third omission is concerned with ethnography. Malthus was an observant traveller and formulated an hypothesis which pervades the whole of the *Essay*. Populations which live on a territory do not reproduce at identical rates, but follow laws which are specific for each ethnic group. Malthus, therefore, opens the door to the study of differential growth rates by ethnicity. Among the societies he mentions are the Christians of Turkey and Persia, the Beduin in Syria, the natives of America, the Samoyeds and Ostiakhs of Siberia, the Uzbeks, Tartars, Turkmen, Kalmuck, Mongols and Kirghiz of Central Asia, the inhabitants of Tierra del Fuego, the Andaman Islanders and the inhabitants of New Holland. But, once again there is no mention whatever of the Jews at a time when the Jews of Eastern and Central Europe, Asia, North America and North Africa could be easily identified as a specific ethnic group with characteristics different from those of other peoples living in these countries. This omission is even more curious when it is remembered that at the time when Malthus was at the peak of his intellectual development, there was also a population explosion among the Jews.

Another curious fact must be mentioned. The Old Testament is cited in the *Essay* only once and without any reference to the Jews. Malthus uses it to illustrate the "obstacles to population among the ancient inhabitants of Northern Europe".

It is not difficult to explain this prudence on Malthus's part. He avoided any mention of Judaism or the doctrine of the Old Testament in order to forestall any attempt to regard his work as a theological treatise, for he wished to escape from the interminable religious polemics on the doctrine of population, which might have been an embarrassment for the diffusion of his ideas.

An analysis of the hypotheses contained in the *Essay* leads to one incontestable conclusion: the doctrine of the *Essay* is completely at variance with traditional Jewish thought. We have mentioned that the imperative duty to reproduce does not, in Jewish religious law, apply to the "peoples of the world", i.e. non-Jews, but that according to the classical Jewish view the attitude to reproduction is positive, and reproduction is regarded as one of God's blessings for his creatures. The pessimism which is implicit in the Malthusian view indirectly questions the wisdom of the Jewish attitude. Far from leading to a flowering of life on earth, human reproduction becomes a threat to the future of humanity, because of the biological and ecological constraints. It is not, therefore, surprising that there should have been disagreement among Jews relating to Malthusian theories and to neo-Malthusianism. The Jews were often a target of the new ideologies of the modern age, and some Jewish intellectuals who had broken with the tradition of the synagogue and of their elders found in Malthus (probably in spite of himself) a base on which to construct a new theology. Thus, an Anglican clergyman, whose views during his lifetime were not generally known among enlightened Jews, became after his death the major source of a new secular ideology and anti-traditional views for the Jewish intelligentsia, in the *Kulturkampf* which divided the Jewish community during the nineteenth century.

Malthusianism in a Jewish environment : Max Nordau

As an example of the connection between Malthusian ideas and the critics of a religious ideology, we may cite one of the great intellectuals of the late nineteenth and early twentieth centuries, Max Nordau (1849-1923), physician, psychiatrist, psychologist, sociologist, philosopher, novelist, poet, dramatist and journalist, who became one of the leaders of the Zionist movement and was a friend and collaborator of Theodor Herzl. Nordau was the archetypical Jewish intellectual who had abandoned the tradition of religious observance and had broken with the doctrine of the synagogue. The son of an eminent enlightened but orthodox rabbi, Nordau found his gurus in Darwin and Malthus, even though he was doubtful about some aspects of their "fatalism". In a celebrated book which he published in 1885[7] Nordau included an essay entitled "A Look Ahead", which was inspired by Malthus and which contained a prophesy based on science dealing with man's future, and which could be considered as an antithesis to the Messianic view, and to give a secular version of the end of the world.

The views he put forward were the following. As a result of migration, powerful nations will either succumb or become the masters of large territories. Only a few great nations will be able to survive, as a result of the "innate vital force of their people." These nations will live at peace, but they will face the problem of earning their daily bread. "There will come a time when in spite of new and improved techniques it will no longer be possible to increase the fertility of the soil, and the problem of earning their daily bread will become a spectre for the nation." Though Nordau admits the possibility of scientific and technological progress, such progress can only serve to delay the fatal day, and he puts the question: "Where then shall we be able to find subsistence for the adults whose lives have been lengthened by the progress of medical science and for the hundreds of thousands of children who are born each year with an insatiable appetite?" He does not think that there will be a decline in the birth rate, because those European peoples which have survived violent wars will possess a biological force superior to those of others, who will face lower standards of living and will inevitably disappear. This shows the limits of Nordau's scientism and optimism: neither a "green revolution" nor a limitation of births will solve the problem of subsistence in the long run. A biologically strong people with a predisposition to survive will inevitably and irresistibly grow in numbers, and such growth cannot be prevented by human artifice.

> It is no accident that some nations are numerous and others weak. In my view, even in the animal kingdom, numbers are a characteristic and essential feature of each species. The fact that the Celts have disappeared almost everywhere, that the number of Greeks never exceeded a few million, that the Magyars, the Albanians, the Basques and the Romansch people of Switzerland have remained low in numbers, proves that these peoples were not possessed of greatness.

International wars, territorial expansion and domination are the result of forces of biological instinct, the struggle for survival in which the fittest survive, applied to the population of the world. This argument demonstrates the influence of Darwin and Malthus on Nordau.

These instinctive forces will lead to a modification of the map of the world and of the geographical distribution of populations. This modification will proceed without any pity for the weak; this is the only proper interpretation of history. Nordau rejects the Jewish traditional teaching on war and the belief in an "immanent justice" which would result in the strong and mighty being humbled and the meek being restored to their legitimate rights when there would be peace. "To weep for the unjust destruction of a weak people", he says, "is sentimentalism. A people will disappear when it lacks the inborn vital force which will be sufficiently strong to overcome the ravages of the environment." (There is here a possible relation with the Freudian concept of the death instinct in which death is seen as resulting from an endogenous process of self-destruction.) The only notion which Nordau retains from traditional Jewish thought is that of historical laws. According to him there is a strict determinism in human history; chance does not play an important part in his system. In fact one of the objections that he raises against Darwinism is that the unscientific concept of chance plays too important a part in the system.

After the destruction of a number of small nations, a limited number of large European states will have been constituted for "the supreme deployment of all organic forces", and there will be a period of peace. However, this peace does not result, as in the traditional messianic Jewish view or in the prophetically inspired vision of pacifism, from a recognition of the legitimate rights of others. It is not founded on altruistic love, but is a kind of equilibrium brought about by understanding and the creation of a "new nature". The territory of each state becomes sacred and exclusive, because it has been determined by an equilibrium of forces and the fear of reprisals against aggression. Therefore, the territory of each state will be regarded as given "an unchanging natural phenomenon . . . as immutable as the Continent and the oceans, and a Russian would think it as impossible to invade German soil, or a German to invade Italian soil as a bird would think of living in the water or a fish in the air".

However, this relatively peaceful phase of economic and cultural development of the surviving Great Powers will once again be faced with the problem of finding subsistence, and the situation will now become more difficult, as a solution through war and conquest will no longer be possible. Therefore, the "surplus population of Europe will spread to where there is least resistance . . . the coloured races . . . fatally condemned to be dispossessed and to be exterminated by the white races". Because of necessity, the spiritual and moral conscience of the West will be appealed to in vain, the "inferior races" are lost and though "missionaries may bring them as many bibles and external trappings of Christianity as they like . . . the white races will be better equipped in the struggle for existence . . . and if they need the lands which at present belong to the more primitive peoples in order to survive, they will take them without any hesitation whatsoever". In the end Europeans will replace the native populations everywhere, but the problem of hunger will once again become acute, because the demographic explosion of the European peoples will continue and Europe will no longer be capable of feeding its excess population. When that happens, the Europeans will eliminate the white colonists in the tropics who had replaced the coloured peoples, for these settlers "will have been weakened by the climate, and after some generations will become an inferior section of humanity". The populations of white settlers will be destroyed systematically, and the law of least resistance will operate, for the descendants of the original settlers will be but pale shadows of their ancestors. "The equator will become like a steam cauldron in which human flesh will be melted down. We have here a renewal of the old story of Moloch." The peoples of the moderate zone will cast some of their children into the fire and will thus be able to obtain a share of prosperity and development. But this, too, will not last foreever, because Nordau believes in a continuous shrinking of the fertile surface of the globe through cooling. This hypothesis probably stems from the second law of thermodynamics, which predicts the end of life. The earth will become progressively colder, and Northern Europe will be left in the throes of a permanent and irreversible ice age and will have to be abandoned as an area for human habitation. How, then, are the peoples to survive? Should they invade the equatorial regions and exterminate their populations, as the original settlers were exterminated and the native populations before them? This will not be possible, because the torrid zones' climate will have changed and they will no longer be "the strangler who kills with a caress"; instead, they will have become the feeders of the human race. There will be a new equatorial civilization, strong, energetic and prepared to fight for its survival. The Nordic peoples who had remained in their original countries will suffer from famines which will become more serious as the earth cools; they will, therefore, look for new lands and will try to vanquish the populations of the equatorial countries. But they will be too late. All the best land will already have been occupied and guarded by members of a new and strong race which has flourished and become more powerful, whereas they themselves will have been weakened by cold and hunger. And Nordau ends with a terrifying description of man's future:

> "...they will camp at the borders of the magic circle like a pack of wolves and will gaze with wild and hungry eyes at the strong and abundant life in front of them, but whenever they cross the border in search of prey, they will be repulsed into their icy desert by the strong masters of the new and blessed earth."

It would be difficult to find a text which is more opposed to the traditional Jewish view of the future of humanity; neither peace, justice nor brotherhood are the fate of mankind, and all this because of the problem of finding subsistence for the population, a problem which is basic to all history. Nordau provides a lucid and disillusioned view of human history as a perpetual conflict. This idea is not completely alien to Jewish tradition, but this tradition does not accept that human nature is unchangeable, nor does it accept the inevitability of continuing conflict. In Nordau's view, the belief in a final victory of peace and reason is a dangerous illusion based on wishful thinking, rather than an observation of the real nature of human relations.

Nordau believes that this illusion must be overcome by increased knowledge and by abandoning the forms and practices of all religions.

The part played by Malthusian doctrine in this is quite clear: it provides a refutation of the conventional lies put forward by religion on the nature of human civilization, a lie which denies the true nature of men and which suggests a solution to the population problem which is absurd, Utopian and unrealizable. It is not difficult to show that this reconstruction of Malthusian doctrines differed from the beliefs of Thomas Malthus himself. However, among the Jews the only aspect of Malthusianism which was regarded as important was the doctrine put forward in the *Essay*; the remainder of Malthus's work which occupied the attention of Christian writers with a social conscience was ignored. The doctrine put forward in the *Essay* was regarded as a scientific refutation of Jewish traditional thinking about population, in which large families were regarded as a blessing and an indication of divine favour. The reaction of traditional Jews who remained faithful to the doctrine of revelation and held it to be compatible with the results of modern science was one of silence. To some extent this may have been due to the fact that many were unaware of Malthus's doctrine during the first decades of the nineteenth century, and others thought that the struggle between Malthusians and anti-Malthusians only concerned Christians, regarding Malthus as a clergyman who was opposed to traditional Christian doctrine. But there was also an absence of theoretical arguments with which Malthus's views could be refuted. Among the Jewish intelligentsia of the nineteenth century, those who studied and critically analysed Malthus's thought were generally Jews who had become assimilated to the cultural environment of their host society, who had been converted to Christianity, or who were indifferent to any religion, e.g. David Ricardo and Marl Marx.

Neo-Malthusian doctrines, on the other hand, were a matter of continuous debate among the traditional rabbis. In orthodox Judaism abortion is permitted where there is a danger to the life or the physical or mental health of the mother, but is not permitted as a means of population control. Some contraceptive methods are permitted in specific circumstances (e.g. where the mother is too young, sick or nursing another child), but neither abortion nor contraception is permitted as a solution to the problem of world population.

Towards an historical psychology of religious mentality

The reception of Malthus's doctrines by the Jews may be used to illustrate a problem in collective psychology. Are religious views and cultural sensibilities the results of previous ethical norms which explain human behaviour, reactions and attitudes, or is the dominant ethic itself the result of a mentality which explains and determines it? Pierre Leroux believes that ethnic factors explain why Jews and Protestants accepted and developed the doctrine which he pejoratively called Malthusianism and by which he meant the dominant commercial spirit of the modern capitalist bourgeoisie. Race lies at the origin of the collective psyche and has determined the Jewish and Protestant ethic. He regards Jews as the embodiment of the capitalist mentality, "industrial individualists and egotists" who use "money to dominate", eternal "adorers of the Golden Calf", Shylocks who measure out their pound of human flesh. Only thus can their fierce egotism in financial and commercial dealings be explained. And a similar explanation holds for their acceptance of Malthusianism, because such acceptance leads to doctrines which justify the poverty of the masses, who are held responsible for their own miseries by overbreeding. In our times, Leroux writes, the Jewish spirit embodied by Judas Iscariot is exemplified by English political economy inspired by Malthus whose primary care is for the benefit of capital.[8]

Leroux finds a connection between the Jewish and the Protestant ethic; both are manifestations of the modern capitalist mentality. He writes:

> It is certain that Calvin and other Protestant theologians who approved lending money at interest, under the pretext of commerce, or what the economists call capital, did so for the same reasons that Jews were allowed to lend to non-Jews by Moses. Protestant states were in a situation of open or concealed warfare against the more powerful and older Catholic countries. To sap the energy of the Catholic countries through usury was a good way to achieve domination. I would not go so far as to suggest that the theologians of the second era of Protestantism preferred the Old Testament to the gospel, or drew greater inspiration from the licence that God granted to the Jews, rather than by the divine spirit found in the gospels, because of the hardness of their hearts, but I do suggest that the spirit of profit, avidity and avarice which animated the descendants of the Saxon and Norman pirates could and did have an influence on Protestant theologians.[9]

Thus, Leroux believes that Protestants accepted the Malthusian doctrine for the same reason as the Jews. Jews and Protestants are seen as the embodiment of an economic and self-seeking individualism, and this explains the popularity of a doctrine which justified individualism and condemned social solidarity, which objected to any action being taken to mitigate the effects of poverty and which criticized philanthropy and encouraged selfishness among the possessing classes.

Leroux's anti-Jewish and anti-Protestant views get the better of his capacities as a scientific observer and researcher.

The justified discredit into which racial theories have fallen includes Leroux's hypotheses. If the hypothesis of an ethnic basis for the Protestant ethic seems altogether improbable, the same is true of a similar hypothesis about the Jews, particularly if account is taken of the varied origins of modern Jewry.

An hypothesis which is less adventurous is to be preferred: at times of crisis and social disruption new ideologies appear to replace older ways of thinking in order to take account of new or newly recognized realities. It is no accident that those Jews who were profoundly influenced by Malthus were also influenced by Comte, Spencer, Darwin, Taine, the positivist school of philosophers and by scientific empiricism. But Malthusianism is not just a theory for modern Jews, it is a crystallization of new forms of behaviour in conjugal, family and social life. The Jewish family is seen as being too large; poverty is caused by a dangerous excess of births, too many or too closely spaced pregnancies lead to premature ageing or ill-health among Jewish women. What was once regarded as a blessing is now seen as a curse. Nordau now abandons science fiction and gives practical advice to Jewish parents, because their families are too large to feed or educate. Malthusian practices become general in the Jewish community in order to restrain the size of families, delay marriage and space or reduce the number of pregnancies. A society in crisis accepts a new ideology of transition and jettisons the values of yesteryear.

Notes

1. P. Leroux (1849). *Malthus et les économistes*. Paris. The first of four essays in this book is entitled "Les juifs, rois de l'époque".
2. Gen. 1, 28.
3. Babylonian Talmud. *The Treatise of Sanhedrin* 56a.
4. Gen. 9, 1.
5. See his commentary on the *Mishne Torah* of Maimonides. *Mishne la melekh*, chapter 10, no. 7, para. 20.
6. Rabbi Menaham Kasher, *Torah Shlema* I, p.167.
7. M. Nordau. *Paradoxe der conventionellen Lügen*.
8. op. cit. in note 7, p.78.
9. ibid. p.42.

14 Malthus as a Theologian: The *First Essay* and the Relation between Political Economy and Christian Theology*

A. M. C. WATERMAN

"Political economy, without God" declared Dr Pusey, "would be a selfish teaching about the acquisition of wealth, making the larger proportion of mankind animate machines for its production".[1] The problem has always been, however, just how to add "God" to "political economy" in any way that continues to make sense of both.

That the difficulty persists is due, in some part, to the failure of theologians to elucidate the relation between the knowledge afforded by the social sciences, if any, and that afforded by Christian theology. The need has not always gone unnoticed. Whately accepted the Drummond Chair at Oxford precisely in order to combat the prejudice against political economy "as unfavourable to Religion".[2] Nearly a century earlier, Bishop Butler's domestic chaplain, Josiah Tucker, had sought to reconcile the theory of international trade with "Divine Providence".[3] But neither made any serious philosophical attempt to meet that need. The historical importance of the last two chapters of Malthus's *First Essay* (1798), therefore, resides in their attempt to supply such an elucidation, which, though unsuccessful, remains to this day the most ambitious and — in the expurgated version by J.B. Sumner[4] — the most influential.

*The Author wishes to acknowledge his obligation to the Christendom Trust for financial support under a Maurice Reckitt Fellowship at the University of Sussex, 1979–1980. He is also grateful to the Rev. J. Drury, Mrs Patricia James and Professor Donald Winch for helpful comments on a preliminary draft, and also to Mr John Pullen for allowing him to see and make use of an unpublished draft of his own paper on Malthus's theology. Neither the Christendom Trust nor any of those who have helped him are to be held responsible for the views expressed in this paper, which are those of the author alone.

MALTHUS PAST AND PRESENT
ISBN 0-12-224670-5

Malthus's own generation drew a veil over his theology. As late as 1807 a clergyman besought Bishop Watson of Llandaff to answer Malthus since no representative of the Church of England had as yet spoken.[5] His enemies preferred to challenge his economics and politics and the very few who attacked the theology of the *First Essay*[6] addressed the wrong targets. His friends appeared to agree with "the opinions of some distinguished persons in our Church" who persuaded Malthus to expunge Chapters XVIII and XIX from subsequent editions of the *Essay*.[7] Somewhat later, James Bonar paid proper attention to what he described as the "moral philosophy" of Malthus[8] but surmised that "perhaps the great economist went beyond his province in attaking the problem of evil".[9] Since Bonar, Malthus's theology has been almost completely ignored. Keynes was interested solely in Malthus's anticipation of his own economic doctrines.[10] A recent article by John Pullen attempts to display the significance of Malthus's theological ideas for a proper understanding of the *First Essay* but does not appraise his method or its results.[11] Despite its title, the recent note by D.L. LeMahieu is really more concerned with the implications of the theology for liberal political thought than with the theology itself.[12] The latest biography merely reports a selection of the contemporary notices.[13]

It is, therefore, my purpose in this paper to evaluate the concluding chapters of the *First Essay* as a serious contribution to Christian theology. The first part examines the problem, and the techniques which Malthus employed for its solution; the second part is a critical appraisal of that solution; and the third part contains a brief account of the subsequent history of Malthusian theology.

I

As Le Mahieu correctly notes, Malthus attempted to construct a "theology of scarcity".

It is now generally acknowledged that the concept of "scarcity" lies at the heart of economic theory.[14] According to the positivist, "mainstream" school of thought, economic models which yield falsifiable hypotheses can be shown to rest upon certain "axioms of choice". Individuals are conceived to choose between alternative goods, implying that both (or all) may not be had. Where there is no choice, either because there is no freedom or no scarcity, economizing behaviour — and, therefore, the science which treats of that behaviour — is impossible. Scarcity is thus a necessary though not a sufficient condition of economics.

This idea was by no means uppermost in the minds of the early political economists however, who tended rather to think in terms of "affluence" and "the wealth of nations". Although the law of diminishing returns — an implication of scarcity — had been formulated precisely by Turgot and was known to French contemporaries of Adam Smith[15] it was the Principle of Population which dramatized for Malthus and his generation the dominance of scarcity in human affairs, and which earned for political economy the title of the dismal science.

Now "the constant pressure of distress on man from the difficulty of subsistence",[16] a proposition thrown up by the "new learning" of political economy, is in seeming conflict with a belief in the omnipotence and benevolence of God upheld by the "old learning" of Christian theology. It was an unintended consequence, therefore, of his demolition of Godwin's utopian fancies that Malthus should be confronted with a new and formidable manifestation of the "problem of evil": how can scarcity (and, therefore, political economy) be reconciled with the existence of a God who is both good and all-powerful?

Malthus approached his problem from the standpoint of natural theology alone, rigorously eschewing any reliance upon "revelation". "It seems absolutely necessary, that we should reason up to nature's God, and not presume to reason from God to nature."[17] This because it is "in the book of nature, where alone we can read God as he is".[18] Although he concedes that "one or two exceptions" of a miraculous kind may have occurred,[19] he insists throughout the *First Essay* that God works according to "general laws".[20] Even those supposed miracles which have occurred may be susceptible of a naturalistic explanation, not excluding the Resurrection itself.[21] "It seems absolutely necessary that the Supreme Being should always act according to general laws" for "the constancy of the laws of nature . . . is the foundation of the faculty of reason".[22] But the sovereignty of natural law is necessary not only for rationality. In a strikingly modern passage[23] Malthus argues that miraculous intervention into nature would be subversive of moral freedom. Human "autonomy", as contemporary theologians would say, is axiomatic.

Malthus owed his epistemology to Abraham Tucker's life-work, *The Light of Nature Pursued*[24] with which he had become familiar as a young man.[25] Tucker began with the premiss that "reason cannot work without materials, which must be fetched from nature"; that we must "begin with the things lying nearest to us . . . which must help us to investigate others more remote"; and that "nature exhibits nothing abstracted to our view, the abstract must be learned from the concrete".[26] Not only the epistemological premises, moreover, but most of the other ingredients of Malthus's apologetic are to be found in Tucker. Indeed, the charge of plagiarism which has so often been brought, rather unfairly, against his political economy[27] could be advanced with about as much justice against his theology.

Tucker's object was to discover a rational basis for ethics. In Volume I (*Human Nature,* in two volumes) he shows that without the prospect of an after-life there are no compelling grounds for right behaviour. His Volume II (*Theology,* in three volumes) attempts to demonstrate, depending as far as possible on "the mere light of reason", that human immortality, and thus the "Re-Enlargement of Virtue"[28] is possible. Crucial to Tucker's vast system is his concept of "mind", in which he locates human identity;[29] which is "spiritual" rather than "corporeal";[30] related to, but not be be confused with the "vulgar" notion of the "soul";[31] and of which "from (her) individuality and distinct existence . . . may be inferred her perpetual duration".[32] Tucker considered the problem of evil, and although he concedes it to be "an inscrutable mystery" which will never be penetrated "as long as there shall be men on earth",[33] he is led to suppose that "God created evil as well as good",[34] that evil may be conceived as a kind of estate tax on happiness,[35] and finally that it is "probably the use of evil . . . to excite the mind to bestir herself in avoiding it".[36] He concludes his discussion of immortality, mind and the problem of evil in this way:

> . . . we may gather from the perishable nature of our bodies and the durable nature of our minds . . . from the method constantly taken by Nature to bring her work to perfection slowly through several stages, . . . from the nature of the mind that it was designed for action, from the nature of action that evil is a necessary inducement to excite it, . . . that a very little quantity of evil may suffice to set the spiritual world in motion.[37]

Although less careful than his master in observing the nice distinctions between "mind", "spirit" and "soul", it was Tucker's vision of the evolution of mind under the stimulus of evil which Malthus took over and made the central feature of his own theodicy. Rejecting the generally accepted doctrine, powerfully advanced by Butler[38] and Paley,[39] that human life is a state of probation, Malthus treats it instead as "the mighty process of God . . . for the creation and formation of mind; a process necessary, to awaken inert, chaotic matter, into spirit; to sublimate the dust of the earth into soul".[40] The "original sin in man" is thus "the torpor and corruption of chaotic matter, into which he may be said to be born".[41] Now since "the wants of the body" provide "the first great awakener of the mind",[42] the scarcity resulting from the Principle of Population has a purpose: for "evil seems necessary to create exertion; and exertion seems evidently necessary to create mind".[43] Not only does the physical evil of scarcity serve to effect the creation of "mind" (that is, in Tucker's conception, genuine human beings) but the attendant "sorrows and distressess" by an analogous process, "generate all the Christian virtues";[44] or, if not, by causing some to produce moral evil, excite "disgust and abhorrence" in others: whence "it seems highly probable that moral evil is absolutely necessary to the production of moral excellence".[45] This neat simultaneous solution of the problems of physical and moral evil still leaves one end untied, however. Those "vicious instruments" who "misapply their talents" and create moral evil may be doing *others* a service: but "both reason and revelation seem to assure us, that such minds will be condemned to eternal death".[46] This raises the question, of course, of why a good and foreknowing God would create human beings predestined to damnation.

Tucker had questioned, "the absolute perpetuity" of divine punishment but had been at pains to argue that this in no way lessened "the discouragement against evil-doing".[47] Malthus's Cambridge tutor, William Frend, had abandoned belief in eternal punishment, along with much else, on becoming a Unitarian in 1787,[48] as had his private tutor, Gilbert Wakefield, some years earlier.[49] Though Otter discounted the influence upon Malthus of "the persons to which he had been entrusted for the specific purposes of education"[50] the approximation of their views on this particular matter to that of Tucker may well have weighed with him.

At any rate, Malthus firmly rejected the possibility that any of "the creatures of God's hand can be condemned to eternal suffering".[51] His actual solution, however, seems to owe nothing to these three but rather to be original, not to say eccentric.

Malthus takes it to be a "moral certainty" that in the process of creation of mind "many vessels will come out of this mighty creative furnace in wrong shapes"; it is inconceivable to "our natural conceptions of goodness and justice" that God would punish these; "it is consonant to our reason" that those vessels which emerge with "lovely and beautiful forms, should be crowned with immortality"; and that those who are "misshapen" (that is, "whose minds are not suited to a purer and happier state of existence") "should perish, and be condemned to mix again with their original clay".[52] Malthus thus commits himself to "annihilationism" which Tucker had considered and rejected[53], and also to a pair of still more doubtful propositions: that God may require *time* to achieve his ends;[54] and that even then, God may and in fact does make mistakes.

The upshot of the matter is, nonetheless, a conclusion which paraphrases Tucker: "We have every reason to think that there is no more evil in the world, than what is absolutely necessary as one of the ingredients in the mighty process".[55] Like Tucker moreover,[56] Malthus, seeing evil as the divinely ordained — or at least permitted — spur to human achievement, supposes that the proper moral response is engagement: "Evil exists in the world, not to create despair, but activity. We are not patiently to submit to it, but to exert ourselves to avoid it".[57]

II

In order to evaluate Malthus's theology both fairly and usefully, it is first necessary to specify the criteria to be used. I shall take it that three distinct sets of criteria ought to be employed in appraising the theological contribution of earlier generations. In the first place, we must inquire whether, in view of his own assumptions, the author is internally consistent and successful in achieving his announced purpose. Secondly, we must consider whether those assumptions, and necessary inferences from them, are consistent with the contemporary canons of orthodoxy by which the author was bound. Finally, if the contribution is to have any applicability in our own day, we must ask whether it meets the standards both of intellectual coherence and of orthodoxy now current. The ideal theologian would satisfy all three sets of criteria. It is sufficient for serious consideration to satisfy the first, and either the second or the third. I shall argue that Malthus fails on all three counts.

In applying the criteria of internal consistency and success within his own terms of reference we must note first that the cogency of the theological portions of the *First Essay* is weakened by self-contradiction and confusion, and, secondly, that the upshot of Malthus's argument is to render vacuous the concept of "evil".

Malthus cites Locke as saying that "the endeavour to avoid pains, rather than the pursuit of pleasure, is the general stimulus to exertion in this life"[58] whence "evil seems necessary to create exertion; and exertion seems necessary to create mind". There are three objections to Malthus's use of this idea. In the first place, it does not seem to make sense to hold that evil, which must be perceptible by humans in order to be effectual, is God's way of creating that "mind" by which, we must suppose, the evil is alone perceived. In the second place, Malthus elsewhere asserts that virtuous acts are produced by *love*, not *fear*,[59] despite his general theme, consistent with the "creation of mind" hypothesis, that God compels us to action of any kind by threat of starvation. In the third place, Malthus also tells us that *self-love* is actually ("the mainspring of the great machine"[60] without relating this motive clearly either to *love* or to *fear*. Other less damaging contradictions occur. The foreknowledge of God is used to rule out the "state of probation" theory of evil, but not the "creation of mind" theory, in which God can and does make mistakes.[61] The claim that human misery proceeds "from the inevitable laws of nature, and not from any original depravity in man"[62] appears to conflict with the assertion that "the original sin of man, is the torpor and corruption of the chaotic matter, into which he may be said to be born"[63] which is the cause of God's allowing evil. And Malthus's approval of the middle class[64] seems inconsistent with the view that "uniform prosperity" tends rather "to degrade than exalt the character".[65]

More serious than any of these, however, is Malthus's failure to achieve his endeavour to "vindicate the ways of God to man" within his own conceptual framework, even granting its coherence. Unlike Butler, Paley or even Abraham Tucker, Malthus was obsessed with the heuristic power and efficacy of natural theology. His more professional and more cautious predecessors carefully hedged their treatment of evil, and were not ashamed to fall back, when necessary, upon the authority of sacred scripture.[66] But Malthus chose solely to "reason up to nature's God" and so was betrayed into a non-solution of the problem of evil. For in his system everything that is commonly thought of and experienced as "evil" has to be regarded as a necessary part of the providence of God, and hence is not *really* an "evil" at all, but a "good".

Writing in 1885 James Bonar felt able to declare that "we cannot find anything in the writings of Parson Malthus inconsistent with his ecclesiastical orthodoxy":[67] but this generous view is impossible to sustain if we submit the theological content of the *First Essay* to serious examination. The criteria we ought to apply, I believe, are first, the Thirty-Nine Articles of the Church of England to which Malthus would have subscribed formally on at least three occasions; and secondly the Vincentian canon — we must hold as *de fide* only those articles *quod semper, quod ubique, quod ab omnibus creditum est* — which as Manning and Marriot[68] and More and Cross[69] have attempted to show was the first principle of Anglican theology from the Reformation to the Tractarians. According to these standards Malthus would seem to be clearly heterodox on four points and of doubtful orthodoxy on a number of others.

In the first place, Malthus, by following too closely Tucker's speculations on the immortality of "mind" whilst ignoring the way in which the latter carefully hedges his position,[70] actually denies the resurrection of the body.[71] This is a mere slip, however, and is in no way essential to his argument. Far more serious is the denial of the incarnation implied by his uncompromising devotion to natural theology. By asserting that "it seems *absolutely necessary* that we reason up to nature's God"[72] he seems to deny the possibility of revealed knowledge; his assumption that "in the book of nature . . . *alone* we can read God as he is"[73] contradicts the New Testament teaching that God is known in and through the Son.[74] Malthus's decision to abstract from the incarnation is consistent with his soteriology. The key passage here is: "Evil exists in the world, not to create despair but activity. We are not patiently to submit to it, but to exert ourselves to avoid it."[75] Because Malthus has emptied the concept of evil of all content. Christ is redundant in his soteriology, which no doubt explains why he is never mentioned or alluded to in the entire *Essay*. Insofar as there is any need for or possibility of "salvation" at all in Malthus's system, it is a Pelagian "salvation by works": "it is . . . the duty of every individual, to use his utmost efforts to remove evil from himself". The last point on which Malthus was unmistakeably heterodox was his denial of the divine omnipotence: God needs time to create man;[76] "evil seems necessary . . . to create mind";[77] God makes mistakes;[78] and "the works of the creator are not formed with equal perfection".[79] Ignoring Tucker's speculation that in view of the problem of evil "we must suppose that there is some other attribute (of God) to moderate between goodness and omnipotence",[80] Malthus chose rather to hold that the traditional attributes "must be in some respects limited".[81]

The foregoing opinions are demonstrably inconsistent with Articles IV and VIII; II; XV, XXXI and IX; and I respectively. Moreover, the doctrines of the resurrection of the body, the incarnation, the atonement, and the omnipotence of God would almost certainly have been held by Anglican theologians of Malthus's day to be authenticated by the Vincentian canon. It is remarkable, moreover, that even his freethinking economist friends, David Ricardo and James Mill, could see clearly that Malthus's position on the last of these matters was simply Manichean.[82]

On three other matters, where the generally accepted teaching is neither specified by the Articles nor guaranteed by the Vicentian test, Malthus's teaching is of doubtful orthodoxy. His doctrine of "man as he really is, inert, sluggish, and averse from labour"[83] seems to call in question the *imago dei*.[84] His view of original sin[85] precludes prelapsarian bliss — and even existence — and seems to imply that creation itself overcomes original sin, which takes away the need of any further redemption. And his "annihilationist" theory of divine punishment,[86] which despite Frend's *Thoughts on Subscription*[87] is not literally ruled out either by the Articles or the Athanasian Creed, is, nevertheless, at variance with what was to remain for another half-century the generally accepted Anglican position.[88]

Notwithstanding his internal inconsistency and dubious orthodoxy — perhaps, indeed, actually because of the latter — it is tempting to think of Malthus as a theologian ahead of his time. Some have thought to have seen a resemblance between his theory of the growth of mind and Teilhard's "evolution of the noosphere."[89] His firm rejection of the supernatural on the grounds that it undermines the moral autonomy of man is very close to the position of "progressive" English theologians of the 1960s, as is his lighthearted attitude towards the formularies and traditional doctrines of the Church of England. In at least two respects, however, I believe Malthus can be shown to have failed to meet the standards which would be applied today: in his uncritical use of natural theology, and in the dualism of his (and Tucker's) concept of "mind".

Hume's *Dialogues on Natural Religion* were actually published in 1779 five years before Malthus went up to Cambridge, but it would be unfair to expect him to have formulated an adequate defence by 1798. Butler had died at about the time that Hume's earliest works began to appear; Paley made no attempt to answer Hume; and in the whole of Tucker's vast work, in which there are continual references to Locke and many to Berkeley, Hume seems not to be mentioned. Today, however, the case is otherwise, and no natural theologian could command attention without first constructing an argument which meets the epistemological objections to his enterprise which have been brought by Hume and later philosophers.

A related but separate point concerns Malthus's use of Tucker's concept of "mind". Quite apart from any strictly theological objections there might be to the dualism of "body" and "mind" (or "spirit"), it has been convincingly argued[90] that the distinction is logically invalid, and hence that the Tucker–Malthus usage is incoherent.

III

The few, obscure critics who publicly attacked Malthus's theology seemed oblivious of the very damaging objections outlined in the previous section. Their structures were directed instead at the supposed insult to "the intelligence and contrivance, in the Author of the Creation" represented by Malthus as bringing "more beings into the world than He prepares nourishment for",[91] and were informed by an uncritical understanding of the divine injunction to "be fruitful and multiply". It was the ease with which Malthus was able to dispose of these accusations in later editions of his *Essay* which seduced the untheological Bonar into supposing that Malthus's orthodoxy was secure.[92]

It seems clear, however, that those unknown but "distinguished persons" in the Church of England who, on reading the *First Essay* privately persuaded Malthus to omit the theological argument from its second edition, must on the one hand have been aware of its inadequacy, and on the other have believed that the apologetic problem presented by the Principle of Population was susceptible of an orthodox solution.

The first to attempt it was William Paley, whose *Natural Theology,* which appeared in 1802 four years after the *First Essay,* attributed "the evils of civil life" to the "constitution of our nature", according to the principle explained "in a late treatise upon population".[93] As he also did the later versions of his *Moral and Political Philosophy*,[94] revised to take account of Malthusian population theory, Paley attempted to soften Malthus"s conclusions by arguing that the limits to growth were "not yet attained, or even approached, in any country in the world",[95] and correctly observed that psychic satisfactions are not subject to physical limitation. The "*distinctions* of civil life" produced by scarcity are partly useful and partly illusory,[96] and moral evil is an unavoidable consequence of human freedom. Moreover, "even the bad qualities of mankind have an origin in their good ones".[97] All this leaves very little of the "evil associated with scarcity" to be reconciled with the divine goodness. What remains, however, is not to be explained in terms of the Tucker–Malthus "creation of mind" hypothesis. Notwithstanding his own generously acknowledged debt to Tucker,[98] the cautious Paley elected simply to ignore that entire agrument, no doubt because he could see all too clearly how impossible the position into which it had led Malthus. He chose instead to reaffirm the traditional "state of probation" doctrine, according to which "our ultimate, or our most permanent happiness, will depend, not upon the temporary condition into which we are cast, but upon our behaviour in it".[99]

Paley's reworking of the theological implications of Malthusian population theory occupies the last seventeen pages of Chapter XXVI of his *Natural Theology*. Part II of J.B. Sumner's celebrated *Treatise*[100] is essentially a vast elaboration of Paley's brief argument, especially as the latter related to "the distinctions of civil life". Having shown that both reason and revelation support the view of this life as "a state of discipline",[101] Sumner goes on to argue that social inequality is best suited "to the development and improvement of the human faculties",[102] and to "the exercise of virtue".[103] It might, therefore, be expected that a benevolent creator would "devise a means" for bringing about inequality; and so, indeed, He does, in the Principle of Population lately set forth in "the comprehensive treatise, in which Mr Malthus has unfolded this important branch of human history".[104] Collateral benefits of the Principle of Population are "the establishment of universal industry" and a "quick and wide diffusion of the benefits of industry"[105] including the propagation of Christianity itself. Protected by his evangelical orthodoxy from the intellectual dangers of exclusive reliance upon natural theology, Sumner affirms of revelation — in implied rebuke of Malthus's simple faith in the "book of nature" — that "no other guide can enter the sanctuary where God resides, or read the book in which His counsels are written".[106] "The experiment of vindicating the moral administration of the universe without the help of a future state, has been sufficiently tried"[107] — another allusion to Malthus perhaps. Sumner is willing to go further than Paley, finally, in explicitly invoking the doctrine of the Fall[108] to account for "natural evil".

The Paley–Sumner restatement of Malthus may therefore be summarized as follows: God places humans in this world as a preparation for "some higher state of existence"; the Principle of Population, by producing scarcity, competition and inequality, provides the optimum conditions for intellectual and moral development and for the spread of civilization; incidental evil is a consequence of the Fall, and in any case" a future state of existence alone rectifies all disorders".[109] What is retained from Malthus's *First Essay* is a recognition of the theological problem posed by scarcity in general and the Principle of Population in particular; the belief that these are necessary to stimulate human nature to exertion and thus to a realization of its capabilities; and the view that the Principle of Population is evidence of God's "contrivance" for replenishing the earth. What is abandoned is the exclusive dependence upon natural theology, together with all the difficulties which resulted from that dependence: the "creation of mind" doctrine, the limitation of divine omnipotence, the heterodox accounts of original sin and eternal punishment, the Pelagian soteriology and the consequent redundance of christology.

Without so much as a trace of overt, public criticism on their part, or of recantation of even acknowledgement on his own, Malthus silently submitted to the expurgation performed by Paley and Sumner. The second edition of his *Essay* in 1803 was published the year after Paley's *Natural Theology:* neither it nor any of the subsequent editions which appeared in his lifetime (1806, 1807, 1817, 1826) contain any of the objectionable material, nor indeed is there any further attempt at a systematic theological exposition, though scattered references to the acceptable ingredients of his theodicy are to be found. In the fifth edition (1817), which came out the year following Sumner's *Treatise*, there is an Appendix in which he admits to having expunged certain unspecified material in deference to the opinions of "a competent tribunal",[110] and which records his admission that the principle of population is "particularly suited to a state of discipline and trial".[111] His final *Summary View* (1830), which reprinted a large portion of the article on Population in the *Encyclopaedia Brittanica*, concludes with a very brief theological argument in which Malthus at last capitulated to the orthodox view. Its aim is to show that the Principle of Population is consistent with "the letter and spirit of the scriptures"; no attempt is made to employ the categories of natural theology; the "light of reason" is restricted to illuminating individual consciences and even then is to be "sanctioned by revealed religion". At its centre is the Paley–Sumner axiom: "It is almost universally acknowledged, that both the letter and the spirit of revelation represent this world as a state of moral discipline and probation".[112]

It is fanciful to construe that "almost" as Malthus's last avenue of escape.

Notes

1. H. P. Liddon (1897). *Life of Edward Bouverie Pusey*, vol. iii, p.389. Longmans, London.
2. R. Whateley (1831). *Introductory Lectures in Political Economy*, p.vii. Fellowes, London.
3. J. Tucker (1776). *Four Tracts on Commercial and Political Subjects*, 3rd Edition, vol. I, p.20. Gloucester.
4. J. B. Sumner (1825). *A Treatise on the Records of Creation: With Particular Reference to the Jewish History, and the Consistency of the Principle of Population with the Wisdom and Goodness of the Deity*, vol. 1. Hatchard & Son, London. Fourth Edition Corrected, vol. 2. Hatchard & Son, London. (Xerox copy of 1816 Edition.)
5. R. A. Solway (1969). *Prelates and People: Ecclesiastical Social Thought in England*, 1783–1852, p.93. Routledge & Kegan Paul, London.
6. Patricia James (1979). *Population Malthus, His Life and Times*, pp.66,

116–121. Routledge & Kegan Paul, London.
7. W. Otter (1836). A Memoir of Robert Malthus. In the Second Edition of T. R. Malthus, *Principles of Political Economy*, p.liii. London.
8. J. Bonar (1885). *Malthus and His Work*, pp.34–40, 317–331. Allen & Unwin, London.
9. ibid, p.38.
10. J. M. Keynes (1933). *Essays in Biography*. Macmillan, London.
11. J. Pullen (1981). Malthus's theological ideas and their influence on his Principle of Population. *History of Political Economy* **13**, 39–54
12. D. L. Le Mahieu (1979). Malthus and the theology of scarcity. *Journal of the History of Ideas* **40**, 467–474.
13. Patricia James, op. cit. in note 6.
14. L. Robbins (1932). *An Essay on the Nature and Significance of Economic Science*. Macmillan, London.
15. J. A. Schumpeter (1954). *History of Economic Analysis*. allen & Unwin, London.
16. T. R. Malthus (1798). *An Essay on the Principle of Population as it Affects the Future Improvement of Society, with Remarks on the Speculations of Mr Goodwin, M. Condorcet and other Writers*. London. The page references are to the Facsimile Reprint of the Royal Economic Society, p.348. Macmillan, London.
17. ibid. p.350.
18. ibid. p.351.
19. ibid. p.391.
20. ibid. pp.127, 158–159, 231–233, 243–245, 246, 362, 391.
21. ibid. pp. 242–248.
22. ibid. p.362.
23. ibid. pp.384–387.
24. Abraham tucker wrote under the pseudonym of Edward Search. See E. Search (1768). *The Light of Nature Pursued*. Payne, London.
25. J. Bonar, op. cit. in note 8, p.324.
26. E. Search, op. cit in note 24, I, pp.xxv, xxviii.
27. cf. e.g. Karl Marx, *Capital*. Penguin Edition (1976), vol. I, p.639. London.
28. E. Search, op. cit. in note 24, II, III, p.491.
29. ibid. II–I, pp.6, 87.
30. ibid. II, I, chapter 5.
31. ibid. II, I, p.117.
32. ibid. II, I, p.112.
33. ibid. II, I, p.236.
34. ibid.
35. ibid. II, I, pp.238–256.
36. ibid. II, I, p.306.
37. ibid. II, I, pp.311–312.
38. J. Butler (1838). *The Analogy of Religion, Natural and Revealed, to the Constitution and Course of Nature*, A New Improved Edition. Chapters IV, V. Chidley, London.

39. W. Paley (1825). *The Works of William Paley, D. D., Archeacon of Carlisle. With a Life of the Author.* In five volumes. Hailes, Bumpus, London. vol. v, *Sermons*, Sermon XXXIII.
40. T. R. Malthus, op. cit. in note 16, p.353.
41. ibid. p.354.
42. ibid. p.356.
43. ibid. p.360.
44. ibid. p.372.
45. ibid. p.375.
46. ibid. p.374.
47. E. Search, op. cit. in note 24, II, III, p.448.
48. Patricia James, op. cit. in note 6, p.32.
49. D. L. Le Mahieu, loc. cit. in note 12, p.20.
50. W. Otter, loc. cit. in note 7, p.xxiv.
51. T. R. Malthus, op. cit. in note 16, p.389.
52. ibid. pp.388–390.
53. Edward Search, op. cit. in note 24, II-I, p.229.
54. T. R. Malthus, op. cit. in note 16, p.352.
55. ibid. p.391.
56. Edward Search, op. cit. in note 24, II-I, p.227.
57. T. R. Malthus, op. cit. in note 16, p.395.
58. ibid. p.359.
59. ibid. p.387.
60. ibid. pp.207, 286, 358.
61. ibid. p.353.
62. ibid. p.207.
63. ibid. p.354.
64. ibid. p.368.
65. ibid. pp.372–373.
66. cf. Edward Search, op. cit. in note 24, I-I, p.xii; J. Butler, op. cit. in note 38, II, chapter 1; Paley, op. cit. in note 38, vol. 1, pp.290–291.
67. J. Bonar, op. cit. in note 8, p.367.
68. (H. E. Manning and C. Marriot) *Catena Patrum III: Testimony of Writers in the Later English Church to the Duty of Maintaining Quod Sempter, Quod Ubique, Quod ab Omnibus Traditum Est.* Tract No. 78 of "Tracts for the Times" by Members of the University of Oxford. vol. IV. 1836-7. New Edition. Rivingtons, London.
69. P. E. More and F. L. Cross (1935). *Anglicanism.* S.P.C.K., London.
70. Edward Search, op. cit. in note 24, II-I, p.7.
71. T. R. Malthus, op. cit. in note 16, p.246. 71. ibid. p.350 (my italics).
72. ibid. p.350 (my italics).
73. ibid. p.351 (my italics).
74. John 10; 30; 14:8-11 etc.
75. T. R. Malthus, op. cit. in note 16, p.395. If "avoid" in this context means "get out of the way of" and "evil" includes the infliction of suffering and death, this would seem to be inconsistent with the willing acceptance of

suffering by Christ, who did no "exert himself to avoid it" (Heb. 5:7–8; 9:26–28; 12:2–13; March 14:36; John 18:4–8, etc.)

76. T. R. Malthus, op. cit. in note 16, p.352.
77. ibid. p.360.
78. ibid. p.378–380.
79. ibid. p.379. cf. Genesis 1: 31 etc.
80. Edward Search, op. cit. in note 24, II-I, p.257.
81. Rogers as cited by Patricia James, in op. cit. in note 6, p.118.
82. P. Sraffa (Ed.) (1952). *The Works and Correspondence of David Ricardo*, vol. VII, pp.212-213. Cambridge University Press, Cambridge.
83. T. R. Malthus, op. cit. in note 16, p.363.
84. However, see ibid. p.294.
85. ibid. p.354.
86. ibid. p.390.
87. James, op. cit. in note 6, p.32.
88. H. P. Liddon, op. cit. in note 1, vol. iv, chapters II, III.
89. P. Teilhard de Chardin (1959). *The Phenomenon of Man*. Book III. Collins, London.
90. G. Ryle (1949). *The Concept of Mind*. Hutchinson, London.
91. Patricia James, op. cit. in note 6, p.437; J. Bonar, op. cit. in note 8, p.365.
92. J. Bonar, ibid. pp.365–367.
93. W. Paley, op. cit. in note 39, vol. I, p.270.
94. ibid. vol. II, chapter XI.
95. ibid. vol. I, p.271.
96. ibid. pp.271–273.
97. ibid. p.274.
98. ibid. vol. II, p.xii.
99. ibid. vol. I, p.284.
100. J. B. Sumner, op. cit. in note 4.
101. ibid. II, II, chapter 2.
102. ibid. chapter III.
103. ibid. chapter IV.
104. ibid. p.103.
105. ibid. chapter VI.
106. ibid. I-I, p.xix.
107. ibid. p.xvii.
108. ibid. II-II, pp.137–139; cf. W. Paley, op. cit. in note 39, I, p.274.
109. W. Paley, ibid. p.282.
110. T. R. Malthus (1817). *Essay*, 5th Edition, vol. 3, p.427.
111. ibid. p.426.
112. D. V. Glass (1953). *Introduction to Malthus*, p.180. Watts, London.

PART 4

Malthusianism

15 The Influence of Malthus on British Thought

T. H. HOLLINGSWORTH

It is something of a surprise to a British writer that there should be an international congress on Robert Malthus[1] at all in the late twentieth century. His name is rarely used by his countrymen today, and there is little prestige even to be gained by claiming Malthus's name for doctrines that he did not advocate, nor for opposing views that he allegedly held. He is regarded primarily as a partisan in a political debate that ended in his own lifetime.

To some extent, this must reflect the British preference for the immediate and concrete and our disinclination to take theory very seriously. Although the first (1798) edition of his *Essay on the Principle of Population* was addressed to a general problem, Malthus showed himself more interested in the practical significance of his ideas in his own country in the second (1803) and later (1806, 1807, 1817 and 1826) editions.[2]

The *First Essay* was originally written, and published anonymously, to remind William Godwin (whose book on Political Justice had appeared in 1793) that any plan for an ideal society must include some means for making sure that population growth does not destroy its perfection in due course. Godwin replied, first in 1801, and eventually at greater length in 1820, but he had few important allies on this general abstract question, which had been raised by Robert Wallace in 1761, as well as by earlier writers.[3] The British public, moreover, was not much inclined to believe Godwin, since his ideas were associated in the popular mind with those of Condorcet and the excesses of the French Revolution, and thus Malthus won an easy victory on this count. The parts of the later editions of the *Essay* that deal with general

MALTHUS PAST AND PRESENT
ISBN 0-12-224670-5

arguments about population growth, and contain discussions of the nature of population growth in various parts of the world, would not be regarded as very important by most of his readers, since it was the custom at the time to begin pleas for particular reforms with preambles of a quasi-philosophical nature (the Constitution of the United States of America comes to mind), which were not to be regarded as more than providing support to the real matter in hand.

The most original contribution of Malthus to the theory of population was his idea that human populations tend to grow in geometric progression whereas food supplies can hardly grow even in arithmetic progression. This received a good deal of attention, but was not effectively refuted. Yet it is really the weakest part of his argument, since the food sources themselves are intrinsically just as biological as the human population and so just as intrinsically liable to grow geometrically. Malthus was fond of remarking that the population of the United States doubled every 25 years, but did not emphasize that US food production was doubling even more rapidly. There is no particular reason to expect an arithmetic growth rate in food production at any stage of development in fact, and Malthus does not give any examples of such a phenomenon. One can readily see that it would be unlikely to grow much faster than population, except in a country developing a massive export trade in foodstuffs. But all this did not really matter for the success of Malthus in winning his main point, that population growth can be a danger to human well-being through pressure on resources, especially those of food.

Malthus had early success in winning over influential people to his main theme. William Pitt, the Prime Minister, was convinced as early as 1803, and so was William Paley, the theologian. Two important possible sources of practical opposition to Malthus were thus removed at the time of the second edition of his *Essay*. It was a great age for British economists, and Sir James Mackintosh, David Ricardo and Sir Edward West broadly supported Malthus. Jeremy Bentham and James Mill, the utilitarian philosophers, also came to agree with him, so that it became accepted that the trap that Godwin had fallen into should be avoided by subsequent writers of an idealist bent.

There was, of course, plenty of opposition to Malthus, especially during the first twenty years or so after the first edition of the *Essay,* but it tended to come from men of lesser eminence, at least in the realm of public affairs. Thus, although the romantic poets, Samuel Taylor Coleridge and Robert Southey, expressed their opposition, they did not need to be taken very seriously, and the novelist Thomas Love Peacock[4] could satirize Malthus but not offer a proper counter-argument.

The serious writers on the subject who opposed Malthus, like James Grahame, John Weyland, and Michael Sadler, carried little weight, and, indeed, their arguments seem to-day very thin. It is true that the prestigious figures of Edwin Chadwick and Nassau Senior differed from Malthus, but only to a limited extent. They wished to modify his ideas, but were not opposed to them in principle.

James Bonar, the author of the first comprehensive study of Malthus[5] is, therefore, probably fair when he says: "It seems clear that in educated circles at least the view of Malthus was as early as 1820 what it was in 1829, 'the popular view', which is quite compatible, as Darwin long experienced, with great unpopularity in particular quarters."[6] Almost before Malthus was known abroad, therefore, he was accepted at home by all but the more eccentric writers, at least in his broad outlines. He remained highly controversial, however, for a reason that interested Englishmen much more than any theoretical tendency for population to grow at any particular rate. This was the great debate over the Poor Law.

An international audience may find it rather obscure to dwell long upon what was purely an English matter (Scotland was quite different), but the question of the Poor Law was a major concern of every British politician between 1795 and 1834, dates which happen to coincide very closely with those of Malthus's adult life. Malthus's Principle of Population came to be judged primarily in the light of what it indicated should be done about the English poor, rather than by more general considerations.

The English Poor Law had originally been established under Elizabeth I in 1601. It was, no doubt, even then in response to growth of population that some system of poor relief had been required. Living standards of the common people had fallen during the sixteenth century, and the phenomenon of "sturdy beggars", as they were called, was widespread. The Elizabethan Poor Law said, broadly, that each parish was responsible for any poor people who had been born there. Local wages and any rates of relief for the poor were fixed by the county magistrates, and workhouses began to be set up in some of the parishes after 1722. Various divergences in the treatment of the poor thus arose, especially whether they were set to work in workhouses or not. This system might work quite well in a largely agricultural country with little internal migration and all the parishes comparable in resources, but the growth of industrialism imposed severe strains upon it. In 1795, the magistrates of Berkshire, meeting at the small hamlet of Speenhamland, a place near Newbury famous only for this meeting, agreed to relieve poor families in proportion to the number of children they had. Many other English counties, but by no means all, quickly followed the Speenhamland precedent.

Malthus's Principle of Population, therefore, soon came to be tested by whether or not there was a tendency for birth rates to be greater in the Speenhamland counties. Unfortunately, clear evidence either way was lacking, partly because birth registration as such did not exist, so that baptisms had to be used instead, and partly because the Speenhamland counties tended to be those where the new industries were not strongly established. They tended to grow rather more slowly than the other counties, but it is possible that Speenhamland encouraged their population growth nevertheless.

The Malthusians, of course, generally argued that relief for the poor in proportion to their family size would only mean that there would be more poor to relieve in the next generation, and that productive work rather than financial relief would be the more effective remedy. Moreover, it was often claimed that the Speenhamland system must lead to more births amongst the poor, and not only to fewer child deaths. It was clear to all that the old Poor Law was in need of reform, since reliance on new interpretations by county magistrates could not be wholly satisfactory, but it was important to decide what kinds to reform would be best.

The Poor Law Amendment Act was at length passed in 1834. It took effective power from the local authorities and increased the role of the workhouse. Poverty became regarded as more of a crime than a misfortune, and the cost to the nation of relieving poverty was henceforth to be kept as low as practicable. The matter having been resolved, and Malthus himself dying at the end of the year, we find a great reduction in the volume of British publications related to Malthus and his ideas thereafter.[7] Malthus had won his battle over the Poor Law and could now be conveniently forgotten. It was also becoming plain that, although population growth in England was quite rapid, food supplies per head were not dwindling. Of course, this was simply because British exports of manufactures paid for food imports, but it served to suggest that any Malthusian limit to population growth might be far off yet.

Indeed, the English economy worked fairly well after 1834, although for unforeseen reasons. Many of those who might have obtained poor relief before 1834 were forced upon the labour market by the new Poor Law, but at just the time when railways began to make migration to the industrial towns much easier than before, as well as giving a great stimulus to trade. Another advantage to the economy at this period was a probable quasi-Malthusian reduction in the birth rate that seems to have occurred between about 1823 and 1832, of which we shall say more subsequently.

Malthus might also have been regarded as completely vindicated by the Irish potato famines of 1846, 1847 and 1849, since the much greater and more widespread poverty of the Irish was well known to everyone, including Malthus, long before the potato crop failed so spectacularly. But most people already believed that Malthus was fundamentally right, so that the potato famines of Ireland could hardly serve as fuel for a non-existent controversy. Instead of the Poor Law, the Corn Laws had by then become the dominant political theme of the day, and economics rather than demography seemed the most immediately applicable social science.

One should perhaps make some mention of Karl Marx at this point, since he was working in England at a time when Malthus was not long dead. Marx believed that rapid population growth was necessary for capitalism to flourish, in order to create a surplus of labour. (Malthusian economics tends to argue that population growth helps capitalism chiefly by maintaining demand for goods and services.) Marx did not want to believe that labourers could restrict their rate of increase (by whatever method) and so improve their bargaining position. Marx seems akin to Godwin and other idealist writers who are more adept at finding fault with a system that really exists than at explaining why no such faults will occur in the ideal systems they propose. Only a total change in human nature will suffice, the likelihood of which always seems doubtful, unless one believes that man is very malleable indeed, which leads to further intellectual difficulties.

It is also a matter of well-attested fact that Charles Darwin read Malthus as a young man and slowly reached his conclusions on the origin of species under the influence of Malthus's ideas. The connection was made through Malthus's identification of the positive and preventive checks to human population, which, Darwin realized, would also apply to plant and animal species. The survival of the fittest in some sense is then inevitable.

However, one element in the story of Malthus's ideas on population remains to be told. It is, of course, ironic that his views should have become generally accepted by about 1820 and yet nothing should have been done as a result, except a change in the Poor Law. Was the population of England growing at an acceptable rate? What of Ireland, where the rate of growth was surely too fast? What of colonies, such as Australia, where the rate of growth might be too slow? Although there was no absence of discussion of such questions, no population policies were debated, except those concerning emigration. The question of the birth rate, in particular, was generally avoided. Indeed, the dissemination of information about birth control was almost entirely illegal. Malthus himself was opposed to all artificial means of contraception on moral grounds, and argued exclusively for "moral restraint", which in practice meant late marriage. (Ironically, the only country to adopt this Protestant idea was Catholic Ireland.)

In the long run, the most important influence Malthus had was probably that on Francis Place, who argued that individual working men would be better off if they had smaller families, and had no doubts about how that goal might be achieved. Place's personal experience of life is relevant to his views on population. He was born in 1771, and was apprenticed to a breeches-maker when he was thirteen. He married when he was only nineteen, and two years later, while helping to organize a strike, almost died of starvation; he was, of course, blacklisted by the employers and unable to find work when the strike ended. By the time he was fifty, he had become the father of fifteen children, five of whom had died in childhood. Although, like Malthus, he was opposed to the perfectionist ideas of Godwin, his own experience had led him to the conclusion that early marriage was highly desirable. He remembered that as a single youth he had been quite unable to live a decent life, and his marriage at nineteen had been the making of him. He, therefore, believed that Malthus's remedy of late marriage was impracticable, although he did not need to be convinced that a large family might mean a lower standard of living. Place published his book on population in 1822, but, apart from a review by Jean-Baptiste Say, it attracted little attention. His main aim was probably to divert working-class leaders from Godwin's views, but only a few hundred copies were sold, and moreover, to a large extent refutation of Godwin had become superfluous by 1822.

Nevertheless, Place's endeavours, stimulated as much by antipathy towards Godwin as by sympathy towards Malthus, bore fruit in a different way. The writing of his book seems to have focused Place's mind on the population problem, and, between 1823 and 1830, Place wrote and distributed practical handbills about contraception, and began to train a small band of disciples. It is no exaggeration to say that in this way Francis Place became the true founder of the birth control movement.

It is not completely clear whether Place's campaign was effective on any significant scale, but it is noteworthy that the rate of population growth between 1811 and 1821 was higher than it was between 1821 and 1831, and also that the proportion of children in the population was appreciably greater in 1821 than in 1841. On both grounds, some reduction in fertility seems probable, although only of the order of from a birth rate of 40 per thousand to one of 36. Although Place did not die until the beginning of 1854, he seems to have become less active as he grew older in the 1830s and 1840s, and the impetus of his birth control movement was lost. But the birth rate did not rise again after the 1830s, and when it began to fall steadily after some 45 years of stability it was not entirely from causes unconnected with Place himself.

Strictly speaking, advocates of family planning, birth control, or contraception, rather than "moral restraint", should be termed neo-Malthusians, since they accept one part of Malthus's ideas while rejecting another. Nevertheless, it is only they who have had much prominence since 1834. The birth control movement spread to America in 1828 through Richard Carlile, a disciple of Place, and Charles Knowlton published anonymously his *Fruits of Philosophy,* a practical medical treatise on contraception, in New York, in 1832. This book sold a few hundred copies each year surreptitiously in Britain until 1877, when Charles Bradlaugh and Annie Besant published a new edition and were prosecuted for doing so on grounds of obscenity. In the three months between their arrest and their trial, 125 000 copies were sold; and, although at first, they were found to be technically guilty of depraving public morals, they won an appeal on the equally technical grounds that the words alleged to be obscene in the book were not set out in the indictment. The steady fall in the English birth rate between 1877 and 1933 was not accompanied, however, by much controversy along Malthusian or even neo-Malthusian lines.

It is true that Bradlaugh's earlier Malthusian League was revived in 1877 and that *The Malthusian* appeared monthly from 1879 to 1921, but they were Malthusian in name only. The Malthusian League eventually ceased activity in 1927, deliberately to make it possible for a National Birth Control Council to be formed that would not be "saddled with a clumsy, anachronistic and inaccurate name or with clumsy, anachronistic, and inaccurate economic theories".[8] *The Malthusian* itself had changed its name in 1922 to *The New Generation,* and, although it did become *The Malthusian* once again in 1949, it expired in 1952.

Apart from attacks on the birth control movement by moralists, who were in fact thoroughly Malthusian in their motives, the only concern shown was a certain alarm expressed from time to time about an alleged progressive degeneration of the British race. The upper and middle classes had begun to reduce their fertility earlier than the lower classes, so that some kind of apprehension (by the former) was not surprising, but any more fundamental questions, of the kind that Malthus himself had raised, have scarcely been considered at all in Great Britain since his death.

The public slowly came to accept Place's position, which is based upon the personal interest of each individual family, rather than on national considerations. Since this had to be done clandestinely for the most part, no clear debate could take place, and no politicians suggested any population policies except in relation to emigration and immigration. Family allowances were eventually introduced, but more with the simple intention of helping parents and children than of producing any increase in the rate of population growth. The Speenhamland experience, moreover, may have suggested that any advantages would be doubtful and the likely effect small.[9] To be sure, certain writers have managed to keep the name of Malthus alive after a fashion, but rarely in a legitimate way. Thus Aldous Huxley wrote of "Malthusian drill" in *Brave New World* (1932) but he really meant Placean contraception. The very word "Malthusian" has almost dropped out of the language during the past forty years.

One may, perhaps, argue that the inattention to Malthus is more apparent than real. His approach may have become so generally accepted that it is followed almost automatically now. Possibly, too, the relative lack of utopian social schemes in English literature since the first edition of Malthus's *First Essay* in 1798 is due to his influence. (England has no natural immunity to utopias, of course; the first, by Sir Thomas More, appeared in 1516.) But if the debt exists, it has become unconscious. Malthus is either forgotten or his views are so well known that his name can be forgotten.

It should also be recognized that the fame of Malthus rests upon his ability to arouse controversy and thus to stimulate others to think about questions of population. His central idea was not new; his arithmetical progression is no more than an approximation at best; he took too little account of technical improvements; and the British, at least, adopted a remedy to excessive population growth that he abominated. The Poor Law was changed in a way to his liking, but it is not clear that the results were especially beneficifal. Thus it would seem wise not to take Malthus very seriously in the late twentieth century.

Notes

1. It is still rather a shock to see him called "Thomas Malthus" in foreign publications, as the second name, Robert, was always used in his lifetime to refer to T. R. Malthus. This habit is quite common amongst modern

English demographers, such as W. Alan Armstrong, J. David Chambers, K. Michael Drake, G. Talbot Griffith, T. Peter Laslett and E. Anthony Wrigley. (The present writer, however, does not object to his own first name, even though he shares it with Malthus.)

It is equally unfair to call him, with William Cobbett, "Parson" Malthus, since his ecclesiastical calling was almost wholly formal. His real life was that of a professor, teaching and writing.

Similarly, Karl Marx was wrong to suggest that he vowed to live a life of celibacy, except for the term of his Fellowship at Jesus College, Cambridge; and Michael Fogarty to say that he had eleven daughters; in reality, he married at the age of 38 and became the father of three children, remarkably consistent with his own theories of population.

2. There have been posthumous reprints in 1872, 1890, 1914, 1958, 1970 and 1973. The 1970 edition is published by Penguin Books, and contains the text of the *First Essay* and Malthus's *Summary View* (1830) edited, with an introduction, by Anthony Flew. The 1973 edition is published by J. M. Dent and Sons in their Everyman Series, and contains the text of the 1826 edition of the *Essay* with an introduction by T. H. Hollingsworth.
3. Giovanni Botero apparently had the fundamental idea as early as 1589 in his book on the grandeur and magnificence of cities.
4. Malthus is made fun of as Mr Fax in *Melincourt* (1817). See especially chapter XXXV, "The Rustic Wedding", in which Mr Fax tries to advise a newly-married couple on moral restraint, without success.
5. *Malthus and His Work,* London. 1885.
6. The quotation is taken from the 1924 reprint, p.363.
7. There is a list of books, pamphlets, and articles on the population question, published in Britain during the period 1793 to 1880 in D. V. Glass (ed.) (1953). *Introduction to Malthus*, London, which runs to 29 pages. The main period of publication was apparently from 1815 to 1834, but after 1860 it become a mere trickle, except for works for or against family limitation, which is scarcely a Malthusian subject in the strict sense.
8. Peter Fryer (1967). *The Birth Controllers*, p.297. Corgi, London.
9. See J. D. Marshall (1968). *The Old Poor Law 1795–1834*, pp.38–42. Macmillan, London.

16 The Rationale Underlying Malthus's Theory of Population[1]

G. HEINSOHN AND O. STEIGER

People who do not need heirs in order to secure their living can remain childless, provided they have access to means of birth control. However, in modern economies — mercantilist, capitalist or socialist — the necessary labour power for their continued existence is provided by procreation within the family, even though these economies are no longer organized on the basis of family units. This is the result of an enforced production of human beings by the state. Its success can be attributed to the elimination of knowledge of techniques of birth control following the liquidation of its practitioners by the systematic extermination of "witches-midwives" between the middle of the fourteenth and the end of the seventeenth century.[2] Witchcraft — clearly distinguished from mediaeval heresy — in early modern times was defined as "sevenfold witchcraft" whose components, without exception, "infect the act of love and the conception in the womb with various sorceries". The seven offences of witchcraft comprised: (1) fornication and adultery (as "training grounds" for sexual satisfaction without pregnancy); (2) rendering men impotent; (3) castration and sterilization; (4) bestiality and homosexuality (as forms of sexual gratification which again do not lead to procreation); (5) contraception; (6) abortion; (7) infanticide (also when masked as child sacrifice).[3] Following the witch trials, the belief in a "natural desire for children" became prevalent, and this belief has dominated scientific analysis since that time to a much greater extent than it did the actual men and women involved in the procreative process.

Thomas Robert Malthus was one of the few theorists of population who was aware of the fact that the "natural desire for children" can be

MALTHUS PAST AND PRESENT
ISBN 0-12-224670-5

modified by human reason, i.e. that in reality such a desire is not natural at all. However, in formulating his Principle of Population, Malthus denounced the use of reason and instead used "natural desire for children" to justify a particular population policy. As far as we know, this has not been recognized sufficiently by interpreters of his theory. It can be shown that Malthus's apprehension that the number of children produced would be insufficient was at least as great as his well known fear of overpopulation.

In 1798 Malthus was the first of the classical economists explicitly to pay attention to the rapid growth of population in England after 1740, and more especially after the beginning of industrialization in 1781. Malthus decisively opposed mercantilist policies, i.e. policies aimed at increasing population:[4]

> Politicians, observing that states which were powerful and prosperous were almost invariably populous, have mistaken an effect for a cause, and have concluded that their population was the cause of their prosperity, instead of their prosperity being the cause of their population.[5]

This criticism is based on a special explanation of the reproductive process among men and which may be regarded as being at the core of Malthus's theory and which runs as follows:

> ... throughout the animal and vegetable kingdoms, Nature has scattered the seeds of life abroad with the most profuse and liberal hand, but has been comparatively sparing in the room and the nourishment necessary to rear them. The germs of existence contained in the earth, if they could freely develop themselves, would fill millions of worlds in the course of a few thousand years. Necessity, that imperious, all-pervading law of nature, restrains them within the prescribed bounds. The race of plants and the race of animals shrink under this great restrictive law; and man cannot by any efforts of reason escape from it.
>
> In plants and irrational animals, the view of the subject is simple. They are all impelled by a powerful instinct to the increase of their species, and this instinct is interrupted by no doubts about providing for their offspring. Wherever, therefore, there is liberty, the power of increase is exerted, and the superabundant effects are repressed afterwards by want of room and nourishment.
>
> The effects of this check on man are more complicated. *Impelled to the increase of his species by an equally powerful instinct, reason interrupts his career and asks him whether he may not bring beings into the world for whom he cannot provide the means of support. If he attend to this natural suggestion, the restriction*

> *too frequently produces vice.* If he hear it not, the human race will be constantly endeavouring to increase beyond the means of subsistence. But as, by that law of our nature which makes food necessary to the life of man, population can never actually increase beyond the lowest nourishment capable of supporting it, a strong check on population, from the difficulty of acquiring food, must be constantly in operation. This difficulty must fall somewhere and must necessarily be severely felt in some or other of the various forms of misery, or the fear of misery, by a large portion of mankind.[6]

• Here it is interesting to note that Malthus made it absolutely clear that if reason had any part to play in human reproduction, "excess population", i.e. the "various forms of misery" when population is increasing to the "lowest nourishment capable of supporting it" should not occur. At the same time, however, he denounced the use of such reason, because it "too frequently produces vice". As we shall show below, the contradiction in Malthus's reasoning is only apparent. It conceals a conscious advocacy of population policy.

It is, therefore, evident that Malthus's Principle of Population embodied in his explanation of human reproduction cited above is valid only in the case of "perfect freedom",[7] i.e. when there is complete lack of rationality and man's "powerful instinct" is not prevented from operating by "doubts about providing for their offspring". In these circumstances, Malthus asserted, population would increase in geometrical ratio, whereas food supplies would, in favourable circumstances, increase only in arithmetical ratio.[8] As a result there would be pressure on means of subsistence and the size of the population would be limited by such pressure. Malthus's principal concern was not to paint a gloomy picture of an absolute surplus population as he realized only too well "that the period when the number of men surpasses their means of easy subsistence has long since arrived, and that this necessary oscillation, this constantly subsisting cause of periodical misery, has existed in most countries ever since we have had any histories of mankind and continues to exist at the present moment."[9]

In his analysis of misery, Malthus was interested in the ratio of the size of the population to the minimum of subsistence in order to determine a nation's wealth:

> Corn countries are more populous than pasture countries, and rice countries more populous than corn countries. But their happiness does not depend either upon their being thinly or fully inhabited upon their

poverty or their riches, their youth or their age, but on the proportion which the population and the food bear to each other.[10]

Here, Malthus assumed a wage which was above the minimum subsistence level (i.e. the supply of food) and which thus favoured marriage which in turn would necessarily result in children. According to him, the number of workers would increase and their average wage fall, but would remain above the minimum of subsistence and thus stabilize their traditional reproductive behaviour. The number of workers would then continue to increase until the wage fell below the minimum level of subsistence. State support for the poor would lead to a reduction in public welfare, even though it was intended to benefit public welfare. Such support, Malthus argued, would raise the income of the unemployed or those who received no wages to the minimum level of subsistence and would thus, once again, lead to a continuation of the old rate of reproduction. The poor would take public support of their minimum wage into consideration — and breed. Since public funds to support a minimum wage are quickly used and only result in general misery, there will ultimately be an increase in mortality.

In order to exclude this source of poverty, i.e. the creation of more unemployment through an excessive increase in the working population, Malthus suggested that the state should dispense with a guarantee of the minimum level of subsistence and make the individual worker personally responsible for the risk of his wage falling below the subsistence level. Such a policy would lead to a change in attitudes towards reproduction. Workers would thus contribute to a reduction in the supply of labour and an increase in wages above the minimum level, so that public welfare was once more safeguarded:

> The object of those who really wish to better the condition of the lower classes of society must be to raise the relative proportion between the price of labour and the price of provisions, so as to enable the labourer to command a larger share of the necessaries and comforts of life. We have hitherto principally attempted to attain this end by encouraging the married poor, and consequently increasing the number of labourers, and overstocking the market with a commodity which we still say that we wish to be dear. It would seem to have required no great spirit of divination to foretell the certain failure of such a plan of proceeding.[11]

Malthus, however, did not propose to reduce unemployment merely by cutting off the traditional support of the poor – one of the mercantilist measures to eliminate the results of the production of human beings at the behest of the state. On the contrary, such a cut-off should be combined with an instruction to follow a lifestyle which did not undermine capitalist prosperity. The aim of such an instruction should be to explain to the wage labourer the relationship that existed between the level of wages and possible family size:

> He may perhaps wish that he had not married, because he now feels the inconveniences of it; but it never enters into his head that he can have done anything wrong. He has always been told that to raise up subjects for his king and country is a very meritorious act. He has done this and yet is suffering for it; and it cannot but strike him as most extremely unjust and cruel in his king and country to allow him thus to suffer in return for giving them what they are continually declaring that they particularly want.
>
> Till these erroneous ideas have been corrected, and the language of nature and reason has been generally heard on the subject of population, instead of the language of error and prejudice, it cannot be said that any fair experiment has been made with the understanding of the common people; and we cannot justly accuse them of improvidence and want of industry, till they act as they do now, after it has been brought home to their comprehensions, that they are themselves the cause of their own poverty; that the means of redress are in their own hands, and in the hands of no other persons whatever; that the society in which they live and the government which presides over it, are without any *direct* power in this respect; and that however ardently they may desire to relieve them, and whatever attempts they may make to do so, they are really and truly unable to execute what they benevolently wish, but unjustly promise that *when the wages will not maintain a family, it is an incontrovertible sign that their king and country do not want more subjects,* or at least that they cannot support them; that if they marry in this case, *so far from fulfilling a duty to society, they are throwing an useless burden on it,* at the same time that they are plunging themselves into distress.[12]

It is clear that Malthus's reasoning, like that of many other writers on population before and after him, was based on equating sexuality with marriage and children, or childlessness with moral restraint, as well as small numbers of children with relative moral restraint. However, this must not be interpreted to mean that this clergyman was blindly biassed by the precepts of Christian morality. His standpoint was based, instead, on a conscious population policy. He knew that abstinence from marriage and childlessness were not "bad" for the individual labourer. Malthus blamed the king who was influenced by mercantilist ideas and policies for encouraging workers to have too large families, but not for encouraging reproduction in general. That Malthus supported a form of production of human beings supervised by the state and at the same time the enforcement of Christian morality, and violently opposed those who wished to separate sexuality from reproduction is made clear in the following passage:

> Indeed, *I should always reprobate any artificial and unnatural modes of checking population,* both on account of their immorality and their tendency to remove a necessary stimulus to industry. *If it were possible for each married couple to limit by a wish the number of their children,* there is certainly reason to fear that the indolence of the human race would be greatly increased, and that neither the *population* of individual countries nor of the whole earth *would ever reach its natural and proper extent.* But the restraints which I have recommended are quite of a different character. They are not only pointed out by reason and *sanctioned by religion,* but tend in the most marked manner to stimulate industry. It is not easy to conceive a more powerful encouragement to exertion and good conduct than the looking forward to marriage as a state peculiarly desirable: but only to be enjoyed in comfort by the acquisition of habits of industry, economy and prudence. And it is in this light that I have always wished to place it.[13]

It is not only this calculated approach to religion which shows that Malthus was fully aware of the fact that labourers did not need children and that he knew of effective methods of contraception. In the *First Essay,* published in 1798 anonymously, for fear of personal trouble,[14] Malthus already opposed the Marquis de Condorcet (1743-1794) who in his *Esquisse d'un tableau historique du progrès de l'esprit humain* had discussed the "natural law of procreation" and asked:

> Does this law of nature apply to man? He alone, among all the animals, has found a way to separate, in the act which should perpetuate the species, the gratification inherent in that act and the procreation which, in other species, is the involuntary cause of it. Not only do the motives of a more permanent and more long-lasting interest give him *the strength to resist this attraction;* but he may yield to it, and foresee the consequences of it. Thus, his will can, *without it even implying great sacrifices for him,* establish in a more pleasant manner for his species that equilibrium which can continue to exist in the others only as a result of violent upheavals and cruel destructions.[15]

Condorcet was an exception among the political philosophers of his day, in openly casting doubt on the equation of sexuality with reproduction. He did not, however, ask the question how this equation had been brought about historically. As Condorcet also discussed methods of contraception, Malthus attacked him:

> Having observed that the ridiculous prejudices of superstition would by that time have ceased to throw over morals a corrupt and degrading austerity, he alludes either to a promiscuous concubinage, which would prevent breeding, or to *something else as unnatural.* To remove the difficulty in this way will, surely, in the opinion of most men, be to destroy that virtue and purity of manners, which the advocates of equality, and of the perfectibility of man, profess to be the end and object of their views.[16]

Malthus's analysis was taken up by Francis Place (1771-1854) in his book published in 1822 entitled *Illustrations and Proofs of the Principle of Population.* Unlike Malthus, however, Place did not attack Condorcet. Instead, he became the first English author to provide systematic instruction in contraception:

> It is time, however, that those who really understand the case of a redundant, unhappy, miserable and considerably vicious population, and the means of preventing the redundancy, should clearly, freely, openly and fearlessly point out the means.[17]

We would add that Place did not come from the upper classes, nor had he received a university education but was a member of a large family whose father was a journeyman baker who had become a court bailiff. Malthus was not impressed by this first neo-Malthusian. In his summing up of the debate on population in the 1830 Edition of the *Encyclopaedia Britannica,* he repeated his arguments against contraception:

> All other checks [despite moral restraint], whether of the preventive or the positive kind, though they may greatly vary in degree, resolve themselves into some form of vice or misery.
>
> The remaining checks of the preventive kind are: the sort of intercourse which renders some of the women of large towns unprolific; a general corruption of morals with regard to the sex, which has a similar effect; *unnatural passions and improper arts to prevent* the consequences of irregular connections. These *evidently come under the head of vice.*
>
> The positive checks to population include all the causes which tend in any way prematurely to shorten the duration of human life.[18]

Malthus applied Christian morality not merely to an advocacy of population policy, but also of education. Even though we recognize today that both prescriptions were failures, we would still like to document how Malthus described, more than 150 years ago, the sublimation of sexuality to parental affection, through the prohibition of sexual activity outside marriage and the recommendation of relative moral restraint within marriage:

> It is a very great mistake to suppose that the passion between the sexes only operates and influences human conduct, when the immediate gratification of it is in contemplation. The formation and steady pursuit of some particular plan of life has been justly considered as one of the most permanent sources of happiness; but I am inclined to believe that there are not many plans formed which are not connected in a considerable degree with the prospect of the gratification of this passion, and with the support of children arising from it. The evening meal, the warm house and the comfortable fireside would lose half their interest if we were to exclude the idea of some object of affection with whom they were to be shared ... In *European countries,* where, though the women are not secluded, yet *manners* have imposed considerable restraints on this gratification, the passion not only rises in force, but in the universality and beneficial tendency of its effects; and has often the greatest influence in the formation and improvement of the character, where it is the least gratified.
>
> Considering then the passion between the sexes in all its bearings and relations, and *including the endearing engagement of parent and child* resulting from it, few will be disposed to deny that it is one of the principal ingredients of human happiness.[19]

Here, we come across what Hajnal has characterized as the "European marriage pattern"[20] the production of a stereotype of woman and the desire for a family culminating in the belief in a "natural desire for children" which did not exist at any other time or anywhere else. The formation of this pattern was, instead, the outcome of an historical process, which was characteristic of and limited to Christian Europe of modern times, and which we have discussed elsewhere:[21] the large-scale persecution and liquidation of the "witches-midwives" between 1360 and 1700, a persecution which persisted on a minor scale in some remote parts of Europe at the time when the *First Essay* was published. Malthus never explained, nor even asked the question of how the "European marriage pattern" arose historically. But contrary to the views of many writers of his time and even of contemporary historical demographers and population economists[22], his analysis gives clear evidence of the fact that he did not regard this pattern as "natural".

Summary

Malthus was one of the few historical demographers and population economists who was aware of the fact that the "natural desire for children" can be influenced by human reason, i.e. that this desire is not in reality "natural" at all. When formulating his "Principle of Population", however, Malthus denounced the use of reason and applied the "natural desire for children" to the advocacy of a particular population policy which has not been recognized by later commentators on his theory. Our paper shows that Malthus's apprehension that man would not have sufficient children was at least as great as his well known fear of misery caused by an increasing population and he, therefore, had to advocate moral restraint, rather than contraception which would have resulted in an increase of childlessness.

Notes

1. This essay is a revised version of chapter E, section 2b, in our book *Menschenproduktion–Allgemeine Bevölkerungstheorie der Neuzeit* (co-authored with Rolf Knieper), Frankfurt a.M., 1979.
2. For a detailed discussion of this historical process see G. Heinsohn, O. Steiger and R. Knieper, op. cit. in note 1; cf. also G. Heinsohn and O. Steiger (1980). "The large-scale murder for the consecration of life. Nine theses on population theory". In *Recent Population Change Calling for Action* (Ed. G. S. Siampos), pp.314–326. Athens.
3. cf. our paper (1982). The elimination of mediaeval birth control and the witch trials of modern times. *International Journal of Women's Studies* 5, 193–214. It refers to J. Sprenger and H. Institoris (1906). *Der Hexenhammer (Malleus Maleficarum,* 1487), part I, p.107. (Trans. J. W. R. Schmidt.) Berlin.
4. The *First Essay* contains a criticism of Adam Smith's assertion of a balanced relationship between welfare and population. *See* pp.303ff.
5. T. R. Malthus (1826). *Essay*, 6th Edition, vol. 2, p.237. London.
6. cf. T. R. Malthus. *Essay*, 6th Edition, vol. 1, pp.2–3 (our italics). In the *First Essay*, Malthus still used a purely biological explanation. "I think I may fairly make two postulata: First, that food is necessary to the existence of man. Secondly, that the passion between the sexes is necessary and will remain nearly in its present state. These two laws, ever since we have had any knowledge of mankind, appear to have been fixed laws of our nature." *First Essay*, p.11.
7. *Essay*, 6th Edition, vol. 1, p.4.
8. ibid. pp.6–7.
9. ibid. vol. 2, p.7.
10. ibid. vol. 1, p.532.

11. ibid. vol. 2, p.289.
12. ibid. p.287 (our italics).
13. T. R. Malthus (1826). *Essay*, 6th Edition, vol. 2, p.479. London. (our italics).
14. cf. D. Levy (1978). Some normative aspects of the Malthusian controversy. *History of Political Economy* **10**, 282ff.
15. Quoted by J. L. Flandrin (1979). *Families in Former Times* (1976), p.226. Cambridge.
16. T. R. Malthus. *First Essay*, p.151 (our italics).
17. Francis Place (1930). *Illustrations and Proofs of the Principle of Population* (1822). N. E. Himes (Ed.), pp.173ff. London.
18. T. R. Malthus. *A Summary View of the Principle of Population,* reprinted in D. V. Glass (Ed.) (1953). *Introduction to Malthus,* p.153. London. (Our italics.)
19. T. R. Malthus, op. cit. in note 5, vol. 2, pp.263ff.
20. J. Hajnal (1965). "European marriage patterns in perspective". In *Population in History* (Eds. D. V. Glass and D. E. C. Eversley), pp.101ff. London.
21. cf. especially the most recent version of our research on the elimination of mediaeval birth control and the witch trials of modern times; see op. cit. in note 3.
22. cf. our papers; (i) (1980) Birth control, witch trials and the demographic transition, or: why historical demography has failed to explain the population developments of modern times; *Diskussionsbeiträge zur Politischen Ökonomie.* No. 23. University of Bremen; (ii) The economic theory of fertility. An alternative approach for an economic determination of procreation. *Metroeconomica* **31**, 1979, pp.271–298; (iii) Population in history and economic theories of population (1979), mimeo., University of Bremen, 1981.

17 Malthus Today

E. VAN DE WALLE

Imagine that Malthus, as did Christ in Ivan Karamazov's tale of the Great Inquisitor, has come back to earth. War, famine and poverty are still rife; inequality, oppression and ignorance continue to be the lot of mankind. Malthus feels vindicated as he walks through the land. Meanwhile, people recognize him and avert their heads in respectful and embarrassed silence. Perhaps in a moment, he will encounter his own Great Inquisitor, a neo-Malthusian who will reproach him for his opposition to contraception. But at this point in our story Malthus is puzzled by some features of the contemporary situation that he had not foreseen.

Three historical developments are in direct contradiction with his theory:

1. The population of the world is much greater than he ever thought possible: the positive checks have not limited the growth of population.
2. The passion between the sexes has abated, or at least, the preventive check in its contraceptive form prevails in a substantial portion of the world.
3. An enormous increase in subsistence has taken place, beyond anything imaginable. This has resulted, for countries such as England, in large improvements in the standard of living.

The positive checks

The relaxation of the positive checks to population runs up against the

MALTHUS PAST AND PRESENT
ISBN 0-12-224670-5

brutal statement of the *First Essay* (p.62):

> With regard to the duration of human life, there does not appear to have existed from the earliest ages of the world to the present moment the smallest permanent symptom or indication of increasing prolongation.[1]

It would be unfair to fault Malthus for underestimating the decline of mortality that was to occur. He argued simply that no available empirical evidence indicated that an increase in expectation of life might even take place. "Such a change may undoubtedly happen. All that I mean to say is that it is impossible to infer it from reasoning".[2] This argument, based on the scientific method, was independent from the "argument of population" which dominates in later editions of the *Essay*, where he recognizes that improvement "particularly with respect to cleanliness and ventilation" had improved the health of the people.[3] Poverty, and the shortage of food, would always check population. An exogenous decline of mortality, caused by innovations in public health and medicine, would simply lead to compensating rises in other causes of death. The stream of mortality could not be dammed. The eradication of one cause of death would simply redirect the flow into other channels. About vaccination, the major life-saving innovation of his time, he wrote:

> For my own part I feel not the slightest doubt that, if the introduction of the cowpox should extirpate the small-pox, and yet the number of marriages continue the same, we shall find a very perceptible difference in the increased mortality of some other diseases.[4]

Malthus would not have understood today's population expansion, because he saw population precariously balanced and subject to what historical demographers have called homoeostatic regulation, or to what in macro-economic models is called the Malthusian equilibrium. A decline of mortality had to be accompanied either by a compensating decline of fertility or by an increase in the production of food.

> It can never, of course, happen that any considerable part of that prodigious increase which might be produced by an uninterrupted geometrical progression should exist and then be destroyed. The laws of nature which make food necessary to the life of man, as well as plants and animals, prevent the continued existence of an excess which cannot be supported, and thus either discourage the production of such an excess, or destroy it in the bud in such a way as to make it scarcely perceptible to a careless observer.[5]

But historically the production of subsistence has kept pace with the geometrical progression. Ester Boserup has provided a refutation to Malthus by pointing out that higher densities can result in the intensification of agriculture and changes in land use and tenure.[6] By providing more labour, larger markets and increased returns to scale, population growth fuels itself for undetermined periods of time, even in a purely agricultural economy. No one today denies that exogenous causes of mortality decline have provided the major impetus for an enormous increase in the numbers of mankind; and the food supply has roughly kept pace. Despite the occasional argument that overpopulation has led to malnutrition and famine, there exists no convincing evidence that the quantity or quality of the diet in the less developed world has deteriorated with the multiplication of their populations.

Contemporary Malthusians have accommodated the population explosion in their restatements of the theory, and they envisage a delayed form of the positive check. Growth will lead to future catastrophes, which will reap the surpluses of population accumulated while the world failed to husband carefully its irreplaceable resources. Pollution, severe environmental deterioration, and the exhaustion of raw materials will cause a "die-back" of unprecedented magnitude. The Club of Rome report (Meadows *et al.*, 1974) for example includes many projections of large declines in the population of the world within the next thirty years. The technical aspects of the projections have been criticized on the basis that improvements in expectation of life, which were based on fairly inexpensive public health measures and on a better understanding of the causes of death, are probably irreversible even if the world's standards of living were severely decreased. Most demographers would not predict large future increases in mortality, except as a result of war, natural catastrophe, or exceptional disruptions of communication and public order. A relapse into high mortality is not incorporated in any of the recent projections of the world population.[7]

The second postulatum

Malthus's next surprise would be the prevalence of voluntary fertility control among Western countries. This is the radical departure from Malthusian morality that allowed European populations to escape from the logic of his forecasts. Much has been written about his rejection of contraception. The most reasonable interpretation is that, like most of his contemporaries, Malthus had very little information or opening of mind towards fertility control; its mental associations were with immorality, extramarital sex and unnatural acts.[8]

Malthus's second postulatum was "that the passion between the sexes is necessary and will remain nearly in its present state". The curious inference he derived from that innocuous statement, was that marriage would remain a constant inclination of men and women, and that fertility would not decline, since it was assumed to be unrestrained within marriage. Of course, natural fertility was a common observation at the time. It took the visionary turn of mind of a Condorcet to think that contraception might some day tamper with the biological determinism of uncontrolled reproduction. Condorcet turned out to be right; neo-Malthusianism refuted Malthus. He failed to see how drastic the decline of fertility would be in the developed countries, and how closely it would accompany their process of development.

A powerful movement today is aiming at reducing the growth rate in the developing world by voluntary means rather than by the threatened action of the positive checks. The name of neo-Malthusianism is increasingly given to a position arguing that slower population growth can itself accelerate the process of development, and that family planning programmes can, on their own, bring down fertility. World opinion expressed in the World Plan of Action at the Bucharest Conference of 1974 holds that economic and social development is a necessary condition for the adoption of family limitation, a position summarized by the slogan: "Development is the best contraceptive". Although a persuasive argument can be made that a change in the structure and functioning of family units must occur before fertility can come down,[9] it is hard to measure the extent to which such a change is already taking place in many countries as a result of better education and increased exposure to external influence. The neo-Malthusian position has been the basis of national and international population programmes, and it is claiming an increasing number of successes. Programme effort has been identified as a major determinant of recent fertility declines.[10]

It is paradoxical that the terms neo-Malthusian (or sometimes Malthusian) have taken a derogatory meaning associated with family planning programmes. Neither Malthus nor the agencies promoting population control for economic purposes would accept the tag; the day when the US Agency for International Development, for example, proudly claims Malthusian ends to its policies is far away. Similarly, Malthusianism has long been a term of opprobrium in some West and East European countries, where it stands for a private, selfish corruption of morals that led to small families, the ageing of the population and in general, to a "demographic collapse",[11] thus deserving the label of "vice" that Malthus himself had bestowed on all checks of the preventive kind outside of "the prudential restraint on marriage." It is certain that the historical decline of fertility has had important consequences on Western economies, some of them negative. An interesting, although unproven hypothesis, is that modern "Malthusianism" has led to labour shortages and to the substitution of technology for labour at the cost of pollution and environmental deterioration.[12] Although the economic and social consequences of very low fertility and excessive ageing may be debatable, no one in the developed world argues seriously for a return to the uncontrolled fertility of the past. The separation of reproduction and the passion between the sexes is a major achievement of modernization.

The difficulty of subsistence

The third surprise of Malthus in his revisit of earth would consist in the improvement of diets and standards of living in England and the developed world. The spectacle of prevailing abundance where he had known scarcity would be so damaging to his theories that it might lead him to revise the Principle of Population as the organizing principle of society. In his view, food was necessary to the existence of man. This is the first postulatum. Nature has been sparing in the room and the nourishment to produce food. Land ultimately is the limiting factor, but by regulating the appropriation of land and the distribution of the product, society and institutions have imposed yet lower limits to increases in the numbers of mankind.

Malthus acknowledged that it should be possible to increase the production of food, secondarily by improved technology, but primarily by better laws and institutions. We are indebted to the ignorance and bad government of our ancestors, he said, for the fact that there still exists a large potential increase in production. Subsistence in England and other European countries of the time could be doubled in the next 25 years, and multiplied by four in a century, according to an arithmetical progression. By removing institutional obstacles to development, mankind could improve its lot and increase its numbers. But only within limits:

> The lower classes of people in Europe may at some future period be much better instructed than they are at present; they may be taught to employ the little spare time they have in many better ways than at the

> ale-house; they may live under better and more equal laws than they have ever hitherto done, perhaps, in any country; and I even conceive it possible, though not probable, that they may have more leisure; but it is not in the nature of things, that they can be awarded such a quantity of money or subsistence, as will allow them all to marry early, in the full confidence that they shall be able to provide with ease for a numerous family.[13]

Later Malthus asserted that the preventive check had contributed to economic advantage in Europe, but only to the extent that it allowed population growth not to exceed the pace of increase in subsistence:

> And probably it may be said with truth, that in almost all the more improved countries of modern Europe, the principal check which at present keeps the population down to the level of the actual means of subsistence is the prudential restraint on marriage.[14]

Malthus would be amazed by the increase in standard of living in Europe since his time. He vastly underestimated the potential of technology to provide food and commodities to the growing populations of the West. Marx and Engels, two generations later, had a better understanding of the forces released by the industrial revolution. Malthus's model relied on human labour and local land as the basic factors of production. He missed the profound importance of the steam engine as a multiplier of human labour. The industrial revolution (and to a large extent the agricultural revolution) were made possible by the reliance on untapped and cheap reserves of fossil fuels as substitutes for labour and land. Agriculture was soon affected because the steamship brought foreign wheat to European markets and broke the link between the production of subsistence, the fertility of local lands, and the rent of the propertied classes. In the long run, fertilizers would push back the bounds of productivity. The use of coal represented the mobilization of millions of mechanical "slaves" to transport grain from the American plains and guano from Peru, to cultivate, process and exchange agricultural products in an enlarged market. Today, at the end of the evolution, it takes 1250 litres of oil per year to feed an American, 0.84 kg of oil to produce and market one kg of bread.[15] Energy, rather than land, has become the main limiting factor to reach an adequate nutrition under current technology in the developing world. It has been estimated, for example, that fertilizers have accounted for 40 per cent of the rise in crop production between the early sixties and the mid seventies, and that the contribution made by bringing new land under the plough amounted to only 17 per cent.[16] Chemical fertilizer requires oil or natural gas for its production.

The Malthusian theory can be adapted to these changed circumstances, as, indeed, it has been. Abundant energy might be compared to abundant land, the situation that prevailed in Malthus's time in the Americas. This he saw as favourable to the expansion of population and to the standard of living until the day of reckoning when the resources would be completely used up. Economic development in the West got a "free ride" from the prodigal use of abundant but unrenewable fossil fuels. The rules of the game were circumvented, but only for a while. The Malthusian theory warns of absolute limits and inevitable scarcity. It reminds us that the need for resources will continue to impose limits to growth, even though technological progress allows substitution and recycling, and may temporarily release the lid.

The developing world appears more vulnerable to resource scarcity, and the low-income, agricultural nations are closest to the situation that Malthus was witnessing. Part of the problem of development is that so much of the available investment must go into supporting population growth rather than increasing productivity. Several economists have described the operation of a "Malthusian trap" or "low level equilibrium trap": small gains in income tend to produce a decline in mortality and a rise in the rate of population growth, which eventually exhausts the initial improvement and pushes the population back to its initial level of income.[17] It has been shown, however, that the mechanism would take a considerable time to dissipate the gain in income. As Preston puts it: "[the Malthusian trap] shuts so slowly that escape seems inevitable."[18]

Malthusianism may have had its greatest influence on discussions of foreign policy. The Irish famine of 1846 had been seen as a natural reaction to previous population growth, and one in which the British government should not intervene, as assistance would only lead to the delaying of an unavoidable adjustment mechanism. Similarly, the notion of triage was abundantly discussed in the 1960s and 1970s: in the same way that wartime field hospitals have to make a choice between those they can rescue and those who are too far wounded to survive, similarly lists of countries were compiled that should be left to the ravages of famine.[19] Food aid, it was advocated, must be limited to those that could be saved. In a twist that the great economist would have approved, it has often been proposed to limit assistance to nations that would implement a programme of population control.

Although these considerations are too controversial ever to have been explicitly integrated into official policies, a great deal of legitimate concern has been raised about the rationale of aid that would lead to the permanent establishment of "basket cases", entirely and permanently dependent on foreign food. This evokes Malthus's position against redistributional solutions. Savane has noted that international aid in the Sahel region is comparable to the Poor Laws, in that it prevents the operation of the positive check of famine. He quotes a study stressing the need to develop the productivity of the area so that it can be self-sufficient: "It is hard to see how the rest of the world could accept to provide permanent and increasing supplies of food to a population whose growth would lead to degradation of the soil on which it lives, and therefore, to a decrease of its own resources."[20] Malthus would not have objected to international solidarity in famine conditions, as long as it did not make the assisted nations dependent nor reduce their ability to cope by their own resources with their problem. About the large sum which was collected in England from the higher classes of society for the support of the poor, he wrote to Samuel Whitbread:[21]

> I should indeed think that the whole, or a much greater sum, was well applied, if it merely relieved the comparatively few that would be in want, if there were no public provision for them, without the fatal and unavoidable consequences of continually increasing their number, and depressing the condition of those who were struggling to maintain themselves in independence.

Malthus the development economist

In describing Malthus's three "surprises", we have identified three avatars of his thought that are still encountered today under the names of Malthusianism or neo-Malthusianism. These include the prediction of a delayed dieback of the population resulting from ecological disasters, the advocacy of fertility control for economic purposes independently of social and economic development, and finally a belief in the scarcity of resources, and the waste of investment to sustain population increase, as limiting factors in economic growth.

It is clear, however, that the persistence of Malthus's influence, and the revival that is now taking place, must be explained by other reasons than the permanence of a few ideas that even their advocates rarely trace back to the *Essay*. I see two reasons, beyond his extraordinary talent as a writer, a polemicist and a scientist. The first is that he was first and foremost a theoretician of the development of agricultural nations, a background where the issues of land scarcity and overpopulation have not abated. The second reason is that Malthus had the uncanny talent to attract powerful adversaries who gave him a role for which neither the cloth nor the temperament predisposed him — that of the arch-enemy of mankind. After having figured as the villain in so many other people's plots, there were bound to be periodic re-evaluations of his arguments for their own sake, rather than as seen through the distortions of his opponents.

It has been noted that the *Essay* starts with a statement of the conflict between the geometric law that governs the growth of population, and the arithmetic law that regulates subsistence; but that the rest is devoted to a description of mechanisms other than famine and a shortage of food that check population:[22]

> It makes little difference in the actual rate of the increase of population, or the necessary existence of checks to it, whether that state of demand and supply which occasions an insufficiency of wages to the whole of the labouring classes be produced prematurely by a bad structure of society and an unfavourable distribution of wealth, or necessarily by the comparative exhaustion of the soil.[23]

For "prematurely" read "in the short run"; for "necessarily" read "in the long run". And the enumeration of premature obstacles constitutes a catalogue of impediments to development that retain their relevance today. Large sections of the *Essay* and the *Principles* consist of descriptions of backward societies of the time and of explanations of their backwardness.[24] Institutional factors such as the corruption and ineffectiveness of despotic governments, the excessive fragmentation or concentration of property, colonialism, protectionism, and monopolies, figure among the main causes of poor standards of living in the world. Ignorance, indolence and improvidence are natural traits of men which can be remedied by public policy, and particularly by education and political liberty. Although Malthus believed that the niggardliness of nature rather than human institutions set the ultimate limits to happiness and wealth, the proximate obstacles, which are institutional in essence, were actually more important. Malthus spoke loudly in favour of a just and enlightened government, civil and political liberty and education for the masses. He backed the existence of privilege in society, particularly in the form of private property, as the only practical mechanism to provide a system of incentives and a refuge against shared poverty. Only this would secure "to a portion of the society the leisure necessary for the progress of the arts and sciences".[25]

It is to this double belief that the roots of social inequality were to be found in a Principle of Population, and that social inequality was necessary to stimulate industry and investment, that Marx and his successors have directed their opposition. We speculated earlier that the virulence of Malthus's detractors may well have kept his reputation alive. Contemporary Marxists in particular have inherited the vigorous opposition of Marx and Engels. The attacks *ad hominem,* the innuendos about Malthus's private life, his alleged plagiarism, his infeodation to Church and financial interests would all be hard to understand unless Malthusianism had hit a raw nerve of the socialist thinkers.

To Marx, an abstract principle of population applicable to all societies was unacceptable. Malthus's overpopulation ought to be blamed on the capitalist mode of production rather than attributed to the operation of an inexorable natural law. The surplus of workers resulted from the substitution of machines for men.

> The reproduction of the working class made new workers cheap and so permitted the bourgeoisie to extract surplus value from their work. But to ask the proletariat to be more responsible was futile, for the very degradation inherent in capitalism ruled out an appeal to their highest nature. The transformation of capitalist to socialist institutions would eliminate the Malthusian dilemma.[26]

The internal contradictions of capitalism led to ever increasing unemployment, until the system was toppled by revolution. The Malthusian hope to remedy this by controlling births would only delay the inevitable. Today, however, neither Malthus's nor Marx's prediction have come to pass in the developed world. The capitalist system has survived its contradictions, and capital accumulation has not led to increased unemployment. Within the system, the Malthusian predictions of a ceiling of subsistence have been refuted by the increase in productivity. But the debate still rages in relation to the less developed countries.

Lenin had suggested that the overpopulation of agrarian Russia was not the consequence of a disparity between population and the means of subsistence, but rather a result of the penetration of capitalism into Russian agriculture.[27]

Similarly, Marxists do not consider population growth as a cause of poverty and unemployment in the less developed world: they are the result of colonialism, imperialism, and the inequal distribution of wealth. There is, of course, nothing here with which Malthus himself would have disagreed; he would have said that the "premature" causes of misery were institutional, and the "necessary" causes were to be found in the Principle of Population. But a hasty interpretation of the Principle has historically been used to justify privilege, class differences in wealth, and unequal terms of trade. Only under private property, said Malthus, would the social system allow "progress of the arts and sciences". His model of the world was based on social inequality and the justification of privilege; the profit motive stimulated investment, but also the exploitation of man by man.[28] Human progress was severely limited by the joint operation of high fertility and of resource scarcity.

Today, Malthusianism has ceased to be a dominant demographic theory in the capitalist world. The free economy has proved capable of generating development even in the presence of rapid population growth. To the accusation that capitalist systems allow exploitation, the standard answer is that the profit motive has been more effective at increasing the size of the cake than have socialist bureaucracies, and that exploitation of man by man when the cake is growing is preferable to oppression by the State, which socialist systems are known to practise occasionally, and a stagnant economy.

Marxists have transferred their hostility to the illegitimate neo-Malthusian posterity of our author. They oppose the use of birth control programmes to relieve economic strains in non-socialist developing countries because this is part of a reformist approach that strives to maintain the *status quo.* "The social meaning of neo-Malthusianism is to distract the workers from the struggle against exploitation and to persuade the proletariat that in order to improve its condition it must abandon the class struggle and find a solution for its difficult position in the small family system. . . .".[29] Moreover, they subscribe, perhaps blindly, to an act of faith that no decline of fertility can occur without a cultural revolution and the development of large-scale industry (Guzevatyi).

Conclusion

Refuted many times, the Principle of Population according to Malthus remains today as an enduring model of the relation between population and the economy. It would be hard to find an article on the subject that does not pay lip service to the great precursor, or does not present his view as a necessary point of departure, however wrong, to which more valid theories are contrasted. Most contemporary demographic treatises continue to discuss him; important theoretical contributions are presented in contrast to his doctrine.[30] A recent discussion of demography and development, gives the following explanation of this success:[31]

> Malthus and the classicists are remembered not because they were right (indeed they were not), but because they helped suggest the notion of a "system" and one in which aggregate economic and demographic change were tied together by behaviour at the family level.

This is a singular achievement.

Notes

1. T. R. Malthus. *First Essay*, p.160.
2. ibid. p.160.
3. He goes on to add: "But these causes would not have produced the effect observed if they had not been accompanied by an increase in the preventive check." *An Essay on Population*, Everyman Edition, vol. 2, p.182.
4. ibid. p.183.
5. T. R. Malthus, *A Summary View of the Principle of Population*. Reprinted in *Three Essays on Population*, pp.53–54. Mentor Books, New York. (The 1830 essay is based on the 1824 supplement to the *Encyclopaedia Britannica*.)
6. Ester Boserup (1965). *The Conditions of Agricultural Growth*. Aldine, Chicago.
7. e.g. United Nations (1979). *World Population Trends and Prospects by Country, 1950–2000*. New York; U.S. Bureau of the Census (1979). *Illustrative Projections of World Population to the 21st Century*. Current Population Reports, Series P-23. Washington.
8. T. R. Malthus, op. cit. in note 5, p.38.
9. Eleanor R. Fapohunda. The relevance of Malthusian ideas to contemporary population dynamics of developing countries: The case of West African countries. MHA, p.185.
10. W. P. Mauldin and B. Berelson (1978). Conditions of fertility decline in developing countries, 1965–75. *Studies in Family Planning* **9** (5), 89–147.
11. G. F. Dumont. Malthus et le collapsus démographique des pays industriels. MHA, p.185.
12. P. Maitra. Malthus re-visited. Population, poverty and pollution. MHA, p.190..
13. T. R. Malthus, op. cit. in note 1, pp.277–278.
14. T. R. Malthus, op. cit. in note 5, pp.42–43
15. F. Monckeberg (1979). Food and world population: Future perspectives. In *World Population and Development: Challenge and Prospects* (Ed. P. M. Hauser), p.133. Syracuse University Press.

16. N. S. Scrimshaw and L. Taylor (1980). Food. *Scientific American* **243** (3), 85.
17. H. Leibenstein (1954). *A Theory of Economic-Demographic Development.* Princeton University Press; R. R. Nelson (1956). A theory of the low-level equilibrium trap in under-developed economies. *American Economic Review* **46**, 894-908.
18. S. H. Preston (1975). The changing relation between mortality and level of economic development. *Population Studies* **29** (2), 231-248.
19. W. Paddock and P. Paddock (1967). *Famine 1975. America's Decision: Who will Survive?* Little Brown, Boston; P. R. Ehrlich (1968). *The Population Bomb.* Ballantine Books, New York.
20. L. Savane. Malthus, Marx . . . Sécheresses et famines dans le Sahel. MHA, p.201.
21. T. R. Malthus. *A Letter to Samuel Whitbread Esq., M.P. on his proposed Bill for the Amendment of the Poor Laws.* Reprinted in D. V. Glass (Ed.) (1953). *Introduction to Malthus*, pp.190–191. Watts & Co., London.
22. *Population and Development Review* **6**, no. 1 (March 1980), p.153. This reference consists extracts from the *Essay* "with modern resonances" devoted to institutional causes of depopulation in the Ottoman empire.
23. T. R. Malthus, op. cit. in note 5, p.35.
24. Y. Breton. Malthus and underdevelopment. This volume, pp.247–253.
25. T. R. Malthus, op. cit. in note 5, p.148.
26. N. Keyfitz (1972). Population theory and doctrine. A historical survey. In *Readings in Population* (Ed. W. Petersen), p.56.
27. United Nations (1973). *The Determinants and Consequences of Population Growth*, p.49. New York.
28. E. Weiss-Altaner. L'exode rural au Tiers-Monde: Est-ce une crise malthusienne? MHA, p.202.
29. B. Z. Urlanis (1970). Marxism and Birth Control. *Studies in Family Planning*, p.1.
30. cf. Ester Boserup, op. cit. in note 6.
31. Nancy Birdsall, J. Fei, S. Kuznets, G. Ranis and T. P. Schultz (1979). Demography and development in the 1980s. In *World Population and Development; Challenge and Prospects* (Ed. P. M. Hauser). Syracuse University Press.

18 Malthus and Underdevelopment

Y. BRETON

It was only after World War II that the concept of underdevelopment began to impinge on the world's consciousness. The urgency, gravity and importance of the problems raised by underdevelopment justified the increasing importance that the discussion of this subject occupied in conferences of international organizations, economic journalism and in academic controversies.

The question which immediately arises is whether underdevelopment is really a new phenomenon, or whether a new term has simply been coined for an old concept. There are some writers who would take the latter point of view and who would stress that since the end of the eighteenth and the beginning of the nineteenth century important economic differences have existed between the richer countries (such as England, France, Holland, the United States) and the rest of the world.[1] The origin of these differences is to be sought in the great changes which shook Western Europe after the discoveries of the fifteenth and sixteenth centuries and the industrial revolution which occurred at the end of the eighteenth and the beginnings of the nineteenth century. There are sufficient references to "backward societies" in Malthus's writings (for instance, in Book I of the *Essay,* and in Section IV of Book II of the *Principles of Political Economy)* to make it clear that he realized that "underdevelopment" existed. Moreover, he tries to explain why some societies were backward and adduces a number of reasons, which we shall consider in two categories : endogenous and exogenous.

1. Endogenous factors

One of the important endogenous factors is the nature of social

MALTHUS PAST AND PRESENT
ISBN 0-12-224670-5

institutions. We shall begin this section by considering the importance of government, continue by discussing serfdom, a feudal institution which had not completely disappeared during Malthus's lifetime, and shall finally deal with private property, a concept which, as the reader will hardly need reminding, was central to classical economic theory and Malthus's thought in particular.

As regards government, bad government could result in economic decline or in stagnation in a state of underdevelopment. This might be brought about by excessive extortion on the part of government or by too heavy taxation which would discourage effort and saving with disastrous economic consequences.[2] A government which was incapable of maintaining public order would make it almost impossible to accumulate capital and, in such conditions, according to classical economic theory, there could be no growth. Only countries which enjoyed peace and tranquillity could grow in wealth and in Malthus's *Essay,* particularly in Book I, many examples are given to support this contention.[3]

As regards serfdom, serfs are almost inevitably indolent and ignorant.[4] Deprived of economic stimulus, they lack the energy and efficiency which is necessary for economic progress, as may be witnessed by the situation in Russia or Poland.[5]

Malthus is full of praise for the institution of private property. "If land were not appropriated", he writes in the *Principles,* "its produce would be very much less abundant, and consequently the producers and consumers would be much worse off".[6] He regards private property as one of the fundamental institutions of society and of civilization,[7] and considers it as natural, even sacred.[8]

Provided man is not robbed of the fruits of his labour, he will be stimulated to effort.[9] Security of property, therefore, is one of the most potent encouragements to the growth of wealth.[10] On the contrary, insecurity of property, whether caused by tyrannical government, weak government, or simply by governments which have enacted bad laws constitutes an obstacle to human economic activity and to the development of habits of providence, as may be seen, for instance in Africa or in Ireland.[11]

However, Malthus had some reservations about large estates, reservations which he built into his theory of effective demand and his conception of the dynamic produced by self-interest. He went so far as to propose the sub-division of large landholdings as a measure to increase productivity.[12] However, there were limits: too large a degree of fragmentation of holdings would be detrimental to an increase in wealth,[13] fatal to production[14] and lead to the risk of excessive population.[15]

Men's energy, Malthus wrote in the *Principles* has differed greatly between different countries and in the same country at different times. Like Ricardo, he believed, that misery was caused by inactivity, and that in order to increase his happiness, men would need to be stimulated to greater effort. For this reason he stressed the need for a profound study of men's attitude to labour.

Malthus believed indolence to be widespread in primitive societies,[16] i.e. among "savages". Nor did he have any doubt that man was naturally indolent in all societies,[17] "really inert, sluggish and adverse from labour", and that he would prefer idleness to the enjoyment of luxuries or the fruits of industry.[18] These views are repeatedly stated in the *Principles*.[19] This natural tendency to indolence and men's marked preference for idleness could be reinforced by other factors, such as political institutions,[20] serfdom,[21] the type of needs, the size of agriculture, the Poor Laws and the natural environment, such as climate or the productivity of the soil.[22]

According to Malthus the most important factor which led to apathy in man was the limited nature of his wants. Indolence in some societies is aggravated by the fact that they have not yet acquired a taste for ribbons, lace or velvet.[23] In populations whose members were satisfied with their level of living the benefits obtained through increased wealth were not worth as much as the luxury of idleness.[24]

In order to overcome indolence and stimulate the desire to work it was necessary to teach a system of morality and religion in which work was given very high esteem[25] and to create new wants.[26]

Malthus believed that this "opening of minds" could be achieved through stimulating commerce between nations.[27] Such commercial exchanges could alter the demand and stimulate new wants in a backward population, whose members would then be prepared to give up some of their leisure time to satisfy them. However, it would be difficult to do this, when the development of new demands was prevented by the values of religions, such as Islam and Hinduism.[28]

On the subject of investment, Malthus believed that the desire to accumulate depended, among other factors, on government. Where there was no faith in government, or where government was poor, rates of interest were high. This was the case in India and in China, where interest was as high as three per cent per month,[29] whereas in England a rate of between three and four per cent per year was sufficient. Malthus believed that progress in the achievement of civil and political liberty in the countries of the East would result in lower rates of interest there.[30]

However, other factors of a social psychological nature, such as lack of prudence were also important. Any accumulation of capital implies that present benefits are sacrificed for the sake of the future. It is, therefore, clear that investment is not encouraged in societies where members see their future as bleak or where there is a considerable degree of uncertainty about future developments. Classical economists and philosophers, as well as other writers, believed that this was the situation in populations of "savages".

Lastly, accumulation would be influenced by environmental conditions. According to Malthus, the nature of underdevelopment in some parts of the world could best be understood by considering the economy in two sectors: commerce and manufactures on one hand, and agriculture on the other. His analysis of relations between the two sectors was more profound than that of other writers of his time. He stressed that in a closed economy any obstacle to normal development in one sector would also effect the development of the other. It was therefore, necessary to try and achieve a balanced growth between these two sectors.[31]

The agricultural development of a region could be held up because of the absence of an important urban centre. Writing about Latin America, Malthus noted that "except in the neighbourhood of the mines or near the great towns, the effective demand for produce is not such as to induce the great proprietors to bring their immense tracts of land properly into cultivation".[32]

An insufficiency of internal effective demand could, according to Malthus, be overcome by opening the economy to international trade by developing export markets, particularly for agricultural goods. In this way, the vicious circle could be broken and the economy set on the road to growth.[33] This was shown by the case of England and the USA.

2. Exogenous factors

Turning next to exogenous factors, Malthus first turned to violence. He writes about the "cruel oppression"[34] practised by the first Spanish colonizers in America. "No settlements", he writes in the *Essay,* "could easily have been worse managed than those of Spain in Mexico, Peru and Quito".[35] This also holds true of the Portuguese administration of Brazil which was governed with "almost equal tyranny".[36]

Adam Smith, too, had protested vigorously against the exploitation and pillage organized by the British and Dutch East India companies in those "ruined and unhappy countries", Bengal and the Moluccas. Malthus, however, was silent on this topic. It may be recalled that from 1804 until the date of his death in 1834 Malthus was Professor of History and Political Economy at the East India Company's college in

Haileybury, where future administrators for the East India Company were trained!

However, it would be wrong to suggest that since the end of the fifteenth century all relations between the richer and the poorer countries were characterized by violence and oppression, such as the enslavement of such peoples as the American Indians or the African Blacks. Equally important and equally efficacious were the asymmetrical "non-violent" influences imposed by the metropolitan economy on colonial economies which it dominated. These consisted of making it impossible for the colonial economies to export manufactured goods to the metropolitan country, either by taxing them heavily or simply by prohibiting their importation, or even by prohibiting the manufacture of goods, e.g. in the case of the North American colonies before the Declaration of Independence, when the English government absolutely prohibited the manufacture of steel in the colonies. Such prohibitions had disastrous effects on the dominated economies, e.g. Ireland. However, possibly for the reasons that we have given above, Malthus does not describe the ruin of the Indian textile industry by competition from the cotton mills of Lancashire at the end of the eighteenth and the beginning of the nineteenth century, caused by the use of obsolete techniques, and he does not express any disquiet at the brutal disappearance of this industry, even though this was one of the most spectacular instances of colonialism and economic aggression during the nineteenth century.

Conclusion

According to Malthus economic development in backward countries would imply profound changes in their economic, political and social institutions, the attitude of their populations to work and in the structure of demand and wants in those countries.[37]

However, he stressed the considerable difficulties inherent in any attempt to change attitude to work,[38] customs,[39] morals,[40] tastes[41] and wants.[42] It would take many years before the "Siberian boor" could achieve the industry and efficiency of an English worker, and powerful and efficient stimuli would have to be applied for this to happen.[43] Moreover, any attempt to civilize and direct the activities of Tartar or black tribes would take a long time and the results would be uncertain.[44] This is the main reason why civilization would prove to be an extremely difficult goal to achieve.

Malthus's analysis of underdevelopment is, therefore, complex, in the sense that he uses many different variables for its explanation and because he gives an important place to the analysis of demand and its static and dynamic interaction with supply.

The world at the end of the twentieth century is very different from what it was during Malthus's time. His explanation of underdevelopment is insufficient for a complete understanding of the actual situation of countries in the third world today. But this does not mean that his theory deserves only to be relegated to a dusty shelf in the museum of forgotten doctrines in the history of economic thought. In spite of its many insufficiencies, Malthus stresses the importance of a number of variables which seem as important today as they did in his own time, even though they are neglected by contemporary economists.

Notes

1. cf. P. Bairoch (1971). Les écarts des niveaux du développement entre pays développés et pays sous-développés de 1700 à 2000. *Revue Tiers Monde* **12** (47).
2. T. R. Malthus. *Essay*, Book III, vol. 2. chapter 14, p.143.
3. ibid. vol. 1, pp.80, 114–115.
4. ibid. vol. 1, p.186.
5. ibid. pp.74–75.
6. T. R. Malthus. *Principles of Political Economy*, p.76.
7. ibid. p.425.
8. ibid. p.410.
9. ibid. pp.309–310; cf. also *Essay*, vol.. 2, p.194.
10. T. R. Malthus, op. cit. in note 6, p.425.
11. T. R. Malthus, op. cit. in note 2, p.89, 93; vol. 2, p.194; T. R. Malthus, op. cit. in note 6, p.350.
12. T. R. Malthus, op. cit. in note 6, pp.373, 426.
13. ibid. pp.375, 376.
14. T. R. Malthus, op. cit. in note 2, vol. 2, p.63.
15. T. R. Malthus, op. cit. in note 2, vol. 1, pp.129, 139.
16. T. R. Malthus, op. cit. in note 6, p.334; T. R. Malthus, op. cit. in note 2, vol. 1, p.26; vol. 2, pp.26, 143.
17. T. R. Malthus, op. cit. in note 2, vol 2, p.26.
18. T. R. Malthus, op. cit. in note 6, pp.321–322.
19. ibid. p.402, 348.
20. T. R. Malthus, op. cit. in note 2, vol. 1, p.143.
21. ibid. p.186.
22. ibid. p.89; vol. 2, p.135.
23. T. R. Malthus, op. cit. in note 6, p.321.
24. ibid. p.334.
25. ibid. pp.309–310.

26. ibid. pp.402–403.
27. ibid.
28. T. R. Malthus, op. cit. in note 2, vol. 1, p.119.
29. T. R. Malthus, op. cit. in note 6, p.156.
30. ibid.
31. T. R. Malthus, op. cit. in note 2, vol. 2, p.76.
32. T. R. Malthus, op. cit. in note 6, pp.339–340.
33. ibid. pp.399–400.
34. T. R. Malthus, op. cit. in note 2, vol. 1, p.42.
35. ibid. p.304.
36. ibid. p.305.
37. T. R. Malthus, op. cit. in note 6, p.351.
38. ibid. pp.339–340.
39. ibid. p.225.
40. T. R. Malthus. op. cit. in note 2, vol. 2, p.210.
41. T. R. Malthus, op. cit. in note 6, pp.348–349.
42. cf. Malthus's letter to Ricardo referred to in J. M. Keynes (1933). *Essays in Biography*, p.98. London.
42. T. R. Malthus. *Essay*, vol. 1, p.10.
44. ibid. p.9.

PART 5

Malthusianism and Socialism

19 Malthusianism and Socialism

MICHELLE PERROT

This paper is not an account of original personal research. It is based entirely on the contributions which have been submitted to this section of the Colloquium, a list of which is given in the Appendix. Eight of the contributions deal with France during the period 1830 to the present day, two with Germany, one with Canada, one with the United States, one with Russia, and two consider general topics such as Social Darwinism and the eugenic movement. All are of considerable epistemological interest. It is unfortunate that there is no paper which deals with Italian Socialism, as controversies about population were widespread in the Italian socialist movement before 1914.[1]

Much work remains to be done on the points of contact between these two doctrines in different countries. Both originate from a discussion of poverty, but the remedies they propose for this evil are totally different. Different reactions in different countries may be explained by differences in their demographic situation, social, cultural or religious factors, family structure and the position of women, and differences in the degree to which the working class movement was libertarian. Thus, in the vast expanse of America, the idea of a limit to subsistence made little sense, and Malthusianism became an expression of moral perfectionism rather than an economic doctrine. We can only sketch these variations in outline; they are more complex than appears at first sight. But before Marx there were a number of links between these two opposing camps. However, since 1830 in the case of England, and since about 1880 in other countries, the debate which was often very bitter was concentrated less on Malthus than on neo-Malthusianism, a movement with practical rather than theoretical ob-

MALTHUS PAST AND PRESENT
ISBN 0-12-224670-5

jectives, and which originated partly from Malthus's analysis as well as from socialism which regarded the control of births both as part of the class struggle and of the fight for the liberty of the individual. We shall attempt to show how and why this turn occurred, and why it was particularly marked in France.

Socialists against Malthus. The hesitations of romantic socialism

In considering the ratio between population and resources as the key variable which explains the existence of misery, Malthus challenged the socialists who looked for a solution to the problem in terms of changes in social organization and the development of productive forces. They were, therefore, forced to discuss Malthus's views early on. However, their discussions were often based on a misapprehension, a situation which is not uncommon when new and shocking ideas are put forward, particularly when these lead to arguments and polemics. Very often they were late in reading Malthus's original text, even after it had become available in translation relatively soon after the English publication, as happened in France, and their reading was often superficial.

Thus, in the book by Pierre Leroux,[2] the references are all at second hand and are borrowed from the writings of the Englishman Charles Loudon,[3] or the French writer Duchâtel. When Leroux cites Malthus, he merely writes: "As Malthus states. . . . " Socialists became familiar with Malthusian ideas through the study of economics; Leroux writes that the Malthusian doctrine is part of the official economics of France.[4] Later they became aware of Malthus through reading Marx, but Marx's interpretation of Malthus was itself controversial. Or, they relied on the celebrated pamphlet of Marcus[5] which under the pretext of refuting Malthus attributed the most atrocious designs to him, such as the asphyxiation of new born children.[6]

Both the author and his doctrine were caricatured. Invectives were common: "the sombre Protestant from sad England" (Leroux), "a reactionary Puritan, the self-seeking defender of the propertied classes, the cruel advocate of 'sweeping the streets clean' even at the cost of massacring the innocent." "Malthusians", writes Leroux,[7] "propose an annual massacre of the innocent, in all families which exceed a size fixed by law". Marx referred to Malthus as "superficial", "a professional plagiarist", "the author of nonsense", "the agent of the landed aristocracy", "a miserable sinner against science", "a paid advocate", the "principal enemy of the people".[8] Proudhon called him "a political assassin".[9] In popular literature or journalism, where incidentally, a Malthusian view of the family was commonly accepted, he was depicted as a type of man eater pictured by Swift, "the black vampire of the night for the poor".[10]

Certain stereotypes are selected from the doctrine. Among them are the analogy of the banquet, cited always as "the extermination of the human species", the theme of the "lottery of life", the view of "moral restraint" as an inhuman or vicious practice, depending on one's point of view, the literal interpretation of Malthus's law regarded as a mathematical regularity and expressed in laborious tables.

However, all these misinterpretations are accompanied by passionate arguments about the problems posed by Malthus: the size of the population, its growth, its subsistence. Even before Marx, Malthus's views were generally condemned. From the French communists to the Russian populists, from Dézamy and Cabet to Milyutinov and Czernichevsky, there was universal opposition. Socialists regarded themselves as continuing the traditions of the Enlightenment and, being resolutely optimistic, refused to recognize any limit to human progress, the forward march of humanity towards the promised land where there would be abundance, the key to happiness. They condemned Malthus as a pessimist and a sceptic. To Malthus's deity and the doctrine of original sin they opposed their faith in science, evolution and growth. Their criticism of Malthus was both intellectual and moral. However, the arguments used and the manner in which the discussion was conducted changed abruptly after the publication of Marx's work.

Before Marx wrote, most of the socialists were romantics. In spite of their criticism of the existing social order they offered a varied view of the future. For France, the complexity of their views is analysed fully by Louis Devance.[11] Among the strongest opponents of Malthus were the Communists (Cabet, Dézamy) and the Christian socialists (Buchez, Leroux). Their objections were based on scientific grounds (once the worker is freed from exploitation, he will be able to ensure the subsistence of his family) and on moral reasons (contraception is a crime against nature or religion). However, many of them did admit that it was possible and even probable that there was a connection between misery and overpopulation. Pierre Leroux himself admitted the validity of Malthus's law. "The only true proposition amongst those which have become undeservedly famous is that which asserts that wherever subsistence is sufficient, under present conditions of morality, population will double every 25 years."[12]

Fourier gives this problem detailed consideration, differing in this from Saint Simon and his followers who do not address themselves to this question at all. The analogy of the antheap and of "pullulation" is familiar to him. He sees in an excess of children, an important cause of misery for the people. "Everything conspires to entrap the father into an antheap of children. At the beginning he is pushed into this position through poverty and despair. The people beget children by the dozen and say "their misery will not be any greater than ours has been".[13]

Although Fourier believes that on a world scale in a socialized economy production will be increased at least fourfold, he does recognize that there is a physical limit to resources. "The world's territory is limited and within the next two centuries it will have to support 5500 million people."[14] Thus, in spite of the "taming of the deserts" which has played such an important part in the romantic imagination, the human species will, in the end, die of congestion and suffocate through excessive numbers. At the end of his anxious discussion of these problems, he concludes with disarming honesty: "I recognize that the wisest among those who have discussed these problems agree with Malthus's view on the nature of this vicious circle, or else confess that they do not understand the problem."[15]

Pecqueur, too, is frightened of an unchecked growth where "it is no longer possible to expect the continuation of civilisation, and where misery would increase without limit, because of large numbers"[16] and he tries to determine an optimum population which would be best for development. Even Proudhon admits that under present conditions, Malthus's law is valid, that misery will overtake production and that it will become necessary to find an alternative equilibrium.

Some German academic socialists, e.g. Schmoller and particularly Wagner, put forward very similar views a few decades later. The latter wrote: "Malthus was essentially correct." He regarded an increase in the standard of living as the best way of developing prudent demographic behaviour.[17]

The main difference between Malthus and the socialists is found when possible remedies are considered. The socialists admit that the danger from overpopulation is real, but they see a solution for this problem in improved social and economic organization, a more advanced technology and a consequent rise in the standard of living which will turn the people away from unbridled sexuality as more varied pleasures becomes available to them. With the exception of Fourier who regards the voluntary restriction of births (though without going into detail) and even abortion as entirely legitimate in order that people should be able to enjoy a satisfactory sex life, socialists rarely saw any value in contraception.

Communists and Christian socialists alike, Cabet and Leroux, as well as Proudhon rejected it with an offended modesty. Proudhon proposed delayed marriage to the age of 28 years for men and 21 years for women or even higher, in accordance with the older demographic patterns which have been adopted in contemporary China; he recommends continence from the age of 40 onwards and praises celibacy which he regards as favourable to creativity. Louis Devance comments: "These views reflect the puritanism and the [anti-] sexual obsession of the author of *La Pornocratie*."[18] In fact, Joseph Garnier regarded Proudhon as one of the most rigorous of Malthusians!

However, beyond these invectives and differences of principle, Malthus and the socialists take a common position on more than one point, and this is due fundamentally to their fear of sex, that great untamed impulse which will overcome all obstacles, unless it is well guarded against. Even Godwin, an avowed opponent of Malthus, considered the enjoyment of sensual pleasures as a sign of a certain primitivism. The best method of taming desire is work "the most powerful anaphrodisiac" (Proudhon).[19] It is the salvation of man and society, because it simultaneously increases resources and reduces the population. The transformation of libido into work, making men toil, is part of the great design which unites Malthus and the socialists.

The Marxist break

As is well known, there is disagreement as to whether Marx had read Malthus. Cagiano de Azevedo says that although Marx's writings do not contain a coordinated account of the relationships between population and the economy, demographic considerations are not absent from his work. In *Capital,* Marx refers to the Principle of Population no fewer than 62 times. Moreover, between 1861 and the end of his life, Marx assembled a series of notes which was intended to result in a conclusion to *Capital.* A section of these notes was devoted to a consideration of Malthus and his theories. Engels, who had been violently critical of Malthus ever since 1844, took up this project but was unable to complete it. It was left to Kautsky to publish this manuscript under the title *Theorien über den Mehrwert,* and a special section of this work was devoted to a discussion of Malthus's views.[20]

However, this is a matter of detail; what is important is Marx's much more radical critique of Malthus. He will have nothing to do with the Principle of Population, which he regards not only as politically pernicious but as scientifically false. A general Principle of Population does not exist, nor even a tendency; there are only different demographic situations corresponding to different methods of production, which are the driving force of history. To advocate birth control is, therefore, an illusion, indeed, a dangerous illusion. Marx denies the existence of a population problem as such. Compared with the hesitancy of the romantic socialists, this denial constitutes an important epistemological break.

However, Marx's ideas and particularly his ideas on the subject of population only took root slowly. Many Marxists remained Malthusians until 1900 and even later. Influenced by the emergence of the neo-Malthusian movement, Marxists began to read Malthus and ceased merely to decry him but took his arguments seriously. This is true of the Russian "legal" Marxists, such as Struve and Bulgakov and of the early works of Kautsky. When studying the Russian agrarian problem, they were struck by the importance of overpopulation as a cause of misery in the countryside. They agreed that Malthus's understanding of traditional rural economies was superior to that of Marx. Bulgakov, partticularly, criticized the view of the virgin territories as constituting a limitless reserve.[21] To him a voluntary limitation of births, i.e. one adopted consciously by individuals and not by government edict seemed altogether desirable. These legal Marxists were chosen as a target by Lenin when he expressed his violently anti-Malthusian views.[22]

A particularly interesting example is provided by Kautsky who was converted to anti-Malthusianism. In a book which he published in 1880 (and which was translated into several languages, e.g. into Italian in 1884),[23] he was convinced that Malthus's diagnosis of the situation was correct. Malthus's main mistake was to underestimate the effectiveness of technical progress: improved economic organization based on an efficient public sector and the development of cooperative production would solve the problem of penury. Following Marx, Kautsky applauded changes in the method of production. But he did not exclude the possibility that birth control might prove to be necessary for a better educated working class and for the emancipation of women. He saw no incompatibility between Malthusianism and socialism. However, this view soon became a minority view among the Social Democrats, where it was opposed both for economic and for moral reasons. Liebknecht thought that a refusal to procreate was immoral. The discussions became more and more bitter; they culminated in 1913 in the idea of a "birth strike" to use the expression introduced by Marie Huot in 1892 and which was taken up in Kolney's pamphlet which was later translated into German.[24] Kautsky objected to this slogan for strategic reasons: the reserve army was not merely a source of labour for capitalism, it was also the reserve army of the revolution, favourable to the aspirations of the working class. Thus, by the beginning of the war, Kautsky had turned into a militant anti-Malthusian. However, his "conversion" was strategic, rather than a recognition that Malthus's theory was false. The enemy was no longer the Reverend Thomas Malthus, but neo-Malthusianism, a libertarian movement, whose appeal to the working class was disliked by the Social Democrats as a threat to the preponderant influence of their party.[24] The fight was no longer directed against an enemy but against a competitor, and the importance of this change must be recognized.

Neo-Malthusianism and socialism

Neo-Malthusianism was more than a doctrine: it was an active movement in favour of birth control with ideas based on the Malthusian analysis. Paradoxically, Malthus's name was given to Leagues and journals and used to support arguments which were very different from his original views. It is almost possible to speak of an anti-Malthusian neo-Malthusianism. Science and hygiene replace God and morality, and birth control is supported both as a movement for the liberation of the individual and as a lever for social revolution. Neo-Malthusianism is opposed to traditional morality and subversive of the existing social order by giving the disinherited masses the supreme weapon, control over their reproduction.

We must distinguish between two different schools of neo-Malthusianism. When applied by government, it becomes a method of controlling populations in order to maximize national welfare; it is conservative, reformist and prudent. (Examples are the German states of the nineteenth century and Holland during the 1880s.) It may be used to avoid "race suicide" (Theodore Roosevelt's theme in the United States about 1905). During the nineteenth century, population statistics were improved in many countries, and in some of them population policies were developed which were not pro-natalist. But another version of neo-Malthusianism, based on ideas of social hygiene, was transformed into the family planning movement. Births should be controlled and family policies adopted which were conducive both to social well-being and stability. This form of neo-Malthusianism did contain some of Malthus's original ideas.

In this paper we are interested in the revolutionary aspects of neo-Malthusianism. These began in England 1820 and 1830, when Francis Place and Richard Carlile[25] attempted to disseminate knowledge of contraception. Their attempts were not welcomed by the British working class. Robert Dale Owen took the movement to America, where it took a completely different direction. In England it was not until 1855 when George Drysdale's *Physical, Sexual and Natural Religion*[26] was published and achieved a great success. After the Bradlaugh-Besant trial of 1877 Drysdale founded the Malthusian League. Many different daughter organizations of this League were founded on the Continent. In England, Paul Robin, an exile from the Commune, met Marx and encountered the neo-Malthusian movement which he introduced into France. The French section was probably the most libertarian and active of all.[27]

The many and varied episodes in the history of these organizations are less important than the personalities involved. Since it began in Western Europe, the development of neo-Malthusianism was linked with industrial growth in European countries with populations of high density. The speed of its development during the 1880s owed much to the Great Depression of that period. Unemployment, which took an important place in its propaganda, was linked to the problem of numbers and of competition. The neo-Malthusians in the industrial countries were more concerned with the problem of employment than with that of subsistence; in these countries full employment meant that subsistence was available, unemployment meant hunger. Fear of want marked the history of all these movements.

Neo-Malthusianism was a dynamic movement and many treatises and pamphlets were written on the subject. Some, e.g. the treatise on sex education by Dr Marestan,[28] and the pamphlets by F. Kolney[29] achieved very large circulations for their period and were translated into many different languages. Did this success signify a latent demand for better knowledge about the body and about sex? Neo-Malthusianism was a well-organized movement, with Leagues, conferences and international congresses. In 1900 an international neo-Malthusian organisation was founded. Their propaganda was well thought out and presented. In France, for instance, militant neo-Malthusians distributed flysheets designed by Paul Robin, popularized the slogan of a "birth strike", used cartoon strips and the cinema and published anatomical illustrations. In a form of direct action, members distributed pamphlets at the factory gates advocating birth control. They concentrated their propaganda on concrete measures, i.e. on the mechanical and chemical methods of controlling conception. Though they were in favour of women being permitted to have access to abortion, they regarded this as a last resort which could be avoided if scientific means of contraception were used. By speaking openly about the body and about sexual matters, the neo-Malthusians shocked the public. They were accused of peddling pornography or, at the very least, indecent publications, even by the Socialists who disliked discussion of such subjects. G.R. Searle regards this taboo on the discussion of sexual matters as the main reason for the profound cleft which separated British neo-Malthusians from the socialists at a time when the practice of birth control was making progress among the skilled workers who were important as members of the Labour Party. Madeleine Rebérioux observes that this may also have been the reason for Jaurès's strange silence of this topic.[30]

Neo-Malthusians were concerned with sexual as well as with social problems; this was one aspect of their modernism.[31] They conducted these discussions in the name of hygiene, the catchword of the period, which could be used to justify everything. They were interested in bodily hygiene, one French member of the movement said "I am a neo-Malthusian, because I am clean". Water played an important part in the contraceptive methods recommended. This made the acceptance of the methods difficult among the poorer section of the population who did not have access to a private water supply. The rather primitive contraceptive methods available at the time presupposed access to a private toilet and this greatly limited their effectiveness.

Birth control was seen as an aspect of moral hygiene as signifying self-control, the mastery of the sexual impulse and respect for oneself and one's wife. It involved "conscious parenthood" [*génération consciente*] to cite the title of the journal founded by Eugène Humbert in 1908. At the base of the movement, there is reprobation of promiscuity, unbridled passion, violations of the marriage bed and the brutality of working class sexuality as it was imagined to be. On this subject, the neo-Malthusians did not differ greatly from Malthus. However, they were not prepared to accept his austere remedies, the aristocratic idea of moral restraint; they claimed, however timidly, the right to sexual pleasure or, at the very least advocated the separation between love and reproduction. They made use of scientific advances which had solved the problems of reproduction. Ovulation was only discovered in the nineteenth century; the discovery was fundamental because it clarified the part of the female, who was no longer regarded as a mere receptacle for the male seed but became a true partner in reproduction. The neo-Malthusians popularized these new discoveries. In this connection, the role of the medical profession was particularly important. Neo-Malthusianism, for better or worse, was a precursor of modern sexology. Although its immediate influence was not great, the significance of the movement for the development of a new science of the body must not be underestimated. I believe that this is the principal reason for the controversy and scandal that it occasioned. It was not only the frightening sense of shame which was so prevalent during a century which was otherwise full of eroticism that was offended, the feeling was that neo-Malthusianism's sacrilegious ideas had made available to mankind the diabolical wisdom of the serpent: the tree of life where the body is exposed in all its nakedness.

Another subversive aspect of neo-Malthusianism is that it affects relations between different social classes as well as relations between the sexes. Through its alliance with the libertarian movement, particularly — though not exclusively — in France, it liberated both the working classes and women by giving them control over their own fertility, a secret which had hitherto been known only to the bourgeoisie and to men (*coitus interruptus* having been the oldest and most widely used method of contraception). To have a family of only one or two children, as was common among the bourgeoisie, meant that the reserve army of labour was reduced, with the consequence that unemployment fell, wages rose and wars caused by overpopulation were avoided. "Fewer hands on the labour market mean higher wages. Let us, therefore, have fewer children." "Large families are unhappy, small families lead happy lives." Thus, said the neo-Malthusian posters in which the workers were called upon to refuse to the Moloch of capitalism "labour fodder, pleasure fodder, cannon fodder". The National Federation of neo-Malthusian Workers, founded in 1910, supported a very active campaign of propaganda through workers' scholarships given by certain trade unions affiliated to the General Confederation of Labour. Some of the unions included in their statutes a clause stating that it was the duty of their members "to have few children". This argument was based not only on the desire to promote the small family (though the notion of the "cost of a child" and particularly that of a good education was basic), but because it was believed that small families would lead to an increase in collective happiness.

The other slogan was that of "voluntary motherhood". "Science has provided a means which enables women not to conceive unless they desire to do so." "There will be fewer abandoned mothers, if women are able to achieve voluntary motherhood." These were some of the slogans used at the time. Many neo-Malthusians regarded it as their duty to stress the primacy of the link between a mother and her child and to play down the idea of paternal responsibility. Paul Robin, Eugène Humbert and Gabriel Giroud were true feminists. The importance of feminism in the neo-Malthusian movement on both sides of the Atlantic must be stressed. Among the women who were most active in the movement were Annie Besant in England, Margaret Sanders and Emma Goldmann in the United States, B.M. Burns and Florence Rowe in Canada, Marie Huot in France (it was she who coined the phrase the "birth strike") as well as Nelly Roussel, Gabrielle Petit with her periodical *La Femme Affranchie* as well as Madeleine Pelletier, a physician who in 1912 advocated women's right of access to abortion which, in her view, was much less dangerous than it was reputed to be, provided that it was carried out under medical supervision, and Jeanne Humbert. It is true that these women only constituted a small minority, even among feminists, who often took a prudish attitude to sexuality: the well-known objections of some women against contraceptive propaganda need an explanation. But it was these activists who insisted on the achievement of "voluntary motherhood". This was not a question of sexual liberation, but rather of the right of women to choose their status freely. By refusing to accept the mother role as the only possible destiny for women, they raised the whole question of the position of women in society[32] with consequences that were explosive.

Although the immediate effects of the neo-Malthusian movement were limited (it would, for instance, be wrong to blame it for the fall in the French birth rate, which preceded neo-Malthusianism), its ideology was seen as a latent threat and led to strong opposition by governments and within the socialist movement, particularly in France. The socialist reaction was divided. The increasing costs of education for the family and a possible future socialist society worried moderate leaders (e.g. Sixte Quenin and Tabouriech).[33] This argument was frequently used after the publication of Pecqueur's book. However, the majority of socialists suspected an attitude which they regarded as "petty bourgeois" and arguments against neo-Malthusianism came to be used which had little in common with Marxism, for example, fears for the vitality of the race and the nation which was seen to be imperilled by the low birth rates of the bourgeoisie. "France will become a nation of Cossacks or Prussians within a century" complained Jules Guesde.[34] Fortunately, the vigour of the proletariat will save France — that generous republic — from the degeneracy of the debilitated and vicious bourgeoisie which is suffering from the ravages of venereal disease. "As much of life as possible to achieve the maximum possible happiness" wrote Emile Zola in his great anti-Malthusian novel *Fécondité*. "We shall increase in numbers and fill the world." And Lucien Deslinières wrote in his description of a future Utopia *L'application du système collectiviste* (1899): "What a prodigious explosion! What a vigorous thrust of little French citizens! It is then that the injunction

'Be fruitful and multiply' will cease to be a vain slogan."[35] Socialism will come to the relief of a God who had become tired on the seventh day of creation.

A large population, a strong people and a healthy race; these were aspects of socialist optimism. Malthus, too, was worried about the quality of the population. Though he cast doubts on Condorcet's thesis of "organic perfectibility", Malthus admitted that some amelioration was possible. "It does not, however, by any means seem impossible that by an attention to breed, a certain degree of improvement, similar to that amongst animals, might take place among men." But he added immediately: "As the human race, however, could not be improved in this way, without condemning all the bad speciments to celibacy, it is not probable that an attention to breed should ever become general."[36] André Béjin has shown[37] how the social Darwinists during the nineteenth century made the transition from an advocacy of control of numbers to that of control of the quality of the population: from the Principle of Population they moved to the Principle of Selection. By stressing the primacy of natural selection and the inexorable laws of heredity, social Darwinists emphasized the problem of selecting for quality in the population. Malthus reserved his particular castigations for those poor who, by reason of sloth, failed to limit the numbers of their descendants.

> The social Darwinists, on the other hand, reserved their disapproval both for the "dysgenic" individuals (degenerates and inferior races which breed too prolifically) as well as for the followers of the eugenic movement who did not breed enough, because in their view wealth is not created through labour but from the excellence of the hereditary characteristics which are transmitted. The true struggle for existence is the struggle for descendants.

So affirms Vacher de Lapouge.[38] He draws an analogy between selection which will correct the errors of nature, and socialism which will correct the errors and injustices brought about by the free market. Both must work together. "Socialism must be selectionist, or it will cease to exist. It will only become possible if human nature changes, and such changes can only be brought about through selection".[39] This is the view of one of the most prominent social Darwinists.

The neo-Malthusians were much more individualistic and less radical. But they often succumbed to the temptations of the eugenic movement. Traces of this can be found in their preoccupation with social purity in, for instance, the Oneida community in the United States, and in the birth control movement which is concerned with the integrity of the race.[40] One of the founders of the neo-Malthusian movement in Canada, R.B. Kerre, writes in *Lucifer*, a journal which in 1907 changed its name to the *American Journal of Eugenics:* "It is necessary to replace a humanity which is begotten by chance and which today is suffering everywhere, by children who are wanted and who are born and educated under satisfactory conditions."[41] For Paul Robin "a good birth, good education and good social organization" are indissolubly linked, and he called his organization the *Ligue de Régénération Humaine*.[42] "The first essential of puericulture (sic) is a proper choice of human stock" read one of the League's pamphlets. Birth is too important a subject to be left to chance.

The persecution of neo-Malthusianism

There are some disquieting features in this advocacy of selection. The neo-Malthusians out-Malthus Malthus. He, as a liberal, puts the onus for finding a remedy on the individual and asks nothing of the state. But it was not this aspect which governments found threatening; some, indeed, used the arguments for their own benefit before 1914.

Neo-Malthusianism was persecuted in some countries, and notably in France, but not for demographic reasons. During the first half of the nineteenth century the ruling classes controlled their own births and exhorted the people, of whose growth they were frightened, to prudent behaviour. Most economists and statesmen were Malthusians. But the situation began to change with the turn of the century. Some of the disquiet was due to the fall in the French birth rate which was seen as weakening France against a victorious Germany and which threatened the economic, and above all, the military strength of the nation. Industrialists only played a very secondary part in this shift of opinion. Those who were important were politicians, such as Senator Bérenger, physicians and demographers such as Bertillon, whose book *La dépopulation de la France* was published in 1911. They attributed to the neo-Malthusian movement responsibility for a situation which was not of its making, e.g. they blamed it for the rise in the number of abortions. The neo-Malthusians paid a price for their association with the libertarian movement, for their anti-militarism, and their proclaimed desire to create a new moral climate, particularly in the sexual sphere, as well as for their links with the direct action school of the syndicalist movement. They were persecuted by associations for the preservation of morality, such as the *Ligue de Moralité publique,* the *Société de Protection contre la Licence des Rues,* or by pro-natalist demographic associations, such as the *Association nationale pour l'accroissement de la population française,* of which Bertillon was a prominent member. Seizures, trials and the arrest of militants were a prelude to the law of 1920 which outlawed all anti-natalist propaganda and drove the movement underground.[43]

Between the world wars, neo-Malthusianism became more isolated than ever. In the Western countries which had been weakened by war and in which the bulk of the population practised birth control and took a sceptical view of life and where Malthusian views had become accepted in some respects (for instance, in regarding wars as being one of the fatal consequences of population pressure), some governments instituted pro-natalist policies and objected to neo-Malthusianism. The socialist parties, which were connected with the middle classes, gladly became defenders of the family and protagonists of motherhood.[44] A part of the feminist movement, which was isolated almost everywhere took shelter behind the respectability of birth control.

It was Lenin who took up the Marxist anti-Malthusian torch and strengthened the condemnation on economic grounds of the socio-political arguments of the pre-war socialists. Neo-Malthusianism was denounced as an example of a petty bourgeois and individualist ideology, which only masked the nature of the process of exploitation.

> The working class is not perishing, it is growing, becoming stronger, gaining courage, consolidating itself, educating itself and becoming steeled in battle ... We are already laying the foundation of a new edifice and our children will complete its construction. That is the reason — the only reason — why we are unconditionally the enemies of neo-Malthusianism, suited only to unfeeling and egotistic petty bourgeois couples who whisper in scared voices: "God grant we manage somehow by ourselves. So much better if we have no children."[45]

However, just as it took time for Marxism to become dominant in pre-war socialism, some time elapsed before communist parties became Leninist. The French Communist party's journal for women *l'Ouvrière* took a general neo-Malthusian line until about 1926. It discussed sex education, free unions and eugenics, cited the works of Nelly Roussel and Madeleine Pelletier and took up the slogan of a "birth strike".[46] In 1927, the French Communist party sprang to the defence of Henriette Alquier, who had been prosecuted for publishing in the journal *Ecole émancipée* articles which advocated contraception for the workers. But, the tone changed in about 1930. *L'Ouvrière,* which resumed publication after a break of about three years, adopted much more traditional attitudes; it linked the feminist movement with fascism, exalted family life in the Soviet Union and objected to neo-

Malthusians who defended the rights of women over their own bodies, as "if anti-physiological processes could be made into a general principle without causing lasting damage".[47] Twenty years later, in 1956, much the same arguments were used in a controversy in which Jacques Derogy, author of *Des enfants malgré nous* (1956, Paris) and a militant communist took up a position favouring birth control as defended by Dr Weil Halé, and was opposed by Maurice Thorez, Jean Fréville and Jeannette Vermersch. "Working class women do not wish to practise bourgeois vices"[48] and "the proletariat desires children" wrote Thorez and Vermersch. It is no exaggeration to regard the anti-Malthusian position as continuing in a straight line from Cabet to Thorez.

The debate between Malthus and the socialists is unending. They share some common positions: a recognition of the social problem and the desire to find a solution, the importance of labour, fear of unbridled sexuality. But on many aspects they take contrary views. Where Malthus thinks of restriction, the socialists desire growth. Malthus puts his trust in God, the socialists in science and technology. Malthus speaks of regulation, the socialists of revolution. Malthus fears the Barbarian crowd in excessive numbers, the socialists see a large population as adding strength to the conquering armies of the proletariat. The two visions of the world are different, with the neo-Malthusians attempting to build a bridge between them in the name of human happiness. By posing the problem of limits to economic growth and wealth and advocating the restriction of births, Malthus opened a discussion which is astonishingly relevant to the problems of today.

Notes

1. cf. Teresa Isenburg (1977). Il dibattito su Malthus e sulla popolazione nell'Italia di fine 1800. *Studi Storici*. No. 3.
2. Pierre Leroux (1849). *Malthus et les économistes, ou y aura-t-il toujours des pauvres?* Paris. Reprint of articles, originally printed in *La Revue Sociale* in 1846, under the title "De la recherche des biens matériels, ou de l'individualisme et du socialisme."
3. C. Loudon (1842). *Solution du problème de la population et de la subsistance, soumise à un médecin dans une série de lettres*. Giard frères. Galignani, Paris. Loudon, a physician, was a Commissioner engaged in the inspection of child workers in English manufacturing industry. He advocated prolonged lactation up to the age of three years as a measure of birth control. Duchâtel (Count Tanneguy) published *De la charité dans ses*

rapports avec l'état moral et le bien être des classes inférieures de la société en 1829. Alexandre Mesnier, Paris. This work was strictly Malthusian in argument.

4. This Malthusian doctrine which is the *official* economics of France, just as eclecticism is its official philosophy, has no help to offer to the poor . . . "other than prisons".
5. Marcus (1839). *The Book of Murder. Vademecum for the Commissioners and Guardians of the New Poor Law throughout Great Britain and Ireland, being an exact Reprint of the Infamous Essay: On the Possibilities of Limiting Populousness,* by Marcus, one of the three. *With a Refutation of the Malthusian Doctrine.* J. Hill, London. Reprinted by W. Dugdale.
6. According to Devance, this pamphlet signed pseudonymously (Marcus) was meant as a caricature and written by an opponent of Malthus. On this, cf. J. Garnier (1857). *Du principe de population.* 2nd Edition, p.195.
7. Pierre Leroux, op. cit. in note 2, p.104.
8. R. Cagiano de Azevedo. Marx et Proudhon contre Malthus. MHA, p.140.
9. ibid.
10. M. Gillet and M. Rozat. Malthus dans la littérature populaire du 19ème siècle. MHA, p.142.
11. L. Devance. Malthus and socialist thought in France before 1870. This volume, pp.275–286.
12. Pierre Leroux, op. cit. in note 2, p.191.
13. F. Fourier (1822). *Traité de l'association domestique et agricole,* cited by L. Devance. Republished as *L'Unité Universelle,* Oeuvres complètes. Anthropos, vol. 4, p.106.
14. ibid. vol. 5, p.557.
15. ibid. vol. 5, p.558.
16. C. Pecqueur. *L'économie sociale* (1839); *Des améliorations matérielles dans leur rapport avec la liberté* (1840). Devance stresses the originality of Pecqueur's thought both on the analytical level, where he is looking for an optimum population which will lead to economic development, and on the level of policy: a system of taxes for over-large families and of allowances for those who choose to educate their children themselves. The concept of the cost of a child and its education is very obvious here.
17. Heinrich Rubner. Tradition malthusienne et socialisme de la Chaire en Allemagne. MHA, p.150.
18. P. J. Proudhon (1875). *La pornocratie ou les femmes dans les temps modernes.* Paris.
19. P. J. Proudhon (1846). *Système de contradictions économiques,* p.385. Rivière, Paris. "Work is the most powerful anaphrodisiac, the more so as it affects both the body and the spirit . . . The indigent are prolific and do little work." Society is, therefore, faced with two alternatives "to be transformed by work into a society of saints, or for civilization to become nothing more than an obscenity, because of the operation of monopoly and misery."
20. R. Cagiano de Azevedo, loc. cit. in note 9.

21. cf. S. Bulgakov (1900). *Capitalisme et agriculture*. Saint-Petersburg.
22. cf. W. Berelowitch. Les lectures de Malthus dans la Russie d'avant la révolution. MHA, p.27.
23. K. Kautsky (1880). *Influence de l'accroissement de le population sur le progrès de la société*.
24. Dieter Groh. Malthusianisme et mouvement ouvrier allemand avant 1915. MHA, p.144.
25. cf., for instance, J. A. Field (1931). *Essays on Population*. Chicago University Press, in particular, the first essay entitled "The Malthusian controversy".
26. *Physical, Sexual and Natural Religion* (1855). By A Student of Medicine. Edward Truelove, London. The work was later republished as *The Elements of Social Science or Physical, Sexual and Natural Religion. An Exposition of the True Cause and only Cure of the three Primary Social Evils: Poverty, Prostitution and Celibacy* by A Doctor of Medicine. By 1892 it had run into 29 editions and over 77 000 copies had been sold.
27. cf. A. Armengaud. Mouvement ouvrier et néo-malthusianisme en France au début du 20ème siècle. *Annales de Démographie Historique* (1966) and *Les Français et Malthus* (1976). Also R. G. Guerrand (1971). *La libre maternité*. Paris. The most recent and best documented discussion is that of Francis Ronsin (1980). *La grève des ventres. Propagande néo-malthusienne et baisse de la natalité en France*. Aubier. See also Francis Ronsin. Between Malthus and the social revolution: The French neo-Malthusian movement. This volume, pp.329–339.
28. J. Marestan (1910). *L'éducation sexuelle*. Paris.
29. F. Kolney (1908). *La grève des ventres*. Paris; (1910). (1909). *Le crime d'engendrer*. Paris; *La société mourante et le néo-malthusianisme*, Paris.
30. cf. G. R. Searle. Socialism and Malthusianism in late Victorian and Edwardian Britain. This volume, pp.341–356. Madeleine Rebérioux. The attitudes of French Socialists to Malthus during the Third Republic. This volume, pp.287–298.
31. cf. Agnès Fine and Marc Lavigne. Le néo-malthusianisme et "la question sexuelle". MHA, p.142.
32. In addition to the sources cited later in this paper, cf. A. McLaren (1978). *Birth Control in Nineteenth Century England*. London; and A. McLaren. Malthusianism and Socialism: Birth control and the Canadian left (1900–1939). MHA, p.146; cf. also Linda Gordon (1976). *A Social History of Birth Control in America*. Penguin Books; and Linda Gordon. Birth control, socialism and feminism in the United States. This volume, pp.313–327.
33. Sixte Quenin (1913). *Comment nous sommes socialistes*. Paris. This was one of the last volumes of the *Encyclopédie Socialiste* published by Compère Morel. In her paper Madeleine Rebérioux traces the progress of neo-Malthusianism among the socialists and particularly the growing importance of the cost of education. E. Tarbouriech (1902) expresses misgivings. *La cité future. Essai d'une utopie scientifique*. Paris; about the cost

to public funds of too high a birth rate and the need it would impose for the economically active population to work harder. He writes: "It would then become apparent that one would need to consider social consequences rather than those for the individual only — this would make all the difference — Malthus's 'moral restraint'." p.301.

34. J. Guesde (1875). *Essai de catéchisme socialiste*, particularly "La fin de la France par la propriété"; cf. also G. Rouanet (October 1889). La dépopulation de la France. *La Revue Socialiste*; the author sees the fall in the French birth rate as the "most terrible of the dangers which threaten the fatherland of the Revolution".
35. Cited by M. Rebérioux, loc. cit. in note 30.
36. T. R. Malthus. *First Essay*, pp. 170–171.
37. André Béjin. Social Darwinists and Malthus. This volume, pp.299–312. Lion Murard and Patrick Zylberman. L'enfer tonique. Société et "dégénération" chez Malthus et Gobineau. (Gobineau had not read Malthus; it is striking that both writers shared the same obsessions.)
38. G. Vacher de Lapouge (1899). *L'argent. Son rôle social*, p.501. Fontemoin, Paris. "The true struggle for survival is the struggle for descendants."
39. H. Vacher de Lapouge (1896). *Les sélections sociales*, p.262. Paris.
40. Linda Gordon, loc. cit. in. note 32.
41. Angus McLaren, loc. cit. in note 32.
42. P. Robin, "Appel aux gens mariés!", cited by F. Ronsin (1980). *La grève des ventres. Propagande néo-malthusienne et baisse de la natalité en France, 19-20è siècles*, p.54. Aubier, Paris.
43. F. Ronsin, op. cit. in note 27.
44. This process is analysed by R. H. Guerrand. Socialisme et malthusianisme en France dans l'entre-deux-guerres. MHA, p.145.
45. V. I. Lenin. The working class and neo-Malthusianism. *Collected Works*, vol. 19, p.237. Originally published in *Pravda*, 16 June 1913.
46. This analysis is based on an unpublished paper by Sandra Dab, "La politique du PCF en direction des femmes entre les deux guerres. Ses conceptions sur le rôle historique de la famille, la place et les droits des femmes". Master's thesis for the University of Paris, June 1980. This paper contains a discussion and summary of the contents of *L'Ouvrière*, which is most interesting.
47. See Dr Rouques in an article in *L'Ouvrière* of March 15, 1935, cited by Sandra Dab, op. cit. in note 46.
48. Annick Peigné, personal communication.

20 Malthus and Socialist Thought in France Before 1870

L. DEVANCE

It has often been said that all French socialists were anti-Malthusian until the end of the nineteenth century and the writings of Paul Robin. This statement is, in principle, true. Malthus conceived his Principle of Population as a scientific reply to the populationism implicit in the communist doctrines of Godwin. The incompatibility between two doctrines, one of which was characterized by its opponents as being nothing more than a shield for the propertied classes against the upsurge of the hungry masses, and another whose aim was to assure a more equal distribution of wealth, hardly needs stressing.

But Malthus's influence on attitudes and behaviour in France was so strong that it would have been surprising if it had left socialist thinking unaffected. In any case, the boundary between socialism and radicalism is fluid; thus, John Stuart Mill was a Malthusian. Catholicism was the other "natural" opponent of Malthusian doctrines, but it may be argued that its opposition was insufficiently vigorous. We need only recall the *Confessor's Manual* by Monseigneur Bouvier and the work of Villeneuve-Bargemont[1] who affirmed that the public interest required "a robust, healthy, intelligent and moral, rather than a large population", and who proposed a return to the institutions of the past, which had delayed marriage as one of their objectives.

No doubt, this explains the indignation of some of the Christian socialists who, together with the communist followers of Babeuf, were among those who denounced Malthus with the greatest vigour.

The two communist writers Buonarotti and Cabet justified their populationist attitudes by reasons of state. To be strong and prosperous, the republic needed also to be populous. Once the people had

MALTHUS PAST AND PRESENT
ISBN 0-12-224670-5

become more virtuous, they would also increase their fertility. Malthusianism was equated with vice, and fertility with moral conduct; a system of values which for all its naturalist and humanist origins was in accord with the traditional teaching of the Church. Buonarotti believed that a necessary condition for a return by the masses to morality was the abolition of large towns; vice prospers in such towns, which are inhabited by parasitic and infertile elements (domestic servants, priests, and artists of all kinds). Cabet advocated the abolition of celibacy which he regarded as anti-social and leading to all kinds of immorality (through seduction and adultery). In the absence of physical deformity, marriage in Icaria (as he called his Utopia) would occur early, at the age of 20 for men and 18 for women. "Concubinage and adultery are crimes for which there is no excuse."[2] The evil of abortion would disappear. The policy to be followed in Icaria would be a type of eugenics, a committee of physicians and of wise men would make experiments with the object of perfecting the human species.[3] This combination of strict sexual morality, populationism and human experimentation to improve the quality of the race seems to have some affinity with the doctrines and practices of German National Socialism.

A similar denunciation of celibacy as anti-social and unnatural may be found in the writings of the communists Lahautière[4] and Pinault.[5] The latter includes Malthusian doctrines among the "popular errors and prejudices" which must be fought.[6] It is an egoistic, inhuman and immoral doctrine which has been refuted by modern developments. The more populous a country, the more active and industrious are its inhabitants "the least populous countries have always been the poorest". A worker produces more than he consumes and this shows that the cause of poverty lies not in an excess of population but in a defective organization of society.

Dézamy condemns the "ultilitarian" doctrines of population, among which he includes those of Turgot, Adam Smith, Bentham, Malthus and Sismondi,[7] in the name of sexual morality. "One step further . . . and they will rehabilitate Sodom and Gomorrah!" "They wish to keep the joys of a family away from those whom they have themselves dubbed proletarians, an appelation which is no more than a bitter derision." Malthus's ideas would lead to immoral sexual practices and constitute a "veritable villainy". But in the writings of his disciples they become truly criminal. Thus, a certain Marcus, author of a pamphlet published in London goes so far as to "preach (in addition to some most disgusting and criminal moral outrages) the murder of the old and infirm, abortion, infanticide etc". In fact, this pseudonymous pamphlet was a caricature, written by one of Malthus's opponents with the intention of being provocative;[8] it advocated the painless extinction of infants in carbonic acid gas, but we must remember that nearly a century earlier, Swift in his satire had already proposed the use of unwanted infants for human nourishment.

Dézamy compares this barbaric desire to prevent "the pullulation of the proletariat" to Pharaoh's massacre of the Israelites or to the killing of the helots by the warriors of Sparta. Such doctrines are not only contrary to good morals but also to "the science of egalitarianism which does away with all fears of overpopulation by demonstrating that famines result from bad government, as do all the other scourges of humanity." By the use of statistics *L'égalitaire* attempted to show that if France were governed according to socialist principles, she could in an average year produce nearly five times as much as she consumed.[9] However, some years later, in his *Code de la communauté,* a work which owed much to Fourier's influence, Dézamy no longer considered the question of an equilibrium of population. In this he differed from Fourier. He forecast and welcomed the general development of chastity within the community. The abolition of "familism" and of "fragmented households" and the realization of "free unions", "perfect equality between the sexes" and the end of "marital domination" would not result in either disorder or debauchery. Science and education would show to all that "only chastity and temperance can conserve health and thus increase and perpetuate our pleasures". Moreover, "gymnastics, intellectual exercises, morals, customs and public opinion would divert human energy from any attempt at incontinence". This materialist and humanist view provided a new justification for the old morality taught by the Church; the idea of a purified and sublimated human sexuality which had become corrupt by a faulty and perverse social organization. Work, civic virtues, a cultured and healthy leisure would result in the continuing reign of virtue and chastity. Such were the dominant themes in socialist as well as in bourgeois literature during the nineteenth century, where savagery and barbarity were equated with sexual malpractice and social harmony with a chastity which would result in demographic equilibrium.

The anti-Malthusianism of the Christian socialists, like that of the communists, is based on an optimistic view of the development of production and on a denunciation of the immorality of contraceptive practices.

Buchez believes that Malthus and the economists were mistaken. "France could maintain three times her present population, and you suggest that poverty is caused by too many children! The only remedy you can see is to castrate men."[10] The Christian physician, however, is more concerned by the debauchery caused by a "depraved sexual appetite". Although this is concerned with some of the fundamental needs of mankind, reproduction and venereal pleasure, it carries within itself the seeds of its own destruction. "Everyone is aware that the abuse or premature use of these powers is damaging to reproduction; it reduces the standing of all those who are guilty of such abuse, makes bastards of their descendants and even renders them incapable of begetting viable offspring." "It is necessary to respect the laws relating to the intercourse of the sexes", writes Buchez, without, however, giving any indication of what these laws are.[11] Thus, a populationist position is not necessarily incompatible with a eugenic policy based on the principles of social hygiene.

Pierre Leroux regarded his critique of Malthusianism which he published in 1846 as particularly important.[12] In contrast to the authors whose works we have discussed so far, he admits the validity of the principle of the geometric growth rate of the population as put forward by Malthus and his disciples. "The only one of the statements among their celebrated propositions which is true is that wherever there is sufficient subsistence, the population will double within a period of 25 years in the present state of human morality." Thus, France would have grown from a population of 27 million inhabitants in 1789 to more than 100 million in 1846. But as the actual population at that date amounted to only 35 million, this showed that 65 million persons were lost to France by misery alone. This loss cannot be attributed to the laws of nature, but to an artificial organization of society in which a handful of individuals are able to accumulate a superabundance of riches, whilst the main body is condemned to languish in want, and to early death. Thus writes Leroux, citing Godwin whose optimism he shared and whose memory he cherished.[13]

Leroux adds that some authors believe that population could double within 15 or even within 10 years. Need one, therefore, fear overpopulation when the system of "industrial feudalism" has been abandoned and been replaced by a socialist society? The answer is in the negative, because agricultural science has shown in its theory of the nitrogen cycle that every human being produces enough manure to produce the quantity of cereals needed for his diet. "The conclusion that the economists should draw from this is that everyone is entitled to subsistence." Leroux condemns the development of agriculture in England where men were driven off the land to be replaced by cattle; animals should be used as a source of power rather than of manure, because the manure produced by humans would suffice.[14] However, he does not discuss the problem of the availability of agricultural land, nor of the density of population. But he agrees that in the present state of morality a doubling of the population every 25 years is a possibility. Unfortunately, he does not develop the point any further. It is not clear whether he suggests in common with the futurologists of his own society, most of whom were socialists, that future fertility would be held in check by the development of chastity.

One of the controversial questions discussed by public opinion in France at the time related to the closure of the "areas of exposure" which could be found near the doors of the foundling hospitals. In a study published in 1825 Duchâtel, who was later to become a minister under Louis Philippe, proposed that the foundling hospitals should be reserved for orphans.[15] So Leroux condemns those who "put morality on the side of Malthus and immorality on the side of St Vincent de Paul".[16] No less vigorously, he took issue with "the false theologians of our time", such as Dupanloup and Lacordaire who were nothing more than apologists for an inegalitarian social system and who were, in truth, accomplices of the Malthusians in their "massacre of the innocent". Lacordaire believed that an increase in the number of monasteries would relieve the burden of population; one of his lectures was entitled "The solution of the social problem through monasticism".[17]

Refusing "to soil his pen" by describing the "obscene details" of the methods recognized by the Malthusians, Leroux confines himself to condemning them because they make it possible for "men to satisfy their instincts whilst violating the laws of nature". To the casuistical atheistic economists, Leroux opposes those members of the Church who, in response to the same problem, did not deviate from the solution put forward in Holy Scripture.[18]

In summary, Christian socialists and the communists criticized Malthusian doctrines on two levels. The first was scientific: even if the law of the geometric increase of population were valid, in a world governed in accordance with the principles of social science the growth of subsistence could be equally rapid. The second objection was on moral grounds. The methods proposed by the Malthusians were immoral, particularly the delay of marriage and what would today be called contraception; the latter method is totally condemned as being contrary to nature and decency. This point of view is very similar to that held by the Church, with a considerable extension of the notion of criminal conduct.

None of the authors discusses the question whether birth control would result in reducing the miseries suffered by the poor, and particularly those of women and children. It cannot be doubted that in a society in which no regular assistance is given to families, the limitation of procreation by members of social classes with modest means constitutes an adaptation to the situation. This was widely recognized, not least by members of the upper section of the working class. The only point on which communists and Christian socialists tended to approximate to Malthusian doctrine was in the praise of continence and the prediction that the practice of continence would increase in the future.

Other socialist theoreticians took a more moderate view of the population problems and did not simply reject Malthus's analysis. Thus, for instance, Fourier discussed the population problem on repeated occasions, unlike Saint Simon and his school who did not consider it at all. Fourier was out of sympathy with those who preached populationism in a society in which there was misery. He reproached the economists (in reality the physiocrats) who attempted to prove "that administrative wisdom teaches us that an anthill of people is desirable".[19] Another quotation will illustrate his lack of sympathy with the Malthusian position. "Everything conspires to entrap the father in an anthill of children. He is pushed into this situation by poverty and despair. People breed children because they think that the children will not have more miserable a life than they themselves have experienced".[20] Fourier recalls that in some societies those who were poor and those who have had too many children were permitted to expose or even to sell them. The Roman Catholic Church did not object to the castration of boys destined to sing in the choir at a time when its dogmas, more severe than those of ancient times, forbade husbands from taking "certain precautions which are dictated by prudence".[21]

Even though Fourier believed that a socialist regime would result in the rapid increase of wealth to four times or more its present levels, he remained preoccupied with the limits of the economy. "The world is finite, and within two centuries its population will probably amount to 5500 million", provided there is general peace and prosperity. Therefore, even though the deserts may be reclaimed, the human species will become overcrowded and asphyxiate through the excess of population. And he adds: "I believe that the wisest writers on this problem are those who, like Malthus, have pointed to this vicious circle, or those who say that they do not understand the problem at all."[22] Fourier does not share Malthus's view on moral restraint; he regards contraception and even abortion as licit. Fourier writes:

> The law, which is already made ridiculous by its injustices is even

more contradictory in its treatment of pregnant girls. They are told that their pregnancy is a crime, as is induced abortion. If they wish to maintain their honour, the only action open to them is abort the foetus before it is alive. I believe that a girl who acts in this way is less culpable than a parent, who with the consent of the Church, mutilates a child in order to make it possible for him to sing in the cathedral, a practice which may be observed in the capital of Christendom.[23]

But in the end Fourier's optimism gains the upper hand. In a socialist society, once the world has reached the maximum population that it is capable of supporting, new factors which are designed to fit new conditions of life will intervene to stabilize the population. Women's health will improve as the number of children they bear diminishes. Fourier believes that experience shows that sickly women are the most fertile (in fact, the reverse is more likely to be true, and Fourier here appears to confuse cause and effect). Moreover, a more liberal system of morality and "female polygamy" would have the same consequences (and here Fourier is supported by researches in comparative demography). In the last analysis, he adds, "new laws which God will lay down in these matters" will be applied.[24] This is on the whole the most likely hypothesis, when account is taken of the development of knowledge, morals and the laws relating to contraception and abortion.

Fourier returns to the population problem in his *Nouveau monde industriel* (1830). Although he asserts that like everyone else, Malthus did not fully understand the problem, he approves of his "wise opinions on the vicious circle". The solution to the problem which he envisages, however, remains the same. But, Fourier adds, "the processes which will be conducive to the control of births under a socialist regime will be so efficient, that it will become necessary to take measures to stimulate fertility, which to-day is regarded with apprehension by the prudent".[25]

It has been said that Fourier was one of Malthus's disciples.[26] This is perhaps putting the case a little too strongly, but in the light of the above remarks the judgement can perhaps be regarded as understandable.

Another writer whose discussion was more elaborate and complex, to the point that it might even seem confused and contradictory, was Pecqueur. His writings are distinguished by scientific seriousness and balanced discussion. He refuses to engage in bizarre provocations or polemics. He attempts to find a synthesis between Malthusian and populationist doctrines, which would be more than eclectic.

In his *Economie sociale,* published in 1839, he admits that population will grow in geometric progression, but actual levels of population will always be determined by subsistence. At present, population is kept in check by the scarcity of means of subsistence. However, the growth of modern technology will result in a universal growth of population. There is no reason to be alarmed by this: "excess population is still far away", "the earth is still too much like a desert". In those regions in which population has been dense for some time, emigration and colonization will provide a safety valve. No limit can be assigned to the total size of the population, nor to the fertility of the soil.[27]

However, right at the beginning of his work, Pecqueur warns:

> If the masses do not exercise sufficient prudence and envisage the consequences of unrestricted reproduction; if morality does not provide them with the strength to impose either a temporary deprivation or a constant check on their legitimate desires and affections, if these two counterbalancing factors were not to apply, then it will not be possible to attain a state of civilization, and misery would fatally apply to the greatest number.[28]

However, some elementary observations moderate his pessimism.

> The wealthy classes have fewer children than the proletariat; raise the conditions of life of the latter to a state of ease, where they will have access to the joys of the heart and the cultivation of intelligence and they will then, too, moderate their sexual appetite.[29] . . . If improvements in the level of living continue, there will be greater providence, less unbridled pursuit of sexual pleasure among the masses.

Here again, we find the theme that sexuality will be sublimated by an increase in culture.

Pecqueur appears to be aware of the necessity of an optimum rate of population growth which would trigger off an increase in the standard of living. He sketches the major features of a project of "national and universal association" and looks forward to a state in which children would normally be brought up in common by society. But "to encourage fathers of families to moderate their reproduction," it may become necessary to make a levy which is proportionate to the number of children on the incomes of producers of either sex.[30] At the same time parents' freedom of choice must be respected and in order to avoid penalizing those who prefer to bring up their children themselves, such parents would be granted a family allowance in addition to their income, designed to compensate them for the additional costs they incur by having children, rather than to stimulate the birth rate. Both the levy and the allowance would have an educative function, as they would take account of the cost of education, and thus incite a sense of economic responsibility in procreative behaviour, which clearly implies a check on the rate of growth. But it must be noted that Pecqueur is opposed to celibacy "which was regarded for too long as a virtue" and which "to-day can only be regarded as a social evil".[31]

Proudhon, in contrast, differs from most of his contemporaries by favouring celibacy. This state is increasingly looked upon as "pure and honourable". Proudhon thought that in its exaltation of virginity, Christianity was prophetic as it was in other respects, and he foresaw an increase in celibacy. "Christianity has revealed to the world the purest form of love in voluntary virginity." "Instigated by the desire of the people, it was a social spontaneity which found its expression in the pronouncements of the Popes".[32]

In general, married men will become increasingly continent. Work will demand an increasing share of their energy, and Proudhon welcomes this. The only religion that he calls for is the religion of work and of the family. "Work is the strongest anti-aphrodisiac, it is the most powerful because it affects both the body and the spirit." The poor are prolific and do not work hard. Humanity is faced with a simple alternative: "through work it can become a society of saints, or through monopoly and misery, so-called civilization will be nothing but an immense obscenity".[33] These quotations show the puritanism and anti-sexual obsessions of the author of the *Pornocratie*. But this does not necessarily make him a Malthusian. His violent diatribes against Malthus are well known. But there are few whom Proudhon did no execrate, and his opposition is directed less against Malthus than against Malthus's disciples. He recognizes that Malthus recommended moral restraint, i.e. chastity, whereas some of his disciples advocated despicable methods. "At bottom, it must be recognized that there is a certain grandeur to Malthus's work."[34] Any doctrine which attempts to separate sexuality from marriage and reproduction, other than that of conjugal continence is totally immoral, including those of the followers of Fourier, Saint Simon and some communist opponents of the conjugal family.

Proudhon admits that Malthus's law is valid in a social system based on monopoly. Misery encroaches upon production. But in a socialist society labour, which is the only true source of wealth, will abolish misery, and a new law of population will operate. Production will grow as the square of the number of workers. However, this revision of Malthus's arithmetic, of which Proudhon was by no means the only supporter, did not prevent him from asking questions about the physical limit of the world's population. However, his solution to the problem was along the lines we have sketched, an increase in celibacy and continence, resulting in humanity reaching an angelic state in which the population would remain stationary. Proudhon esteems marriage no less than he does celibacy. For him marriage is a social and moral sacrament and is indissoluble. He is the only socialist theoretician who absolutely condemns divorce. But men should not marry before the age of 28 years, nor women before the age of 21. After the age of 40 men should become completely continent. (It may be noted that Proudhon wrote this in 1846, just before he married at an age exceeding 40 years and became the father of three daughters.) Thus, a couple's fertile period would last for only 12 years. It should be rare for families to have more than five children. From this figure, losses due to sterility, premature widowhood and accidental death must be deducted (about 1.5), deaths before reaching the age of reproduction (2.5) and births averted by celibacy (0.5). Thus, Proudhon calculates, 4.5 deaths per family must be subtracted from five. In such a situation, population would grow by ten per cent per generation, i.e. every 30 years, or double every three centuries. Throughout, the increased practice of continence and celibacy will develop, men will become like angels, and chastity and disdain for material possessions will develop at the same time as virility.[35]

Joseph Garnier, a liberal economist and supporter of Malthus, wrote of Proudhon: "Having quarrelled with Malthus and refuted Malthus's opponents at the same time, he arrived at conclusions which were even more severe than those of Malthus, so that the most ardent Malthusian economist would be prepared to agree with many pages of his *Contradictions*.[36]

We have shown the wide range and diversity of opinions of theoretical socialists on Malthusianism. There are two reasons for opposing Malthus, depending on whether or not Malthus's law of population is accepted (most of the writers do so), and on whether or not a policy of refusing aid to the poor and advocating delay in marriage is accepted. Most socialists do not agree to a discouragement of marriage, though some, like Proudhon, advocate a delay in the modern Chinese manner, or recommend taxing parents in accordance with the number of their children. Another distinction is between those who do and those who do not accept the legitimacy of contraception and abortion. Most reject these practices in the name of morality and the natural law, and therefore join the traditional stance of the Church. However, Pecqueur is in favour of contraception and Fourier accepts both contraception and abortion.

All authors, except Fourier, favour continence. They all believe that misery is not caused by excess population, but that the reverse is true: fertility and poverty will decrease in parallel.

Socialists did not fail to be influenced by Malthus. Malthusian practices were prevalent at the time among the middle and upper working class. Finally, there were considerable similarities between the opposition of the communists and the Christian socialists, which continued during the succeeding century.

Notes

1. J. P. Villeneuve-Bargemont (1834). *Economie politique chrétienne*, vol. 1, p.244.
2. E. Cabet (1855). *Opinions icariennes sur le mariage*, p.5.
3. E. Cabet. *Voyage en Icarie* (Ed. Anthropos), pp.122–123.
4. R. Lahutière (1841). *De la loi sociale*, p.65.
5. Pinault (1843). *La Fraternité*, p.137.
6. ibid. p.119.
7. *L'Egalitaire*, 1840.
8. J. Garnier (1857). *Du principe de population*, 2ème ed., p.185.
9. *L'Egalitaire*, No. 2, p.43.
10. P. Buchez (1833). *Introduction à la science historique*, p.29.
11. ibid. p.264; P. Buchez (1839). *Essai d'un traité complet de philosophie*, vol. 2. p.549.
12. P. Leroux. *Malthus et les économistes; ou y-aura-t-il toujours des pauvres?*
13. ibid. pp.191, 322, 323.
14. ibid. pp.218, 219.
15. C. Duchâtel (1825). *La charité.*
16. ibid. p.95.
17. ibid. pp.167, 234ff.
18. ibid. pp.104–105.
19. C. Fourier (1822). *Traité de l'association domestique et agricole.* Republished under the title *L'unité universelle* (Ed. Anthropos), vol. iv. p.105.
20. ibid. p.106.
21. ibid.
22. ibid. vol. 5, pp.557–558.
23. ibid. vol. 4, p.107.
24. ibid. vol. 5, p.558.
25. C. Fourier (1830). *Nouveau monde industriel* (Ed. Anthropos), pp.38, 335, 337–338.
26. P. Proudhon (1846). *Système des contradictions économiques* (Ed. Rivière), p.351.
27. C. Pecqueur (1839). *Economie sociale*, pp.147–149, 162, 174–175.
28. ibid. p.19.

29. C. Pecqueur (1840). *Des améliorations matérielles dans leur rapport avec la liberté*, p.131.
30. C. Pecqueur (1842). *Théorie nouvelle*, pp.699ff, 728, 749.
31. C. Pecqueur, op. cit. in note 27, p.288.
32. P. Proudhon, op. cit. in note 26, p.385.
33. ibid. pp.373-372, 386.
34. ibid. pp.347-348.
35. ibid. p.379. In his *De la justice*, 11ème époque, p.306, Proudhon advocates a minimum age at marriage for men of 26 years.
36. J. Garnier, op. cit. in note 8, p.293.

21 The Attitudes of French Socialists to Malthus during the Third Republic

MADELEINE REBÉRIOUX

Until the last decades of the nineteenth century, socialists in general and French socialists in particular, passionately rejected the doctrines associated with the name of Malthus. It would, however, be a mistake to regard this opposition as being purely "dogmatic", or, to use the terms employed by the neo-Malthusians at the beginning of the twentieth century, "Marxist". To demonstrate that such a view would be in error, we need only look at, for example, Pierre Leroux's book *Malthus et les économistes,* or at Proudhon's *Les contradictions économiques.* The same dislikes can be found in one of the great articles appearing in *La Revue Socialiste* in which, four years before his death, Benoit Malon discussed Malthus and in which he expresses his horror of bourgeois society and of the evils for which it is responsible.[1] Malthus is anathematized even more strongly than Ricardo or Leroy-Beaulieu against whom Guesde hurled invectives at nearly the same time.[2] Guesde's first and violent denunciation of Malthus dates back to *L'essai de catéchisme socialiste* which was published in 1875[3], long before he had any contact with Marx or his disciples.

Malthus and his school are regarded as "fathers of the new Church" and as representatives of economic orthodoxy. It matters not, whether their views are correct or not, or whether the concept of the "reserve army" should or should not be analysed in accordance with the Malthusian model. What is intolerable is the view of the *Essay's* author that the laws which govern the affairs of men are as "natural" as those which apply to other living beings. The suggestion that the human population will grow faster than the means of subsistence likens men to animals and regards them as part of nature whose laws are not to be

MALTHUS PAST AND PRESENT
ISBN 0-12-224670-5

denied. This view is used to legitimize a policy of *laissez faire* and to justify objections to any intervention on the part of society to help the oppressed. Malthus is the father of non-interventionism and of economic liberalism. As Malon writes, forecasting the methods of propaganda which came to be used later "one must not weary of repeating" the abominable phrases in which the essence of Malthus's doctrine is expressed. His words reveal Malthus as a veritable "man-eater". The example of the banquet is often cited.

> A man who is born into a world already possessed, if he cannot get subsistence from his parents on whom he has a just demand, and if the society do not want his labour, has no claim of *right* to the smallest portion of food, and, in fact, has no business to be where he is. At nature's mighty feast there is no vacant cover for him. She tells him to be gone, and will quickly execute her own orders if he do not work upon the compassion of some of her guests.[4]

The significance of the instinctive anti-Malthusianism which is common to all socialist schools and which was welcomed by the "suffering masses" can be better understood by adopting a somewhat wider perspective. Malthus's name is linked with those who oppose any intervention by the state against the mineowners or the ironmasters. Thus, Jaurès, an ally of Jules Guesde, elected by the miners and peasants of the Carmausin to represent them and who, according to Barrès, could be regarded, during the early 1890s, as the leader of "the young",[5] attempted to draw a distinction between collectivism, "the concrete manifestation of socialism"[6] and what he called "general socialism". "I call him a socialist, who advocates the energetic intervention of society in economic relations in order to support the poor and the disinherited against the strong, the forces of capital".[7] This very broad definition includes all those who rejected the doctrines of Malthus and Léon Say, and who, from Sismondi to Marx, from Proudhon to Malon and Guesde, believed in the autonomy of social facts and in the possibility of influencing them.

Nonetheless, since the 1880s this anti-Malthusian stance was in retreat. Among the socialists it yielded little by little to a different type of analysis which became more prominent during the pre-war period. No longer was Malthus denounced as Public Enemy Number One of the proletariat; less general[8] and more diverse attacks on him, which were much less flamboyant, bore witness to the emergence of new attitudes. These new critical analyses in the first place led to a different interpretation of Malthus's writings. Secondly, along with the revival of interest in the future (it must be remembered that any vision of the future is rooted implicitly in a criticism of the present, for what would be the value of thinking about tomorrow if it were merely a repetition of today?) during the last decade of the nineteenth century grows the rift between the criticism of what the Malthusian choice implied for contemporary French society and the growing concern for the sentiments and behaviour likely to be witnessed once the socialist society has been achieved.

This new interpretation of Malthusian doctrine is connected with the retreat of economic liberalism and the advances made by interventionist doctrines. The elections of 1889 brought into power a party which was protectionist[9] and when even Paul Leroy Beaulieu was touched by the sufferings of people in the countryside the politicians tended to abandon liberal doctrines. The Catholics, too, wished to made gestures favouring the workers, and most of the Radicals under the leadership of Léon Bourgeois attempted to unite under a banner in which the state was regarded as the provider of security.[10] A number of parties thus attempted new ways to spike the socialists' guns. Previous objections fell into disuse and it was no longer necessary for socialists to denounce the author of the *Essay on Population*.

Malthus is no longer pictured as a cannibal, nor even as one who advocated the death of the proletariat. In 1909, it was even possible for Dr R. Vargas to explain to a meeting which adopted conclusions directly opposed to those of Malthus, that the reverend gentleman was "a good fellow", who adored his children and wished to improve the lot of the lower classes by preaching the gospel of fertility reduction to them.[11] Accusations now tend to be put forward in the calmer and more objective tone of sociological discussion. After each census, and particularly after the Census of 1896 which revealed for the first time an excess of deaths over births, and which led to the foundation of the *Ligue de la Régénération Humaine*,[12] and on the other side of the spectrum to the *Alliance nationale pour le relèvement de la population française*, some socialists began to share the disquiet expressed by the pronatalists including a number of statisticians, physicians and sociologists. However, the discussion of Malthusian doctrines was not limited to these problems. There were two different approaches.

Lafargue was practically the only writer to adapt for his own purposes the analyses of Marx and Engles on the nature of society and the social reasons for industrial overpopulation, "justly called by Engels the reserve army of capitalism"[13] and on the use for this purpose of mechanization, "that terrible weapon of capitalism". More frequently, socialists who were critical of Malthus opposed his certainties with some stubborn facts, relating both to subsistence and to population. As regards the birth rate: its general fall in Europe, which was evident to those who were not blinded by the French situation[14] and which could be demonstrated by statistics, "the most revolutionary of all the sciences",[15] justified the view of Godwin and Chernichevsky[16] against those of Malthus. And as regards subsistence, one could cite the enthusiasm and unshakeable confidence in the potential of science of Elisée Recluse, the anarchist geographer, which was shared by Compère Morel and the physician Oguse, both followers of Guesde[17] and by Désiré Descamps.

"Our agriculture", writes Descamps, "is still in its infancy . . . until science will have transformed its methods and multiplied the fertility of the soil tenfold, twentyfold, one hundredfold".[18] In 1913, Compère Morel affirmed that the earth was sufficiently large, its soil sufficiently rich and its population sufficiently industrious to "multiply the means of subsistence and public wealth infinitely". The socialist sympathizer and scientist, Charles Richet, in his forecast of the future *Dans cent ans,* published in 1892, makes the same point in a less exalted way but no less confidently. Even if the population of the world were to be multiplied by ten during the twentieth century, "the riches of the earth and the sea would be capable of providing sufficient nourishment for these larger numbers" (p.156). How much can be achieved by a good rotation of crops![19] Moreover, it is not necessary to rely on the morrow, for produce is already abundant today, as Dr Oguse wrote in 1907, the year of the wine growers' revolt, "Every moment the fertility of the soil and with it the wealth of France is increasing."

Socialist neo-Malthusians considered that national statistics supported them in their view of the wealth of France. During the 1890s they began to take the national interest explicitly into account. It was in 1893 that the followers of Guesde added the word "French" to the seal of the Labour Party, but Guesde had already, since the 1880s, denounced the voluntary restriction of births as being equivalent to national suicide.[20] At the other end of the socialist spectrum, Gustave Rouanet in an article published in the *Revue socialiste* for October 1889 almost pathetically regards the fall in the French birth rate as the "most menacing" of all the dangers which "threaten the country of the Revolution". Rouanet candidly admits that in this he is not expressing a specifically socialist point of view: he is defending "the vital interests" of his country. France owes her influence to her "genius", but also to the "formidable armies" which she could raise in 1793, when her population amounted to 27 per cent of the population of Europe. Today, France is weakened in face of her powerful neighbours (there is no difficulty in guessing who was meant) when her population amounts to only 13 per cent of that of the European continent.

However, whether considered from a military point of view like Rouanet or as part of a much larger dynamic system like the young Guesde, purely French interests were not the only arguments used by socialists. Malthusian doctrines were regarded as menacing civilization itself. In any case, what would be the fate of civilization without France? These views can be found throughout the pages of the *Revue socialiste* from the date of its foundation to 1914, from Malon to Fournière, Andler and Albert Thomas. They were supported on the eve of the war by the groups gathered around Andler which were responsible for the publication of the *Cahiers du socialisme*, and also by those who published with Albert Thomas the collection *Documents du socialisme*. For instance, in 1910 Robert Hertz published a pamphlet in the *Cahiers du socialisme* series, entitled *Socialisme et dépopulation*. This pamphlet by Robert Hertz which was circulated by the SFIO was called "the most absurd of all the anti-Malthusian pamphlets" by Georges Hardy,[21] Paul Robin's brother-in-law. Hertz was part of the vitalist movement in which Romain Rolland, Elie Faure and the young Jean Richard Bloch were prominent, and his views were close to those of Andler who, one year later, organized a conference on Socialist Civilization.[22] In Hertz's view the fall in the birth rate carries with it the downfall of innovation. France is one of the group of older countries which will lack the vital energy required to bring about a strong socialist civilization. It is also possible to detect in his pamphlet and in some simpler articles in the socialist provincial press[23] an undertone of disquiet of "civilized populations" at the risk of becoming inferior to the prolific coloured peoples, if Malthusian practices were adopted: those people with black or yellow skins, colonized or semi-colonized, to whom, for good measure, the Russian *muzhiks* were added.

However, these writers find some difficulties in objecting to Malthus purely on the grounds of French interests and of civilization. When his doctrines had been opposed in the past on behalf of the oppressed classes and when Socialist opponents of Malthus had claimed to support a system of values different from that of the *Alliance contre la dépopulation*. Therefore, they generally fulfilled their basic duty[24] to question Malthusian doctrines on behalf of the working class, worn down by excessive work and excessive numbers of children, who until they reached the age of twelve years or so were a liability to those responsible for bringing them up.

Several writers, indeed, were squarely indignant that socialists did not confine their objections to this point which affected the working class. It is not surprising that the followers of Guesde should have been upset by the views of Rouanet or Hertz. But even the invocation of the class struggle or the proletariat or membership of the Guesdist faction were insufficient to achieve unanimity on a subject as complex and divisive as Malthusianism.

By the end of the nineteenth century Guesde's followers hoped to play a part in relation to the trade unions similar to that of the Social Democratic party in Germany. At that time Lafargue and Guesde put the most important stress on achieving the eight-hour day.[25] This objective was to be achieved not with a view of reducing the reserve army of labour[26] (or, at least, not officially), but in order to limit the time when the productive forces destroyed themselves and the future of the race by overproduction. These tactics were designed to turn against the owning classes the hypocritical complaints which they had voiced against the rising tide of Malthusianism among the proletariat.[27] Paul Brousse advocated similar objectives but used different tactics. His was a municipal socialism, founded on the development of public services and for him there was only one solution to the problem of the falling birth rate, that society should make itself responsible for all workers' children. "The birth rate will recover", he wrote, "on the day when a child ceases to be a liability and becomes an asset".[28]

However, as neo-Malthusianism made headway among the working class it drew supporters outside the ranks of anarchists and their sympathizers, for instance, Sixte Quenin who had been chosen by Compère Morel to be his collaborator in editing the *Encyclopédie socialiste*.[29] In one of the last volumes entitled *Comment nous sommes socialistes,* the Deputy for Arles posed the problem of working-class Malthusianism in very simple terms and with as little ideology as possible. What assistance could be provided to compensate for the "total sacrifice" that a child entailed.[30] His reply seems self-evident to him, but ranges him in the opposite camp to his editor. But the reply may not have been as self-evident as it seemed. Only Georges Sorel attempted to solve the dilemma at the time: according to him it was precisely the willingness to accept such a "sacrifice" that constituted the greatness of the proletariat and gave it a reserve moral force which would enable it to save humanity from the threat of degeneracy. Because of their parents' sacrifices, workers' children are a force for moral progress and a renunciation of children through neo-Malthusian practices by workers would constitute more than a fault: it would mean an abandonment of the socialist future. However, as Gaston Pirou[31] in a sharply worded article put it, this was very much a theorist's view. But it does not seem any more "theoretical" than the qualifications used to condemn neo-Malthusianism by others.

Let us consider these objections briefly. No socialist, not even Sixte Quenin or Madeleine Pelletier, supported neo-Malthusianism wholeheartedly. On the eve of the war, when the discussion was fiercest, four principal objections were put forward. It was an anti-French and, therefore, an anti-humanitarian solution. This was the view of the right wing of the SFIO, of whom Robert Hertz was a good representative. Those who, like Rouanet or Désiré Descamps, saw it as an expression of the dominant culture in French society regarded it as a petty bourgeois solution to the problem. It implied a cult of saving which was put forward by the republican school-system and the bourgeoisie and an attachment to private property, which was one of the reasons why the radicals had broken with the socialists. The more orthodox followers of Guesde used much simpler arguments: Vargas and Compère Morel regarded neo-Malthusianism as merely a "reformist" solution to the problem. "Reformist" was the all-pervading adjective used by this faction for any policy which was marginal to the achievement of socialism through gaining votes and reading the doctrine; it could be applied to the struggle for peace or for the struggle against alcoholism. This general denunciation obviously took away a great deal of its appeal. Lastly, Sixte Quenin who, whilst dissenting from some of their views, remained with the followers of Guesde, and Ernest Tabouriech,[32] an intellectual whose feminist sympathies made him sympathetic to some aspects of neo-Malthusianism, regarded neo-Malthusian practices as a useful solution for the individual but of no social significance. The social problem would remain unsolved and these practices could not, therefore, be regarded as socialist.

What of the future? What did French socialists think about population in the future socialist society, given their views about Malthus and neo-Malthusianism? There was "La Sociale", the Utopia of proletarians, which so many authors in novels and essays endeavoured to render not only desirable but credible during the twenty years or so around the turn of the century. Not all the socialists agreed. The Guesdists continued to stress that it was imprudent and dangerous to speculate about the future. However, Compère-Morel, who was the guardian of orthodoxy, wrote: "From the entrails of modern society, the future will emerge".[33] When the demand exists, the hope for the future is a necessary condition for daily action. We shall follow the steps of Jaurès and Kropotkin, Deslinières and Rouanet, Tabouriech and Sixte Quenin, Lafargue (who in this as in other matters is somewhat idiosyncratic) and Madeleine Pelletier. These pair groups are not used for rhetorical purposes only: each of them illustrates a different nuance and sometimes more than a nuance of socialist thought.

Jaurès and Kropotkin, whose names have frequently been coupled,[34] believe in abundance and in this respect, as Jaurès has shown,[35] are the intellectual successors not only of Saint Simon but of Marx himself. Under a socialist regime, there will be luxury which will be achieved in a number of ways, in the first place through the disappearance of those who live on unearned incomes and those who today limit production in order to maintain high prices (Kropotkin). However, Jaurès does not completely share the confidence of Kropotkin and others.[36] He believes that it savours of the utopian to believe in a prodigious growth of production which would result solely from different social arrangements[37] and on many occasions[38] he considers the ways in which production would be organized in a socialist France so that potentials for a good life were fully realized. However, as I noted with some surprise, he remains silent about the need for an abundant population.[39] He may agree with Rouanet that the population problem will disappear under socialism, when society will be capable of achieving a balance between population and subsistence gradually as required by internal and external conditions.[40] Neither Rouanet nor Jaurès, however, reveal any trace of the exuberant dream formulated by a provincial politician who later became a Guesdist, Lucien Deslinières, who published in 1899 a long work on *L'application du système collectiviste,* in which he wrote: "What a prodigious explosion! What a vigorous thrust of little French citizens! It is then that the injunction 'be fruitful and multiply' will cease to be a vain slogan".[41] This flood of beautiful babies will come about because society will make itself responsible for the maintenance of each infant which will be taken from its mother early in life, and through the prohibition of both prostitution and women's employment. Although this programme may not be equally pleasing to all, it is similar to the celebrated military Utopia of the American author Bellamy.[42]

Sixte Quenin or Tabouriech were not impressed, in spite of the difference between themselves. Both feared the possibility of a human antheap, which Deslinières appeared to welcome. To show the magnitude of the risk, Sixte Quenin pictures a France with a population of 1000 million, a possibility which he thinks would follow from the abolition of war, epidemics and alcoholism.[43]. There would be other risks. An ecologist before his time, Sixte Quenin deplores "the inability to find a silent and solitary place anywhere, where the workers could recover from the stresses of urban life" and in spite of his confidence in progress, he sees the risk of famine looming over the horizon.

Fortunately, the neo-Malthusians will be there and Sixte Quenin, believing in the superiority of politics and culture over love, expects that their practices will not only render sexual relations less fecund but also less frequent. Tabouriech, whose *La Cité Future* is sub-titled "A Scientific Utopia" is concerned about the pressure that a large increase in the birth rate would place on the budget and about the need for the working population to nourish these children and to provide the necessary investment. And he concludes by returning to Malthus (but, dare I say it, a socialized Malthus): ". . . it will [then] be possible to practise Malthus's moral restraint but for social rather than for individualist reasons, and this makes all the difference".[44]

Though advising his readers to beware of Sixte Quenin, Tabouriech agrees with him on some points. He doubts whether it will become necessary to follow a social (i.e. official) Malthusian policy. He places his hopes in a voluntary restriction of marital fertility. But he differs from Sixte Quenin and some other writers by taking "the woman's" side. Without going into great detail: in a socialist society women and men will be equal and reproductive behaviour will, therefore, be influenced by women's attitudes. Together with Viviani and Lafargue, Tabouriech is the only member of the older French socialist school to have sympathy for the feminist point of view. Though not all socialist writers were as coarse as Doctor Oguse[45], there were few who followed Bebel[46] who would have allowed women the right to regulate their own lives and their fertility and who hoped that they would be given the means to do so in a socialist society. Among the anti-Malthusians whom we have mentioned only Désiré Descamps who has already been cited several times took that view,[47] as did Lafargue. We need only cite the celebrated article *Conjungo*,[48] where the charming Laura's husband paints a picture of a socialist matriarchy in which women regain the pre-eminence which they enjoyed in more primitive societies and in which they will have the right to choose their mates and to realize their full desire in a glorified maternity

There can be little doubt that after 1890, the contradiction between the laws of Malthus and the silent practice of his "deadly secrets" was somewhat of an embarrassment to the French socialists. Clearly, the reverend English gentleman was mistaken, but their sense of life, confidence in progress, hope for the future, and the element of *machismo* which was part of their mental make-up hardly predisposed them to congratulate themselves on the erroneous nature of his forecasts. They limited themselves to using the threat of a diminution of the working class and of the end of bourgeois ideology. Once the conditions of the workers had been planned and society collectivized, individualism which was the common element in Malthusianism and neo-Malthusianism, would be in retreat.

But there were many differences and nuances in different socialist groups, not excluding the anarchists. Many of the most eminent socialists, among them Jaurès and Vaillant, chose to be silent on the subject. Perhaps their modesty, resulting from a bourgeois origin, was responsible. The development of neo-Malthusian practices by the working class made it difficult to keep the debate at an abstract level.[49] Perhaps they were conscious that they might fall into a trap. Among those who discussed the subject, their anti-Malthusianism separated them from the trade unions. It is clear, however, that on the eve of World War I, neo-Malthusianism had made striking progress. This simple truth is born out by at least one strong element in the ongoing debate: the delineation of a future society.

Notes

1. B. Malon. La civilisation bourgeoise et ses aboutissants. *Revue socialiste*, November 1889, pp.513–538.
2. cf. J. Guesde. *Le collectivisme au Collège de France.*
3. A recent discussion of Guesde's and Lafargue's views may be found in a paper by Léon Garni. Jules Guesde, Paul Lafargue et les problèmes de la population. *Population*, Nov.-Dec. 1979, 1023–1043.
4. T. R. Malthus. *Essay*, 1803 Edition, pp.531–532; cited by K. Smith, *The Malthusian Controversy* (1951), p.57. London.
5. In *Le Journal* on 20 January, 1893, Barrès appealed to "the young" to rally under the leadership of Jaurès.
6. J. Jaurès. Collectivisme et radicalisme. *Revue socialiste*, March 1895. This article, which was intended to be the beginning of a book which was not, however, ever completed, was later reprinted with four others in volume 1 of "Etudes socialistes". *Oeuvres de Jean Jaurès* under the direction of M. Bonnafous.
7. Lettres de Jaurès. *Dépèche de Toulouse*, 16 October, 1893.
8. See F. Ronsin. Between Malthus and the social revolution: The French neo-Malthusian movement. This volume, pp.329–339.
9. On this point cf. chapter 7 of R. Schnerb (1970). *Libre échange et protectionnisme*. Presses Universitaires de France, Paris. Series *Que sais-je?*, 3rd Edition.
10. I have used a paper given by J. Gaillard at the seminar of P. Vigier and S. Bernstein on February 23, 1979.
11. R. Vargas (1909). *Que devons nous penser du néo-Malthusianisme?* Groupe

d'études sociales de Montpellier, p.20. Some years later Compère Morel recognized in Malthus only the views of a "good bourgeois conservative". cf. Contre le néo-Malthusianisme. *Le Socialisme*, 16 Feb. 1913. This article was reproduced in the volume of the *Encyclopédie socialiste*, edited by Sixte-Quenin.

12. P. Robin was late. In England, the Malthusian League was founded in 1877, and in the Netherlands the first Malthusian organizations were founded in 1884.
13. cf. his two articles in *L'Egalité*, 26 Feb. 1882, and 24 Sept. 1882.
14. The sociologist Julius Wolf noted in the *Revue d'économie politique* (1902) (No. 6) the difference between the "civilized countries of Europe" and the "less civilized countries, such as Russia".
15. J. Guesde's article "La fin de la France par la propriété" was republished in 1899 in *Le Socialisme au jour le jour*.
16. W. Godwin (1820). *Recherches sur la population*. N. Tchernichewsky. *Critique de l'économie politique*. Guesde made much use of the latter volume.
17. cf. particularly Dr Oguse. Socialisme et néo-Malthusianisme. *Revue socialiste*, August 1907.
18. D. Descamps. Le problème de la richesse. *Revue socialiste*, April 1899.
19. Since 1875, Guesde used the example of England in support of this thesis. See *Essai de catéchisme socialiste*.
20. J. Guesde, loc. cit. in note 15.
21. This was the true name of Gabriel Giroud. cf. *Néo-Malthusianisme et socialisme* (1910).
22. Hertz is not widely known, even though he had published a major article on the Fabian Society in the *Revue socialiste* in November 1911. His pamphlet has been discussed for the first time by A. Armengaud (1966) in his pioneering article: "Mouvement ouvrier et néo-Malthusianisme au début du XXème siècle". *Annales de démographie historique*, 7–21.
23. For instance, the anonymous articles published in January, 1907, in *Le travailleur socialiste de l'Yonne*.
24. Even Hertz devotes some pages to this topic. The only exception is G. Rouanet who is obsessed by the problem relating to France.
25. P. Lafargue. *L'Egalité*, 26 Feb. 1882, and particularly the explanation of the motives given by Guesde on May 22, 1894, in support of his Bill to limit the length of the working day to eight hours.
26. They maintained that the reason for its existence was social and not sexual.
27. cf. for instance the anger of Henri Turot at the populationist sermon preached by *Le Temps* to the workers after the Census of 1896. "Whether you are rogues or fools, can you not see who should be asked to make these sacrifices?" *Petite République*, 7 Aug. 1896.
28. P. Brousse. Les Malthusiens. *Petite République*, 10 Aug. 1896.
29. On the *Encyclopédie socialiste* see Madelene Rébérioux (1976). Guesdisme et culture politique. *Mélanges d'histoire sociale offerts à Jean Maîtron*. Editions ouvrières, pp.211–228.

30. Sixte Quenin (1913). *Comment nous sommes socialistes*, p.287.
31. For an intelligent summary of his views see G. Pirou (1911). Théoriciens et militants. *Revue politique et parlementaire*, pp.130–142.
32. E. Tabouriech (1902), *La cité future. Essai d'une utopie scientifique*, p.484.
33. Preface to Sixte Quenin, op. cit. in note 30.
34. cf. the message from Jaurès to Kropotkin in *La Dépèche de Toulouse* on August 12, 1896, the day after the anarchists had been expelled from the Socialist International at the London Congress.
35. Particularly in the last article of the "Suite" published in 1895–1896 in the *Revue socialiste*.
36. cf. D. Descamps. Le problème de l'amour'. *Revue socialiste*, July 1897; *see* also the article by Compère Morel published in 1913 and already cited. "The revolution will bring riches beyond expectation for all."
37. J. Jaurès. La production socialiste; *see* Bonnafous, op. cit. in note 6, p.375.
38. In 1893–1894 in the *Dépèche de Toulouse*; in 1895–1896 in the *Revue socialiste*; in 1898 in *Cosmopolis*; and in June 1906 in Parliament.
39. On this subject, I have only been able to find very occasional references in *L'Humanité* in June 1912 and May 1913, all linked to political changes.
40. G. Rouanet (Oct. 1889). *Revue socialiste*, p.396.
41. L. Deslinières (1899). *L'application du système collectiviste*, p.497.
42. *One Hundred Years Later* or *The Year 2000* was translated into French three times in 1891; in the USA it sold 400 000 copies within three years.
43. Sixte Quenin, op. cit. in note 30, p.229.
44. E. Tabouriech, op. cit. in note 32, p.301.
45. He ridiculed those who advocated the prevention of births because of the sufferings of the mother, by saying that "constipation, too, caused suffering" and suggested in opposition to Paul Robin, the foundation of a *Ligue de régénération humaine par les laxatifs*; cf. Dr Oguse, loc. cit. in note 17.
46. In his book *Woman and Socialism* which is more frequently cited than read, Bebel states among other things: "Strong and intelligent women nowhere wish to be subject to the decrees of providence and to pass the best years of their lives in a state of pregnancy or with a child at their breast."
47. In a socialist society women will not become mothers, unless they wish to do so for physical or moral reasons. Children will be born not to satisfy a handful of exploiters, but for the good of humanity as a whole. *Le problème de l'amour*. loc. cit. p.35.
48. P. Lafargue. Conjungo. *Le Socialiste*, 30 June 1901.
49. In his Montpellier pamphlet, Vargas writes: "This doctrine seems to me to occupy too important a part in the preoccupations of some revolutionaries, or at least those who may be considered as the most serious revolutionaries. It becomes invase, over-important and corrosive."

22 Social Darwinists and Malthus

A. BÉJIN

I

Though there is no lack of studies dealing with the relationship between the theories of Malthus and Darwin,[1] only a few have traced the connection between Malthus's treatment of population problems and that of the authors who have been called Social Darwinists and who wrote towards the end of the nineteenth century.[2] It is not surprising that this should be so. There has not as yet been a systematic analysis of the different cross-currents of thought (liberal, eugenic, racist, social imperialist, selectionist) among the Social Darwinists and particularly among European Social Darwinists, which would make it possible to study the points on which they were in agreement and those where their opinions diverged. Moreover, most historians of the social sciences regard Social Darwinism as an intellectual blind alley and believe that sociology had to detach itself from the ideas put forward by the Social Darwinists in order to be able to start afresh. Though this point of view is debatable, there is less disagreement that on the political side the ideas of Social Darwinism have been used to legitimize Nazi totalitarianism. The defeat of this totalitarian faction by a totalitarianism at the opposite end of the political spectrum has meant that less attention has been given to its underlying ideas, whereas many writers have studied the predecessors of communist thought. Moreover, those few authors who have attempted to trace the origins of Social Darwinism have generally confined themselves to considering the relationship of Darwin's theory and that of the sociologists who relied upon it, and have not gone as far back as Malthus, thus depriving themselves of an interesting perspective.

MALTHUS PAST AND PRESENT
ISBN 0-12-224670-5

In order to undertake a systematic analysis of the similarities and differences between Malthus's demographic writings[3] and the ideas of the Social Darwinists I shall first attempt to delineate the principal propositions put forward by Malthus which Darwin and his disciples accepted and, secondly, consider the changes in those ideas that the "liberal" and the "socialist" school of Social Darwinists respectively came to accept. The discussion will be confined to European authors. However, a discussion of the ideas of the American school of Social Darwinists, which have been studied more systematically than those of the Europeans,[4] is likely to yield similar results. Although the Social Darwinists accepted Malthus's theory of population as a point of departure, they were led to modify his views about the definition of nature, man, the struggle for existence, the role of the state and the notion of progress so that their position in the end was very different from Malthus's.

Though Malthus's theory is by nature dualist in character, in some aspects it approaches a monist point of view. God is the creator of nature and has imposed general laws upon it. Man, with his interlinked body and mind, differs from other animals not merely because he possesses "natural rights" but also because he possesses reason and a moral conscience. However, like other members of the plant and animal kingdoms he is subject to unchangeable natural laws, of which one of the most important is the Principle of Population. This Principle applies to each individual member of humanity and not to collective groups, such as nations, classes or ethnic groups. It operates through three types of check to population growth. The relative importance of each of these checks varies in different periods of history. However, they are always present and it is a mistaken view to attribute the evils which result from them to the imperfection of human institutions. They are natural evils, that is to say, they are part of the will of God who, through their operation, stimulates men's activities and thus makes progress possible. However, progress which will essentially be achieved in the moral sphere can only be limited.

We now consider these views in greater detail

1. A modified dualism

If we term philosophical doctrines which distinguish and allow for the co-existence of God and Creation (the world, nature), mind and matter, as "dualist", as opposed to the "monist" doctrine which presupposes the essential unity of all these elements,[5] it would appear that Malthus's views were essentially dualist. However, some of the "concessions" that Malthus makes may be seen to favour monism particularly from the moment when the doctrine of creation of species is questioned.

> As we shall all be disposed to agree that God is the creator of mind as well as of body, and as they both seem to be forming and unfolding themselves at the same time, it cannot appear inconsistent either with reason or revelation, if it appear to be consistent with phenomena of nature, to suppose that God is constantly occupied in forming mind out of matter . . .[6]

2. Nature and man

Malthus does not define man in the first place by his "natural rights", nor by his "duties" (though he prefers to discuss the latter), but in terms of the laws which govern his nature. These laws are no different in essence from those which apply "in other parts of animated nature".[7] They are he says "nearly" unchangeable: ". . . we know from experience that these operations of what we call nature have been conducted almost invariably according to fixed laws."[8] Moreover, this constancy of natural laws is indispensable if man is to use his powers, particularly the power of reason: "that faculty which enables us to calculate consequences."[9]

> The constancy of the laws of nature, or the certainty with which we may expect the same effects from the same causes, is the foundation of the faculty of reason . . . If God were frequently to change his purpose . . . a general and fatal torpor of the human faculties would probably ensue.[10]

The most important of these laws are "the mighty law of self-preservation",[11] "the apparently narrow principle of self-love",[12] the "principle of benevolence" which serves to soften the "partial evils" resulting from the operation of the principle of self-love, but which cannot be substituted for it.[13] Above all others, however, is the law which regulates the relationship between two of the most powerful and general desires of mankind, which are according to Malthus "the desire for food" and "the passion between the sexes".[14] This is the celebrated Principle of Population:

> Population, when unchecked, increases in a geometrical ratio. Subsistence increases only in an arithmetical ratio.[15]

This Principle of Population implies "a struggle for existence a perpetual struggle for room and food".[16] But a number of commentators have interpreted this struggle in a way different from Malthus. For him the struggle for existence is a *consequence* of the Principle of Population, not a law from which the Principle may be deduced. Moreover, it cannot be legitimated, particularly when it takes the form of war, "that great pest of the human race",[17] by an appeal to some "right of the strongest".[18]

Together the operation of these laws of nature tends to promote the "general good" and to increase "the mass of human happiness".[19] They rest on the principle of private property. This principle is not, in Malthus's view, a natural right, but it "must be considered as the most natural as well as the most necessary of all positive laws"[20] and on a regulatory force which tends to bring individuals back on the "right road": that "great *vis medicatrix reipublicae*, the desire of bettering our condition, and the fear of making it worse".[21]

3. The operation of the checks

What impressed Malthus in the first place was not the struggle for existence but the variety and profusion of nature,[22] "the prodigious power of increase in plants and animals".[23] As the aspect which is of value to man is necessarily limited by the scarcity of territory and "the diminishing and limited power of increasing the produce of the soil",[24] the growth of human population is checked in a way which leads to a struggle for existence. From the second edition of his *Essay* onwards, Malthus distinguishes three checks which need not here be considered in detail,[25] viz.:

a. "positive checks" which lead to a rise in mortality and involve "misery" and/or "vice";
b. "preventive checks" which lead to a limitation of births and which may be sub-divided into those which are "vicious" (e.g. contraception) and those which are "virtuous", i.e. moral restraint which leads to a decrease in nuptiality.

Though Malthus believes that it is inevitable that one or other of these checks will operate to reduce population growth, the preventive checks, whether vicious or virtuous, are subject to human volition. Thus, though the checks are necessary, it is not possible to determine absolutely which of them will be operative. Their operation cannot be analysed by means of a chain of causes and effects which are rigidly linked together, because it will depend on a choice informed by conscience and, therefore, there is some degree of freedom. This is a most important point, because it makes it possible in theory to formulate a "strategy" for the use of these checks. It would not be possible to consider such a "strategy" unless there were some degree of freedom of choice at the margin. However, the choice of such strategies must, according to Malthus, be left entirely to the individual. This is particularly true of moral restraint, the preventive check which rests on individual continence and which an individual imposes on himself until such time as he is able to support a family.

4. Who is affected by the checks?

The checks which we have described are regarded by Malthus as essentially applying to quantities (of human beings). This concept is based on an individualist abstraction (only individuals are considered and they are regarded as equal), but is by no means self-evident. It would be perfectly possible to think of checks which apply to qualities (physical, intellectual or moral) and the majority of Social Darwinists accepted this point of view.

Malthus thought of the Principle of Population as a game which humanity played against nature (i.e. the environment). The population consists of individuals.[26] Groups of individuals, such as families, classes or nations, are regarded by Malthus as constructs rather than as possessing a real existence. All individuals are equal, as each has been created in God's image. They are, therefore, equal in the face of death. In its efforts to adjust the growth of human populations to the growth of subsistence, nature claims its share of human lives. As nature itself is subject to the laws of God, it cannot prefer any particular type of human victim. All are of equal worth and nature will be content with a given *number* of hostages. Malthus does realize that in this game against nature, some individuals are, to use Orwell's phrase, "more equal than others". For Malthus there are no "fittest" individuals, but some categories of men seem to him to be more exposed to the reprisals of nature, in particular "the lowest orders of society".[27] However, nature is not systematically partisan. The process of adjustment is quantitative, rather than qualitative. Thus, the game against nature is not a Hobbesian struggle of each against each, rather does it consist of an antagonism between any one individual and all others. The positive check which may claim a particular individual as a victim does not result from the actions of another particular individual but from the pressures exercised by all his fellow men. Thus, the concept of a struggle does not really fit this situation. One must use a completely different metaphor to describe this adjustment process, which takes account of the important random element in it. Malthus himself used the metaphor of a lottery, though most of those who commented on him have preferred the concept of a struggle as this seems to fit in better with Darwin's ideas. The image of a lottery is found in at least two places in Malthus's works.

> . . . it has appeared that from the inevitable laws of our nature some human beings must suffer from want. These are the unhappy persons who, in the *great lottery of life*, have drawn a blank.[28]

> If the lowest classes of society were thus diminished, and the middle classes increased, each labourer might indulge a more rational hope of rising by diligence and exertion into a better station; the rewards of industry and virtue would be increased in number; the *lottery of human society* would appear to consist of fewer blanks and more prizes; and the sum of social happiness would be evidently augmented.[29]

The metaphor of a lottery may imply the existence of a struggle or rather of a conflict between the interests of different individuals: the net gain of one player is paid for by the stakes of all the others. Moreover, this does not exclude the possibility of choosing a strategy of action: if each ticket in a lottery stands the same *a priori* chance of winning, it would still be possible to increase one's chances of gain by foresight and industry so as to secure several of these tickets. Paradoxically, in the lottery of life one can increase one's chances of success as easily by vicious practices (contraception etc.) as by virtuous ones (such as foresight). However, according to Malthus, such behaviour would be self-defeating, for the fraudulent gain of a few extra years of life would diminish the chances of happiness in the next world. For the non-believing neo-Malthusians, practices which to Malthus appeared vicious came to be regarded as virtuous.

5. The evolution of different checks

Though Malthus alludes to the properties that characterize all living species (and, in particular, to their natural fertility), his main concern is with man. The demographic consequences of predatory animals on human populations seemed to him to be negligible, and he did not, therefore, discuss predation between different species. However, one aspect of predation was central to his thought, though he presented this in a way which conceals its essential nature. That aspect was the relationship between man and those animals which he uses as food, and the reification of animals as "food" plays down the idea of predation. Malthus did not regard man sufficiently as part of nature to consider him as a beast of prey on other species.

Thus, Malthus confined his discussion to relations within the human species. We have stressed that he used the metaphor of a "lottery" rather than a "struggle". Those who produce too many children and/or consume too much of the limited amount of subsistence available might be regarded as "struggling" against those who have fewer children or who make smaller demands on resources. But this struggle (which often cannot be noticed) is mediated by scarcity; the excess fertility of some creates scarcity which will affect all. However, it is unnecessary and perhaps even undesirable to extend the notion of "struggle" to cover this point. It would suggest an attenuation of the historical changes that have taken place in the operation of the Malthusian checks.

According to Malthus these checks at first "in past times and in the more uncivilized parts of the world"[30] consisted of the positive checks, especially of wars and only later were they transformed into preventive checks, both vicious and virtuous. The general outline of this scheme of development is clear. Misfortunes (particularly wars) and vice will retreat and be replaced by virtue. Population control will evolve in the direction of prevention of growth and become internalized. In sum "bad" violence, directed against others which will correct growth is replaced by "good" violence, against the self and which will prevent growth. We are a long way from a doctrine which glorifies war and regards it as the principal means of population control. This liberal and relatively optimistic view, which postulates the existence of a growing capacity for self-control among individuals, also presupposes that the influence of institutions — and particularly that of the state — on individual conduct is strictly limited. It also explains the well-known opposition of the reverend gentleman to the poor laws[31] and makes it possible for us to understand why Malthus strongly objected to any measures designed to compel individuals to adopt even virtuous methods of prevention. "Prudence cannot be enforced by laws, without a great violation of natural liberty, and a great risk of producing more evil than good."[32] Thus, Malthus thought it wrong to use the poor laws to help those poor who did not voluntarily limit their families, but equally wrong to impose such a limitation on them by law. The best way was to let nature take its course. "When nature will govern and punish for us, it is a very miserable ambition to wish to snatch the rod from her hand and draw upon ourselves the odium of executioner."[33] On the other hand it was perfectly licit to attempt to persuade the poor to adopt responsible attitudes towards reproduction by providing them with a good education.[34]

6. On the possibility and nature of progress

Malthus distinguished two aspects of progress which he believed man to be capable of, progress in happiness and progress in morals. As regards the former which he conceived in utilitarian terms, happiness could not increase indefinitely. "In human life we are continually called upon to submit to a lesser evil in order to avoid a greater."[35] According to Malthus, the rate of population growth itself was a major indicator of the sum of happiness. ". . . there is not a truer criterion of the happiness and innocence of a people than the rapidity of their increase."[36] However, the rate of growth and, therefore, the amount of happiness in a population is limited for humanity as a whole by the Principle of Population.

The natural design is good, because the limit that the Principle of Population imposes on the rate of growth and, therefore, on happiness also acts as the spur which enables man to achieve the other kind of progress, moral progress. But in this sphere, too, progress can only be limited. ". . . the vices and moral weakness of man can never be wholly overcome in this world."[37]

It is possible to conceive of other types of progress, particularly progress in man's physical and intellectual faculties. Malthus, however, firmly rejected the possibility of indefinite organic improvement in man. His most virulent criticisms of Condorcet and Godwin relate to this point.[38] In this respect, the views of the Social Darwinists differed radically from those of Malthus.

II

These views of Malthus, which we have sketched briefly in the preceding section of this paper, were modified both by the liberal (Clémence Royer) and the socialist (Enrico Ferri, Karl Pearson, Georges Vacher de Lapouge among others) school of Social Darwinists. These are discussed below.[39]

1. From a modified dualism to monism

God is not included in the scheme of the Social Darwinists, or at most his attributes are transferred to nature and history, or, to put it more precisely, to the history of nature: evolution. Evolution leads not only to the elimination of some species, but also to the creation of new ones. Natural laws are not longer regarded as fixed rules imposed by the Creator, but as evolutionary rules which characterize natural development.

2. From fixed to changing natural laws

Darwin and the Social Darwinists are not content to look at the history of nature, but believe that natural laws themselves have undergone an evolution which is difficult to trace, particularly in their application to human societies. The latter are regarded as entities which derive from nature but which have become partially independent from it. Thus reason, the faculty which, according to Malthus, enables us to foresee the consequences of our actions, becomes paralysed. History is subject to the unpredictable play of forces and becomes fundamentally irrational. To comprehend history one must not think of general laws, but in terms of a "destiny" which some consider to be predictable, but others believe cannot be understood in a completely rational manner. The time for a new type of oracle has come.

3. Rational and moral man changed to a beast of prey and subject to instinct and subordinated to class, nation and ethnic group

Darwin and the Social Darwinists have overcome the theoretical differences which distinguish men from animals. Like Malthus, they do not define man in terms of his "natural rights". It is known that he is subject to a slow process of development, in which reason is only one of the facilities of adaptation.

Social Darwinists do not approach the study of man from considering any type of animal. Their favourite reference is the beast of prey. They are almost obsessional in what we may call *polemomorphism*. Life is likened to a perpetual struggle and international society to a jungle in which individuals, but also groups of individuals such as classes, nations and ethnic groups, devour one another.

4. From a nature in which equilibrium is achieved through variety to a nature based on inequality

Malthus views inequalities as one of the manifestations of the infinite variety of nature: ". . . those roughnesses and inequalities, those inferior parts that support the superior . . . contribute to the symmetry, grace and fair proportion of the whole."[40] But the Social Darwinists believe that nature is characterized by inequality, rather than by variety.[41]

5. Divergence of interests between individuals, but chiefly between classes, nations, ethnic groups and species in the struggle for life.

This change of view can be illustrated in many ways. According to Clémence Royer, constant growth and development is attained through the victory of the superior and the disappearance of inferior groups and through the competition of equal groups.[42] Enrico Ferri, an admirer of Karl Marx, views the class struggle, even if it were to become attenuated, as a necessary aspect of the struggle for existence.[43] However, another socialist, Karl Pearson, one of the exponents of what has been called social imperialism, considers that the energy spent on the class struggle is lost to the inevitable struggle between different nations and ethnic groups. "The true statesman has to limit the internal struggle of the community in order to make it stronger for the external struggle."[44]

6. From the principle of population to the principle of selection and the law of heredity

In his formulation of the Principle of Population, Malthus envisaged a quantitative adjustment of population to means of subsistence. In replacing this concept by the principle of selection[45] and the "inexorable law of heredity",[46] the Social Darwinists stress the qualitative selection of the fittest. Whereas Malthus particularly condemned those poor who, because their poverty was the result of idleness, did not limit their offspring, the Social Darwinists were particularly vehement about the dysgenic effects of the high fertility of the "degenerate" and "inferior" races on one hand, and the low rate of reproduction of those with valuable hereditary characteristics, which they could transmit to their offspring, on the other. The true struggle for existence is the struggle for offspring,[47] wrote Vacher de Lapouge. And, writing of those "eugenists" who voluntarily reduced the size of their families: "The unforgivable sin is infertility."[48] This point of view would have seemed strange to Malthus for whom "it is not the duty of man simply to propagate his species, but to propagate virtue and happiness".[49]

7. From *laissez-faire* to methodical selection

The liberal Social Darwinist Clémence Royer did not think that natural selection operated satisfactorily in modern societies. It, therefore, becomes necessary to use the law to enforce conditions which will make it possible for natural selection to operate and be effective. But in order to do so, it will be necessary to allow unlimited personal liberty.[50] But for interventionist Social Darwinists Royer's suggestions are inadequate. The evil (the excessive attenuation of the process of natural selection) has gone too far. Most "social selection" has dysgenic effects. Salvation (which, however, in the pessimistic views of Vacher de Lapouge will only be temporary) can only be achieved through methodical selection, based simultaneously on the eugenic principles enunciated by Sir Francis Galton, and on socialism. "As a practical measure selection consists of correcting the deleterious consequences of natural selection and so leads to an increase in the numbers of the fittest and most beautiful. In this it is analogous to socialism which consists of correcting the natural consequences of economic development in order to achieve social perfection".[51] "Socialism will be and must be selectionist or it will not be able to exist, it can only be achieved when men have changed from their present state, and this can only be done through selection."[52]

8. From limited moral progress to unlimited racial progress or to inevitable degeneration

"My choice is made. I believe in progress!" Thus wrote Clémence Royer at the end of the foreword to the first French edition of *The Origin of Species*.[53] And she returned to this subject in a later book in which she stated that a return to a "free" struggle for existence would make it possible "to achieve a divine race which will govern the earth justly in joy and in peace".[54]

The collectivist school of Social Darwinists was more circumspect if not more definitely pessimist. For Karl Pearson "this dependence of progress on the survival of the fitter race, terribly black as it may seem to some of you, gives the struggle for existence its redeeming features; it is the fiery crucible out of which comes the finer metal".[55]

But it is Vacher de Lapouge who shows most clearly the distinction between the foolish Promethean hopes and the lucid nihilism of the mass of Social Darwinists and the essential parts of Malthusian doctrine: Malthus's sense of what was fitting, his ideal of self control, his humbleness in the face of creation. The man of the Social Darwinists saw himself as a God, able to create new races. But this God cannot overcome his own mortality.

> Evolution . . . does not tend towards continuous improvement, it

tends towards nothing . . . There is no heaven even on earth. Science must not be asked for more than it can provide. It can give man knowledge and power. But it cannot directly influence happiness: for that we must ask the priest, the magician, the drug pedlar and the seller of alcohol and above all the gunsmith, that merchant of suicide.[56] . . . Systematic selection appears to be the only measure which will make it possible to escape the coming mediocracy and the final decay . . . Pride must stop. If man is a potential God, then this God is mortal and although future progress cannot be foreseen his end is sure to come. Once the sun has ceased to make the earth, the mother of all things, fertile, the hour will have struck and death will come to freeze the last of these prodigious geniuses, the brain pregnant with universal science defeated by matter![57]

1. cf. particularly the paper by P. Vorzimmer (1969). Darwin, Malthus, and the theory of natural selection. *Journal of the History of Ideas* **30** (4), 527–542.
2. W. Petersen (1979) in his book *Malthus*. Harvard University Press (Cambridge, Massachusetts) devotes a few pages (pp.224–230) to this topic which do not, however, in my opinion cover the essential points.
3. We refer to the *First Essay* (1798), the 7th Edition of the *Essay* (1872) and the *Summary View* (1830).
4. See particularly R. Hofstadter (1955). *Social Darwinism in American Thought*, Revised Edition. Beacon Press, Boston.
5. E. Haeckel (1892). *Le monisme, lien entre la religion et la science. Profession de foi d'un naturaliste.* (Translated into French by G. Vacher de Lapouge (1897). Schleicher, Paris.
6. T. R. Malthus. *First Essay*, p.355.
7. T. R. Malthus. *A Summary View* reprinted in D. V. Glass (Ed.) (1953). *Introduction to Malthus*, p.122. Watts, London.
8. T. R. Malthus, op. cit. in note 6, p.127; See also p.392.
9. ibid. pp.215–216.
10. ibid. p.362.
11. ibid. p.190.
12. ibid. p.286.
13. ibid. p.294.
14. T. R. Malthus. *Essay*, vol. 2, p.154.
15. T. R. Malthus, op. cit. in note 6, p.14.
16. ibid. p.48.
17. T. R. Malthus, op. cit. in note 14, p.164.
18. T. R. Malthus, op. cit. in note 7, p.176.

19. ibid.
20. ibid. p.177.
21. T. R. Malthus, op. cit. in note 14, p.257.
22. T. R. Malthus, op. cit. in note 6, p.15.
23. T. R. Malthus, op. cit. in note 7, p.121.
24. ibid. p.122.
25. T. R. Malthus, op. cit. in note 14, vol. 1, p.14.
26. For a clear illustration of Malthus's individualism, *see* T. R. Malthus, op. cit. in note 14, vol. 2, p.169.
27. T. R. Malthus, op. cit. in note 6, p.71.
28. ibid. p.204. (my italics).
29. T. R. Malthus, op. cit. in note 14, vol. 2, p.254 (my italics).
30. T. R. Malthus, op. cit. in note 14, vol. 1, p.315; cf. also T. R. Malthus, op. cit. in note 7, p.158.
31. T. R. Malthus, op. cit. in note 6, pp.83–84.
32. T. R. Malthus, op. cit. in note 7, p. 155.
33. T. R. Malthus, op. cit. in note 14, vol. 2, p.202.
34. ibid, pp.210–215, 249–250.
35. ibid. p.192.
36. T. R. Malthus, op. cit. in note 6, p.108.
37. ibid. pp.264–265.
38. ibid. pp.163–167 and p.380.
39. We refer to the following: Clémence Royer (1862). Preface to the translation of Darwin's *Origin of Species (De l'origine des espèces)* Paris; C. Royer (1870). *Origine de l'homme et des sociétés.* Paris 1870; La nation dans l'humanité et dans la série organique. *Journal des Economistes* **40**, 119. Nov. 1875, pp.234–249; Enrico Ferri (1894). *Socialisme et science positive (Darwin Spencer, Marx).* French translation by V. Giard and E. Brière, Paris, 1896; K. Pearson (1905). *National Life from the Standpoint of Science,* 2nd Edition. London; G. Vacher de Lapouge (1896). *Les sélections sociales.* Paris (1899) *L'Aryen. Son rôle social.* Paris.
40. T. R. Malthus, op. cit. in note 6, p.378.
41. cf. C. Royer, Préface, loc. cit. in note 39, p. lxi; G. Vacher de Lapouge, L'*Aryen*, op. cit. in note 39, p.511.
42. C. Royer, *La nation, . . .* loc. cit. in note 39, p.249.
43. Ferri, op. cit. in note 39, pp.70–71, 45.
44. K. Pearson, op. cit. in note 39, pp.54, 46, 60–61, 66, 95.
45. This expression may be found in Darwin (*The Origin of Species* (1859). Penguin Books, Harmondsworth, 1968, p.130), who refers to "natural" and "sexual" selection.
46. K. Pearson, op. cit. in note 39, p.23.
47. G. Vacher de Lapouge, *L'Aryen*, op. cit. in note 39, p.501.
48. G. Vacher de Lapouge, *Les sélections sociales*, op. cit. in note 39, p.307.
49. T. R. Malthus, op. cit. in note 14, vol. 2, p.210.
50. C. Royer, *Préface*, in note 39, p.lxii.

51. G. Vacher de Lapouge, *L'Aryen*, op. cit. in note 39, p.504.
52. G. Vacher de Lapouge, *Les sélections sociales,* op. cit. in note 39, pp.262.
53. C. Royer, *Préface*, op. cit. in note 39, p.lxiv.
54. C. Royer, *Origine*, op. cit. in note 39, p.587.
55. K. Pearson, *National Life*, op. cit. in note 39, p.26.
56. G. Vacher de Lapouge, *L'Aryen*, op. cit. in note 39, p.512.
57. G. Vacher de Lapouge, *Les sélections sociales* in note 39, pp.489–490. About Lapouge's theories see my paper "Le sang, le sens et le travail: Georges Vacher de Lapouge, darwiniste social, fondateur de l'anthroposociologie". *Cahiers Internationaux de Sociologie* **73**, Juillet-Déc. 1982, 323–343.

23 Birth Control, Socialism and Feminism in the United States[1]

LINDA GORDON

The histories of Malthusianism as a set of ideas, and of neo-Malthusianism as a social movement, both of which sometimes influenced policies, differed substantially in the USA and in Europe. One reason, of course, is the fear of *under*-population which was predominant in the United States at least until World War II. Another reason, which will be discussed in this paper, is that the idea of controlled reproduction was presented to the American public primarily by socialists and feminists. The result was that the basic project of controlling reproduction was much more closely associated with radicalism in the USA than in Europe.

The American language symbolizes this radicalism. "Neo-Malthusianism" is almost a foreign phrase in the United States. For the last 65 years, the term "birth control", invented by the socialist feminist Margaret Sanger, has been the generic term used for controlled reproduction, despite attempts in the 1940s to substitute "family planning" in order to deradicalize the programme. Before Sanger's campaign, the feminist slogan, "voluntary motherhood", predominated; and earlier there were various socialist and communitarian slogans, often associated with Free Love or some other form of sexual heterodoxy.

The illustration of differences between America and Europe is, however, only one aspect of this paper. A more important objective is to evaluate critically the way in which the notion of controlled reproduction has been conceptualized throughout the modern world. Different aspects of this history have been conflated under one general rubric — called neo-Malthusianism in Europe, birth control in the

MALTHUS PAST AND PRESENT
ISBN 0-12-224670-5

USA — in a manner which masks conflict and obscures the real human motives and interests involved. This conceptual confusion occurs among scholars and participants, opponents and protagonists of controlled reproduction.

At least four distinct perspectives on controlled reproduction may be distinguished at different times and in different countries: neo-Malthusianism, or population control, a concern to regulate growth rates of populations on a large scale; eugenics, with the object of regulating reproduction differentially between different social groups in order to improve the hereditary quality of the human species; birth control, a campaign to provide control over conception as a means of achieving greater sexual, economic and personal freedom for individuals, particularly women; and family planning, aimed at increasing family stability and prosperity, through planned births. None of these perspectives has been entirely independent of the others, but each has been autonomous and each has at certain times and in certain places been dominant in social policy. At times they have been mutually supportive, at others in conflict.

In different countries these different aspects of controlled reproduction have appeared in different sequence and relative strengths. Everywhere, however, the conflation of different tendencies, the obscuration of different political purposes in ideas relating to and campaigns for controlled reproduction, have led to ideological rather than critical interpretations of the historical process. It is also true, of course, that the ideologies *create* both the confusion and the analytic failure. Even those who forgot the anger aroused by Malthus and the neo-Malthusians should see from the controversies about abortion during the 1970s that issues in the control of reproduction stimulate intense passions, which create impelling ideologies. Some have argued that population control is nothing but an imperialist conspiracy against colonial rebellion. Others believe that family planning and the small-family norm is an inevitable, evolutionary process of "modernization". Feminists, past and present, sometimes believe that it is sex, specifically the sexuality of women, that is the essential issue, rather than reproduction. These and many other erroneous simplifications would be less prevalent were it not for the fact that many scholars and journalists continually miss the complex history and politics of campaigns for controlled reproduction.

The primary object of this paper, then, is to insist on the complexity of the history of controlled reproduction in the recent past. This will be illustrated with reference to the situation in the USA and the fairly obvious implications for European history will not be stressed. At the same time this paper offers the only Marxist contribution from the United States, and the only feminist contribution altogether, at this conference. I shall have to ask readers to bear in mind several variables at once, and to look for the evidence in other places,[2] as only conclusions can be presented here.

To maximize the clarity of this many-purposed presentation, five historical moments in the movement for controlled reproduction in the United States will be defined. These periods are both essential and chronological; each is identified with a socio-political stance, at a particular period. None are sharply delineated. Since the categories are not the subject, but the reality they organize and reveal, one must not require them to be perfect. They are imperfect, overlapping representations. They are: (1) utopian socialism and perfectionism; (2) the nineteenth-century women's movement; (3) socialist feminism of the first decades of the twentieth century; (4) "planned parenthood" and population control, 1930 to 1970; and (5) the revival of feminism during the 1960s and 1970s.

I

British neo-Malthusianism came to the United States in the 1820s and was immediately integrated into the utopian and feminist programme of the early socialists. The long-term influence of this kind of experimental socialism without class consciousness in the United States was an important factor in the different history of controlled reproduction in the "new world". Robert Dale Owen, the son of Robert Owen (who in turn had probably been directly influenced by Francis Place), moved to the United States and quickly became allied with Frances Wright, an utopian feminist, in both publication and community-building projects. Their social network established a connection between demands for controlled reproduction, utopian communalism, and feminism, a connection which marked not only the *ante bellum* reform movement but was also an important aspect of the autonomous women's movement which emerged after the Civil War.

To these trends was added the religious radicalism of the Second Great Awakening, an heretical perfectionism, and it was perhaps this that altered the Europian neo-Malthusian contribution most sharply. In its original sense, "perfectionism" referred to the belief of the revivalists that human beings could, through conversion (today it is called "being born again"), become perfect in earthly life. Perfectionism soon became the mode of secular as well as religious reformism, demanding and fully expecting quick achievement of liberating transformation. The perfectionists rejected the scepticism of the old world, which was engendered by the greater solidity of class distinctions, and the persuasively long history of human suffering. Perfectionism also produced a tendency to view individual reforms as carrying the potential for curing social ills, the view that a single level of change could make a reality of Utopia. As Sylvester Graham recommended a whole-grain and fruit diet, as Mary Gove Nichols recommended therapeutic baths, as the revivalists recommended a new breathing-in of Christ, so some thought that controlled reproduction could create a new humanity. They looked forward to this transformation on both individual and social levels, through spiritual as well as biological change.They believed that amative but non-procreative sex required of its practitioners a self-control that was liberating, and provided a transcendent intensity of experience. Many of them also experimented with control over human breeding — eugenics — made possible by control over sexual intercourse, and believed they could establish a superior human "stock".

The principal methods recommended by the perfectionist reformers for controlling reproduction were not mechanical devices but alterations in sexual intercourse itself.[3] Male continence, "karezza", periodic abstinence and *coitus interruptus* were not invented by these reformers; they are ancient methods, the last being the most common contraceptive technique in the world. But the reformers' endorsement of them, and exploration of new non-procreative sexual techniques, has great importance for the future of controlled reproduction in at least three ways. First, they put sex into the group of relations which could become the object of conscious social planning.[4] Secondly, they advanced justifications, secular and religious, for the value of non-procreative sexual intercourse (such as animal magnetism, sedular absorption, electrical exchange). Thirdly, by emphasizing the spiritual value of non-procreative sexual relations, they provided a basis for later feminists to insist on mutual free choice as a precondition for intercourse to be moral.

Thus in the United States there was a socialist tradition which incorporated sexual and other forms of cultural and personal radicalism within a vision of social justice and (a pre-class conscious form of) workers' control. Ironically and unfortunately, that tradition was weakened and even attacked by both feminists and socialists later. One explanation might point to the greater economic inequality and suffering during the late nineteenth century. But this explanation fails when society is considered from women's point of view, for the labour and suffering produced by too frequent and uncontrolled pregnancies and maternal responsibilities were hardly superficial or minor in relation to other forms of oppression. A more satisfactory explanation would have to take account of the ancient culture that treated the man's point of view as the only one, thus diminishing the esteem given to both biological and social reproductive labour; the difficulty women have experienced in conceiving their own unpaid domestic labour as a social rather than a natural phenomenon, and in seeing themselves as a social group in itself (let alone for itself); and the widespread tendency of working-class organization in advanced capitalism towards economism.

II

The feminist emphasis on voluntary sexual relations had been strong since the 1840s, it was usually connected with other reform issues, such as the right to divorce or to custody of children. During the 1870s it became identified with a demand for controlled reproduction, "voluntary motherhood". Since the contraceptive method advocated by the feminists was abstinence, the voluntary-motherhood programme has been miscontrued by many historians as exclusively inimical to sexuality. Closer scrutiny shows that it was more complex. These feminists shared with earlier perfectionists a confidence in the possibility of justice on earth, and the inclusion of intimate relations in the "political". They differed from earlier perfectionists in their identification of male supremacy as the form of domination and wickedness which bore the greatest responsibility for the corruption of the world and of the human species. As regards sexual and procreative activities, they, too, argued that both individual and social, spiritual and biological, transformation would result from the emancipation and honouring of women. Sexual intercourse with an unwilling partner was demeaning and corrupting, and women's freedom to choose sexual relations had to begin with their freedom to refuse them. To be sure, they displayed hostility to sexuality, but this was directed against the specific, historical, male-dominated sexual experience of most women of their time and culture. Many feminists defended sexual activity in the abstract, spoke up for the propriety of women's sexual desires, even sided with the advocates, of "free love" and believed that a healthy, non-obsessive sexuality would promote peace and social cooperation. Furthermore, these feminists incorporated the eugenical, hereditarian beliefs common to all reformers during the nineteenth century (including socialists), and argued that free, respected motherhood would produce superior children.

The advocates of voluntary motherhood were absolutely pronatalist. They were not Malthusian and did not even emphasize family limitation. From the 1840s to the very end of the nineteenth century, European Malthusianism was remarkably lacking in influence in the United States.

After the civil war many feminists preserved an anti-capitalist attitude that had been strong among pre-War reformers who had reacted against the destruction of traditional relationships by mass production and wage labour. But even those feminists with socialist leanings at this time were remarkably lacking in class consciousness. They believed in the unmodified universality of the "bonds of womanhood"[5] — and what issue and need was more universal among women than that for controlled reproduction? Thus their commitment to sex-and-family issues, by contrast to "public" issues such as suffrage, employment or education, tended to push them away from an analysis of class (or race) conflicts.

III

The movement for women's rights in the United States split during the early years of the twentieth century into factions which supported and those which opposed birth control. Fundamentally at issue was not population, but sex. This split had always existed in the United States feminist movement in embryo; one tendency was influenced by "free love", communitarian and utopian-anarchist traditions towards sexual radicalism; the other, by far the stronger, towards "social purity". Both sought to elevate the status of women, but supporters of the latter group believed that the traditional family, normative motherhood and sexual chastity were women's best defence. As long as sexual abstinence remained the exclusive method of birth control, as in the feminist programme during the nineteenth century, their unity was unbroken. But feminist solidarity ceased on this issue when European radical writers on sexual matters began advocating contraception. Their counterparts in the United States found themselves alienated both from the suffrage and the socialist movement. Thus, a network of socialist and anarchist feminists was formed outside existing organizations between 1905 and 1915 as a distinct tendency on the US Left, and a new phase in the history of controlled reproduction began.

To the ultimate legitimation of controlled reproduction they contributed both an ideology of sexual freedom (as a form of personal fulfilment and social protest) and a large if short-lived mass movement for birth control. Their ideology was influenced by many European radical thinkers about sexual issues, such as Reich and Hirschfeld, Ellis and Carpenter, but they were closest to the German writers in associating sexual repression with class exploitation. Like all oppositional ideologies, this feminist form of radicalism on sex reflected (and perhaps ultimately reinforced) some of the changed requirements of capitalism itself. Monopoly capitalism transformed the composition, structure and style of its labour force, including many more women, multiplying white collar jobs, and encouraging consumption. Thus the rejection of an older ideology of sexual repression in favour of greater permissiveness towards quick and various earthly gratifications was also an affirmation of a new "lifestyle" compatible with the new political economy. In particular, the increasing popularity of sexual permissiveness and controlled reproduction (important in increasing heterosexual activity) seemed to fit the needs and aspirations of new social groups: single employed women, upwardly mobile children of the working class or the small-town petty-bourgeois, professionals, white collar workers of both sexes.

At the same time, other groups put forward a demand for contraception without a radical perspective on sexual matters; particularly the rapidly increasing number of women in the labour force, many of whom came home from their work to carry virtually the same burden of housework and child care as non-employed women. Thus, the conditions of marriage and family life began to make lack of control over conception, except at the cost of limiting one's sexual activity, seem intolerable.

Between 1914 and 1916 a mass movement for "birth control" sprang up, dominated by socialists, mainly women, with energetic rank-and-file organizing activity. There were agitation and direct-action groups in every major city and most large towns of the United States. Birth-control activists broke the law and were arrested, conducted political legal defences, and opened (often illegal) clinics which supplied contraceptives, thus antagonizing the conservative medical profession most of whose members were opposed to birth control.

Most American socialists remained opposed to birth control. Although the movement was not mainly Malthusian, its opponents often put forward anti-Malthusian arguments which had become classic: that the movement would weaken the nation by reducing its population. Socialists added that it represented an attack on the working-class family, an attempt to reduce the numbers of that class, to transform anger at exploitation into self-blame for poverty — another weapon in the arsenal of the ruling class. Supporters of birth control also used class arguments. The most common was that upper-class women *did have* access to contraception through private physicians but that this knowledge was kept secret from the workers in order to keep wages low (the old wages-fund theory) and to maintain the number of army recruits. Socialists were also divided, with the majority being in opposition, about the tactics of the birth-control movement. By and large the birth controllers sided with the militants to the left of the socialist party or in the left wing of the party, in their preference for direct action over electoral tactics. Probably the most common complaint against the birth controllers, however, was that the issue of reproduction was simply not *political.* To its socialist opponents, the feminist (non-Malthusian) demand for birth control seemed strictly personal: it concerned intimate relations which ought to be private. At best there was a certain anti-totalitarianism in this view; a less charitable interpretation would be that it represented uncritical acceptance of the originally bourgeois notion of the family as a haven from economic and political strife.

The struggle over birth control, therefore, took place within as well as between social classes. A century earlier it seemed that those workers who favoured birth control represented a higher stratum within the developing working class; Place's followers reflected an artisan culture of individual self-help rather than collective, class action. By the early twentieth century such an argument could no longer be maintained. Workers who favoured birth control were generally more class-conscious, more politicized and more radical than those who opposed it.

If the views of working-class activists about birth control are to be believed, it was issues relating to sex and family rather than class consciousness or demographic concern that were sharper in this division. The most fervent arguments against birth control were, ironically, the same in the working class as in the middle and upper classes: it would give women too much power to leave their families and to reject their domestic duties. It would threaten to reduce the differences between men's and women's standards of sexual conduct. Ironically, the arguments in favour of birth control among socialists were more class-specific and did not so much resemble arguments from other class and political positions. The birth-control activists argued that unlimited childbearing depoliticized women, who, therefore, acted as a conservative brake on working-class activity; that men's dominance weakened solidarity not only among the whole working class but even among men; that working-class children were being deprived by being born into such large and often unwanted families.

To the extent that large-scale social control of population growth was at issue in this period, the focus was on eugenic or qualitative rather than on quantitative control. The eugenists had been arguing, since the mid-nineteenth century, that there was danger of under-reproduction of "superior stock" and over-reproduction of "undesirables", such as Catholic European immigrants. Eugenists feared "race suicide" — race used here ambiguously, referring ostensibly to the "human race" and at other times to white Anglo-Saxon Protestants. The eugenists offered a programme consisting of two parts: "positive eugenics," encouraging more reproduction among the "fit", and "negative eugenics", discouraging reproduction among the "unfit". "Race suicide" received greatest public notice when President Theodore Roosevelt decried it in 1905, and it remained a fear at the height of birth-control activism between 1914 and 1917. In response, the birth controllers themselves manipulated the argument, pointing out that the differential birth rate made it irrational to keep contraception from the poor, while the rich practised it.

In this "race suicide" form of population concern, one sees the effects of another American peculiarity: its multi-national character had been manipulated (originally through slavery, now through a variety of forms of labour and economic divisions) to make racial and ethnic distinctions central to status, and to produce a pervasive racism. An hypothesis worth consideration, surely, is that population concerns in the United States have consistently been fought out more along racial and ethnic than on avowedly class lines.[6] (We must put aside for now the larger question of the extent to which race–ethnic conflicts *are* in fact class conflicts.) The lack of a clear and continuous class dimension to the controversy about controlled reproduction is also, of course, a product of the generally non-socialist forms of working-class organization in the United States. This phenomenon (or non-phenomenon since the usual formulation refers to what the American working class does not do, rather than what it does) would be better understood if the sexual and reproductive issues were included in the analysis. A class dimension to the conflict might have produced a division simply between bourgeois population controllers and their proletarian opponents. But it might also have brought about a lasting feminist programme for birth control that could be seen to be independent of the establishment's population control policies.

In fact, socialists were active — on either side — in the controversy in the United States over controlled reproduction only when they were in alliance with feminists, or were themselves the carriers of feminist ideas. The period just discussed, before World War I, was the last in which socialists played an important role in this issue. For the sixty years or so since then, socialists have not been distinguishable from liberals on these issues.

IV

The American birth-control movement became gradually more neo-Malthusian in orientation between 1920 and 1960, but this process, too, was complex. Increasing concern with population control coincided and interrelated with the professionalization, masculinization, and deradicalization of the movement. These characterizations should not be seen as moralistic. There was no conspiracy. Many factors were involved in this change: the general suppression and internal weakening of the left after World War I; the gradual winning over of many men of wealth and influence to the importance of birth control; the Great Depression and the concern it produced about over-multiplication of the poor; United States immigration restrictions. We shall discuss the effects rather than the causes of these events on the United States birth-control organizations.

In the 1920s national organizations became dominant over autonomous local ones, and popular participation declined along with direct-action tactics. Money became more plentiful and paid staff did more and more of the work; they and their national organizations in turn increased their dependence on large monetary contributions, and money-raising became an activity of the birth-control organizations. Men increasingly outnumbered women as staff workers and later as board members. Propaganda directed at liberating women from involuntary motherhood became infrequent, even actively avoided by the 1930s, as was class-struggle rhetoric. In general, by 1925 the birth-control organizations would not be said to be any longer part of the left — in contrast to their unequivocal position ten years earlier — although leftists continued to be more strongly in favour of birth control in their opinions than either liberals or conservatives. The depression of the 1930s resulted in government taking an interest in contraception for the first time, as a neo-Malthusian measure to stabilize and ameliorate difficult conditions.

This process produced a genuinely new campaign by the 1940s, centralized in the Planned Parenthood Federation. Its ideology was primarily family stability, recognizing now, however, that this stability could only be achieved with a permissive attitude towards sexual enjoyment without fear of conception, and substantial respect for women's wishes within marriage. Planned Parenthood's attitudes towards women's independence, sexual or economic, were overwhelmingly negative for at least two decades. Nevertheless, the pressures of the economy were nudging more and more women into the paid labour force and increasing demand for contraception. The manufacture and sale of contraceptives was legalized, state by state, and quickly taken over by large pharmaceutical corporations. Contraception was big business, and had become quite respectable among married people. This stabilization function of contraception was to some extent limited by a hiatus in the delivery system: the Planned Parenthood Federation's policy of declining to offer services to the unmarried. As non-marital sexual activity steadily increased, the sale of condoms by chemists could not keep pace, and illegitimate pregnancies continued to remain numerous as did illegal abortions.

By the 1940s, also, the size and rate of growth of the population became a matter of concern for the United States. The depression undermined the old view that steady population growth was good. Furthermore, United States international dominance and political/military activity in defence of its economic and ideological interests throughout the world made the world's population problems a threat to the United States. The Planned Parenthood Federation became Planned Parenthood-World Population, thus completing the appearance of uniting all interests in controlled reproduction in one harmonious international organization.

V

From the mid-1960s onwards, a women's liberation movement once again changed the terms of understanding of proposals for controlled reproduction. Feminists, at first, shared an anti-natalist bias with population controllers (a bias quite reversed by feminists a decade later). Unlike the population controllers, however, feminists viewed demands for birth control as part of an overall campaign for women's self-determination. The feminist birth-control programme at its outset was not theoretically or historically sophisticated about the many uses of controlled reproduction. Nevertheless, it immediately, though unintentionally, began to loosen the ideological knot which united and subordinated the many aspects under the rubric of population control. That separation is far from complete, and many — perhaps most — liberal feminist spokeswomen for birth control do not distinguish their demands from those of population control, cost-cutting, or social stability.[7] However, the process of separating the feminist and libertarian issues accelerated as abortion became the chief feminist demand.

Abortion had not previously been part of any programme for controlled reproduction — neo-Malthusian, eugenic, feminist, or family-planning. It had, however, been a nearly universal part of the *practice* of controlled reproduction. Until the mid-nineteenth century abortion was considered to lie within a spectrum or continuity of control practices. From about 1840 in the United States, abortion gradually became distinguished from "prevenception", and condemned morally and legally, as a result of a concerted campaign led by ministers and physicians.[8] While a large number of illegal abortionists thrived, and abortion was common in the lives of women of all classes, few supported legalization until the 1960s.

The contemporary drive for abortion rights was a response to several factors which emerged between 1920 and 1960: first, a great increase in teenage sexual activity without contraceptives;[9] secondly, a great increase in the number of families absolutely dependent on two incomes, and in families headed by a woman,[10] either circumstance making it no longer easy for mothers to stay at home with unplanned babies (these phenomena increased the demand for abortion among married women whose attempts at contraception had failed); thirdly, the relative underdevelopment of contraception, in terms of safety, ease of use, and the sex education and attitudes required for its use.[11]

Although a generally effective and relatively safe measure, abortion has been supported more enthusiastically by feminists than by population controllers.[12] Abortion gives individual women a high degree of control over reproduction, unmediated by men, technology, sexual mores, or population planning policies. Thus libertarians of the Right as well as of the Left tend to support abortion in the United States today.[13]

It may be fitting to close with some comments about the contemporary anti-abortion movement, for studying it underlines the necessity of a complex analysis of what reproduction control has meant politically. As in the nineteenth century, so today, opponents of controlled reproduction often perceive its different implications more clearly than its supporters. The anti-abortion movement is part of a traditional opposition to voluntary motherhood and the "woman movement" at least a century old. It is *not* primarily anti-neo-Malthusian although its most anti-statist parts are hostile to eugenic policies (as, for example, in the recent victory of the Right to Life movement in forcing the "March of Dimes" to discontinue funding genetic testing and counselling of pregnant women, particularly amniocentesis) and to foreign aid of any kind. It is *not* consistently opposed to family planning. It *is* consistently anti-feminist, most of it lined up against the Equal Rights Amendment, day care centres, divorce, sex education, affirmative action (a federal law requiring active recruitment of women and minorities for jobs and educational places), non-marital sexual relations and homosexuality. Once again it might appear that in the United States, unlike much of the rest of the world, class issues drop out of controversies about control of reproduction, whilst feminist and sexual issue are central. The importance of the anti-abortion campaign within the "New Right" confirms this pattern; observers note that leaders of the "New Right" manipulate the "social issues" (such as abortion, the Equal Rights Amendment, busing for racial integration) to obscure the class dimensions of their programme.[14] But such a distinction between feminist and class issues is misleading, for it constricts our understanding of what is a class issue, and replicates a mistaken view of the class struggle as pertaining exclusively to relations in production, and fought only by wage labourers. If, as has often been remarked, feminism was uniquely powerful in the United States during the nineteenth and early twentieth centuries, the strength of women was closely related to the economic development of the United States, its rapid transformation into a highly industrial, and later technological and internationally dominant power. As an example, I shall conclude with a brief historical problem of interpretation as an instance of the integration of feminist and class issues.

During the early twentieth century, at the height of the race-suicide panic, two conflicting causal theories for the decline of the birth rate among the "middle classes" were offered: one blaming feminism for inciting women to shirk their duty to reproduce, the other blaming the economy which made large families no longer practical. Many journalists, scholars and physicians joined the debate on one side or the other. The truth is, of course, that the two theories were describing different aspects of the same historical phenomenon. Feminism itself grew from the upward mobility that made smaller families more economic. If women, instead of men, had been considered by these writers and social theorists to be the "typical" individual of the families in which birth rates were low, there would have been no mystery nor controversy. To have asked women with small families whether feminism or class mobility was the cause would have introduced a false distinction. Nor were these women, when married, likely to have been in conflict with their husbands about desired family size. Identifying professional attainment as a status symbol, their husbands increasingly shared their small-family preferences, for these men demanded different things of their wives and children than their fathers. A contemporary expression of this understanding, written by someone with enough nostalgia still to sign himself "Paterfamilias", argued in 1903:

> I have four children . . . It happens that we (*sic*) are able to care for four, not quite in the style in which two could have been maintained, but . . . sufficiently well for us to maintain our social position, which is very dear to us . . . If a time should come when we had to give up our present style of living (which, practically, means our friends . . .), I would consider it, perhaps, the most serious day of my life. So far as can be judged at present, the only thing that might threaten such an event would be the appearance, say, of a couple of more children.[15]

It is an important fact about American socialism that at this time it still mainly condemned small families — thereby, perhaps unintentionally (if ignoring of subordinates can ever be "unintentional"), also condemning women's advancement. For example, consider this socialist attack on a physician who supported birth control in 1907: "Dear Doctor, . . . Human life is more than money, is a man justified in killing his own children because his business fails?" At its greatest strength during the early twentieth century, American socialism took an entirely nostalgic and wistful view of the family, in contrast to socialists a century earlier who dreamed of a radical transformation of the family and personal relations, which could liberate women. American non-feminist socialists today are still deeply divided on that issue, and their divided views about controlled reproduction reflect their ambivalence.

Notes

1. A slightly edited version of this paper appears in *History of European Ideas*. Pergamon Press, Oxford. (Forthcoming).
2. This paper is in large part a summary of aspects of some of my articles and my book, *A Social History of Birth Control in the U.S.* Viking and Penguin, (1976–1977). That book contains references and I have, therefore, omitted reference notes here, except when drawing material from sources not noted in the book.
3. These alterations were seen as valuable in themselves, not merely as contraceptive techniques. See note 4 for references about their ideas as sexual reformers.
4. Linda Gordon (1976). *Woman's Body, Woman's Right: A Social History of Birth*

Control in America, chapter 4. Viking, New York; Hal Sears (1977). *The Sex Radicals. Free Love in High Victorian America.* The Regents Press of Kansas, Lawrence.

5. Sarah Grimke signed her *Letter on the Equality of the Sexes and the Condition of Women* in 1837 with the *double extendre* "Thine in the bonds of womanhood", referring both to the fetters of female subordination and the ties among women.
6. This hypothesis does not imply that Britain or other European countries lacked concern for problems relating to the quality as well as the quantity of the population.
7. See, for example, chapter 15 particularly, in Lawrence Lader (1973). *Abortion II: Making the Revolution.* Boston, Beacon Press; various statements of Karen Mulhauser, president of NARAL, for example in *In These Times* Chicago, April 4-10, 1979.
8. James C. Mohr (1978). *Abortion in America. The Origins and Evolution of National Policy*, chapters 3, 5, 6 and 7. Oxford University Press, New York; Linda Gordon. Why nineteenth-century feminists didn't support "birth control" and twentieth-century feminists do: Feminism, reproduction, and the family, in *Rethinking the Family.* (1982) Longman, New York.
9. The number of illegitimate births in the US, for example, grew from 90 000 in 1940 to 407 000 in 1973, from 3·5 per cent of all births in 1940 to 13 per cent in 1973. Data from Heather L. Ross and Isabel V. Sawhill (1965). *Time of Transition. The Growth of Families Headed by Women*, p.2 and tables 1-D and 1-L. The Urban Institute, Washington, D.C.
10. Since 1950, families headed by a woman have grown almost ten times as fast as two-parent families. In 1940, the number of such families came to 1 859 000, or 5.3 per cent of all households; in 1974, they were 9 291 000, or 13.3 per cent.
11. The underdevelopment of contraception is argued more fully in Linda Gordon, loc. cit. in note 8.
12. It has been argued, in the 1970s as in the 1870s, that feminists are selfish and callous to the issues of respect for human life in their support for abortion. That argument does not hold up to examination. For example, feminists have been continuously and disproportionately to their share in the population represented in peace movements, charities and other ameliorative social activism, on behalf of men as well as women. Furthermore feminists have often been castigated by the same opponents for their excessive softness and desire to temper suffering and preserve life without regard to its toughness or worthiness.
13. Allen Hunter and Linda Gordon. Sex, family and the New Right: Anti-feminism as a political force. *Radical America* **11** (6), Winter 1977–78, Cambridge, Massachusetts.
14. A. Hunter. In the wings. New Right organization and ideology. *Radical America* **15** (1)–(2), January-April, 1981.
15. This and the following excerpt are quoted in Linda Gordon, *Woman's Body*, op. cit. in note 4, pp.152 and 158.

24 Between Malthus and the Social Revolution: The French Neo-Malthusian Movement

F. RONSIN

The great majority of French neo-Malthusian militants originated in the various socialist and revolutionary movements and did not renounce their previous political opinions when they began their struggle for the voluntary limitation of births. Although the literal meaning of the word "neo-Malthusianism" signifies nothing more than a reinterpretation of Malthusian doctrines, in France the term has been strongly affected by the symbiosis between Malthusian and socialist doctrines. It is possible to think of French neo-Malthusianism as a left turn of Malthusianism in the direction of revolution.

There were considerable obstacles to this change of course. Malthus's work is dominated by his desire to oppose the developing movement of socialism and to prevent the confrontation between social classes which he foresaw. Moreover, he did not lack disciples, including some in France, who rallied round his doctrines in order to maintain the existing social order. The socialists, on the other hand, seemed unalterably opposed to Malthus. The reactionary implications of his work were only too evident, and socialists did not share his fear of an insufficiency of resources. Their confidence in the infinite bounty of nature was inherited from the eighteenth century and was transformed into an equally optimistic belief that science and technical progress would be successful in solving all the problems which might face a society that was organized in accordance with a "harmonious system". Moreover, these "architects of a future society" took the view that sexuality and its consequence, fertility, were not intrinsically class

MALTHUS PAST AND PRESENT
ISBN 0-12-224670-5

phenomena but natural forces which related primarily to a person's private life and not the class struggle.

That population problems were taken into consideration by a number of French socialists is a sign of the difficulties faced by this school of thought, after their prophecies had met with a number of set-backs. We must remember the catastrophic results of the Revolution of 1848, the destruction of the Paris commune, the grotesque epilogue of the First International, the folly of the Boulangists and the failures of "propaganda by example", as the anarchists who favoured terrorist attacks called their activities. The situation may be illustrated by an anecdote related by Gabriel Giroud, Paul Robin's son-in-law and biographer. When Bakunin abandoned the political struggle, he sent a valedictory letter to the Jurassian Federation in which he wrote: "During the past few years, more new ideas have emerged in the International than are necessary to save the world, if ideas alone were sufficient to save it, and I defy anyone to think of new ones." In the margin of the book in which this letter of Robin's friend, who was critically opposed to Malthusian doctrines, was printed, Robin wrote: "Nothing is said by the International about the limitation of population growth, or about good births."[1] Moreover, Robin thought that his own actions, so far from contradicting socialist doctrines, were indispensable to the socialist struggle.

In this paper, we shall attempt to give a series of exmples which will show how French neo-Malthusians attempted to reconcile their socialist convictions with their efforts to limit the number of births, and how they introduced demographic considerations into their revolutionary strategy and we shall assess the effect of their political opinions on the struggle for the dissemination of contraceptive information.

Paul Robin and Eugène Humbert

Paul Robin had a long history as a militant revolutionary before he was converted to Malthusian doctrines. His record as a fighter for socialism was regarded as sufficient by no less a person than Karl Marx to propose him for membership of the General Council of the International, and his election to that body was unanimously approved. Although he originated from a catholic bourgeois family — one of his uncles was an admiral and another a canon — Robin was converted to socialism at an early age. A former student of the *Ecole normale supérieure* he held teaching appointments at La Roche-sur-Yon at Brest, but attracted unfavourable notice because of his political sympathies and his educational innovations. At the age of 28, he resigned from the teaching profession and went to Brussels for the Students' Congress of 1865. It was during his stay in Belgium that he became a member of the International in 1866. However, three years later the Belgian authorities declared him an undesirable alien, because of his involvement in the social struggle. He joined Bakunin in Geneva, became a member of the Social Democratic Alliance and collaborated in the publication of the Journal *L'Egalité*. Having somewhat imprudently returned to France in 1870, he was imprisoned following the third trial of the militant members of the International. He was set free on the proclamation of the Republic and returned to Belgium. Unable to join the insurgents in Paris, he then returned to his family in Brest before taking refuge in London because he feared reprisals would be taken against him. He became a member of the colony of revolutionaries who had fled to England from all corners of Europe. However, he only remained a member of the Council of the International for a short period; after a year he was expelled, together with his anti-authoritarian comrades. It was at that time that, without abandoning his previous convictions, he became a convert to Malthusian doctrines.

Robin joined the Malthusian League which had been founded by Charles Drysdale in 1877 and threw himself into its propaganda with the enthusiasm which was characteristic of all his actions. It was only natural that he should address himself to his former revolutionary friends in the first instance. He was convinced that the neo-Malthusians had discovered the deficiency in revolutionary theory which had hitherto prevented its success. "Prudence [in reproduction] is to be desired as much in the daily industrial struggle, as in the fight for the day of the social revolution, which will, I hope, come soon."[2] He was surprised and disappointed at the indifference, and sometimes the outright hostility, with which his new ideas were received in socialist and libertarian congresses. He could not understand the reasons which led the main socialist periodicals to reject the articles which he submitted and, indeed, to oppose them. Though he never ceased to be a member of the revolutionary movement, he accused it with increasing frequency of being led by narrow-minded men who were incapable of achieving a radical change in society. Indefatigably he repeated his thesis, that human happiness could be achieved only if three problems were solved, in this order and in this order only, viz: (1) good birth; (2) good education; (3) good social organization. This, in sum, was his theoretical point of view and governed his political actions. He devoted his main efforts to furthering the cause of neo-

Malthusianism. As a professional teacher he had also completed a piece of educational research (particularly in Cempuis), but the principal object of his activities had always been the achievement of a libertarian socialist society.

In contrast to Robin, Eugène Humbert came from the working class. His youth was spent in conditions of extreme poverty; his mother who was a tobacco worker in Nancy suffered considerable privations in her efforts to bring up two children on her own. His education did not extend beyond primary school and he was apprenticed to his uncle as a cobbler at a very young age. It was at his workplace that a fellow-worker introduced Humbert to anarchist theories. His first militant activities took place in a small group and the first periodical in whose publication he participated was addressed to workers in the trade, *Le tire pied.* Humbert devoted all his spare time to political activities and to educating himself, and was helped in his efforts by the two brothers Reclus who lived in Nancy. In 1896, at the age of 26, he left Nancy for Paris. On arrival, he immediately established contact with anarchist and neo-Malthusian circles, of whose existence he had learned through reading some of Paul Robin's pamphlets. However, it took him several months to alter the views on birth control which he had formed as a result of his communist libertarian convictions and to accept the need for a voluntary limitation of births as a necessary condition for the overthrow of the social order. From that moment, most of his activities in which Jeanne Humbert, who later became his wife, participated, were devoted to neo-Malthusian propaganda and the dissemination of contraceptive information, but both remained convinced and militant active anarchists.

This brief account of the intellectual history of Robin and Humbert shows how the old pupil of the *Ecole Normale,* the intellectual bourgeois and friend of the founders of socialism with his messianic theoretical views, became associated with the young proletarian who was in revolt against capitalism. Their collaboration played an important part in the early political orientation of the French neo-Malthusian movement and its early successes. Robin, with his effervescent spirit was the visionary genius; Humbert was the indefatigable administrator and organizer who was responsible for the rapid progress of the *Ligue de la régénération humaine* and for obtaining an audience for its views. They shared libertarian ideals which were put forward in their propaganda and their journal *Régénération,* and their appeal and influence, therefore, tended to be confined to the syndicalist and revolutionary movement. The whole editorial team of that journal belonged to the same ideological persuasion and when after the break between Robin and Humbert *Génération consciente* was founded and some new organizations set up to compete with Humbert their political orientation remained the same. All, including some independent propagandists such as Jean Maresttan, wished to show that only minor adjustments to socialist theory were needed to make it possible to be both socialist and neo-Malthusian. There were numerous publications in which they justified their position which, however, proved unacceptable both to the more dogmatic socialists and to the orthodox Malthusians. We shall discuss some of these to illustrate how some socialists regarded Malthusian doctrine, rejected some of its aspects and tried to use others for their own revolutionary purposes.

The controversey between Alfred Naquet and Gabriel Giroud

In 1910 a pamphlet entitled "Neo-Malthusianism and Socialism" was published by *Génération consciente,* containing articles that had previously appeared in that journal. These included Naquet's paper entitled "Malthusianism, neo-Malthusianism and Socialism" and Giroud's reply "Neo-Malthusianism as a Preliminary to Socialism". Naquet was 76 years old at the time; a Blanquist and member of Bakunin's secret society *Fraternité internationale,* he had been Professor of Medicine before being elected to the Chamber of Deputies for Vaucluse between 1871 and 1883 and subsequently became a senator.[3] Gabriel Giroud had been at school in Cempuis and married Robin's daughter. He shared his father-in-law's ideas, but was even more insistent that the limitation of births was the most important goal to achieve, before all other social developments. He was the most articulate representative of a particularly intransigent form of neo-Malthusianism and tended to regard other forms of the political struggle with some degree of contempt.

In his paper, Naquet reaffirms the view that even if the neo-Malthusians were to be successful in their attempts to reduce the French birth rate, their success would have no practical effect unless it were preceded by world revolution.

> If France were to be depopulated, whilst the population of Germany continued to grow, we would be invaded by the peaceful influx of Germans who would take over the spaces left empty by Frenchmen. This would not necessarily be a bad thing: Germans are as good as Frenchmen. But the result of this restriction of the French birth rate would be nil.[4]
>
> The only chance of a successful conclusion would be the existence of a

> World Federation. But even then it would only need . . . women to have unlimited numbers of children, for misery to return.

Misery would be followed by "acquisitiveness" and the "reconstitution of private property". This is the hazard that socialism is faced with, unless it takes account of Malthus's Principle of Population "the guiding light which is needed to study all projects of social reform". Neo-Malthusians and socialists should be allies "because neither can achieve anything without the help of the other"

Giroud could not agree. He was not concerned with the distant and hypothetical prospect of world revolution, but considered that obstacles faced socialists at the present moment in their desire to achieve social progress.

> To-day, revolutionary actions and strikes tend to be ineffective, because the workers in revolt have to contend with "the reserve army of capital" . . . This army has not been created by capitalists, but is the result of workers' sexuality. It is the workers who replenish it through their incontinence and who furnish the capitalists with the means with which to perpetuate their serfdom.

Giroud believed that socialist efforts to explain to the workers that their misery was due to exploitation by capitalists were unlikely to be successful, and an appeal for a struggle to end would not succeed as long as large numbers of workers continued to have large families, whom they were unable to support or educate even though they exhausted themselves with work. Socialism could not be achieved unless the workers were first given access to contraception.

A careful reading of the two texts shows that they are not contradictory. It is not the authors' intention to discourage militant workers by suggesting that their struggle was bound to fail because of the existence of a vicious circle. Naquet did not oppose neo-Malthusian propaganda; all he said was that it would not be sufficient by itself to lead to a transformation of society. Giroud, on the other hand, supported the socialists in their struggle, but believed that it would not be successful unless births were limited in the first instance. Unity was, therefore, essential. What other conclusion would the reader draw from a pamphlet which contains the declarations of faith of a socialist neo-Malthusian and a neo-Malthusian socialist?

Madeleine Pelletier and Armand. Revolutionary neo-Malthusians against Malthus

Theories seem to have a charm which it is difficult to resist. But, unlike the Malthusians, the neo-Malthusians were men and women of action. They not only made propaganda for neo-Malthusianism, but combined their efforts with the sale of contraceptives and with the dissemination of contraceptive knowledge to the public. Indeed, the costs of their propaganda efforts were largely met from their commercial activities, and this would appear to show that there existed a real unmet need among the French public for birth control, that is to say for an easy limitation of fertility. What was the use of stressing the implications of fertility movements for the revolution? Their convictions were firm and the arguments brought forward could only strengthen them: a low birth rate would make *revanche* more difficult, i.e. it lessened the likelihood of war; it reduced the reservoir of available labour, i.e. it weakened capitalism; it increased recourse to immoral practices, i.e. it liberated the human spirit from taboos and constraints. Is the Principle of Population the basic force in human history? Would it be a matter of importance if it were possible to act efficiently to reduce population growth? Many neo-Malthusians completely abandoned Malthusian doctrines. In the Federation of Workers' Neo-Malthusian Groups (FWNMB), which was founded during the winter of 1910-1911 and made spectacular advances until 1914, Malthus's doctrines were freely and sometimes acrimoniously discussed, but Giroud wrote about their journal *Rénovation:* "When *Rénovation* accidentally discusses the doctrine of neo-Malthusianism, it is clear that it is completely ignorant of the subject."[5] Madeleine Pelletier's article entitled "Neo-Malthusianism and Socialism",[6] published in the July 1911 issue of *Rénovation,* is an excellent example of this socialist type of neo-Malthusianism, which does not accept any of Malthus's arguments.

> When neo-Malthusianism took a concrete form with the writings of Paul Robin, it was possible to explain the opposition of the socialist party. Robin regarded neo-Malthusianism as a social theory complete in itself. Subsistence, said Malthus, and Robin echoed his sentiments, was the key factor . . . However, voluntary restriction of births is not necessarily linked to a particular social theory. . . . The worker with a large family is generally badly housed, badly nourished, wallows in filth and, depressed by his unending misery, he seeks refuge in alcohol and lives like an animal. How is it possible to teach a man about socialism when he is in a continuous state of semi-intoxication? . . . To-morrow they will shout "long live the emperor Louis Napoléon", just as to-day they shout "long live Guesde", "long live Jaurès".

Rénovation was by no means exceptional. The journal of the FWNMB put the case most strongly and is indicative of a development which was found in all French neo-Malthusian organizations between 1908 and 1914. Eugène Humbert, though he accepted Malthus's arguments for himself, was clear that a neo-Malthusian could advocate the prudential check without worrying about the equilibrium between population and subsistence. More and more frequently, articles in *Génération consciente* stressed the immediate need to disseminate a knowledge of contraception in order to achieve ideals which were foreign to Malthus's thought: the social revolution, social progress, pacifism, feminism. Similarly in February 1911 Albert Gros who edited a periodical called *Le Malthusien* published an article by Ernest Armand[7] entitled "Malthusianism, neo-Malthusianism and Individualism" which made it crystal clear how little individualist anarchists in the neo-Malthusian movement thought of Malthus.

> The old Malthusian thesis advocated moral restraint, sexual abstinence and delayed marriage. We leave these policies to those who are frightened of life, those who are contemptuous of the flesh, those who would deny pleasure. Individualists do not concern themselves with what the population of the earth will be in 1000 years' time. It will be for the population of the year 2000 to solve the problems posed by the relationship between population and means of subsistence. The misery, suffering and oppression that men see everywhere will be sufficient to convince those who think that the fewer dependants a human being has, the more independent will he become of those who exploit and dominate him. Conscious parenthood is a means of resistance against oppression and the determinism imposed by external conditions.

Thus, the work begun by those Malthusians in England who preferred the practice of contraception to moral restraint continued in France and led some neo-Malthusians to abandon the Principle of Population and advocate birth control within the context of the social struggle.

Limits to the freedom of expression

The first world war put a sudden stop to the activities of the French neo-Malthusians. Gabriel Giroud tried to continue his work, but the different periodicals that he edited, were immediately banned. Shortly after the conclusion of peace, the law of July 31, 1920 was enacted, which prohibited all anti-natalist propaganda and made the publication of information about and the sale of contraceptives and abortifacients illegal. From that time onwards, the authorities were able to use this law to suppress the activities of militant neo-Malthusians. Up to then, prosecutions against them had been brought under the provisions of the laws against pornography. It is not the object of this paper to analyse the pretexts which the police and judicial authorities used to bring prosecutions, but the zeal with which they administered these regulations shows their opposition clearly. But Paul Robin, the founder of the neo-Malthusian movement, was not significantly affected by this: he was convicted several times, but only slight penalties were imposed. Nor did Gabriel Giroud's many pseudonyms deceive anyone, and yet he was never convicted but allowed to retain his post as a teacher. Eugène Humbert, on the other hand, was closely watched and became a victim of persecution. The FGNMB was prosecuted a number of times during its brief existence. This apparent inconsistency was quite deliberate. In spite of his revolutionary past, the authorities regarded Paul Robin as an anachronism and as respectable. Giroud was above all a Malthusian. Though both might exercise some small influence in reducing the level of the French birth rate, they could in no way be regarded as constituting a threat to the established social order. Humbert's case was different. Since his young days in Nancy he had been noted on police files as a dangerous anarchist and he continued to suffer from this reputation throughout his life. The FGNMB, too, disturbed the authorities as its members were essentially revolutionary and anti-militarist trade unionists. In a police report dated January 31, 1914, there appear the names of 61 members of the FGNMB in Auxerre, 43 of whom were described as convinced and notorious anti-militarists of whom nearly half were syndicalists.[8] On February 4, 1911, the Chief Prosecutor of the Court of Appeal in Brest said that the group there consisted of some 15 members all of whom were employed in the dockyard and who belonged to libertarian groups. The revolutionary activities of some of the French neo-Malthusians stimulated the vigour with which they were repressed. Their affiliation also enables us to understand why the teaching of contraception was prohibited in France for a period of almost 50 years. During the inter-war period the weakening of the libertarian movement and the preponderance of reformists and Leninists in the various parties of the left led to the neo-Malthusians becoming isolated. The communist party remained faithful to the condemnation of Malthusian doctrines by Karl Marx, a condemnation which had been reiterated by Lenin, and was extremely hostile to the neo-Malthusians in its bitter struggle with the anarchists. The parties of the left did not propose to abrogate the restrictive laws of 1920 and 1923 once they achieved power, even though they had violently denounced them earlier, and population statistics showed that their spirit flagrantly contradicted the aspirations of the great majority of French citizens. It is interesting to compare the experience of France with that of Britain.

Unlike their French counterparts, British neo-Malthusians did not identify themselves with any particular political doctrine and it was, therefore, not possible to counter neo-Malthusian propaganda by linking it with subversive revolutionary activities. Moreover, since the end of the first world war, the British movement had been strongly influenced by Margaret Sanger and increasingly concentrated on advocacy of birth control. In 1922, the Malthusian League's journal changed its title from *The Malthusian* to *The New Generation.* In the following year, the founders of the Malthusian League resigned and this heralded the end of Malthusianism. In 1926, the League ceased all propagandist activities. The movement for the liberalization of the law and the dissemination of contraceptive information was no longer based on political grounds, but on considerations relating to individual liberty and social progress. It appeared that the legal status of contraception had not influenced the birth rate greatly; the only obstacles to its acceptance were moral ones. In 1930, the Church of England agreed that birth control to prevent undesired pregnancies could be regarded as licit in certain circumstances, and the government authorized the dissemination of contraceptive information.

The development in France was similar, but happened some decades later. In spite of Jeanne Humbert's valiant efforts to continue her husband's work, the neo-Malthusian movement in France disappeared shortly after the end of the Second World War. It was replaced by the French family planning movement, which concentrated its energies on legalizing contraception, and which regarded itself as politically neutral and free of any Malthusian influence. It obtained a considerable amount of support from the progressive movement and from the Protestant community. It was able, therefore, to open it first information centres, though these were strictly speaking illegal, without being prosecuted. At the presidential election of 1965 all the candidates declared their support for a revision of the law and in 1967 the passing of the Neuwirth law made the sale of contraceptives and the dissemination of information about contraception legal. However, the legislators were anxious to prevent a resurgence of neo-Malthusianism and took care to include in Article 5 of the new law, a blanket prohibition of all anti-natalist propaganda. Not a single one of the deputies and senators, irrespective of their political views, criticized the openly anti-democratic nature of this provision of the law.

Notes

1. G. Giroud (1937). *Paul Robin, sa vie, ses idées, son action*. Paris.
2. The first neo-Malthusian appeal by Paul Robin was published as *La question sexuelle*. London, 1878.
3. cf. *Dictionnaire biographique du mouvement ouvrier français* (Ed. J. Maitron). Editions ouvrières, Paris, 1976.
4. Note the extreme prudence with which Naquet expresses his views, in order not to support the Germanophobes and ardent "patriots" of this period.
5. *Rénovation*, No. 9., 15 December 1911, letter signed G. Hardy.
6. Madeleine Pelletier had belonged to the Socialist International since 1906. As a feminist and revolutionary she took an active part in neo-Malthusian propaganda. She later became a member of the communist party and was arrested in 1939 for procuring abortions. She died insane in the hospital of Perray-Vaucluse. cf. *Dictionnaire biographique* cited in note 3.
7. Ernest Armand (whose real name was Juin) began as a member of the Salvation Army but became one of the most interesting personalities in the individualist anarchist movement. Remaining a militant libertarian until the day of his death in 1962, he devoted much of his energy to defending the cause of sexual freedom. cf. J. Maitron (1975). *Le mouvement anarchiste en France*. Revised Edition. François Maspéro, Paris.
8. This list is reproduced in my book *La grève des ventres. Propagande néo-malthusienne et baisse de la natalité française — XIX–XX siècles*. Aubier-Montaigne, Paris, 1980. On neo-Malthusian workers' groups, see also F. Ronsin. La classe ouvrière et le néo-malthusianisme: l'exemple français avant 1914. *Le mouvement social*, January-March 1979.

25 Socialism and Malthusianism in Late Victorian and Edwardian Britain

G. R. SEARLE

In the first part of this paper I shall employ the term "Malthusianism" to designate those who took it as axiomatic that poverty would speedily disappear once wage-earners began to have no more children than they could afford to maintain in comfort. These people can be divided into two groups. First, there were the strict followers of Malthus who believed that population should be brought into balance with the means of subsistence by deferred marriage and sexual abstinence. Secondly, there were the "neo-Malthusians" who sought, to control fertility within marriage by disseminating knowledge about contraception. In Britain, the latter were organized around the Malthusian League, which during the forty years following its foundation in 1877 was the only body which promoted the cause of birth control.[1]

No socialist, one would have thought, could have sympathized with either of these groups, since no socialist could admit that overpopulation was the main cause of poverty; for socialism assumes that poverty and degradation are the inevitable consequences of an economic system which keeps the majority of people in a state of subjection to the small minority who own the means of production. Between these two creeds there seems to be an impassable chasm. And, in fact, the relationship between socialists and Malthusians was predominantly one of hostility throughout the period under discussion.

Socialists were particularly scathing about the strict Malthusians who urged the poor to make prudent marriages. Robert Blatchford, the editor of *The Clarion,* was speaking for them all when he argued that prolonged celibacy was "unnatural" and that only "a coward or a slave" would subject himself to it solely from economic motives; "if

MALTHUS PAST AND PRESENT
ISBN 0-12-224670-5

the state of things in England to-day makes it impossible for men and women to love and marry", he asserted, "then the state of things in England to-day will not do".[2] In any case, as nearly all sympathetic observers of working class life, whether socialists or not, were agreed, the casual poor and the unskilled labourers for whom "prudence" might seem to be most necessary, were precisely those least capable of responding to Malthusian exhortations. "That a man with 24s a week is unwise to have six children is perfectly true", wrote the Fabian Mrs Pember Reeves, "but, then, what sized family would he be wise to have? If he were really prudent and careful of his future he would, on such a wage, neither marry nor have children at all."[3] The overcrowded conditions in the parental homes from which most labourers came, a lack of social amenities and of recreational outlets, as well as the force of custom, all drove the poor into marrying early and setting up a home of their own; children were then born "as a matter of course".[4]

But would this have happened if the Malthusian League had presented the case for birth control more effectively, angling its arguments towards those poverty-stricken members of the working class who stood in greatest need of its counsels? It is interesting to observe that, when in the autumn of 1913, the Malthusian League held a series of open-air meetings in a depressed area of South London, Southwark, the response which it elicited suggests the existence of considerable latent support for the "neo-Malthusian" message. One of the lecturers who took part in this campaign, Mrs Bessie Drysdale, noted that, while the economic, medical and eugenic aspects of the question had only a minority appeal, audiences invariably responded to "the common sense argument of cutting one's coat according to one's cloth, and the moral one of bringing no children into being consciously to suffer".[5] A fellow worker noted, in addition, that it was when the lady speakers told the people of what unlimited families meant for women and children that the attention was greatest. "What she says is true, God bless her!", called out one working man.[6] Evidence from a number of sources suggests that working class women who encountered Malthusian propaganda wanted, above all else, practical information about how to prevent conception.[7]

Yet not until 1913 did the Malthusian League meet this demand, mainly because of the fear that it would be prosecuted for distributing obscene literature. It has become customary for later commentators to criticize the League for showing itself so timid. This ignores the fact that it required considerable courage in the late nineteenth and early twentieth centuries to make out in public even a general theoretical case for family limitation. More valid is the criticism that the small band of enthusiasts who composed the League insisted on presenting birth control "as a logical extension of Malthus's economic teachings": a strategy which expressed their deeply held conviction that Malthus's law of population provided a solution to all the country's difficulties and that all other purported remedies were dangerous fallacies.[8] This fatally crippled the League's propaganda efforts. Working-class audiences did not want instruction in political economy, even in the form of bright and simple leaflets. Bessie Drysdale and other League speakers realized that this was the case, but it did not cause them to change their approach. The consequence of this was that not only did they fail to capture significant working class support, they also came into open conflict with the various socialist societies, in particular the Marxists of the Social Democratic Federation (SDF).

With characteristic perverseness, on those rare occasions when the Malthusian Leaguers were given the chance of addressing a socialist meeting, they invariably refused to adapt their message to their audience. For example, Dr Binnie Dunlop told the Southwark branch of the British Socialist Party in September 1911 that he could not agree with those sociologists who regarded neo-Malthusianism as simply meaning family limitation; he emphasized instead the League's official view that Malthusianism rested on Malthus's law of population and was not merely a matter of personal inclination.[9] Why did League speakers behave in this way? Some might argue that the Malthusians were perfect examples of Victorian "faddism", that is to say they were enthusiasts for a cause whose enthusiasm was so strong that they were apt to express impatience and contempt for others who did not share it.[10] This led them to dismiss both the protectionism favoured by many members of the Conservative Party and the social welfare policies of the pre-war liberal governments.[11]

But the League's quarrel with socialism ran deeper than that. For, not content with contending that family limitation would automatically lead to higher wages and improved economic conditions, the Malthusians also took the view that, if the workers were able to control their numbers, they could save and then buy land or the means of production, and so become capitalists themselves. Such a process, they argued, would probably bring about an increase in the number of small firms conducted on cooperative or co-partnership principles, tending still further to diminish the distinction between Capital and Labour.[12] This analysis, of course, derived from the more conservative pages of John Stuart Mill's political economy. Also deriving from Mill was their prediction that any lessening of population pressure would tend to lower rents and so reduce the income of the landowners, who were depicted as a "parasitic" class; but workmen and capitalists, it was claimed, both stood to gain from family limitation. It is now obvious why the Malthusians particularly disliked socialism; for it was their belief that socialistic experiments would actually encourage the multiplication of the poor by lessening the effect of those economic forces which recommended family limitation to their self-interest.[13]

It is hardly surprising, therefore, that most socialists should have detested the Malthusian League and all that it stood for. Significantly, it was socialists, along with a handful of "Mrs Grundys", who came out on the streets to heckle when the League launched its South London campaign.[14] The Leaguers, for their part, were only too ready to perpetuate the vendetta. The organization's monthly paper, *The Malthusian,* gleefully recorded every trade union setback and every quarrel within the socialist ranks; poetic retribution was being visited upon foolish and obstinate men who refused to accept "true" economic doctrine, the Malthusians believed. On the eve of the war the Leaguers could even delude themselves into supposing that socialism was rapidly losing its popular following and that they were gaining at its expense![15]

What were the arguments with which the socialists sought to refute their Malthusian critics? Marx himself, it will be recalled, had argued that Malthus's so-called "law of population" was "a law peculiar to the capitalist mode of production", corresponding to the process of capital accumulation, and thus not of universal validity.[16] Perhaps because they found this line of reasoning too sophisticated to be of propaganda value, few British Marxists used it. Instead, they tended to rely on Lassalle's concept of an "iron law of wages", which asserted that under capitalism wages would be kept down to the lowest standard of subsistence which people would accept. From this, they deduced that working men who limited their families would simply make it possible for employers to cut wages.[17] Interestingly enough, the Malthusians did not reject the premisses underlying this argument; they merely sought to modify it by showing that "economy in reproduction" was the one and only way in which working men could render Lassalle's law inoperative.[18]

But for the majority of British socialists who stood outside the Marxist tradition, it was thought sufficient to refute the notion that overpopulation caused poverty. Julia Dawson employed a *reductio ad absurdum*; if the Malthusians were correct, she told her *Clarion* readers, "every large family would be poor, and we should have Kaiser Bill and other royalties coming to our doors begging for bread". "It is the unequal distribution of wealth and work which is the cause of poverty", she added.[19] Socialists often developed this point by insisting that there was plenty of food in the world, if it were only properly distributed. A common ploy was to cite Prince Kropotkin, who had claimed that by intensive culture it would be possible to grow more than enough food for everyone[20] — a claim extended by Herbert Burrows, who was prepared to argue that the Mississippi Valley alone could supply sufficient wheat to feed the entire human race![21]

In addition, social reformers and socialists alike were struck by the coincidence between areas with high birth rates and areas with high death rates. Perhaps, thought Charles Booth, the death of a child, especially if it were a baby, tended to bring about the birth of another; hence, "if child mortality could be checked the birth rate would certainly be reduced, and a terrible waste of every kind would be prevented".[22] Socialists, predisposed to believe that the solution to all difficulties lay in a radical improvement of the social environment, also noted that there was an inverse relationship between fertility and income. From this they deduced that higher wages and better living conditions *automatically* brought about a reduction in the birth rate. This was the conclusion reached by the Webbs in *Industrial Democracy,* which includes a discussion of differential fertility within the working class.[23] Many other socialists followed the Webbs' lead. Thus, Mrs Pember Reeves wrote in 1913: "... for those who deplore large families in the case of poor people, it must be a comfort to remember a fact which experience shows us, that as poverty decreases, and as the standard of comfort rises, so does the size of the family diminish. Should we be able to conquer the problem of poverty, we should automatically solve the problem of the excessively large family."[24] This oft-repeated argument clearly worried the Malthusian Leaguers. In response, they could do no better than to suggest that the statistics of differential fertility were being misinterpreted and that cause and effect were being reversed; in other words, it was not the case that artisans had smaller families than labourers because they earned more money, but rather that they "had maintained high wages because they had taken advantage of the knowledge that was made public by the Knowlton trial and limited their families."[25] This argument was easily demolished. In desperation, the Malthusians were driven back to the thesis that, though comfort might, indeed, constitute a very powerful "preventive check", this check only operated when the workers had "won" their comfort through their own exertions; the poor, however, would not modify their behaviour simply because other people or the state had improved their circumstances for them.[26] The Malthusian

Leaguers clearly believed that social progress must necessarily follow, but could not precede, the widespread acceptance of the individualistic virtues of thrift, prudence and self-help.

The most telling socialist criticism of Malthusianism during the early twentieth century, however, was to ask why real wages were declining despite the fact that the birth rate had continued to fall steadily from the late 1870s onwards. The Malthusians might reply that this trend had still scarcely affected the family life of unskilled workers, among whom the most harrowing forms of poverty and destitution were to be found. This was true enough, but this argument tacitly admitted that family limitation pure and simple was not the most pressing problem of the hour and that a consideration of the likely social consequences of differential fertility was of greater relevance. This was the background to the development of eugenics in the ten years before 1914.[27] It is interesting, therefore, to observe that the Malthusian League enthusiastically incorporated elements of eugenics into its own creed, and that even socialists were in some cases attracted by the eugenists' claim to possess the key to racial betterment.

One final possibility is that socialists disliked Malthusianism, in *all* its manifestations, because they had a vested interest in "destabilizing" the economic system. Members of the League did, in fact, sometimes allege that socialist agitators were inciting the poor to have as many children as possible in the hope that the resulting misery would bring the socialist revolution nearer.[28] In general, however, there is little evidence that socialists believed that a high birth rate amongst manual workers would help their cause. Indeed, it was far more common for them to urge working class parents to "go on strike" so as to deprive both the capitalists and their allies, the warlords, of necessary manpower.[29] The strain of anti-militarism in prewar British socialist thought was, of course, very strong. And although socialists did not take the Malthusian view that overpopulation was the principal *cause* of war, they did recognize that the fecundity of the poor, by creating a plentiful supply of cannon fodder, made it easier for wars to be sustained. For this reason alone, socialists were likely to welcome any downturn in the birth rate.

There were also some who were prepared to argue publicly that family limitation would directly promote working class interests. Thus, an anonymous member of the Daily Herald League wrote to *The Malthusian* saying that, in his opinion, socialists and trade unionists should make family limitation part of their propaganda; for, he argued, "if the workers didn't have more than two children per family they would obviously be much better off, even under the present system, and they would be better able to work for the Socialist Revolution, especially their overburdened wives".[30] On another occasion a trade unionist wrote in to make the point that workers who drank or had large families could not be expected to give a good account of themselves in labour disputes: "the misery caused by large families trying to exist on strike pay of a few shillings a week has broken many a strike".[31] Here was an argument for birth control which would not have spontaneously occurred to the Drysdales and other leading ideologues of the Malthusian League! Of even greater interest was the viewpoint of another socialist who rejected as nonsense the notion that socialist leaders wanted cheap support and food for revolution; on the contrary, he argued, "it is in the slums that one finds the greatest ignorance, the greatest poverty, and the largest families, *and* the least support for socialism."[32] This remark is worth examining with some care, because, if true, it suggests that, whereas socialism may have been flatly opposed to the economic contents of the Malthusian creed, it enjoyed a much closer relationship with the practice of family limitation itself. For the rest of the paper I shall, therefore, concern myself with Malthusianism in its other meaning, namely, birth control.

The socialist correspondent quoted above was clearly correct in his assertion that before 1914 family limitation had not made much of an impact upon the slums where the poorest members of the working class lived. The Registrar-General was able to show, using fertility data for 1911, that whereas the birth rate for skilled workers was 153 per thousand married males aged 55 and under, it was as high as 213 for unskilled workers.[33] The fertility of particular occupational groups was affected, not just by income and social status, but also by the availability or otherwise of work for married women; thus, birth rates were very low in many of the textile towns of Lancashire, while coal-miners, not on average a particularly badly paid body of men, had exceptionally large families. But it remains broadly true that amongst the wage-earning population there was an inverse relationship between income and fertility.[34] And a major reason for this disparity was that artisans were more inclined to practise various forms of birth control (including abortion) than the casual poor, who, so contemporary observers often noted, tended to view artificial checks to conception with disgust. Charles Booth, who shared that disgust, thought that the London poor were influenced in matters of sexual conduct "by superstition of the same character as that which brings the poorest kind of women to be churched, 'because they don't want a miscarriage next time' ".[35] The cultural divisions within the working class community created by income differentials also owed something to differences of religion; in London, for example, a large sector of the casual labour force consisted of Irish immigrants who, as Roman Catholics, had additional reasons of their own for rejecting all available means of family limitation. However it be explained, this divergence of behaviour survived into the inter-war years. An oral history project has revealed that those members of the working class who had "a fatalistic attitude to family size" and "expressed little ambition for their children", coming in the main from the poorest strata of the community, tended not to practise birth control; while it was the skilled from the working and lower/middle classes, anxious that their children should receive a secondary education or possessing ambitious leisure needs, who were more likely to see the advantages of birth control.[36]

What substance was there in the socialist correspondent's other claim, that socialism had little support in the slum districts of the big cities? Historians of the labour movement would broadly accept this proposition. For example, Gareth Stedman Jones has shown that the London Marxists of the SDF drew their support mainly from better-off craftsmen, but were not establishing any hold over dockside labourers and other casual workers before the First World War.[37] Similarly, the Independent Labour Party (ILP), the largest of the socialist societies, relied to a great extent on young, unionized workers, as can be seen from this description of one of the Glasgow branches: ". . . except for an odd teacher and a few shop assistants, the members were all working men and their wives. For the most part the men belonged to the skilled trades . . . and were nearly always known as exceptionally good and steady working men. They were active trade unionists to a man. The ILP was not attracting as yet what are called the 'unskilled workers'."[38] To a lesser extent this was even true of the trade union movement itself. Thus, the casual poor still had little contact with organized Labour, and could not be relied upon to support *any* kind of progressive politics. Some socialist and trade union leaders on the eve of the war were doubtful, for this very reason, whether in the immediate future they stood to gain electorally from the enactment of universal male suffrage.[39]

There is a sense, therefore, in which Malthusianism and socialism were in direct competition for the allegiance of the same social group: the skilled working man who was literate, intellectually curious about the state of the world and desirous of improving his position in it. The commitment of the Malthusians to *laissez faire* economics meant that there could never be a synthesis of the two creeds.[40] Nevertheless, both shared certain characteristics. For example, the leaders of both the Malthusian League and of the SDF were in many cases secularists, who explicitly attacked the providential view of life and the fatalism and passivity which this engendered; and both did so by invoking so-called "laws of social development" and ascribing scientific status to their own propaganda work.[41] Perhaps it is this deeper compatibility which explains why some labour activists were able, against all odds, to treat even the *economic* teaching of Malthusianism with qualified approval. Thus, when the Women's Labour League debated the whole issue of family limitation in 1913, there were members who were prepared to put the Malthusian — and, incidentally, the eugenic — case for smaller families.[42] One would suppose that the feminist aspects of birth control propaganda must also have appealed to some socialists, though not probably to the SDF, which remained at best insensitive to the women's viewpoint. Finally, as we have already seen, it was possible for socialists to advocate family limitation on the grounds that this rendered the working class better equipped to fight for its own emancipation.

Some historians, however, would find it necessary at this point to draw a contrast between Malthusianism, which offered the industrious workman an escape from poverty, and socialism proper, which promised the redemption of the working class as a whole. Thus, Angus McLaren, in his important book on *Birth Control in 19th Century Britain,* has pointed out that what worried many socialists about the case for family limitation was its implied "individualism".[43] This point is well worth making, but to press it too far would obscure the true relationship between socialism and Malthusianism, which was a remarkably complex one. It is not a case of "bourgeois individualism" competing with the group loyalty and class solidarity generated by the Labour Movement. For there was a large residue of "bourgeois moralism", if one wants to call it that, within British socialism itself.

This can be clearly seen if, instead of treating family limitation in isolation, one studies it in connection with the contemporary debate about how best to cope with the social problems caused by heavy drinking. There are many similarities between the two issues. After all, Malthusians and temperance reformers were middle class moralists of a similar psychological type. Each group was trying, in its own particular way, to rescue the poor from their degradation by educating them in the necessity of responsible behaviour. Indeed, the attack on working men who "wasted" their money on beer almost exactly parallels the strictures passed on poor families who produced more children than they could raise in comfort. To put it in a nutshell, alcohol and excessive fertility were both social evils which could be treated as examples of "self-inflicted poverty".[44]

Now, obviously no socialist could accept that the poor, taken in the mass, were in some way to blame for their own misfortunes; and the standard response to accusations of this sort was to show how drunkenness and reckless procreation were the *consequences* of the poverty visited upon the poor by a vicious economic system. But here unanimity ended. Some socialists rejected the case for temperance *in toto;* Robert Blatchford, for example, argued in *Merrie England* that though a sober man might succeed in life better than a drunken man, it did not follow that if everyone were sober wages would increase[45] — a line of argument which seems to assume the existence of "an iron law of wages". It comes as no surprise, then, to learn that, in general, Blatchford was also unsympathetic towards the case for birth control.

But few socialists adopted so intransigent a position. Indeed, nothing is more striking about the early Labour Movement than the large number of its leaders who were abstainers. This characteristic was particularly pronounced in the ILP, where very few branches sold alcohol at all in their club rooms. But J.B. Brown has shown that many trade union leaders shared this disapproval of heavy drinking; they did so, first, because they thought that the drunkard was likely to be contented with his lot, and, secondly, because they believed that intemperance tended to sap the effectiveness of men on strike.[46] This brings us to a broader issue. All socialists were agreed that a bad social environment lowered people's character; but it could also be argued that only a transformation of the character of working men and women would give them the strength and "vision" to challenge the *status quo.* That is why socialists like Philip Snowden of the ILP thought that socialism and temperance should advance hand in hand.[47] The result was a curious blend of moral exhortation and economic determinism.

Such a blend was in fact characteristic of many aspects of working class politics at the end of the nineteenth century. The active leaders of the trade union and cooperative movements, for example, tended to turn their backs on the rough and disorderly aspects of the older popular culture in their pursuit of "respectability"; thrift, prudence, sobriety, a commitment to education and so on all enjoyed their high esteem. Since socialism requires its adherents to practise "deferment of gratification" on an heroic scale, it is even more dependent upon these "bourgeois" virtues. But, of course, before being taken up and assimilated by the politically conscious manual workers active in the socialist movement, the "virtues" in question must first have been reinterpreted and adapted to fit the realities of working-class life. R.Q. Gray has shown this process of adaptation taking place in the late Victorian period amongst the "labour aristocracy"[48] — the very group in which, as we have seen, political radicalism and the practice of family limitation had both secured a firm and significant foothold before the end of the nineteenth century.

It would be satisfying if we could round off this paper by demonstrating that socialists were, indeed, more likely to practise birth control than other working men who were not socialists. But, necessarily, evidence for or against this proposition is extremely difficult to find. A gentleman stood up at one of the Malthusian League's meeting in 1906 and asserted that "most of the English socialist leaders had small families, although they would not admit that such limitation, if general, would be a remedy for poverty".[49] Given the nature of the life led by these men, it would not be surprising to find that they had taken steps to ensure that their efforts to "spread the faith" were not unduly hampered by domestic obligations. I have looked into the family circumstances of 15 of the most prominent labour leaders and working class socialists and have found that they married, on average, at the age of 25 and produced 4.3 surviving children. The group includes a couple of Roman Catholic trade unionists, O'Grady and Connolly, who produced nine and seven children respectively. But the most prolific of them all was actually an Anglican, George Lansbury; in his old age he grudgingly came to accept the case for birth control, but not before he had fathered 12 children. At the other extreme was Snowden, who married at the age of 40 and was childless. No very clear pattern emerges from all this.

About the predominantly professional middle-class Fabian Society it is easier to generalize. The Malthusian Leaguers often acknowledged that the Fabians were sympathetic to family limitation and even preached it *sub rosa*.[56] We also know that several of the leading Fabians deliberately opted for a childless marriage. In addition, there is the evidence of a survey, which the Society organized in 1906, under prompting from George Standring, who was also prominent in the Malthusian League.[51] A questionnaire went out to between 600 and 700 people who were confidently expected to reply, asking whether, and if so why, they controlled their fertility. The questionnaire elicited 302 "significant replies", involving 316 marriages. Of these marriages 242 (76.5 per cent) were declared to be "limited", though the methods employed were not enumerated. This is interesting as far as it goes, but not all the respondents were actual members of the Fabian Society, though the others were presumably sympathizers. In occupational terms the respondents ranged from skilled artisans at one end of the social scale, to professional men and small property owners at the other.[52] All that one can deduce with any certainty is that Fabian members and their friends seem to have behaved much as other people from the same social background.

A final question must be asked. Why, if socialists stood to gain on balance from the practice of family limitation spreading among their potential working-class supporters, did they not come out openly in its favour? In part, the answer must be that many socialists, especially those of the SDF, had come to accept the Malthusian League's contention that family limitation was logically bound up with *laissez faire* economics. But this would not explain the attitude of the ILP leaders, whose campaigning activities were concentrated in provincial areas, outside London, where they would not have collided with the Malthusian Leaguers. In any case, the ILP's stance was not one of hostility so much as one of silence and evasion.[53] Even otherwise vocal and argumentative spokesmen like MacDonald and Snowden, who held strong views on a wide range of issues, seldom if ever touched upon the subject. It is true that the members of the ILP, especially female members, made the fight for women's rights an integral part of the socialist programme. For example, Ethel Snowden, who was both a feminist and a socialist, insisted that women had an absolute right over themselves after marriage and were not obliged to surrender their bodies at their husbands' command. But this seems to have been an appeal to men to exercise sexual self-restraint and to treat their wives with greater "chivalry". Significantly, in a book devoted exclusively to the modern feminist movement, Ethel Snowden manages to omit any mention of contraception.[54] Calculating prudence rather than prudishness is probably the main explanation here. The ILP were seriously committed to winning seats on representative bodies, and were, therefore, well advised to keep clear of birth control, which was "a potential vote loser", as Robert Dowse and John Peel rightly argue.[55] Moreover, socialists had particular reasons for caution, since their enemies were ever on the lookout for evidence of "immorality"; for example, the atheism of some socialist leaders was given great prominence in anti-socialist literature. Before 1914 the topic of birth control was one which could not be raised in polite society, and had the socialist societies incorporated it into their programmes they would only have damaged their chances of securing a large popular following.

After the war the climate of opinion changed, and it was now possible even for professional men like medical practitioners publicly to advocate birth control without destroying their reputations.[56] Nevertherless, the Labour Party remained deeply divided over this subject in the inter-war period. In 1924 the Labour Minister of Health, John Wheatley, who, significantly, was a Roman Catholic, flatly rejected the suggestion that maternity and child welfare clinics should be empowered to give contraceptive advice to married women in cases where further pregnancies would injure their health.[57] Then, two years later, a Labour backbencher, Ernest Thurtle, moved that leave be given to bring in a bill which would authorize local authorities to incur expenditure, when deemed expedient, in conveying knowledge of birth control methods to married women who desired it. While appealing to MPs on all sides of the House, Thurtle said that it was as a socialist that he introduced his bill. But it was also as a socialist that another Labour MP, James Barr, stood up to oppose him; Barr also reminded his colleagues that the recent Labour Party Conference, on the advice of the Executive, had agreed by a majority of 771, 000 votes that the subject of birth control must be left to the individual conscience, since by its nature it could not be made a party political issue.[58] The Commons summarily rejected Thurtle's motion; 44 Labour MPs voted against, as against 27 who supported it, on a 47 per cent turn-out — a distribution of opinion similar to that within the Conservative Parliamentary Party.

Eventually, it is true, the second labour government produced the important memorandum, 153 MCW of 1930, which gave the advocates of birth control the concession for which they had long been pressing. But this reform was unobtrusively put through by administrative decree, before opposition from within or outside the party could be effectively mobilized.[59] No doubt fear of alienating working-class Catholics played its part in discouraging the Labour Party leadership from officially identifying itself with the now highly vocal birth control lobby. In addition, Dowse and Peel believe that the Labour Party was influenced by the conservatism of much working-class opinion, which disliked birth control as a threat to "the male orientation in the family".[60] Many working-class people were also conservative in the sense that they recoiled with embarrassment from any frank and open discussion of sexual issues. It is interesting, in this context, to learn that Lansbury, a late convert to birth control and a supporter of Thurtle's motion, still retained "a typically Victorian unwillingness to discuss sex, and the mechanics of contraception disgusted him" — or so we are told by his biographer and son-in-law, Raymond Postgate.[61]

It is clear that during the inter-war years the division of opinion on the question of birth control did not coincide with party political allegiances to any marked degree, and the same may also have been true of the late Victorian and Edwardian periods. Moreover, even when critics of birth control *debated* the issue in terms of class and political strategy, that does not necessarily *explain* why they took up that attitude in the first place. Similarly with the proponents of family planning. The formation of sexual attitudes may be more dependent than is often recognized on the sort of psychological impulses which have so far proved resistant to the analytical techniques of political history.

Notes

1. Rosanna Ledbetter (1976). *A History of the Malthusian League, 1877–1927.* Columbus.
2. R. Blatchford (1902). *Britain for the British*, pp.132–133. London.
3. Mrs Pember Reeves (1913). *Round About a Pound A Week*, pp.219–220. London.
4. e.g. B. Seebohm Rowntree (1901). *Poverty: A Study of Town Life*, p.174. London; C. Booth (1902). *Life and Labour in London: Final Volume: Notes on Social Influences*, p.46. London.
5. *The Malthusian*, 15 February 1913.
6. ibid. 15 June 1914.
7. Thus, when Julia Dawson of *The Clarion* gave space in her "Woman's letter" to the Malthusian Leaguer, Mrs Alice Vickery, her postbag was filled with letters, many of which asked the question: "How can I limit my family?" (*Clarion*, 24 February, 10 March 1900).
8. A. McLaren (1978). *Birth Control in Nineteenth-Century England*, p.109. London.
9. *The Malthusian*, 15 November 1913.
10. On "faddism" see D. A. Hamer (1977), *The Politics of Electoral Pressure*, p.1. Hassocks.
11. On protection, see *The Malthusian*, June 1905. The only good *The Malthusian* could see in legislation like the National Insurance Bill was that the cost might force the recognition of the population difficulty upon those who had to pay the lion's share of the taxes, i.e. the middle classes, and encourage them to come out as open supporters of Malthusianism (15 May 1911).
12. ibid. 15 February 1913, 15 March 1913, 15 May 1914.
13. ibid. 15 March 1914.
14. ibid. 15 June 1913.
15. ibid. 15 December 1913.
16. See discussion in H. A. Boner (1955). *Hungry Generations: The Nineteenth Century Case Against Malthusianism*, p.190. New York.
17. e.g. Fairchild of the British Socialist Party, a persistent critic of the Malthusian League, argued that "if the working classes limited their families, their wages would go down, because they would be able to live on less!", so *The Malthusian* reported with incredulity (15 December 1913).

18. *The Malthusian*, 15 April 1914.
19. *Clarion*, 10 March 1900.
20. *The Malthusian*, 15 February 1914.
21. ibid. June 1906. Herbert Burrows, of the SDF, often came out in opposition to Malthusian economics, but that did not prevent him from acknowledging that "in individual cases limitation of the family was good": Rosanna Ledbetter, op. cit. in note 1, p.93.
22. C. Booth, op. cit. in note 4, p.20.
23. S. and Beatrice Webb (1897). *Industrial Democracy*, pp.637–43. London.
24. Pember Reeves, op. cit. in note 3, p.158.
25. *The Malthusian*, 15 March 1914. The Knowlton trial refers to the famous trial of 1877 in which Charles Bradlaugh and Annie Besant were prosecuted for publishing Charles Knowlton's birth control pamphlet, *Fruits of Philosophy*.
26. ibid. 15 May 1913.
27. G. R. Searle (1976). *Eugenics and Politics in Britain, 1900–1914*. Leyden.
28. e.g. an article in the left wing *Daily Herald* advocated large familes among the working classes as a way of creating rebels against the capitalist system (*The Malthusian*, 15 May 1914).
29. An example is given in McLaren, op. cit. in note 8, p.176.
30. *The Malthusian*, 15 March 1914.
31. ibid. 15 July 1914.
32. ibid. 15 April 1914. The correspondent was James P. M. Millar.
33. National Birth Rate Commission (1916). *The Declining Birth-Rate*, p.9. London.
34. For further discussion, see T. H. C. Stevenson (1920). The fertility of various social classes in England and Wales from the middle of the nineteenth century to 1911. *Journal of the Royal Statistical Society* **83**, 401–432.
35. C. Booth, op. cit. in note 4, p.46.
36. Diana G. Gittins (1975). Married life and birth control between the wars. *Oral History* **3**, 63.
37. G. Stedman Jones (1971). *Outcast London. A Study in the Relationship Between Classes in Victorian Society*. Oxford.
38. S. Pierson (1973). *Marxism and the Origins of British Socialism*, p.209, Ithaca, citing J. Paton (1936). *Proletarian Pilgrimage*, p.199. London.
39. e.g. J. Ramsay MacDonald, cited in M. Pugh (1978). *Electoral Reform in War and Peace, 1906–18*, p.30. London.
40. A rare example of a man who declared an allegiance to both creeds was George Standring. But, significantly, he ended up by seceding from the Malthusian League, and founding a journal of his own. A. McLaren, op. cit. in note 8, pp.110, 113; Rosanna Ledbetter, op. cit. in note 1, pp.72–74.
41. On the place of birth control in secularist propaganda, see F. B. Smith (1967). The atheist mission, 1840–1900. In *Ideas and Institutions of Victorian Britain* (Ed. R. Robson), pp.219–20.

Interestingly, secularism provided a political apprenticeship for those who would later become prominent Malthusian Leaguers and for many first-generation socialists. Annie Besant involved herself in *both* causes.

42. *Women's Labour League: The League Leaflet*, July, September, October, November, December, 1913.
43. A. McLaren, op. cit. in note 8, p.169.
44. J. B. Brown (1973). The pig or the stye: Drink and poverty in late Victorian England. *International Review of Social History* **18**, 380–395.
45. R. Blatchford ("Numquam") 1893. *Merrie England,* p.75. London.
46. J. B. Brown, loc. cit. in note 44, p.390.
47. ibid. p.394. For Snowden's and the ILP's views on this matter, see C. Cross (1966). *Philip Snowden*, p.94. London.
48. R. Q. Gray (1973). Styles of life, the Labour aristocracy and class relations in later nineteenth century Edinburgh. *International Review of Social History* **18** 428–452, especially pp.451-452.
49. *The Malthusian*, July 1906.
50. ibid. 15 December 1913; see also Rosanna Ledbetter, op. cit. in note 1, pp.101–104.
51. *The Malthusian*, January 1907.
52. S. Webb. *The Decline in the Birth Rate* (Fabian Tract no. 131: March 1907).
53. The ILP did eventually give official endorsement to birth control—in 1926.
54. Ethel Snowden (1911). *The Feminist Movement*. London.
55. R. E. Dowse and J. Peel (1965). The politics of birth control. *Political Studies* **13**, 179. When Thurtle's motion came before the Commons in 1926 Philip Snowden voted for it. But MacDonald, who was anxious that the party should not associate itself with the family planning movement in any way, abstained. See Rosanna Ledbetter, op. cit. in note 1, p.114.
56. J. Peel (1964). Contraception and the medical profession. *Population Studies* **18**, 133–148.
57. R. E. Dowse and J. Peel, loc. cit. in note 55, p.185.
58. *Hansard*, 5th Ser., 191, cols. 849–858: 9 February 1926.
59. R. E. Dowse and J. Peel, loc. cit. in note 55, pp.184–191; Rosanna Ledbetter, loc. cit. in note 1, pp.228–229.
60. R. E. Dowse and J. Peel, loc. cit. in note 55, p.182.
61. R. Postgate (1951). *The Life of George Lansbury*, p.242. London.

PART 6

Malthusianism and Darwinism

26 Malthus and Biological Equilibria

R. KEYNES

The first impact of Malthus on the thinking of biologists can be dated with some precision, for on 28 September 1838 Charles Darwin made the following entry in his *Third Notebook on Transmutation of Species*, the sentences in brackets being added at some later date:

> 28th. (I do not doubt every one till he thinks deeply has assumed that increase of animals [is] exactly proportionate to the number that can live.) We ought to be far from wondering of changes in numbers of species, from small changes in nature of locality. Even the energetic language of Decandolle does not convey the warring of the species as inference from Malthus — (increase of births must be prevented solely by positive checks, excepting that famine may stop desire.) — in nature production does not increase, whilst no check prevail[s], but the positive check of famine & consequently death . . . Population is increase[d] at geometrical ratio in far shorter time than 25 years — yet until the one sentence of Malthus no one clearly perceived the great check amongst men. (there is spring, like food used for other purposes as wheat for making brandy. — Even a few years plenty, makes population in man increase & an ordinary crop causes a dearth.) Take Europe on an average every species must have the same number killed year with year by hawks, by cold &c. — even one species of hawk decreasing in number must affect instantaneously all the rest. One may say there is a force like a hundred thousand wedges trying to force every kind of adapted structure into the gaps in the economy of nature, or rather forming gaps by thrusting out weaker ones. (The final cause of all this wedging, must be to sort out proper structure, & adapt it to changes. — do that for form,

MALTHUS PAST AND PRESENT
ISBN 0-12-224670-5

which Malthus shows is the final effect (by means however of volition) of this populousness on the energy of man.)

It is unfortunately impossible to be able to identify the particular sentence of Malthus to which Darwin refers, but he marked several in his own copy of the 1826 edition of the *Essay* that is preserved in the Cambridge University Library. In any case, the marked copy is probably not the one that he read in 1838, for a note in his hand on the flyleaf records that he only acquired it in April 1841. So I can only say that it seems to have been the potential for geometric growth of populations that especially caught his attention.

Darwin later credited Malthus with having provided him with the primary stimulus for the concept of natural selection, when in his *Autobiography*[1] he wrote:

> In October 1838, that is, fifteen months after I had begun my systematic enquiry, I happened to read for amusement Malthus on Population, and being well prepared to appreciate the struggle for existence which everywhere goes on from long-continued observation of the habits of animals and plants, it at once struck me that under these circumstances favourable variations would tend to be preserved, and unfavourable ones to be destroyed. The result of this would be the formation of new species.

There is, however, room for discussion as to why a reading of Malthus should have been needed to trigger this line of thought. The "struggle for existence" was not a new idea, for Darwin had with him on the Beagle five years earlier a copy of Lyell's *Principles of Geology* in which he would have read: "In the universal struggle for existence, the right of the strongest eventually prevails; and the strength and durability of a race depends mainly on its prolificness, in which hybrids are acknowledged to be deficient." It is true that Lyell's struggle for existence was a combat between different species rather than one between individuals of the same species, but his thesis that there was an intense struggle in Nature was very forcibly put, and cannot have escaped Darwin. Another point is that Darwin must have been aware of Malthus's views long before he actually read the *Essay* from citations in Humboldt's *Personal Narrative,* another favourite book. This is perhaps reflected in the remark on the Fuegians that he entered in his journal for 25 February 1834:[2] "They are surrounded by hostile tribes speaking different dialects; and the cause of their warfare would appear to be the means of subsistence."

Historians of science in search of an explanation for the influence of

Malthus on Darwin, for example Himmelfarb, Herbert and Manier,[3] have explored the subtleties of the differences between their philosophies in some detail. The only contribution that I can make to the argument is to suggest that one should not discount the possibility that 28 September 1838 was one of those all too rare occasions when an idea already dormant in the mind suddenly surfaces, and afterwards seems so obvious that one cannot understand why it did not emerge sooner. It may be observed that Darwin was not really expecting Malthus's *Essay* to provide serious information about the problem that was currently occupying him, and yet that one seminal sentence released the essential clue.

Be that as it may, when during an attack of fever at Ternate in the East Indies in February 1858, Alfred Russel Wallace independently hit upon the idea of natural selection, he was similarly indebted to Malthus, for as he explained in his autobiography:[4]

> One day something brought to my recollection Malthus's *Principles of Population,* which I had read about twelve years before. I thought of his clear exposition of "the positive checks to increase" — disease, accidents, war, and famine — which keep down the population of savage races to so much lower an average than that of more civilized peoples. It then occurred to me that these causes or their equivalents are continually acting in the case of animals also; and as animals usually breed much more rapidly than does mankind, the destruction every year from these causes must be enormous in order to keep down the numbers of each species, since they evidently do not increase regularly from year to year, as otherwise the world would long ago have been densely crowded with those that breed most quickly. Vaguely thinking over the enormous and constant destruction which this implied, it occurred to me to ask the question, why do some die and some live? And the answer was clearly, that on the whole the best fitted live. From the effects of disease the most healthy escaped; from enemies, the strongest, the swiftest, or the most cunning; from famine, the best hunters or those with the best digestion; and so on. Then it suddenly flashed upon me that this self-acting process would necessarily improve the race, because in every generation the inferior would inevitably be killed off and the superior would remain — that is, the fittest would survive.

In general, animal populations remain stable over relatively long periods of time — long, that is, in relation to the lifetime of a single generation, though not, of course, on an evolutionary time scale. There are naturally exceptions to this statement when external conditions change abruptly or when a species changes its range and quickly exploits a new environment. I have in mind the spectacular population explosion of the collared dove in England, whose arrival from south-east Europe was a closely guarded secret among British ornithologists not so many years ago and which is today rapidly becoming a pest. There are also well recognized situations where there is a regular cyclical variation arising from the interaction between predators and their prey.[5] But long-term stability is the usual rule. It follows that either fertility or mortality or both must be subject to appropriate regulation by factors determined by population density, and the problem for biologists is to discover how such control mechanisms operate.

As far as mortality is concerned, straight death by starvation often intervenes in the animal kingdom, and there are also instances where the toll of disease rises sharply with population density. The other side of the coin is of greater interest in today's discussion, and a point that certainly concerned Darwin was the relationship between the fertility of a population and its food supplies, for against the passage in the *Essay* quoting Muret's conclusions on checks to population in Switzerland he noted: "This is much the same as to say well-fed are less fecund." In a human society where the basic biology is obscured, if I may so put it, by sociology, this may in fact be true, but for animals it is not, and there is ample evidence that when food supplies are inadequate, the rate of increase of all living organisms tends to slow down.

Professor Jewell discusses studies on populations of large herbivores in Africa which show that over a wide range of species, their densities are well adjusted to the available nutritional resources. With some assistance from enhanced mortality when food supplies fail, this is partly brought about through a direct physiological relationship between levels of nutrition and reproductive performance, affecting the age of puberty, the incidence of pregnancy in young females, and the calving interval. However, this is far from the whole story, for there are in addition behavioural adaptations in specific food preferences which minimize interspecific competition between, for example, grazers and browsers, and enable the whole spectrum of plants to be fully exploited. Grazing by one species may even facilitate use of the land by another. Such animal populations cannot be considered in isolation, but must be regarded as a well-knit community which shares out its resources by suitable ecological separation and overlap. The question may be raised whether there is any useful analogy between animal and human communities in this respect.

Professor Wynne-Edwards considers the problem of self-regulation in populations of red grouse. These are herbivorous birds, and once again there is a close correlation between the supply in a given season of the buds and shoots of heather that form their staple diet and the size of the population, which, since grouse are territorial, means the area occupied by each male. Wynne-Edwards's thesis is that population density in this species is regulated by a complex sequence of events with an important component of behavioural adaptation, in which the food supply, acting presumably through hormone levels, determines the agressiveness of the males when they compete for their territories in the autumn, and so adjusts the number of pairs that will breed in the following year. The number of young produced per unit area is also related to the food supply, but thanks to the prior adjustment that has taken place in the area of each territory, the heather is never over-exploited and irreversibly damaged. In this way, at the sacrifice of the substantial surplus of birds who are unsuccessful in the autumnal battle for territories and do not survive the winter, the community as a whole assures itself of an adequate supply of food in the following season. Homeostatic mechanisms of this kind for regulating animal numbers are unlikely to be confined to herbivorous species, but also apply to carnivores.

Many other examples of ways in which animal populations tend to be self-limiting in size through the operation of innate physiological and behavioural mechanisms in a wide spectrum of species ranging from primates to meal worms, will be found in Lack's classic study on *The Natural Regulation of Animal Numbers*. The question that I now have to consider is whether similar rules apply to man. It is not at all easy to answer and has, indeed, given rise to some controversy, bedevilled as it is with the difficulty of disentangling the various ways in which the complex behaviour patterns of human populations are apt to modulate the basic biology. Two points that strike me as a strictly neutral physiologist are: first that one must try to discount any evidence relating to populations that are not truly living at subsistence level, and secondly that it is not just the total calorie value of the food intake that has to be taken into account, but also its quality, that is to say its protein content, that really matters in this context. With these important reservations, it would greatly surprise me if the physiological mechanisms inherited by man from his ancestors were any different from those of the rest of the animal kingdom. I am, therefore, ready to be convinced by the evidence assembled by Dr Frisch for the existence of a direct connexion between food supplies and human fertility, operating through hormonal mechanisms.

In conclusion, although one can derive some comfort from the biological lesson that there are ways in which, without any conscious or moral effort, all populations do tend to restrict their growth in their own long-term interest, the problem remains as to how he is to rescue himself from the Malthusian dilemma. But in an area where economics, sociology, ethics and biology interact in such an appallingly difficult fashion, the biologist must be forgiven if he occupies a back seat.

Notes

1. Nora Barlow (1933). *Charles Darwin's Diary of the Voyage of HMS Beagle*. Cambridge University Press, Cambridge.
2. ibid.
3. Gertrude Himmelfarb (1962). *Darwin and the Darwinian Revolution*. Doubleday, New York; Sandra Herbert (1971). Darwin, Malthus and selection. *Journal of the History of Biology* **4**, 209–217; E. Manier (1978). *The Young Darwin and his Cultural Circle*. D. Reidel Publishing Co., Dordrecht.
4. A. R. Wallace (1908). *My Life*. Chapman & Hall, London.
5. D. Lack (1954). *The Natural Regulation of Animal Numbers*. Oxford University Press, Oxford.

27 Species Diversity and Environmental Carrying Capacity Amongst Large Mammals and the Shift of Equilibria by Man

P. A. JEWELL

In his autobiography, Darwin wrote of his indebtedness to Malthus and his chance reading of the *Essay on Population* that crystallized his ideas on the elimination of unfavourable variations. Darwin's theory of natural selection and survival of the fittest now illuminates the whole of biology and it is appropriate to consider whether Darwinian ideas may not now, in reciprocation, have relevance to the condition of man. In recent years there has been renewed interest in man as seen in the context of his biological evolutionary history[1,2] and expressed in the current interest in sociobiology.[3]

An examination of animal populations could hardly be expected to give any hint of how an escape might be found from the Malthusian dilemma, because such studies confirm the universal operation of limited resources. Nevertheless, animal populations do exhibit many adaptations that defend them against overpopulating their environment, and, conversely, animal communities show a high degree of integration that ensures the maximum use of resources, particularly the food resources.

Large mammalian herbivores in Africa

I take large mammalian herbivores as an example, and will concentrate attention on the African savannas. This extensive biome includes habitats comprised of open-canopy scrubland, tall-tree grassland and

MALTHUS PAST AND PRESENT
ISBN 0-12-224670-5

treeless short-grassland and receives a mean annual rainfall ranging from 450 to 2000 mm with from $7\frac{1}{2}$ to $2\frac{1}{2}$ months of aridity. Striking correlations have been demonstrated between the density of large herbivores and rainfall. For a single species, for example the buffalo[4], a high positive correlation exists between their density in different parts of East Africa and mean annual rainfall (Fig. 1). The extremes are 1 buffalo per 4 km^2 at Mkomasi Reserve with 445 mm rainfall to 23 buffalo per 1 km^2 at Mount Meru with 1968 mm rainfall. Both places are in Tanzania. Rainfall, in turn, is highly correlated with the growth of plants and it is this primary production that comprises the limiting factor.

In a more extensive application of this principle[5] a plot of the total biomass of large herbivores against rainfall, taking twenty-four different wildlife reserves in East Africa, shows a highly predictive correlation (Fig. 3). Biomass ranged from 1000 to 20 000 kg km^{-2}. Here two new factors contribute to the standing crop biomass that is attained: one is the diversity of species of herbivores that occupy a given area, and the other is the occurrence of a few species of very big mammals, such as elephant, hippopotamus and buffalo.

Ecological separation and ecological overlap

The savannas of Africa support an exceptionally large number of species of large herbivores. Frequently up to twenty species may co-

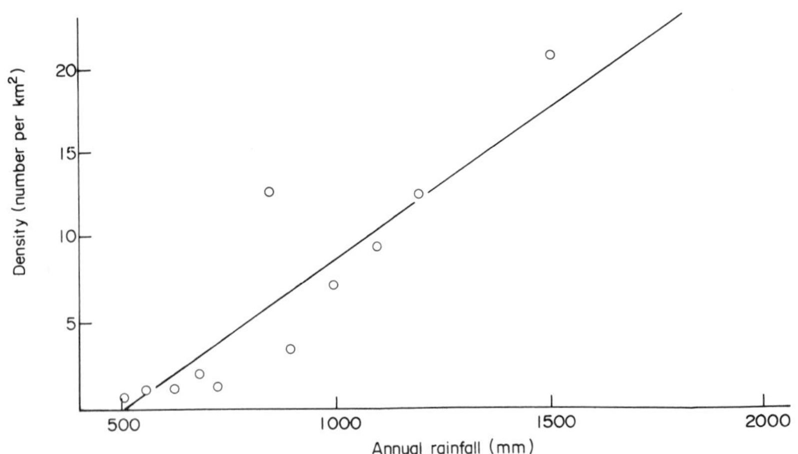

FIG. 1. The mean crude density of buffalo in different areas of eastern Africa. Significance of correlation ($P<0.001$).
(From Sinclair, 1977.)

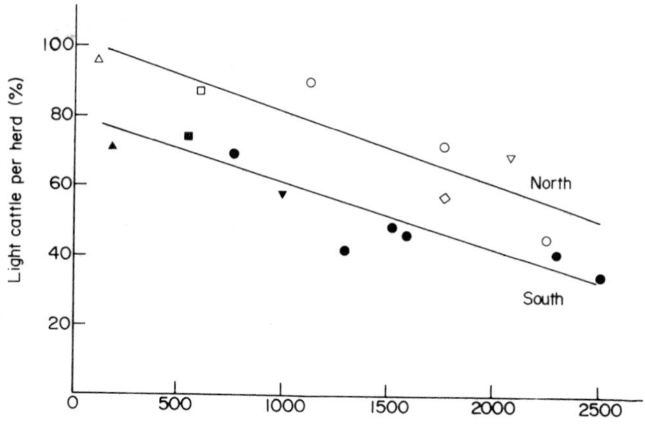

FIG. 2. The relation of percentage light cattle in herd to altitude. Open symbols are for sites in Northern Kenya, black symbols are for sites in Southern Kenya. (From Finch and Western, 1977.)

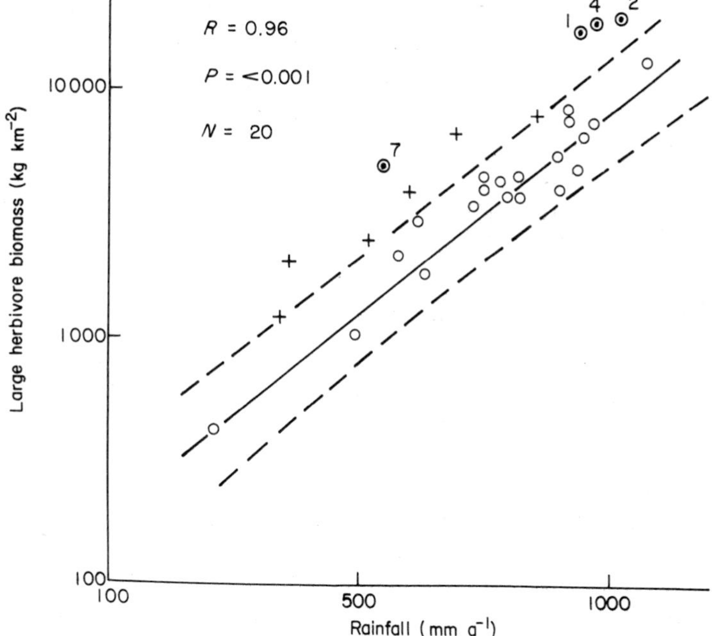

FIG. 3. Carrying capacity in African savanna areas plotted on a log scale and taken from Coe *et al.* (1976). Certain exceptional areas (⊙ and +) are omitted from the calculated regression because like Rwenzori NP (2) they have exceptionally favourable soil and rainfall or Amboseli (7) have an inland drainage basin. The pastoral areas (+) were not adjusted to conform to the other data.

exist in a single ecological unit. Superficially there would appear to be intense competition between species and they do share resources. For example wildebeest, zebra and buffalo, in the Tarangire Reserve in Tanzania all make intensive use of the palatable grass *Cynodon dactylon*. The buffalo, however, demonstrates the first respect in which competition is avoided as they eat less of the open ground grasses like *Sporobolus marginatus*, more of the tall grasses like *Setaria*, and proportionately much more of the woodland species of grass.[6]

The more obvious separation in diet between grazers and browsers removes competition between them completely. Hartebeest will select 96 per cent grasses as food plants, whereas dikdik select 80 per cent of their intake from shrubs and trees. The height at which browsers feed allows them to complement each other in their offtake so that dikdik, lesser kudu, eland and giraffe exploit the whole spectrum of plants from field layer to canopy. The habitat preferred by each species permits a wide and distinctive distribution in space since most areas are comprised of a mosaic of such environments (Fig. 4). Moreover, the herbivores show spatial preferences through time, and often aggregate at the ecotone, or transitional zone, between plant communities.

By this feeding behaviour large herbivores achieve a reduction in competition between them that may be called ecological separation and that is the basis of their effective use of all resources. It is an example of adoptive niche occupancy but the niches are not exclusive. On the contrary there is also marked ecological overlap and this gives stability to the system as a whole.[7]

Grazing succession and facilitation of energy flow

The sequential use of an area in an annual cycle by an array of herbivores dominated by different species at different times permits further specialization and reduction of competition. A well-documented illustration of such a grazing succession is that of the Rukwa Valley, Tanzania, with its salt lake and open plain that is subjected to annual flooding.[8] As the flood recedes, lush vegetation is exposed but it is far too rank for the smaller herbivores to use. The larger species, however, particularly the elephant and buffalo, move into this area, feed on the grasses and trample it excessively and stimulate growth at the leaf table. This usage creates pastures of shorter grass onto which the lighter herbivores can move. As the dry season advances, the heavy grazers, joined by zebra, move onto the exposed pastures of the lake bed. The zebra are able to graze on coarse grasses like *Sporobolus spicatus* that grow in the most saline areas. Topi, eland, puku and reedbuck can now feed and are able to use the cleared areas. The intensive grazing of these swards keeps the grasses growing and also ensures that the area is always moving towards a grazing climax. Flooding provides for natural recovery.

The manner in which grazing by one species may facilitate use by another has been intensively studied in the Serengeti in Tanzania.[9] In the grasslands along the western border of the plains, the migratory wildbeest convert a senescent grassland into a highly productive com-

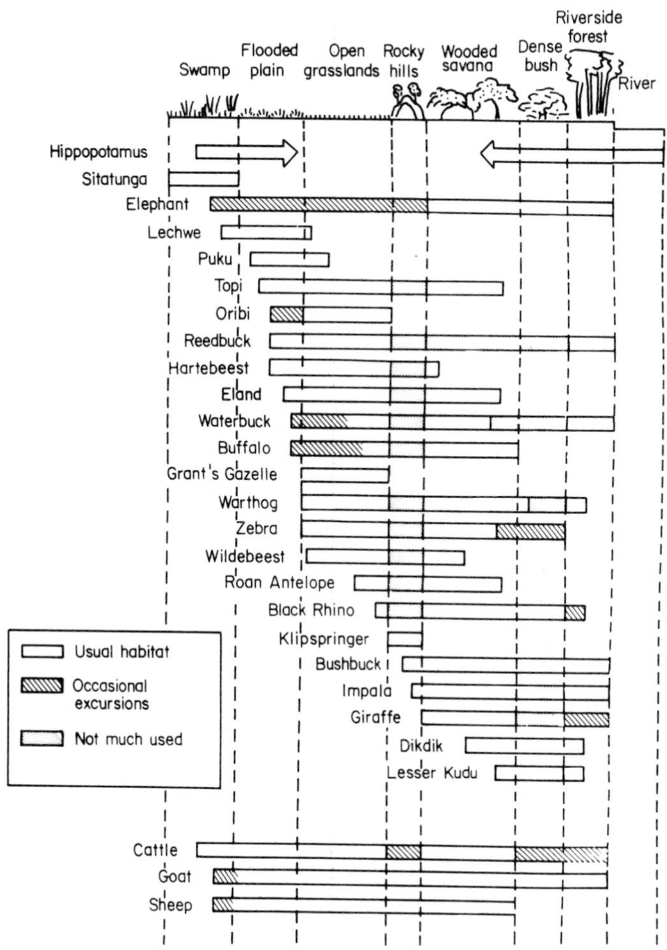

FIG. 4. A diagrammatic representation of the ecological separation and overlap of species of herbivores, both wild and domestic in representative East African habitats.

munity. As the wildebeest pass through the area they have a seemingly devastating effect on the herbiage, reducing its green biomass by 84 per cent. During the following months, however, the grazed areas sustain continuous new growth whilst ungrazed areas show a decline in the biomass of vegetation. The regrowth after grazing is a result of vigorous tillering and it is into these areas that Thompson's gazelles move after leaving the plains to the East. The gazelle could consume significant amounts of foliage in areas previously grazed by wildebeest during the following 30 days, whereas they appeared to take no food from the ungrazed areas. It seems likely that the association between these two species is an important contributory factor to the very high biomass of herbivores that this area of the Serengeti can sustain.

The density of grazing wildebeest is the key operative factor in the productivity of the Serengeti ecological unit as a whole.[10] In recent years there has been a spectacular increase in the density of herbivores. In 1971-1972 the wildebeest numbered about 770 000; in 1977 there were 1 400 000. Buffalo, 65 000 at the former time now number 75 000. Topi numbers have increased two or three fold. The numbers of giraffe have doubled. The major factors in this change are as follows:

1. The populations have been free of rinderpest since 1962 following an extensive vaccination programme amongst domestic cattle in the surrounding areas. The fact that the growth in numbers appears to have been fairly constant at round about 11 per cent per year[11] suggests that several improving factors are at work and that no limiting factor has yet been reached (see Fig 5).
2. Close grazing by the increased density of wildebeest removes excess grass cover and so reduces the incidence of fire. However, this must be seen against the background of
3. a series of good years in which there has been no severe drought and in which primary production has steadily sustained the increasing numbers of herbivores.
4. Wildebeest are tending to improve the productivity of their grazing in the manner described above and this appears to continue provided that rainfall is adequate.

This sequence of events has improved the food available to browsers, particularly the giraffe, by reducing fire damage to acacia and other bushes, by permitting extensive regeneration, and stimulating a regular green flush.

These current increases in the density of herbivores in a particular wildlife area are a compelling example of the potential for population growth that is immediately expressed when limiting factors are relaxed. Prior to this relaxation, and despite endemic rinderpest, the availability of food limited numbers. Clear evidence was found in the very poor body condition of sections of the populations (wildebeest and buffalo in this case). Moreover, theoretical calculations of the metabolizable energy of forage that was available to the community of herbivores showed that it fell short of requirements in the dry season.[12] If a sequence of drought years supervenes now there will undoubtedly be a devastating mortality. To borrow words from Malthus, and considering these classes of animals: " . . . the distresses which they suffer from the want of proper and sufficient food . . . must operate as a constant check to incipient population. And that these are the true causes of the slow increase of population . . . will appear sufficiently evident, from the comparatively rapid increase that has invariably taken place, whenever these causes have been in any considerable degree removed."

Domestic stock and pastoralists

The density of cattle may be considered in relation to rainfall (and presumed pasture production) making use of national livestock surveys that, for Africa, must be based on FAO estimates.[12]

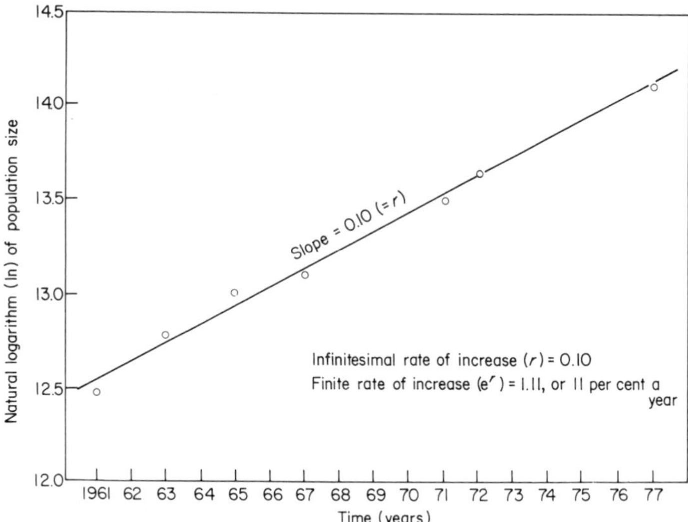

FIG. 5. Population growth of wildebeest in the Serengeti plotted as the natural logarithms of population size against time in years. The average rate of increase is found from the slope of the regression line.

The relationship proves to be similar to that discussed earlier, but the regression line for cattle falls well below that for wildlife biomass. This is to be expected as other domestic species and the density of persistent wildlife should be added to the national cattle densities. In some areas, however, eastern Ethiopia being an example, cattle biomass exceeds the "optimum carrying capacity" by more than 100 per cent. Where tsetse fly is present the cattle densities are severely depressed.

The cattle and small stock managed by pastoralists are often at densities that are at the upper limit of carrying capacity. There are two reasons for this. The terrain may be overstocked and the herbivores are using up the "capital" standing crop of plants by browsing perennials and by destroying woody plants.

The limiting resource in arid environments is water, both that directly available for drinking and that indirectly available through plants. A precarious balance has been achieved by traditional pastoralists and they, like hunter-gatherers, are some of the few human populations in the world to-day that still exhibit a density-dependent adjustment to resources. In minor ways, through management of their stock, pastoralists can extract more from the system than wild herbivores. An example was recorded in aerial counts of herbivores in southern Kenya in relation to distance from water. It was found that within a distance of 5 kilometres of water, wildebeest were at a density of 14 per km^2, cattle 15 and sheep and goat 23 per km^2. Numbers of other species were much lower. Zebra apparently were able to move much further away, but this was rarely the case for wildebeest. The cattle, sheep and goats on the other hand, because they were herded and presumably therefore driven away, were found at higher densities in the range from 5-10 kilometres from water where there were 25 cattle and 9 sheep or goats per km^2.

A further subtle adjustment that maximizes the productivity of cattle is seen in relation for coat colour. Experimental physiological work shows that light-coated cattle suffer less heat stress in the dryer, more arid areas than do dark-coated cattle. On the other hand, dark-coated cattle appear to be in some ways metabolically more efficient, their growth rates may be faster, they do better at higher altitudes where heat stress is less, and they recover faster after falling into poor condition during a drought. There is, therefore, a balance between the colours that is optimal under different conditions of heredity and altitude. These optimal ratios are approximated in the herds owned by the Masai and other pastoralists[13] (see Fig. 2).

The adjustments achieved by pastoralists are extremely sensitive to disturbance. Providing extra boreholes for water, for example, leads to immediate over-grazing of the natural primary production. A similar result is obtained by the ill-considered elimination of tsetse fly, the carriers of trypanosomiasis, that prevent cattle from entering many regions of Africa in which environmental stability is highly fragile. It is these equilibria that should not be disrupted, and man should adopt positive policies to protect them.

Changes in fertility of wild large mammals in response to changing population density

It is well established that when food supplies are inadequate most mammals, including women and men[14], produce fewer offspring. Breeding seasons are strongly accentuated in environments where food supply fluctuates regularly. The very presence of a breeding season, as opposed to aseasonal reproduction, shows that selection of individuals has worked to alleviate the detrimental effects of poor nutrition on the reproductive processes of the population concerned. In consequence there are few documented examples of major malfunctions of reproduction in wild species that can be directly attributed to nutrition.[15] A remarkable contrary circumstance is recorded for the impala antelope. When the Kariba Dam was built in Rhodesia and a lake formed, many small populations of impala were marooned on temporary islands that rapidly ran out of adequate browse. On one such island this culminated in a die-off of impala but even under these unfavourable conditions 93 per cent of adult females had conceived and 75 per cent of yearling females.[16] Despite these observations, a more subtle relationship between food of good quality and fertility has been recorded. In a study of Grant's gazelle, Thomson's gazelle and Coke's hartebeest on a ranch in Kenya, when feeding conditions were good, 98 per cent of a shot sample of females (36 individuals or more of each species) were either pregnant and/or lactating. The gazelles showed a distinct peak of conceptions when the standing crop biomass of the grass/herb layer was highest. The hartebeest showed an incidence of pregnancy of 76 per cent in contrast to an incidence of 50 per cent in females of the same species on the nearby Athi plains where rainfall was lower and the plains were more heavily used by herbivores.[17]

A further circumstance affecting fecundity and fertility in wild mammals is density itself. It has been shown experimentally, using captive rodents, that reproduction stops when density rises greatly, and this in the presence of abundant food. In the wild it is often not possible to dissociate the effect of rising density and falling food availability following from its increased consumption. A reduction of reproductive performance in a population may be expressed as (a) a later age of puberty; (b) a lower incidence of pregnancy in young age-classes of females, and (c) an increased calving interval. It has been only rarely recorded in large wild mammals subjected to nutritional stress that reproduction may cease earlier in an individual's lifetime, that loss of embryos is greater, or that the incidence of sterility is higher.

Examples of sub-maximal reproductive output

Puberty, calving interval, and age-specific pregnancy rate

The elephant provides a well-documented example[18] of response to environmental stress. In five separate populations in East Africa mean ages at puberty for both males and females were 11, 12½, 14, 18 and 20 years. The mean calving interval in female elephants ranged from three to eight years and in the series of populations there was an increasing proportion of inactive adult females. All these functions were correlated with increased environmental deterioration and the elephant is one of the few wild mammals in which a "menopause" has been recorded, and has also been shown to be density- or habitat-dependent. The maximum individual calving interval recorded was 13 years, and attainment of sexual maturity was 34 years. Such an individual might have only two or three offspring in her lifetime with a high probability of one or more of these dying before sexual maturity.

For other species of African large mammals information is not nearly so complete, but statistically valid samples are available for some reproductive functions.

For lechwe *(Kobus leche)* populations in Zambia (11) the mean pregnancy rates in the first mature age group (yearlings in this case) were:

	Pregnancy rate
Rapidly increasing population (captive)	1.00
Increasing population (Bangwenlu)	0.67
Stable population (Kafue flats)	0.36

Similar differences have been recorded in wildebeest[19] but it is uncertain whether the differences would exert much impact on the dynamics of the populations. Very old wildebeest cows have been reported to be not pregnant, but in other studies there have been no signs of reproductive senescence, even in females older than 16 years.

The buffalo is a species that can be sensitive to nutritive conditions because its gestation period is 11 months. When a post-partum interval to next conception is added, individuals can get out of phase with the cycle of the seasons. In Uganda there are two wet periods in the year with corresponding growth of grass. In one population of buffalo in a productive area the mean calving interval was 18 months. In another area of unfavourable coarse grass, the calving interval was 24 months[20].

Finally, in these examples from African mammals, another instance of the perverse failure of nutritional stress to suppress population growth may be given. Populations of the nyala (*Tragelaphus angasi),* in Zululand, have outstripped their food resource by overbrowsing. Under these conditions the larger males, with higher growth rates and metabolic requirements, die off at a proportionately higher rate. The effect is to reduce the male segment of the population, yet enhance the population's capacity for recovery through the better feeding conditions that are created for females.[21]

Summary and conclusions

In this summary I will reverse the order in which topics are presented in this paper. There is good evidence from populations of large mammals to show that nutrition affects reproductive performance. Although population growth is suppressed, however, numbers do not become adjusted to food resources without the intervention of enhanced mortality. But facts presented in the early part of the paper do show that on a very broad scale the density of large herbivores is adjusted to the resource of food.

Animal populations should not be considered in isolation but in an ecological context and in the middle section of this paper I illustrated how different species can share resources by forming a functional community, exhibiting ecological separation and overlap. As early as 1927, Elton emphasized in his classic book on *Animal Ecology*[22] that it is convenient to have some term to describe the status of an animal in its community, to indicate what it is *doing* and the term used was "niche". It was the numerous herbivores, with many other animals dependent upon them, that were denoted as the "key-industry".

Elton was concerned with animals of similar occupations, rather than of similar or separate species, and he drew an analogy between natural communities and human communities. The analogy was explored in real terms by Golley[23] who plotted the number of species (occupations) present in forests against the increasing numbers of individual trees, and also the number of yellow-page entries (occupations) in towns of increasing size (in terms of numbers of people resident) against the town populations. There was a difference in the form of the relationship (regressions) for the two plots; in human communities the diversity of occupations increases more rapidly as numbers of people rise. Perhaps this analogy does no more than emphasize our increasing divergence from the fundamental activity of food production. It seems questionable whether this diversity leads to stability, as it does in natural communities of animals and plants.

Notes

1. D. Morris (1967). *The Naked Ape*. Cape, London.
2. R. Ardrey (1966). *The Territorial Imperative*. Atheneum, New York.
3. E. O. Wilson (1975). *Sociobiology, the New Synthesis*. Harvard University Press, Cambridge, USA.
4. A. R. E. Sinclair (1977). *The African Buffalo*. University of Chicago Press, Chicago.
5. M. J. Coe, D. H. Cumming and J. Phillipson (1976). Biomass and production of large African herbivores in relation to rainfall and primary production. *Oecologia (Berl.)* **22**, 341–354.
6. H. F. Lamprey (1963). Ecological separation of the large mammal species in the Tarangire game reserve, Tanganyika. *East African Wildlife Journal* **1**, 63–92.
7. B. H. Walker (1980). Ecology and management of Savanna ecosystems in South-Central Africa. In *Human Ecology in Savanna Environments* (Ed. D. R. Harris). Academic Press, London and New York.
8. D. F. Vesey-Fitzgerald (1960), Grazing succession among East African game animals. *J. Mammal* **41**, 161–172.
9. S. J. McNaughton (1976). Serengeti migratory wildebeest: Facilitation of energy flow by grazing. *Science* **191,** 92–94.
10. P. A. Jewell (1980). Ecology and management of game animals and domestic livestock in African savannas. In *Human Ecology in Savanna Environment* (Ed. D. R. Harris). Academic Press, London and New York.
11. J. J. R. Grimsdell (1978). *Ecological Monitoring Handbook No. 4*. African Wildlife Leadership Foundation, Nairobi, Kenya.
12. D. Bourn (1978). Cattle, rainfall and Tsetse in Africa. *Journal of Arid Environment* **1**, 49–61.
13. Virginia Finch and D. Western (1977). Cattle colour in pastoral herds: Natural selection or social preference?. *Ecology* **58**, 1384–1392.
14. Rose E. Frisch. Population, nutrition and fecundity. This volume, pp.393–404.
15. R. M. F. S. Sadlier (1969). The role of nutrition in the reproduction of wild mammals, *Journal of Reproduction and Fertility*, Suppl. **6**, 39–48.
16. G. Child (1968). *Kariba Studies*. National Museums of Rhodesia.
17. C. R. Field and L. H. Blankenship (1973). Nutrition and reproduction of Grant's and Thomson's gazelles, Coke's hartebeest and giraffe in Kenya.

Journal of Reproduction and Fertility, Suppl. **19**, 287-301.
18. R. M. Laws, L. S. C. Parker and R. C. B. Johnstone (1975). *Elephants and their Habitats*. Clarendon Press, Oxford.
19. C. A. M. Attwell (1977). Reproduction and population ecology of the blue wildebeest *Connochaetes Taurinus Taurinus* in Zululand. Ph.D. thesis, University of Natal, Pietermaritzburg.
20. J. J. R. Grimsdell (1973). Reproduction in the African buffalo, *Syncerus Caffer*, in Western Uganda. *Journal of Reproduction and Fertility*, Suppl. **19**, 303–310.
21. J. L. Anderson (1978). Aspects of the Ecology of Nyala. Ph.D. thesis, London University.
22. C. Elton (1927). *Animal Ecology*. Sidgwick & Jackson, London.
23. F. B. Golley (1966). The variety of occupations in human communities compared with the variety of species in natural communities. *Bulletin of the Georgia Academy of Sciences* **24** (i), 5pp.

28 Self-regulation in Populations of Red Grouse, *Lagopus l. scoticus (Aves-Galliformes)*

V. C. WYNNE-EDWARDS

1. A hypothesis under test

Thomas Malthus rightly surmised that in the absence of other effective checks, populations of living organisms must in the end be limited by the space and nourishment available. He was, however, wrong in assuming that there is a constant tendency for "all animated life" to increase beyond that limit. During the last 50 years it has become clear that there are many kinds of animals, including top predators, which could, if their numbers were to increase freely, overexploit their food resources and harm the renewal of future crops, or perhaps even exterminate the food producers altogether. At the same time the evidence has grown, much of it by experiment, that animals can often effect a self-regulation of their populations by influencing their natality, emigration and mortality rates. Contemporary man stands in conspicuous contrast to most animals in not having effective adaptations for curbing population growth.

In 1962 I published an hypothesis[1] that the population regulation of animals is normally a homeostatic process; it depends on automated programs of the brain which cause changes in their physiology and behaviour; these in turn result in adjusting the population density, keeping it as nearly as possible in parallel with alterations in food supplies which may occur from time to time and place to place. The basic programs are genetically coded, but they can be modulated by feedback from the outside world regarding the current availability of food, the individuals' nutritional condition, and the nature and conse-

MALTHUS PAST AND PRESENT
ISBN 0-12-224670-5

quences of their interactions with other individuals. The brain then adjusts their reproductive activities or their competitiveness towards their associates, as appropriate.

Competition with conspecifics had a central place in the hypothesis. In the first place the intensity of such competition is density-dependent and provides a reliable feedback index to the participants. Contests between animal rivals tend to be formalized and conducted according to conventions which decree threat and display, rather than fighting and bloodshed. The goals for which the rivals compete are also conventionalized; they are essentially qualifications that will give the winners a right to citizenship, feeding or reproduction. The qualifications can be concrete like territories or other exclusive sites and possessions, or abstract, determining personal status, and deciding who is to rank above whom and win privilege from it. Very often both kinds of goal merge together.

The hypothesis predicted that these goals have been interposed as substitutes or tokens, by means of which the population density can be manipulated and the demand for food controlled, in order to shield the resources from pressure and at the same time maintain an adequate standard of living for all members that have obtained the right to it. If individuals are programmed to regard winning a territory as the only way of gaining a place in the habitat or breeding, it is clearly possible to put an artificial limit to the number that qualify per unit area. Provided their programs direct them to take territories that are ample in terms of the food resources they contain, the actual means of subsistence can be conserved indefinitely, barring catastrophes. When there is not enough room for all the candidates to win a place, the losers are simply excluded. Varying the reproductive rate and the exclusion rate thus take over as the main executive mechanisms for achieving homeostasis.

The most surprising concept in the hypothesis was the conclusion that this world of artificial aspirations, of formal competition for qualifications of property and rank, by which individuals are coerced into conserving the means of subsistence, is the original social world and reveals the primary zoological purpose of social life.

2. The red-grouse research project

The functional aspects of population homeostasis are open to direct investigation, and within a year of the hypothesis being conceived in 1955 two research projects had been started. The more successful, on the red grouse, was initiated in 1956 and is still in progress. It has been grant-aided from public funds since 1959, first by the Nature Conservancy and afterwards by the Natural Environment Research Council.

The red grouse is a well-known and economically valuable game-bird in Scotland. It is a sub-species of the circumpolar willow grouse, *Lagopus lagopus,* but differs conspicuously from the other sub-species by having no white plumage at any season. It inhabits moorlands dominated by ling heather, *Calluna vulgaris,* which are very extensive in Scotland, especially in the eastern highlands. The moors are mostly between 300 and 1000 m above sea-level, and are almost entirely treeless. The Callunetum forms a small-shrub heath, with vegetation 10 to 30 cm deep. Red grouse are large birds, normally weighing 0.6 to 0.7 kg; they are often noisy and can easily be made to fly by a well-spaced line of men and gundogs moving across the heather. The research study areas have been chosen for their topography, which has to be fairly smooth and slightly saucer-shaped, so that the grouse seldom fly out of sight and can thus be accurately counted. The birds are large enough to carry numbered tags on their backs, like footballers, or else small radio-transmitters. From 1963 onwards the research team have had a 3000-ha moor under their own control, on which there has been no shooting, except for experimental purposes. The team have also facilities for keeping small groups of birds in captivity.

Red grouse are almost entirely herbivorous like all the Galliformes; over 90 per cent of their food is *Calluna.* They are selective feeders, picking off just the young shoots and buds which are the only parts containing enough protein; but the amount of cellulose and lignin they have to digest at the same time assures them of abundant metabolizable energy. *Calluna* is an evergreen and has a growing season from April to September; thus the winter food of the grouse is a dormant standing crop.

3. The territorial system

The species of *Lagopus* are all typical territorial birds. Each October the cock red grouse compete to obtain individual territories on which to live through the winter and spring, and breed in early summer. They display to the neighbouring cocks in short ritual flights and on the ground, erecting the brilliant scarlet combs above their eyes and making loud aggressive calls. They also move about and confront and chase one another. Each tries to win and hold his chosen piece of ground; but in an average year fewer than half of them are successful. The winners divide up the habitat, and occupy it in an almost continuous mosaic. The losers have no place to call their own because the same process is taking place on every moor; so that eventually they become outcasts. The hens do not compete, but the successful cocks admit a quota of them as future consorts to share the habitat with them, and they reject the rest. This means that the population becomes sharply divided into haves and have-nots, an establishment and a surplus.

For the next two months or more the surplus birds are tolerated fairly well by the establishment provided they stay hidden for an hour or two at dawn while the established cocks are going through their daily routine of territorial display and defence. Later in the day the outcasts are allowed to feed, more or less unmolested. But as the winter progresses hostility against them intensifies until it lasts all day, and they get so frequently challenged and moved on by territory owners that they have not time to select their food adequately and their weight and condition decline. They lack security and fall easy victims to foxes and raptorial birds. An early investigation showed that winter deaths from predation were nine times as heavy on outcasts as on established birds[2]. Other outcasts succumb to malnutrition, and by April all but a small remnant are dead.

The majority of territory owners retain their holdings through the winter, but there is some slight mortality among them which is generally made good by replacing each of the individuals that goes missing by the best-preserved outcast locally available. Replacement happens within a few days in the late autumn when there are still plenty of fairly healthy outcasts, but it can take some weeks in the early spring. The cocks and hens form pair-bonds some time between February and April, and nesting takes place on the territory in May. The young hatch out in late May or early June. As soon as they do so the territorial system disintegrates, and the parents appear free to lead the chicks away in any direction. Most of the infantile mortality occurs during the first 15 days; the young that survive this period make rapid growth. Family groups break up in August and the parent cocks that have finished moulting may resume their customary dawn displays on their old territories.

The young are by this time fast approaching adulthood and are beginning to prospect for possible territory sites. Their acquisitive activity is likewise confined to the mornings, after which they may wander at large alone or in flocks for the rest of the day. Evidence from telemetry suggests that they prefer to get as close as possible to the site where they were hatched. For example, of two young brothers that were fitted with transmitters one clearly dominated the other, but they both finished up by winning territories next to each other, the dominant one actually occupying most of his father's former holding plus some additional ground. Consolidating the territory appears to be a gradual process, and it was not till 4 November that this dominant young cock actually ousted his father, who was never seen again and presumably became an outcast.[3] That date coincides with the time when the heavy winter mortality of outcasts normally begins. The bumper months of heather growth and superabundant food are, of course, over, and shorter days are forcing the established birds to become still more selective in their diet. They probably need the exclusive use of their feeding territories, and it could be this that finally precipitates the fixing of the boundaries.

The astonishing result of this protracted contest is that, on the average, over half the August adults are not only excluded from membership of the next season's breeding stock but condemned to die from starvation, predators or disease during the winter. The grouse by their concerted actions thus determine both what the density of potential breeders per square kilometre shall be, and which individuals are to live and which to die in achieving it. As far as we know, the annual homeostatic adjustment depends wholly on the established males. How they select which females are to share the habitat with them and which are to be expelled is not known, but it must entail their individual recognition, and presumably selection, by the local males. During the next four to five months the favoured hens can be described as candidates elect; they form temporary associations with particular males but their final pair-bonds remain in the balance, possibly awaiting a reassessment of the food supply when the worst of the winter has passed. The established quota of females is usually a little smaller than that of the males and eventually leaves some males unmated in the breeding season; but in years when the food supply is exceptionally good the sex ratio can swing the other way, and a few cocks are found to have two mates.

The exclusion process is, by my definition, essentially social, because it is mediated by the participants themselves through conventional competition. It throws an unexpected sidelight on the classical checks to population increase as recognized by Malthus and after him by Darwin. In the vast majority of deaths, as far as adult grouse are concerned, starvation, predators and disease are acting just as secondary agents, usefully mopping up an unwanted surplus offered to them by the social system.

A few of the outcasts escape their death sentence by filling accidental gaps left by casualties in the establishment. Experimental shooting of territorial birds between the late autumn and the spring, even when a sample area has been completely cleared, is followed by re-colonization at the same density as before, as long as there are outcasts around capable of taking the territories over. But establishment on a territory is virtually the only route to survival.

4. Population density varies with food supply

The quality and quantity of the new growth produced by the heather varies from year to year and also from place to place, and as a result a greater density of grouse can be safely sustained in some years or places than others. Population homeostasis results in adjusting the density accordingly. The territories taken by individual cocks vary much in size even in the same year and place. Some cocks rank higher or are more aggressive than others; and those nearer the bottom of the scale which barely managed to win a place in the establishment at all may be left defending a holding of barely viable size. Some high-ranking cocks win especially favoured sites, rich in good food and good cover, and they do not, therefore, need to hold enormously large areas; and again the boundaries of some territories are found to conform in part with natural features which are adopted to separate them from their neighbours. Territory area is consequently somewhat loosely correlated with individual status.

The experiment has been made of implanting a small pellet of male sex-hormone beneath the skin of a territorial cock in the spring, and it resulted in his expanding his territory by 75 per cent at the expense of his weakest neighbours.

When the same was done at the same season to an outcast cock he forced his way into the establishment and survived until the summer, but his territory was small and he did not breed.[4]

It is possible by watching the interactions of individually marked cocks for many hours and weeks to map the approximate boundaries of territories over an area as large as 50 ha. Either by this method or by the much simpler alternative of counting the established cocks per unit area the average territory size for the given sample area and year can be found. If this is repeated on the same study areas for a number of years the average is found to go up and down by a factor of two or three times and occasionally more. Grouse moors in the eastern highlands of Scotland generally carry individual territories varying from less than one to more than five ha; the averages mostly fall between two and four ha.

A climatic event of some severity occurred soon after the research began and gave the first clue to the cause of the annual and local variations. There was a long spell of bright cold weather during th months of 1958, when large expanses of the *Callunetum,* unprotect the usual blanket of snow, were exposed on south-facing slopes to sun each day; the heather leaves transpired but the roots were locked in frozen soil and could not replace the moisture lost. The result was a major die-back which greatly reduced the amount of new growth produced in the summer that followed. When October came the cock grouse took territories about twice the size they had held the previous year, making room for only half as many birds to establish themselves. It looked like cause and effect, as if the birds were going to need larger territories if they were to obtain the usual amount of good-quality food, and at the same time avoid doing further damage by overexploiting the heather that had survived the frost.

There was another similar pointer. One of the study areas consistently held higher grouse numbers than any of the surrounding moors; and the heather there was growing in soil derived from a basic bedrock whereas the soil on other moors was acid. Biochemical tests showed that the heather from the base-rich soil contained 25 per cent more nitrogen and 36 per cent more phosphorus than heather samples from the acid soils.

This suggested the possibility of inducing a change in grouse numbers experimentally by applying an agricultural fertilizer to the moor to upgrade the food-value of the heather. It would be necessary to work on a large scale so that the experimental ground would carry a big enough sample of territories to yield a significant result. After a series of pilot trials the first experiment was started in 1965 on a particularly uniform 32-ha expanse of moor, half of which was treated with calcium-ammonium nitrate and half left untreated as a control. The outcome was that 18 months later the grouse established on the treated area had risen from 7 to 17 territories, whereas there were still only seven on the control.[5] Other similar experiments showed that the enriched heather becomes so attractive to herbivores of all kinds that unless the fertilized ground is enclosed by a fence the *Callunetum* is likely to be demolished by domestic sheep and cattle and the grouse actually driven away.

The fertilizer experiments demonstrated beyond doubt that a strong correlation normally exists in the red grouse between population density and food supply. The four main postulates of the initial hypothesis have thus all been confirmed, namely (i) that the density is controlled from within by the members of the population themselves, (ii) that they do it by competing conventionally for "artificial" territories, (iii) that these are substitutes for the means of subsistence they represent, and can be made to vary in size by varying the plane of nutrition available, and (iv) that the territorial system expels the population surplus which is normally present each autumn as a result of reproduction.

5. Reproduction

Nutrition during the months of March to May is crucial to the subsequent success of reproduction. The hens need to build up their body-weight in advance and the food supply often sets a limit to how far this preconditioning is realized. They start increasing their food intake in March and at the same time reduce the food-particle size, presumably because they are selecting for a still higher protein content. Much depends on whether the spring comes early or late and how soon the heather resumes its growth and thus augments the food supply. By the time the hens are laying eggs in May their food consumption reaches twice the normal, requiring some 30 000 pecks a day.[6]

How much food there is in March and April depends on antecedent events — on the biomass of new shoots produced the previous summer, on how much of it has since been eaten by the primary consumers (including grouse), and how much destroyed by the weather. The hen's reserves and daily diet in May decide when she can lay the first egg, how many she will lay and how viable the eggs will be. As a result of collecting first clutches of eggs from wild birds in order to hatch and rear them in captivity the unexpected fact emerged that the perinatal mortality rate in the incubator and brooder-pen closely parallels the rate in the wild on the moor. In other words, eggs vary in quality or viability, as a result of variation in the mother's nutritional condition. In years of good spring feeding, therefore, the breeding success tends to be good and vice versa.

The measurement of breeding success that has been adopted is the ratio of young birds to old birds in August, at the time the young are reaching their full size; and in a sample run of five years on two adjacent moors the "young-to-old ratios" varied between 0.7 and 2.4 to 1, with an average of 1.5 to 1. Over many years and with many study areas counted each year there has never failed to be a surplus of grouse to evict by the time the October-November contest comes round.

Factors other than nutrition of females also influence the number of viable recruits produced. A primary factor is obviously the density of breeders per square kilometre. Then, as has already been stated, some established males only obtain small territories, and although the owners survive the winter they fail to mate. This may be because in

March and April when the food resource is under the greatest stress there would not be enough food on a small territory to meet the requirements of two birds. The cock also increases his food intake then, at the same time as the hen. These smallholder cocks simply fail to mate at the usual time, though not for want of available hens, as has been confirmed many times. The probability that matelessness is correlated with the food supply is supported by the fact that in years of poor spring feeding the sex-ratio in the breeding population may swing, as stated earlier, as far as 1.4 cocks per hen, whereas when the spring feeding is well above average the ratio tends to go the other way, e.g. 0.9:1, because some of the dominant cocks have accepted two mates.

There are years when soon after the eggs hatch the adults lead their broods away to a considerable distance — how far has not been ascertained. The male parents mostly return quite soon, but not all the adult females come back and still fewer of the young. In August, among large samples of grouse shot by hunters, males may again predominate, but whether this and the emigration of hens and young are connected is not known.

Whatever the existing density of the breeding population has been in our region, they have been able to produce an autumn surplus. (There is one exception, where the young have been afflicted with an introduced tick-borne disease.) The ratios of young to old birds tend to reflect the current state of the food resource and so does the size of the surplus. A possible limiting condition against maximizing the production of young would be that the peak number of full-sized birds in the late summer should not overtax the production of food nor leave a depleted standing crop for those that have to depend on it in the winter. There is evidence that the exodus of broods of chicks, just mentioned, is strongest in summers that precede a population decline, that is, when the food resource is waning and the probability of becoming established on one's own native heath is likely to be below average. From an evolutionary point of view the export of emigrants that establish themselves elsewhere is a constructive event; but most grouse in most year-groups are in fact remarkably sedentary, the males even more so than the females.[7]

6. Discussion and conclusion

The investigations briefly summarized here were publicly supported for the improvement of game management, but were designed equally for testing the "animal dispersion" hypothesis. Both needed an answer to the same question: What determines the numbers of grouse? That the research has got so far in finding the answer owes most to the skill and perseverance of the research team, some of whom have shared in it for more than 20 years. But a factor second only to that is the unusual simplicity of red-grouse ecology, above all in the birds' rapid maturation and short lifespan, their normal sedentariness and their virtually monophagous plant diet.

During the last ten years or so a new sequence of events has taken place, which cannot yet be fully accounted for. It was a strong fluctuation in numbers on the best known of all the study areas, where the population built up for four successive years to reach unprecedented densities and then declined for another four to the opposite extreme. It appears not to have been wholly due to variations in quality and quantity of food, though in retrospect one must regret that the monitoring routines of the earlier nutrition-study period had by then been relaxed. It produced other unprecedented maxima, in emigration rates, failure of cocks to mate, and winter losses among the establishment. Taken as a whole it suggests that the model of grouse population dynamics built up over the previous 15 years was too simple, although it was valid as far as it went. One must look to the future for an explanation.

We have seen the main predictions of the hypothesis all confirmed. Population density is at all times (including the recent fluctuation) regulated by social interaction, and in the red grouse specifically by the males: the females merely comply. The regulatory machinery depends on conventional competition for individual territories, once a year, and as a general rule the territories have been shown to be correlated inversely in size with the amount of protein food per unit area. The correlation is generally demonstrable in the field and has been verified by experiment. The territories fill the habitat with the result that surplus birds, unable to find room to establish themselves, are squeezed out. Thus, a quota of breeders are installed each autumn for the ensuing breeding season. The surplus is very large, on the average bigger than the breeding quota, and most of its members die.

The number of young produced per unit area is also related to the state of the food supply, but it is never so great as to exceed the expected summer carrying capacity of the Callunetum; and there has never been any indication, summer or winter, that the food resource has been damaged by the grouse through overexploitation. Describing the control as homeostatic seems justified because normally, at any rate, it matches the autumn density against the standing winter crop.

There are four inferences or conclusions that seem of particular relevance in the context of Malthus' *Essay*. The first is that control systems of this type are not confined to the red grouse. Their characteristic component parts are widely recognizable in the animal kingdom. In the simpler invertebrates they tend to be less obvious, whereas in the arthropods and vertebrates they are often conspicuous. This suggests that population homeostasis is a very old phenomenon and that it has been progressively developed by evolution. Many populations, especially of smaller and more prolific animals, are in practice held in check by predation much of the time, but most of them probably have homeostatic adaptations to call into play when predation fails to suffice. Some species that would appear to be perpetually checked by predation have been shown in fact to use homeostatic programs to vary their productivity, according to whether predation is heavy or light. The classical Darwinian checks on population increase — starvation, predation, disease and climate — are no doubt often largely secondary killers, as they are in the red grouse.

All animals including carnivores derive their supplies of energy, and the materials from which proteins are made, from the primary production of plants. Many are capable of overexploiting their food sources, meaning that by consuming too much they can harm the renewal of future crops. To these species population homeostasis must be a paramount advantage, giving them the only reliable kind of insurance that future food supplies will be sustained. Even animals that consume non-living foods, such as nectar, carrion and detritus, can benefit by replacing a free-for-all scramble for food by an assured and apportioned right to it.

In the grouse the exclusion of the surplus results from a competitive process in which one individual confronts and dominates another. Each of them makes a perceptive judgement of how the other one rates, compared with himself, and, usually without needing physical contact or a trial of strength, decides whether he wins or loses. What each discerns in the other must have a genetic component and social competition must consequently make a large contribution to the total sum of natural selection. In the red grouse it eliminates, on the average, over half the autumn population. Each is judged as a whole individual and, taking the population at large, the genotypes of winners and losers are both likely to vary widely in their make-up.

This is of course the special kind of self-imposed selection on which the evolution of personal adornments depends and which Darwin called sexual selection. It applies to male versus male and female versus female as much as to the choice of mates of one sex by the other. Ideally it should be eugenic, so that success fell to those with the highest qualities of survivorship against dangers of every kind, and less dependable genotypes were eliminated; and perhaps in the course of time these have become the qualities that inspire awe in rivals and ardour in suitors.

It will be recalled that population homeostasis must depend on innate programs in the central nervous system which are capable of being modified by sensory inputs and operate through endocrine and behavioural channels. Acquiring homeostasis has made it necessary for the object of rivalry among competitors to be diverted away from winning the limiting raw materials themselves towards artificially contrived, limiting qualifications instead. Thus, rights to citizenship, food and reproduction have come to accrue to individuals which compete successfully for property and rank. For this reason it seems inappropriate to regard plants and microbes as being social, for they still compete directly for the means of subsistence, which in general they are in no danger of destroying by overexploitation. They have no need of sociality.

This leads us to the point of being able to assign a primary zoological function to sociality: that it is a necessary condition for the transfer of objectives just described and so achieving a homeostatic regime. Accordingly one could define a society biologically as "an oganization capable of providing conventional competition between its members". If this is valid it fills a large gap since there is no other even tentative explanation.

Finally, the palaeolithic peoples who survived into the scientific era all appear to have possessed some kind of homeostatic mechanisms, though their controls depended on the exercise of traditional rules that governed marriage, conception and perinatal mortality.[8] The innate brain programs and physiological controls of their pre-human ancestors must have gone much earlier, as part of the release from automation that accompanied the evolution of the cerebral cortex and rational thought. Man appears simply to have dropped his traditions of homeostatic behaviour, once the neolithic agricultural revolution had made denser populations both sustainable and advantageous. Now, just a few millennia later, we begin to realize how transient and deceptive such presumptions were.

Notes

1. V. C. Wynne-Edwards (1962). *Animal Dispersion in Relation to Social Behaviour.* Oliver & Boyd, Edinburgh and London.

2. D. Jenkins, A. Watson and G. R. Miller (1963). Population studies on the red grouse, *Lagopus lagopus scoticus* (Lath.) in north-east Scotland. *Journal of Animal Ecology* **32**, 317–376.
3. A. N. Lance (1978). Survival and recruitment success of individual young *cock red grouse Lagopus l. scoticus* tracked by radio-telemetry. *Ibis* **120**, 369–378.
4. A. Watson (1970). Territorial and reproductive behaviour in the red grouse. *Journal of Reproduction Fertility,* Suppl. **11,** 3–14.
5. G. R. Miller, A. Watson and D. Jenkins (1970). Response of red grouse populations to experimental improvement of their food. In *Animal Populations in Relation to their Food Resources* (Ed. A. Watson), pp.323–335. British Ecological Society, Symposium number 10. Blackwell, Oxford and Edinburgh.
6. C. J. Savory (1978). Food consumption of red grouse in relation to the age and productivity of heather. *Journal of Animal Ecology*, **47**, 269–282.
7. D. Jenkins, A. Watson and G. R. Miller (1967). Population fluctuations in the red grouse *Lagopus lagopus scoticus. Journal of Animal Ecology* **36,** 97–122, from which most of this information is derived.
8. A. M. Carr-Saunders (1922). *The Population Problem.* Clarendon Press, Oxford.

29 Population, Nutrition and Fecundity

ROSE E. FRISCH

The number of live births that a married couple produce during the course of their entire reproductive lives (the total fertility ratio) is a valuable supplement to the crude birth rate because it provides an insight into the many biological and social factors which can affect fertility (Fig. 1). This is particularly true for developing countries, where the total fertility ratio at different socio-economic levels could be expected to differ: it may be as low as two or three births in the higher socio-economic groups whose members tend to practise efficient contraception, and as high as six or seven live births in the lower socio-economic groups. However, even the higher values are still well below the maximum of 11 to 12 live births found in well nourished, non-contracepting populations, such as the Hutterites[1] (see Figs 1 and 2).

The total fertility ratio may be below the theoretically possible maximum for a number of reasons. The fecundity of females or males may be below the maximum. The level of reproductive capacity may vary from zero to 100 per cent in response to ordinary environmental factors, such as the quality and quantity of food, the presence of chronic or acute disease, physical work and altitude, and by intrinsic factors such as age (Fig. 1). Alternatively, only a small number of children may be desired. Differences in the desired number of children may be influenced by their value, the cost of children, religious beliefs, by the level of mortality in infancy up to the fifth birthday and/or perceived reproductive capacity. Thirdly, social customs, such as a taboo on intercourse during lactation or visits of the wife to her parental home may decrease the risk of conception. Age at marriage may affect the frequency of intercourse and, therefore, the risk of concep-

MALTHUS PAST AND PRESENT
ISBN 0-12-224670-5

tion. A late age at marriage is also associated with declining fecundity (Fig. 2). In developing countries, women marry at relatively young ages, so this last factor is not usually a limiting one in the lower socio-economic groups.

Each of the factors listed above, may be limiting the total fertility ratio either singly or in combination (Fig. 1). The effects of socio-economic factors have been demonstrated and discussed by many

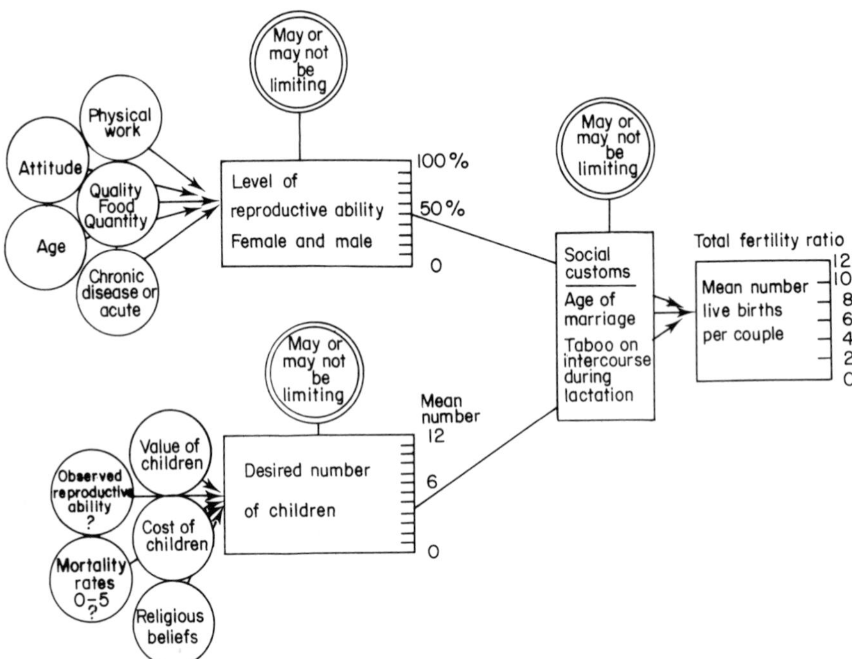

FIG. 1. The mean number of live births per couple (total fertility ratio) may be influenced by the (1) level of reproductive capacity and (2) the desired number of children. Each of these may, in turn, be influenced by many other factors, nutritional factors, age or the value of children. Each of the major factors may be limiting; alone or together, or in interaction with social customs such as age at marriage. Social customs, too, may or may not be limiting. The reproductive capacity of well-nourished couples may be 100 per cent, and yet they may only have two children because that is the number they desire and they use contraception efficiently. The total fertility ratio of poorly nourished couples may be about five children, as is found among Bush people of the Kalahari desert; however, the number of children they desire is greater than five. The Bush people say: "God is stingy with children" (cf. N. Howell (1979). *The Bush People*. Academic Press, London and New York). The main limiting factor for Bush women may be a reduced level of reproductive capacity resulting from under-nutrition and high levels of physical activity.

authors.[2] In this paper, we shall focus attention on the possible limiting effects of the biological factors on the mean number of births of a couple during their whole reproductive lives.

The average number of births to poorer couples in many developing countries is today about six or seven,[3] and this is similar to that observed in the past for poor couples in countries which are now developed.[4] As a result of the improvement in mortality following the introduction of public health measures in developing countries, an average family size of six or seven children per couple results in a very rapid rate of population growth.

Nutrition and natural fertility

It has long been recognized that natural fertility differs in different populations[5] and explanations for this phenomenon have been given in terms of differences in general health and food intake, without the mechanism which results in different fertility being specified.[6] Mauldin cited the findings of Mahalanobis and others which suggested that at certain periods of Indian history, low fertility may have been due to

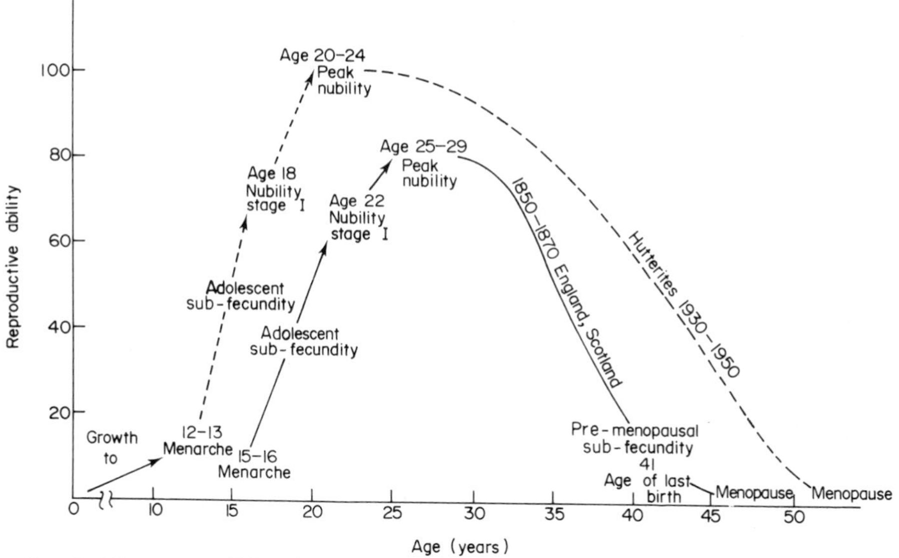

FIG. 2. The curve of female "procreative power" (variation of the rate of child-bearing with age) during the middle of the nineteenth century, compared with that of the well-nourished non-contracepting Hutterites. Hutterite fertility results in an average of 10 to 12 children per couple; the fertility curve for 1850–1870 in about six to eight children. (Reprinted, with permission, from *Science*, **199**, 1978).

impaired fecundity resulting from low levels of consumption.[7] Gopalan and Naidu related malnutrition to relatively low fertility in India.[8] Chen *et al.* showed in a prospective study that in that essentially non-contracepting population, fertility in Bangladesh was correlated with the food supply.[9] Similarly, Wilmsen has reported that seasonal variations in births among the Kalahari Sen were correlated with seasonal changes in dietary intake.[10]

I have suggested a possible mechanism which would explain variations in natural fertility in terms of the effects of environmental factors, and especially nutrition, on the age at menarche and at menopause and on the efficiency of reproductive events during the life cycle.[11] Historical data relating to nutrition, growth, age-specific fertility rates and the age at which reproductive events occur show that slow growth to maturity of women and men, caused by undernutrition, hard work and disease is correlated with a shorter and less efficient reproductive life span compared with that of a well-nourished population (Fig. 2). Women and men who have been under nourished can be identified by a later age at completion of growth (20-21 and 23-25 years respectively), compared with that of contemporary well-nourished members of the same sex, who complete their growth at ages between 16 and 18 and 20 and 21 years respectively.[12]

Historical data for these slower-growing women also show that, compared with well-nourished women, they have children at longer intervals, reach menarche later and menopause earlier and that the incidence of relative and absolute sterility among them is higher. It is suggested that undernutrition and "hard living" may have been the entire or partial explanation of fertility below the maximum in English and Scottish populations during the middle of the nineteenth century.[13]

A shorter and less efficient reproductive pattern has also been observed among the poorer populations of many developing countries when data on age at menarche,[14] age at menopause[15] and length of birth intervals[16] and pregnancy wastage[17] are available. Some of the principal biological factors are considered below. The discussion is necessarily brief and no account is taken of the interaction between these factors and social factors, or mortality, although the importance of the latter factors is recognized.

Undernutrition and adult reproductive function

Data relating to both normal and anorexic women show that a loss of body weight of 10 to 15 per cent below the normal weight for height which represents a loss of about one-third of body fat, results in amenorrhoea.[18] Data for obese women show that excessive fatness, too, can cause amenorrhoea. Too little or too much fat is, therefore, associated with the cessation of reproductive function in the human female.[19]

A weight loss of between 10 and 15 per cent, which results in nutritional secondary amenorrhoea in normal women does not amount to starvation; many ballet dancers, runners and models maintain themselves at this level.[20] Fluctuating weight gain and loss around the minimum weight for height results in irregular cycles.[21] Nutritional amenorrhoea differs from post partum amenorrhoea, as will be shown in detail below.

It should be noted that other factors, such as emotional stress, can also affect the maintenance or onset of menstruation. Menstruation may cease without weight loss and may not resume in some women, even though the minimum required weight is attained.[22]

Male reproductive capacity, too, is affected by a decrease in calorific intake and subsequent weight loss. Healthy male volunteers who reduced their calorific intake by 50 per cent over a period of six months, first experienced loss of libido, then a decrease of prostate fluid and later a decrease in the mobility, motility and longevity of sperm. The

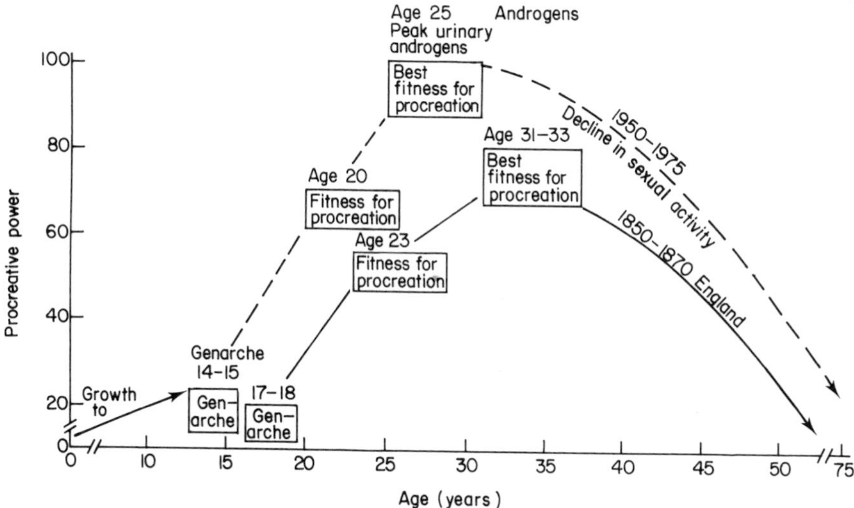

FIG. 3. Hypothetical curve of male reproductive capacity for modern males, and males during the period 1850–1870, based on ages of peak height velocity, completion of height growth and hormonal data for modern males and the relation to ages at menarche of the female in Fig. 2. (Reprinted, with permission, from *Science*, **199**, 1978.)

most severe effects were associated with a weight loss in the range of 25 per cent of normal weight for height?[23] Undernutrition also delays the onset of sexual maturation in boys,[24] as it does in girls.[25]

The fecundity of both men and women falls with increasing age (Figs 2 and 3). The decline in men may be more rapid with undernutrition, as is found for women.[26]

Nutrition, age at menarche and menopause and biological consistency

During the last century the age at menarche has fallen by about three to four months per decade.[27] The average age at menarche of girls in the United States is now about 12.6 years. In 1900 it was about 14 years. In 1850, in Britain, the figure was about 15 to 16 years and varied with socio-economic status, richer girls experiencing menarche earlier.[28]

Menarche normally occurs after a period of rapid weight gain during the adolescent growth spurt. Since it is associated with the attainment of a minimum weight for height apparently representing a critical fat/lean ratio, factors which slow the rate of growth also delay menarche. Such factors are: undernutrition, high altitude, hard physical work, disease, twinning (twins usually grow more slowly than singletons).[29] Norwegian statistics on changes in age at menarche between 1830 and 1930 show that class differences in age have tended to disappear as menarche began to occur earlier. This would be expected as diet and modes of living in the different social classes became more equal.

The well-established relationship between undernutrition, altitude or disease and the delay of menarche would have little demographic significance in populations where girls marry at the age of 16 years or older,[30] if it were merely an isolated reproductive phenomenon. However, historical data and information from contemporary undernourished populations show that this is not an isolated event. A later age at menarche *in a population* is usually associated with a longer period of adolescent sterility, a higher frequency of nutritional amenorrhoea when food supplies are marginal, more pregnancy wastage,[31] a longer period of pre-menopausal sub-fecundity and an earlier age at menopause, e.g. 45-47 years against 50-51 years for women in well-nourished societies.[32]

The secular change in age at menopause, about three years, is about the same as the change in age at menarche during the last hundred years. The change is less marked for age at menopause, however, since it amounts to only about six per cent, compared with a change of between 20 and 25 per cent for age at menarche. In historical populations, where this type of biological profile is found, the maximum of the age-specific fertility distribution also occurs later and is at a lower level than is well-nourished societies[33] (Fig.2).

Post partum amenorrhoea. Factors affecting the resumption of menstruation after parturition

After the birth of a live child, the period of post partum amenorrhoea of a lactating, undernourished woman is longer to a varying degree which depends on other interacting factors than that of a lactating well-nourished woman.[34] Lactational amenorrhoea is endocrinologically and physiologically different from the nutritional amenorrhoea caused by weight loss which has been described by Frisch and McArthur.[35] The weight for height for a lactating woman after childbirth is well above the *minimum* weight for height necessary for menstruation because she has just had a successful pregnancy. In addition, it has been shown that American and European women's weight gain during pregnancy includes an increase in fat deposition[36] (Fig. 4). The changes in weight for height associated with the length of the period of post partum amenorrhoea and the resumption of menstruation while lactating are not yet known for any racial or ethnic group, nor is the extent of interaction with the suckling stimulus at different nutritional levels.

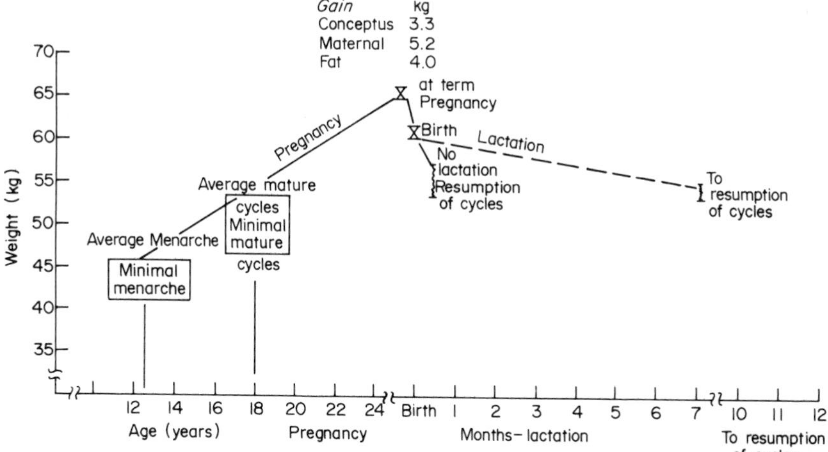

FIG. 4. Scheme of changes in weight (approximate) for a woman 160 cm tall, from the age of onset of menstruation to pregnancy and birth of the first child. Little is known about the mechanisms controlling the time of resumption of regular ovulatory cycles of lactating women, particularly in relation to their nutrition.

However, it is neither necessary nor expected that lactating women should have to gain weight before resuming normal, ovulatory cycles. Only women who ate so poorly, or worked so hard physically while lactating, that they lose a great deal of weight would have to gain weight before resuming menstruation. (Such women's weight for height might then be below the threshold weight for regular cycles.) Preliminary information for Zaïre indicates that heavier women resumed menstruation sooner than did lighter women of the same height.[37]

Differences in the amount of suckling[38] undoubtedly affect the length of amenorrhoea. The biological interaction, however, is difficult to unravel: for example, a lighter baby may want to suckle more often, but a heavier baby may also want to take nourishment more often depending on the amount of milk available, and this in turn can be affected by parity, age and nutrition.[39]

An explanation for the relatively short interval between the early death of an infant and a new pregnancy even in the undernourished populations of Bangladesh[40] may be found in the increase in body weight and fatness which takes place normally during pregnancy.[41] This increase in fatness, in addition to the increases gained during the adolescent spurt and later maturation[42] would increase the probability of a second pregnancy occurring after a short interval, if the infant dies soon after birth.[43]

Possible biological mechanisms

The findings suggest that physical differences in the rate of growth result not only in a displacement of the age-specific fertility curve in time, but also in a difference in the ultimate level: the faster women (and men) grow, the earlier and more efficient is their reproductive capacity. Experiments in which rats were fed high-fat and low-fat diets, the fats being substituted isocalorically for carbohydrates, demonstrated this biological mechanism. Rats on a high-fat diet matured sexually (first oestrus) significantly earlier than did those on a low-fat diet.[44] Carcass analysis of the rats showed that at maturation those rats on a high-fat diet were relatively fatter than the rats who had been on a low-fat diet.[45]

Conversion of weak androgens to oestrogen by aromatization is known to take place in human adipose tissue.[46] Adipose tissues may, therefore, be a significant extragonadal source of oestrogen. Also, differences in relative fatness affect the pathway of metabolism of oestrogen to more or less potent forms.[47] Women who are well nourished, particularly those on a diet containing a high percentage of calories from fat[48] may have higher levels of the more potent oestrogens than do poorly nourished women on a low fat diet.[49]

Human reproduction reconsidered? Significance

The usual biological explanation given for the relatively low fertility that has been observed for the lower socio-economic groups in Britain during the middle of the nineteenth century and in poor agricultural societies is the use of "folk contraception", usually *coitus interruptus.* This cannot be disproved. However, the physical and reproductive data suggest an alternative explanation wholly or in part: the effects of undernutrition and "hard living" on reproductive capacity.

Undernutrition, rather than the widespread use of folk contraception, may also be the explanation, wholly or in part, of why a completed family size of six or seven children is found in many developing countries today.[50] If this is so, the need for family planning programmes is much greater than has been realized[50] since the concept of fertility control may not be present in some groups of an undernourished population. The data also suggest that when couples are well fed and their potential fertility is high, whilst infant mortality is low, there is interest in and receptivity to the idea of efficient means of contraception.

Notes

1. J. W. Eaton and A. J. Mayer (1953). The social biology of very high fertility among the Hutterites. The demography of a unique population. *Human Biology* **25**, 206–264.
2. A. J. Coale (1972). *The Growth and Structure of Human Populations. A Mathematical Investigation.* Princeton University Press, Princeton.
3. W. Brass (1974). Population size and complex communities, with a consideration of world population. In *Population and its Problems: A Plain Man's Guide*, (Ed. H. B. Parry).
4. E. A. Wrigley (1969). *Population and History.* Weidenfeld and Nicolson, London; D. V. Glass (1966). Fertility and population growth. *Journal of the Royal Statistical Society* **A 129**, 210; J. M. Duncan (1871). *Fecundity, Fertility, Sterility and Allied Topics.* 2nd Edition. A. & C. Black, Edinburgh.
5. L. Henry (1961). Some data on natural fertility. *Eugenics Quarterly* **8**, 81–91.
6. A. J. Coale, op. cit. in note 2; also A. J. Coale (1974). The history of the human population. *Scientific American* **231**, 40–51.

7. W. P. Mauldin (1960). The population of India: Policy, action and research. *Economic Digest* **3**, 15.
8. C. Gopalan (1960) and A. N. Naidu (1972). Nutrition and fertility. *The Lancet* **ii**, 1077–1079.
9. L. C. Chen *et al.* (1974). A prospective study of birth interval dynamics in rural Bangladesh. *Population Studies* **28**, 277–297.
10. E. N. Wilmsen (1978). Seasonal effects of dietary intake on Kalahari Sen. *Federation Proceedings* **37**, 65–72.
11. Rose E. Frisch (1975). Demographic implications of the biological determinants of female fecundity. *Social Biology* **22**, 17–22; (1978a). Population, food intake and fertility. *Science* **199**, 22–30; (1978b). Nutrition, fatness and fertility. In *Nutrition and Human Reproduction* (Ed. W. H. Mosley), pp.91–22. Plenum Press, New York.
12. Rose E. Frisch (1978b), loc. cit. in note 11.
13. Rose E. Frisch (1978a), loc. cit. in note 11.
14. cf. Rose E. Frisch (1975), loc. cit. in note 11; A. K. M. Chowdhury, Sandra L. Huffman and G. T. Curling (1978). Malnutrition, menarche and marriage in rural Bangladesh. *Social Biology* **24**, 316–324.
15. Rose E. Frisch (1975), loc. cit. in note 11; R. H. Gray (1976). The menopause, epidemiological and demographic considerations. *The Menopause* (Ed. R. J. Beard), p.25. University Park Press, Baltimore.
16. Chen *et al.,* loc. cit. in note 9; R. G. Potter *et al.* (1965). Lactation and its effects upon birth intervals in eleven Punjab villages. *Journal of Chronic Diseases* **18**, 1125–1140.
17. C. E. Taylor, J. S. Newman and N. O. Kelly (1976). Interactions between health and populations. *Studies in Family Planning* **7** (3), 94–100.
18. Rose E. Frisch and J. W. McArthur (1974). Menstrual cycles: Fatness as a determinant of minimum weight-for-height necessary for their maintenance or onset. *Science* **185**, 949–951; J. W. McArthur *et al.* (1976). Endocrine studies during the refeeding of young women with nutritional amenorrhea and infertility. *Proceedings of the Mayo Clinic* **51**, 607–616.
19. Rose E. Frisch (1977). Food intake, fatness and reproductive ability. *Anorexia Nervosa* (Ed. R. Vigerski), pp.149–162. Raven, New York; (1977). Fatness and the onset and maintenance of menstrual cycles. *Research in Reproduction* **9** (6), 1.
20. J. Mayer (1974). Personal communication; L. Vincent (1978). Personal communication; cf. also Rose Frisch, G. Wyshak and L. Vincent (1980). Delayed menarche and amenorrhoea in ballet dancers, *New England Journal of Medicine* **303,** 17–19.
21. See references cited in note 18.
22. Rose E. Frisch and J. W. McArthur, loc. cit. in note 18.
23. A. Keys *et al.* (1950). *The Biology of Human Starvation*, vol. 1, pp.749–763. University of Minnesota Press, Minneapolis; M. W. H. Bishop (1970). Aging and reproduction in the male. *Journal of Reproduction and Fertility*, Supp. 12, 65–87.
24. Rose E. Frisch and R. Revelle (1969). Variation in body weights and the

age of the adolescent growth spurt among Latin American and Asian populations in relation to calorie supplies. *Human Biology* **41**, 185–212.
25. ibid. cf. also Rose E. Frisch (1972). Weight at menarche: Similarity for well nourished and under-nourished girls at different ages, and evidence for historical constancy. *Pediatrics* **50**, 445–450.
26. cf. Rose E. Frisch (1978), loc. cit. in note 11.
27. J. M. Tanner (1962). *Growth at Adolescence*, 2nd Edition. Basil Blackwell, Oxford; G. Wyshak and Rose E. Frisch (1982). Evidence for a peculiar trend in age at menarche. *New England Journal of Medicine* **306** 1033–1935.
28. Rose E. Frisch (1978a), loc. cit. in note 11; also loc. cit. in note 29.
29. Rose E. Frisch and R. Revelle (1971). Height and weight at menarche and a hypothesis of menarche. *Archives of the Diseases of Childhood* **46**, 695–701.
30. J. Bongaarts (1978). A framework for analyzing the proximate determinants of fertility. *Population and Development Review* **4**, 105–132.
31. C. E. Taylor and J. S. Newman, loc. cit. in note 17; E. Siegel and N. Morris (1970). The epidemiology of human reproductive casualties with emphasis on the role of nutrition. In *Maternal Nutrition and the Course of Pregnancy*, pp.5–40. National Academy of Sciences.
32. Rose E. Frisch (1978b). loc. cit. in note 11; R. H. Gray loc. cit. in note 15.
33. Rose E. Frisch (1978b), loc. cit. in note 11.
34. L. C. Chen *et al.*, loc. cit. in note 9; R. G. Potter *et al.*, loc. cit. in note 16; C. E. Taylor *et al.*, loc. cit. in note 17; R. Buchanan (1975). Breast-feeding: aid to infant health and fertility control. *Population Reports*. Series J, No. 4. J–49–J–69; J. Knodel (1977). Breast feeding and population growth. *Science* **198**, 1111–11115.
35. Rose E. Frisch, loc. cit. in note 18.
36. F. E. Hytten and A. M. Thomson (1970). Maternal physiological adjustments. In *Maternal Nutrition and the Course of Pregnancy*, pp.41–73. National Academy of Sciences.
37. M. Carael (1978). Relations between birth intervals and nutrition in three central African populations (Zaïre). In *Nutrition and Human Reproduction* (Ed. W. H. Mosley), pp.365–384. Plenum Press, New York.
38. H. Mosley (1977). The effects of nutrition on natural fertility. In *Natural Fertility*. (Eds H. Leridon and Jane Menken), pp.83–105. I.U.S.S.P. Liège.
39. R. Buchanan, loc. cit. in note 34.
40. H. Mosley, loc. cit. in note 38.
41. F. E. Hytten and A. M. Thomson, loc. cit. in note 36.
42. Rose E. Frisch (1976). Fatness of girls from menarche to age 18 years, with a nomogram. *Human Biology* **48**, 353–359.
43. N. Howell (1976). Toward a uniform theory of human paleodemography. In *The Demographic Evolution of Human Populations* (Eds R. J. Ward and K. M. Weiss), pp.25–40. Academic Press, London and New York.
44. Rose E. Frisch, D. M. Hegsted and K. Yoshinaga (1975). Body weight and food intake at early estrus of rats on a high-fat diet. *Proceedings of the Natural Academy of Sciences* **72**, 4172–4176.
45. Rose E. Frisch, D. M. Yoshinaga and K. Yoshinaga (1975). Carcass

components at first estrus of rats on high-fat and low-fat diets: body water, protein and fat. *Proceedings of the National Academy of Sciences* **72**, 4172–4176.

46. A. Nimrod and K. J. Ryan (1975). Aromatization of androgens by human abdominal and breast fat tissue. *Journal of Clinical and Endocrinological Metabolism* **40**, 367–372.
47. J. B. Brown and J. A. Strong (1965). Effect of nutritional status and thyroid function on the metabolism of oestradial. *Journal of Endocrinology* **32**, 107–115; J. Fishman, R. M. Boyar and L. Hellman (1975). Influence of body weight on estradiol metabolism in young women. *Journal of Clinical Endocrinology and Metabolism* **31**, 989–991.
48. Rose E. Frisch, D. M. Hegsted and K. Yoshinaga, loc. cit. in note 44.
49. Rose E. Frisch, D. M. Yoshinaga and Y. Yoshinaga, loc. cit. in note 8; L. C. Chen *et al.*, loc. cit. in note 9; Rose E. Frisch (1975), loc. cit. in note 11.
50. Rose E. Frisch (1978), loc. cit. in note 11.

Index

N

U

V

W

Y